SERIOUS MIN

RICHARD MCLAUCHLAN

Serious Minds

The Extraordinary Haldanes of Cloan

HURST & COMPANY, LONDON

First published in the United Kingdom in 2022 by
C. Hurst & Co. (Publishers) Ltd.,
New Wing, Somerset House, Strand, London, WC2R 1LA
Copyright © Richard McLauchlan, 2022
Foreword © John Campbell, 2022
All rights reserved.

Printed in Great Britain by Bell and Bain Ltd, Glasgow

The right of Richard McLauchlan to be identified as the author of this publication is asserted by him in accordance with the Copyright, Designs and Patents Act, 1988.

Distributed in the United States, Canada and Latin America by Oxford University Press, 198 Madison Avenue, New York, NY 10016, United States of America.

A Cataloguing-in-Publication data record for this book is available from the British Library.

ISBN: 9781787387928

This book is printed using paper from registered sustainable and managed sources.

www.hurstpublishers.com

To Sabrina, Magnus and Arvo, who have helped me to understand the meaning of the word 'family' more than any book ever could.

CONTENTS

Family Tree: The Haldanes of Cloan	viii
Foreword by John Campbell OBE	xi
Introduction	1
1. Hard Times	13
2. Family Matters	29
3. The World in Black and White: 1860s and 1870s	47
4. The Declaration of Independence: 1880s and 1890s	75
5. A New Century: 1900–1905	103
6. The Haldane Missions, Part One: 1906–1914	123
7. The Haldane Missions, Part Two: 1906–1914	139
8. The Motto Comes True: 1914–1918	161
9. Changing of the Guard: 1918–1930	189
10. Living Tradition: 1930–1945	219
11. The Long View: 1945 Onwards	255
12. What Makes a Haldane?	285
Appendix: The Forebears of Robert and Mary Haldane of Cloan	307
List of Illustrations	311
Acknowledgements	317
List of Referencing Abbreviations	321
Notes	325
Bibliography	357
Index	369

The Haldanes
as named in this book,

Robert Haldane of Cloan
(1805–77)

surnames Haldane

Richard Burdon
(1st Viscount Haldane of Cloan)
(1856–1928)
'Bo'
'Uncle Richard'
'Lord Haldane'

George Abercromby
(1858–75)
'Geordie'

John Scott = (Louisa) Kathleen Trotter
(1860–1936)   (1863–1961)
'Johnnie'   'Maya'
'Uffer'

surnames Haldane

John Burdon Sanderson   **Naomi Mary Margaret** = Gilbert Richard Mitchison
(1892–1964)   (1897–1999)   (1894–1970)
'Jack'   'Nou'   'Dick'
'JBS'

= (1) Charlotte Burghes (née Franken)
       (1894–1969)
= (2) Helen Spurway (1915–78)

surnames Mitchison

Geoffrey	Denis Anthony	(John) Murdoch	(Sonja) Lois	Nicholas Avrion	Valentine Harriet Isobel Dione
(1918–27)	(1919–2018)	(1922–2011)	(1926–)	(1928–)	(1930–)
'Geoff'	'Denny'	'Murdo'		'Av'	'Val'
	= Ruth Gill	= Rosalind Wrong	= John Godfrey	= Lorna Martin	= Mark Arnold-Forster
		'Rowy'	(div.)		
	four children, incl. Graeme & Terence	four children, incl. Sally & Neil	two children	five children, incl. Tim & Hannah	five children

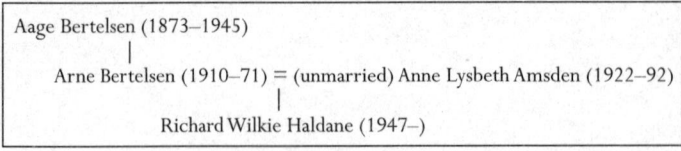

Aage Bertelsen (1873–1945)
|
Arne Bertelsen (1910–71) = (unmarried) Anne Lysbeth Amsden (1922–92)
|
Richard Wilkie Haldane (1947–)

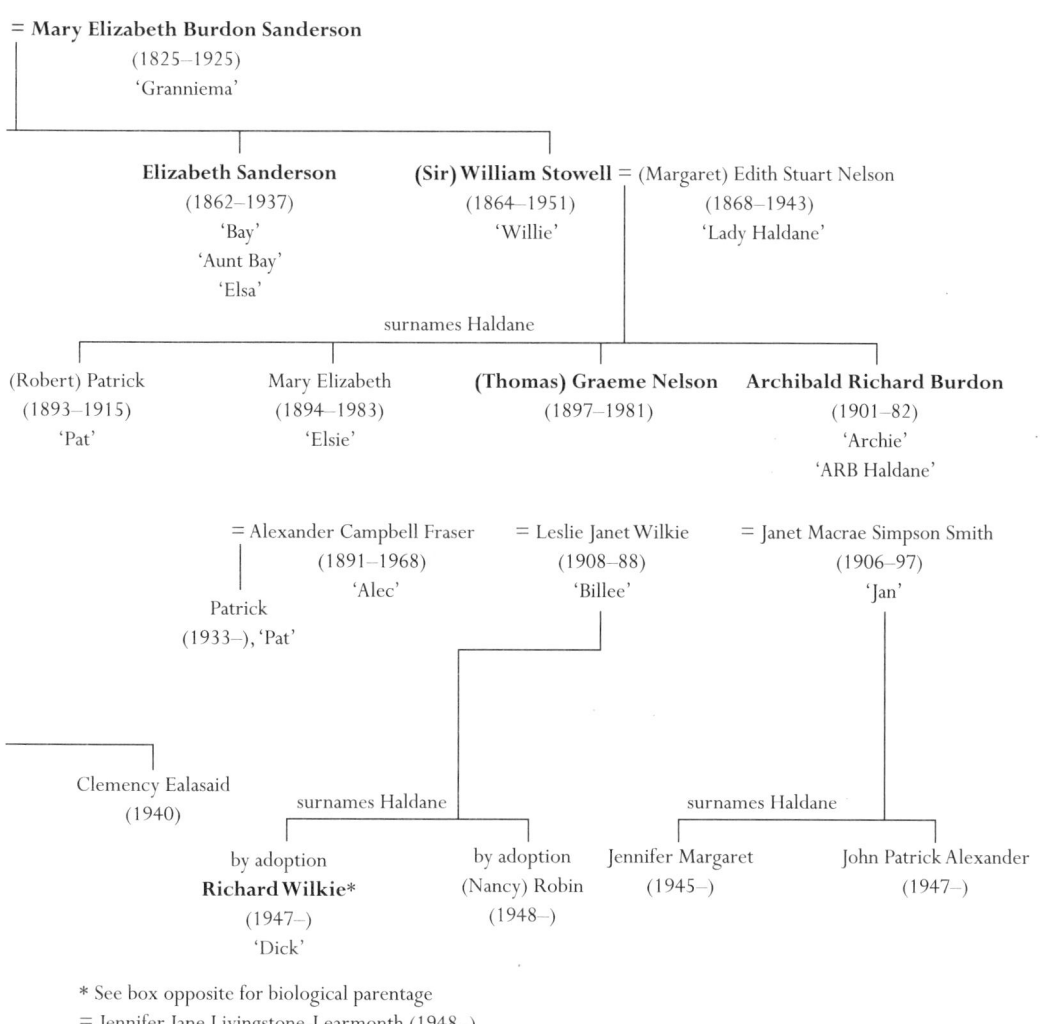

FOREWORD

John Campbell

This book is the culmination of Richard McLauchlan's seven-and-a-half years' travels in the footsteps of an exhilarating and extraordinary family, the Haldanes of Cloan. That journey began in early 2015 when Richard agreed to assist me in the preparation of my book *Haldane: The Forgotten Statesman Who Shaped Modern Britain*, published in 2020, also by Hurst. His contribution started in researching the archival papers of the subject of that book, my hero Richard Burdon Haldane, Viscount Haldane of Cloan. But Richard's exceptional talent soon meant his role expanded and he became my close collaborator on all aspects of the book.

Lord Haldane was just one of many remarkable Haldanes. He and his siblings triggered a golden age of multigenerational achievement within the family—as thinkers, writers, scientists, and public servants. They came to take their place amongst Britain's 'intellectual aristocracy' alongside famous dynasties such as the Huxleys, the Trevelyans, and the Keyneses. The family's diverse contributions to our national and international life provide not only fertile ground for historians, but also a precedential example for those in public life today. For this, and for the many wonderful and compelling stories within the following pages, I commend this book to you.

These stories embrace both the astonishing highs and the turbulent lows which comprise the warp and weft of all family life. As Richard surveys the Haldanes over the last 170 years, with all of

FOREWORD

their intellectual curiosity, individual eccentricities, and practical ubiquity, he weaves together some beguiling insights into what it is to be a member of such a heavyweight clan. His work is not just an exercise in sociology or history. As the story unfolds, it provides inspiration to all who would aspire to leadership in every field of endeavour.

John Campbell OBE
May 2022

INTRODUCTION

The rain lashed against the thin windowpanes of Cloan. The adult occupants of the house, Robert Haldane and his wife Mary, glanced up momentarily from their religious texts to observe the assault, then resumed their reading. It was cold inside, but they didn't mind. They had been bred to accept the discomforts of the body. With eternity on their minds, what was a bit of rain and a passing chill?

The children, meanwhile, were warm and cosy, tucking into fresh roast potatoes. They were not inside the house. They were amongst the trees up the hill behind Cloan, in a snug shelter made from requisitioned wood, tarpaulin, and moss. A fire burned brightly, with a makeshift fireplace of brick to lend the scene an aura of respectability. Here the potatoes crackled as they browned to a delicious crisp. The children were proud of their creation and gloried in their independence. They even invented their own special language and a 'Song of the House', marking them off from the outside world.[1]

There were five of them around the fire, wearing the traditional country garb for upper-middle-class Scottish children of the 1870s; the four boys in hard-wearing knickerbocker three-piece suits with tam-o'-shanter caps, the girl in thick woollen stockings tied with garters beneath numerous petticoats of flannel. All wore buttoned-up leather boots.

The eldest of them, Richard, known as Bo, was a pale boy with a high voice and a serious demeanour. Yet his dry remarks were laced with humour and his narrow mouth with its thin lips could quickly contort into a mischievous smile. He guided proceedings with a courtly, as well as portly, air. His scarlet stockings bulged with large calves.

The second eldest, Geordie, held himself with less reserve. Indeed, he was the very life of the party. With his square and slightly jutting jaw held aloft, he led the singing of the house song and outshone the others with his voice and musicality. He brought joy to all he did, and intelligence too; for he was known as the genius of the family. Within a few years, he would be dead.

Next was Johnnie, with his head in the clouds of smoke. He didn't have much time for the singing. He was too busy examining the way his lungs reacted to the inhalation of the fumes. The intense look of concentration on his face rarely left him. Every moment was teeming with possible data, begging to be understood. He was best left to get on with his experiments in peace.

Then came Elizabeth, known as Bay, desperate to keep up with the older boys. She gazed with wonder as an argument broke out, amazed at the versatility of her brothers' minds. But wait, she had something to offer too. Her voice ought to be heard. She butted in. The boys listened with reluctance. Unfortunately for them, her point was a good one, as it always was.

Lastly, Willie sat at the far end of the fire, a little boy with a perturbed look on his face. He had noticed a fault in the construction of the log house. Water was slowly seeping in and soon there would be a puddle. Uninterested by the serious debate underway, he crept silently back out into the rain to find fresh moss for the roof, prepared, if necessary, to dig a ditch for irrigation purposes.

Such was life for the Haldane children as the wet autumn evenings drew in. Happy, yes, but remote, inward-looking, somehow set apart. Under those few bare branches warmed by the fire sat some of the most remarkable children of their generation, who, as adults, were not just shaped by the age in which they lived but shaped it themselves in varied and profound ways. Richard would go on to create the army that helped defend the gates of Paris against the German onslaught many autumns later in 1914, and would lay the foundation stones of much that we take for granted in modern Britain, most notably our education system; Johnnie would help invent the first gas mask and save countless lives on the Front; he would so transform our understanding of respiration that he would make it possible for human beings to ascend safely to the highest heights and the lowest depths of the world; Elizabeth would successfully battle for the rights of women, secure positions of honour previously viewed as unsuitable for her sex, and outstrip intellectu-

INTRODUCTION

ally most of her contemporaries; and Willie would oversee the practical affairs of the others to allow their lives of unremitting public service to continue unhindered, and pick up the title of Crown Agent of Scotland and a knighthood along the way. We can only imagine what Geordie, the so-called genius, might have done.

Subsequent to them came personalities no less remarkable. Johnnie's children, Naomi and Jack (remembered today as Naomi Mitchison and J. B. S. Haldane), would lead the way in literature and science respectively, advancing—with bravado and humour—some of the most unpopular views of their time, many of which are now taken for granted, whether they be the right of women to birth control or the possibility of human reproduction without sex. Naomi's own children, as Mitchisons, carried on the tradition; with less drama perhaps, but with equal purpose and no less intellectual acumen. As Naomi put it, 'It is easy and comforting to have nice soft wool pulled over one's eyes… The Haldanes were fairly good at noticing the wool and scrubbing it off. I think the same may be true of the next generation of Mitchisons!'[2] All three of Naomi's sons who survived into adulthood became professors in the sciences (the daughters, following their mother, became writers). According to one of her son's witty children, there was a time when 'a third of a ton of human flesh answered to the name of Professor Mitchison'.[3] From Johnnie's uncle, Sir John Burdon Sanderson, onwards, the family could boast of six Fellows of the Royal Society across four generations. The only son of Naomi not to be elected to that illustrious institution, Denny Mitchison, has recently received the following assessment of his scientific legacy for his path-breaking contribution to the treatment of tuberculosis: 'His work has saved more lives than any other person who is alive today.'[4]

Willie's sons, too, proved impressive. Many Scots of an historical bent will have read A. R. B. Haldane's classic works on Scotland's past, if not his beautiful books on fishing. Not many, however, will know that his ever-retiring brother, Graeme (T. G. N. Haldane), helped establish the National Grid. He was the first engineer in Britain, possibly in the world, to construct, monitor, and document the performance of a heat pump system for space heating.[5] He knew Albert Einstein, J. J. Thomson, and even Franklin D. Roosevelt.

These tales of achievement all go back to that husband and wife at their religious texts, sitting in a draughty Cloan. The marriage of Robert and Mary brought together two strains of characteristics that, when combined, proved astonishingly potent. I am not, however, making grand or facile claims about the genetic component of this. As Professor Avrion Mitchison reminded me in an interview, we can't make verifiable claims about the extent to which 'Haldane characteristics' were (and are) inherited and compare them with the extent to which nurture played a role. We must be content with a very large dose of uncertainty on this point. It is true that genetic differences between people play an important part in differences in intelligence. A major UK study has shown that, by adulthood, genetic differences are responsible for roughly two-thirds of people's differences in intelligence (interestingly, they contribute to a fairly small amount, two-fifths, of people's differences in childhood).[6] It would therefore be foolish to let our uncertainty relegate the importance of Robert's and Mary's genes. They play a key part in our story, but it must remain a silent part. We just don't know exactly where the genetic factors end and the environmental factors begin.

What we can be certain of is the fact that, for the Haldanes, *place* was (and is) enormously important. For, transcending Robert and Mary and their descendants, we find the main protagonist of our story: that north-west-facing farmhouse, grown to baronial proportions, called Cloan, which stands like a sentinel overlooking the 'Lang Toun' of Auchterarder in Perthshire, Scotland. It was there that the monumental matriarchy of Mary Elizabeth Haldane was established and endured for nearly three-quarters of a century. It was to this woman and to this home that so many gave their allegiance, returning season after season for stimulation, inspiration, and rest. Her children, when staying in adulthood, would impart to Cloan something of that aloofness which had been theirs in the log house up the hill. That is not to say they didn't have many guests with them over the years. But their insistence on discussing topics of the highest cultural significance, their banning of the standard recreational games of most country houses, and their day-long treks across heather and hill gave Cloan an Olympian feel, as if it were a place cut off from the pursuits of ordinary mortals. And, with their aging and saintly mother bed-bound high in her 'upper chamber', dispensing wisdom to the prime ministers and archbishops who

INTRODUCTION

would climb the winding staircase to sit beside her, there was the added sense of some holy pilgrimage site. For many, Cloan was sacred ground.

When Graeme Haldane's son, Dick, finally put the house up for sale in 2014, the man who bought it was no stranger to the place. His name was Neil Mitchison, Naomi's grandson, whose own daughter, bearing the name of her great-grandmother, was announced Young Woman Engineer of the Year in 2014. She was awarded 'for her inspirational work with laser warning systems for military aircraft'.[7] A strong and intelligent female with a scientific bent, at the van of her field, applying herself to the task of finding solutions to real-world defence challenges and receiving a public honour for it? A tradition continues, it seems.

* * *

There has been an explosion of interest recently in this exceptional family. In 2019, Jenni Calder published an updated version of her sensitive and insightful biography, *The Nine Lives of Naomi Mitchison*, under the new title *The Burning Glass*. In the same year appeared *A Dominant Character: The Radical Science and Restless Politics of J. B. S. Haldane* by Samanth Subramanian, a book positively dripping with exhilarating anecdotes. Then 2020 saw the publication of John Campbell's *Haldane*, a weighty study—which I was proud to be involved in as Campbell's collaborator—of Naomi and JBS's uncle, Lord Haldane (the Bo of our fireside scene). The book is justly subtitled *The Forgotten Statesman Who Shaped Modern Britain*. But, as yet, no book on the family itself has appeared.[8]

Noel Annan, in his influential essay on the 'Intellectual Aristocracy', has named the Haldanes of Cloan as a key branch of that illustrious group.[9] Other families Annan mentions—the Trevelyans, Darwins, and Huxleys, for instance—have already had their stories told in print.[10] But with Calder's, Subramanian's, and Campbell's books now in stock at every good bookseller, is there anything new to say on the Haldanes of Cloan?

Thankfully, even the most thorough biographer couldn't chronicle all the exhilarating stories that seem to pullulate around the Haldanes. And, despite the recent publications, there is a distinct lack of accessible biographical material on some family members who rightly deserve to have their stories told. Elizabeth Haldane's life, for example, was so full of incident and interest that it begs for its own full-scale biography. This book exploits these lacunae, not least because Elizabeth, like her mother Mary before her and her niece Naomi after, was one of the most powerful female forces of her time. As *The Times*, very much in the voice of the period, said upon her death: 'Few women… could have met so many eminent men on such terms of equality.'[11] Indeed, a striking aspect of the history of the Haldanes of Cloan is the fact that the women in the family made nearly as much of an impact on society as the men, with very many more obstacles in their way. This alone makes the story worth telling for today.

Another problem now becomes evident. Naomi Mitchison alone wrote eighty-five books. The number of her brother JBS's books and scientific papers totals well over four hundred. That is to say nothing of their extensive journalism, nor the vast array of publications by the generations before and after them in the family. The Haldanes of Cloan have had a passion for the pen. This has been shared with a passion for action. Mary Haldane's children were relentlessly practical. To create an organisation, invent an apparatus, manage a hospital, or chair a Royal Commission appeared to come as naturally to them as breathing. A book that documented all their achievements would be of *War and Peace* proportions.

And with most of the family members leaving lengthy paper trails in their wake, what about the seemingly endless archives of letters, cuttings, photos, memoranda, draft manuscripts, and so on? Lord Haldane never tired of paraphrasing Goethe as follows: 'He who would accomplish anything must limit himself.'[12] The coronavirus pandemic has made limitation unavoidable. Libraries and archives were closed or had very restricted access across the years that this book was in preparation. Travel was reduced to its bare minimum, rendering a number of research trips impossible. I was fortunate to have spent many months prior to the pandemic engaged in archival research for *Haldane*, and this present book draws extensively on the fruit of that research. Though archival sources for the views and actions of other family members are less prominent, two factors have helped offset this. The first is the deep archival work of previ-

INTRODUCTION

ous biographers, and to them I am greatly indebted. The second is the kind assistance of Haldane and Mitchison family members, in their willingness both to take part in lengthy interviews with me and to provide material from their private collections. Consequently, despite the constricted research conditions, a fair number of previously unseen stories and little-known facts are now brought to light for the first time.

These various strands of investigation into multiple lives reveal aspects of the Haldane story that individual biographies have not quite been able to expose. One has already been mentioned: the cross-generational impact that the women in the family have had upon society. Interestingly, too, it becomes clear that certain life stories or characteristics recapitulate themselves in different individuals over time—as when, in a sonata, a theme restates itself in modified form later in the piece. As each generation radicalises the ideals of the one before, we find that the continuities of approach are just as remarkable as the genuinely new elements that are introduced. Indeed, in many cases, the continuities make the discontinuities possible. By studying these patterns, we discover something of the ambiguities of what it means 'to continue a family tradition'. And so we find that the Haldanes of Cloan *as a family*—certainly not just Lord Haldane—shaped modern Britain. A primary aim of this book is to relate the connected achievements of individual family members to the times in which they lived and to show the ways in which they moulded the world around them. Theirs was no passive acceptance of the status quo; the world changed because of their presence in it. The Haldanes, 'In the long rush of driving time', may have been 'blown like the thistle-down', as Naomi wrote in a poem about her brother. She ends, however, with the words, 'But shaping the way we are blown, / Shaping the wind that blows us.'[13]

Furthermore, to trace the web of people amongst whom the Haldanes moved is to trace much of the history of modern Britain and, indeed, many other parts of the world. Because their range was so wide—encompassing politics, philosophy, science, literature, defence, law, education, and agriculture—and their prominence so great, their social networks read like a *Who's Who* of their age. Even if we were to discount the extraordinary networks of Lord Haldane, which extended from the likes of Oscar Wilde at one end to Field

Marshal Douglas Haig at the other, we would still have to mention—if we are to do justice to the other family members—writers such as Aldous Huxley, Ernest Hemingway, W. H. Auden, and Doris Lessing; scientists such as the Nobel Prize-winners Niels Bohr, Peter Medawar, and James Watson; royalty and politicians such as Edward, Prince of Wales, Hugh Gaitskell, and the first prime minister of India, Jawaharlal Nehru. The Haldanes of Cloan were equal parts movers and shakers within this colourfully populated world.

These are some of the major themes that will weave their way through the following pages. This is not a series of mini-biographies, it should be said. I want to tell a story, a story of how one remarkable woman, marrying a man of ancient family gripped with a passion for Truth (note the capital), instilled in her children qualities of selflessness and public service on the one hand and of intellectual integrity and dogged individuality on the other; and how that generation put those attributes to such exemplary use, while passing them down to their own children with consequences they could never have foreseen, so that what was once a respectable and strongly religious Whig family of the Scottish gentry could be transformed, in the persons of Naomi and JBS, into radical socialists, espousing the nationalisation of the land, open marriages (in Naomi's case), and the abolition of the Abrahamic religions. There is even, at one stage, the suggestion of incest between Naomi and JBS. Graeme Haldane—whose own virginity, as this book reveals for the first time, was taken by his cousin Naomi, in an act that was consciously carried out by the latter as a demonstration of her left-wing politics—shared some of these socialist leanings. Graeme repeatedly asked his brother Archie (A. R. B. Haldane) for help in getting rid of his money. He didn't want to live as a rich man.

It could be argued that a lot of these changes were simply a result of the inevitable historical progressions of a century ravaged by war, in which old privileges, certainties, and institutions were no longer tenable. But this view does not reckon with the fact that very often it was a Haldane who was leading the argument for their downfall. Indeed, there was something written into the spirit of the Haldanes of Cloan that pushed their logic and their lives to these places before others reached them. This was not originally a Haldane trait; it took

INTRODUCTION

Mary Elizabeth Haldane (née Burdon Sanderson), of Northumbrian rather than Scottish stock, to introduce this questing element into the family. Again, I am unable to make any claims about the genetic element here. JBS was less reticent when accounting for his father's character: 'insofar as J. S. Haldane's unusual qualities were genetically determined, the genes came from his mother'.[14] Naomi was similarly confident; a comparison between Mary's descendants and the descendants of Robert Haldane's first marriage to Jane Makgill appeared conclusive:

> Those by his [Robert's] first wife continued in the solid Haldane tradition with honour and courage and honesty, but with the children of the second marriage other genes came into the family tree. None of the descendents [sic] of Granniema [Mary Haldane]—my grandmother—were ever quite content to leave things as they were. We all wanted to dig deeper and this disquiet and divine curiosity which, in the early and mid-19th century, turned people towards theology, later brought them to digging down to other foundations, above all to science. But also to politics…[15]

Chapter 2 will provide some nuance to this claim, but in Naomi's view it is clear that nature rather than nurture played the dominant role in these dynamics. As she saw it, her obedient religious forebears, the Burdon Sandersons, harboured the seeds of revolution within their DNA.

What is certainly true is Mary's abiding presence in the family to this day, nearly a hundred years after she died. Just as T. H. Huxley dominated in the imaginations of his celebrated offspring well after his own death—'the *persona* of past culture still influencing the present', as Ronald Clark put it[16]—so too Mary Haldane, born in the same year as Huxley, continues to shape the parameters of the possible and the proper in the minds of her great-grandchildren and their children.[17] This may explain why a forebear who died in 1925 is still known by the intimate title of Granniema.

Having said all this, Mary and Robert's youngest grandson, Archie, took a different route within the family; he was 'quite content to leave things as they were'. A quiet, traditional life by river and glen was what he wanted. This may have been largely due to the death of Archie's beloved older brother Pat, killed in action in 1915, which created in him a hankering for a lost, more innocent world.

This raises the question, 'What does it mean to be a Haldane of Cloan?' Nothing makes the question more concrete than the story of the current head of the family, Dick Haldane's adoption by Graeme and Billee Haldane in 1947. As we'll discover in the final chapter, it is a remarkable and moving tale of wartime infidelity, family secrets, suicide, and reconciliation. Indeed, it is a tale of personal discovery, of finding that the head of the family is literally a half-Dane (the origins, it was once said, of the Haldane name itself), and of shame being turned into pride. That said, Dick's story is not a neat rounding off that will quietly answer some of the reader's understandable questions on the nature/nurture dispute. On the contrary, it serves to emphasise the inescapable complexity of inheritance and of all family life. For the Haldanes, as for most families, the search for belonging—the quest to understand one's relationship to those who have come before and to come to terms with that relationship—has been a painful one for each generation. Dick's story is best understood as the current chapter in that long and difficult history.

* * *

A final issue is worth noting. One wouldn't blame a reader new to this dynasty for confusing R. B. Haldane with A. R. B. Haldane, or J. S. Haldane with J. B. S. Haldane, or indeed Mary Elizabeth Haldane with Elizabeth Sanderson Haldane. Moreover, many in the family share the same first name and a number have pet names which were more often used than their first names. It would be nice to be able to find one name for each which is distinct enough to avoid confusion, but I fear that this can only lead to a standardising that would be inappropriate for the narration of the story. One practice I will follow will be to avoid using childhood names which lasted into adulthood when writing of people in their professional capacity. Thus, although Elizabeth Haldane was mainly known by her family as Bay or Aunt Bay (and sometimes as Elsa), it would feel unnatural to refer to her in this way when discussing her work for, say, a Royal Commission. Similarly, Elizabeth's brother John was

INTRODUCTION

familiarly known as Johnnie, but I will use John when speaking of his scientific work. One exception to this rule will be their brother Willie, of whom it feels unnatural to write William even with regards to his professional life. To provide extra clarity I have added within the opening family tree the different appellations of the book's characters. This tree—along with the tree in the Appendix, which traces the forebears of Robert and Mary mentioned in Chapters 1 and 2, and the children of Robert's first marriage—will I hope help to clear up the occasional moments of confusion that may arise when trying to understand the sometimes complex relations within the family.

To tell a story that covers so many individuals, who achieved so many things, and to do so without regurgitating recent publications, will inevitably mean many omissions. It is my hope that the story told will prove interesting and entertaining enough to send readers to the more exhaustive biographies of particular Haldanes for further details, and, where biographies are yet to be written, encourage those confident with words to rise to the challenge.

1

HARD TIMES

When Mary Elizabeth Burdon Sanderson was born on 9 April 1825, at Rotherfield near Tunbridge Wells, the south-east of England was bathed in light. Wild flowers were in abundance and everywhere fresh verdure flourished. Nearly one hundred years later, she recalled: 'My parents used to call me their sunny child, as there was so much sunshine surrounding my birth.'[1]

Her love of flowers never left her, and many felt her to be forever enfolded by the regenerative forces of budding new life. As Mary's granddaughter, Naomi Mitchison, wrote to her Aunt Bay—Elizabeth Sanderson Haldane, Mary's daughter—in April 1926, almost a year after Mary's death:

> I think you must find all this Spring weather rather a mockery at Cloan—it all seems such a very short time ago! Flowers seem most curiously and particularly associated with her, don't they? I expect, for instance, that Geoff [Naomi's eldest son] will always remember her in a kind of bower of colour and scent. I do—and the few special ones she would always have by her.[2]

Mary's passion for flowers was passed down to both Elizabeth and Naomi, a constant within a rapidly changing world. Mary was born seven years before the Great Reform Act, at a time when only half a million men had the vote in Great Britain, and twelve years before Victoria became Queen. Lord Liverpool's Tory administration ran the country, right up to the northern tip of Shetland, out of Westminster. Legislation was only just being brought in to limit children under the age of sixteen to twelve hours of work a day in the cotton mills.[3] Those at the other end of the social spectrum, with some form of educational choice, had only six universities from which to choose. Inequalities were such that between 1837 and 1844, as Mary passed through her teenage years, more than a million British people are believed to have starved to death simply from lack of employment (and this was followed by the Irish potato famine).[4]

Mary's descendants would play leading roles in putting much of this right. Certainly, her verdant beginnings seemed to promise much. You would be forgiven for anticipating that her legacy was rooted in a childhood of privilege and perpetual sunshine, metaphorical or otherwise. There was privilege certainly. The three generations of family preceding her included Lord Mayors of London and Newcastle; a well-known judge of the High Court of Admiralty, Lord Stowell (1745–1836); and his brother, the long-serving Lord Chancellor, Lord Eldon (1751–1838). Her father, Richard Burdon, had won the famous Newdigate Prize at Oxford around the same time that Shelley was being sent down for his atheistic pamphleteering, while her mother, Elizabeth (whose maiden name, Sanderson, was added to her husband's surname upon their marriage in 1815), was a considerable heiress.[5] Elizabeth was banned in her youth from developing 'the usual accomplishments of a young lady' and instructed instead in Latin and Greek, 'and other subjects considered suitable for a masculine mind', alongside her Clapham classmate, the future Lord Macaulay. Mary recalled her mother's 'clear intellect and power of influencing others'. Elizabeth had 'a strong will of her own'—a trait that was to become very common amongst the women of the family.[6] It was at her mother's feet that the young Mary read Voltaire in French, completing *The History of Charles XII*, *The Age of Louis XIV*, and the two volumes of his *History of the Russian Empire Under Peter the Great*. Both parents placed a great emphasis on the development of a high culture.

The houses of Mary's youth seemed to proclaim these distinctions. West Jesmond, which in Mary's early years was still 2 miles distant from Newcastle upon Tyne, rises with expansive Gothic intensity from the ground, its buttresses, parapets, and battlements declaring a kind of leaping solidity.[7] It would be hard to live there and not feel special. The family's other house, Otterburn Dene, was a small shooting lodge stranded amidst the vast Northumberland moorland, where Richard, Elizabeth, and their children would relocate during the spring and summer. It could only be reached by one solitary cart-track across the endless heath, which was scattered with bone-filled stone cists and ancient burial mounds.[8] Its isolation amidst these signs of death said something a little darker about the lives of the Burdon Sandersons.

* * *

Mary's father, Richard, was a man of striking character. Upright in bearing, with dark brown hair and large grey eyes, he had a distinguished appearance. He was noted for travelling in a carriage pulled by four brown horses with black legs. He paid the greatest care to every aspect of his turnout and deportment. Mary remembered that 'He was athletic and had a well-proportioned figure, a very neat leg and ankle and a good foot, so that he both walked and danced well, as well as being a good oarsman and pugilist. He was always very carefully dressed.'[9] As Mary's sister-in-law, Lady Burdon Sanderson, remarked, 'he had the charming manner and dignified courtliness of an earlier generation'.[10]

He had been brought up in hardy ways. His eighty-year-old grandfather would take him out riding, but while the octogenarian struck out on his bounding steed, Richard was forced to follow on a lowly mule, having received strict instructions never to say—or even think—that he was afraid as he hurtled towards the hedges and ditches. Richard, from then on, 'never knew what fear was'.[11] He was sent to his prep school in Ovingham at six years of age, where the day began with the headmaster, Mr Birkett, calling out: 'All out to bathe, boys.' Each one was taken hold of by a foot and plunged into the River Tyne without a moment to protest. After the Grammar School at Durham and a glittering undergraduate career at Oriel (he was only nineteen when he won the Newdigate), he was elected a Fellow of his college in 1813 and won the Chancellor's Prize for an English Essay the following year. Disappointingly, Richard, soft of voice, was prohibited from reading the essay at the Encaenia ceremony that year (when honorary degrees are given) as was customary for the prize-winner. In the audience were, among several other members of royal houses, Tsar Alexander I of Russia, the King of Prussia (Frederick William III), and the Prince Regent, afterwards George IV. Richard's substitute did not read it well.[12]

In the same year that he was awarded his Fellowship, Richard was appointed Secretary for Presentations (the Lord Chancellor's advisor on senior appointments in the Church of England) by his uncle, Lord Eldon—the Lord Chancellor himself. In 1814, Richard was also made a Commissioner in Bankruptcy. Uncle and nephew were very close. Eldon had lost his own son, John Scott, but found in Richard a striking resemblance to him; with Richard he sought to fill the void. Upon their marriage, Richard and Elizabeth took a house in Montague Street, off Russell Square, on account of its proximity to Bedford Square where Eldon lived. It was a time of political protest, as the prospect of universal male suffrage entered into public debate. Eldon, an arch-Tory, was *persona non grata* in the eyes of those sympathetic to the expansion of the suffrage. During a particularly riotous period, he asked Richard to accompany him on his walk to the House of Lords. They got there safely, but not before a shot was fired at the Lord Chancellor, passing through the skirt of Richard's coat.

The dangers of Richard's position were, in his own estimation, more spiritual than physical. His role in the Lord Chancellor's department was one that often functioned on the basis of political rather than religious considerations. Candidates seeking preferment for a particular living within the Church (that is, clergymen who desired 'higher' roles, such as canon, archdeacon, dean, or bishop) regularly staked their claims based on the service they had given to the political party in power at the time.[13] Sometimes livings would even go to the highest bidder, with various presents offered to the Chancellor and even to Richard himself as a way of ensuring his goodwill. They had the very opposite effect. Richard's devotion to the Word of God in the Scriptures had been steadily growing over this period, under the influence of the evangelical churchman Charles Simeon (friend of Robert Haldane's father, incidentally), and through reading the works of the Calvinist preacher William Romaine. Each called for an ever more exacting allegiance to the literal words of the Bible. Richard simply could not reconcile the practices he was witnessing in his professional life with the ideals he encountered in Scripture for God's church on earth. Something had to give. It was his profession. Richard decided not only to resign his Secretaryship, but also—though he would come to regret this—his Commissionership in Bankruptcy. As Mary wrote (and it is a significant passage for this study): 'My father was not one to flinch, even if the sacrifice cost him almost his life. He was devotedly attached to his uncle, and his work was congenial to him, but he felt he must give it up, cost him what it might; and he did so.'[14]

Eldon, on hearing the news, did not leave his room for three days. Deeply distraught, he could not comprehend what would prompt a man with so promising a future to do such a thing. He and his brother Lord Stowell assumed that their nephew must have gone mad. Richard was agonised by the thought of hurting others by his actions, and became bedridden with fever. He was persuaded by his wife that a change of scene was needed for recuperation; the couple went to Tunbridge Wells, and following his recovery they decided to settle in the area. It was here that three of their four children—first another Richard, then Jane, then Mary—would be born.

Clearly, Richard Burdon Sanderson was a man of deep seriousness. Yet he could have his rare comic, if not ridiculous, moments. During his courtship of Elizabeth, for instance, he was 'anxious to find out if the young lady was good tempered'.[15] It was winter, and Richard and Elizabeth found themselves walking in a glistening white garden. Richard ever so graciously guided his intended beneath a snow-laden tree and proceeded with vigour to shake a branch over her beautiful bonnet of white crêpe. We are told that the young lady, still a teenager, 'took the deed in such good part that he felt he was on sure ground in choosing her as the partner of his life'.[16]

Despite what we might think about this escapade, Richard was a lovable man. He could not bear to give pain to others, and he had a deep bond with animals. Wherever he was, there were sure to be a rabble of dogs and an elegant horse close by. He was devoted to his wife, only leaving her to overnight elsewhere once during their entire married life of nearly fifty years. He would read to his children in the evenings from Milton's *Paradise Lost* and Pope's Homer. Richard, however, was a perfectionist and could be easily irritated. When he taught his youngest son Greek, he showed 'extreme impatience' with any false answer, instilling in the boy his own lifelong sensitivity to little errors.[17] Richard was very proud of Mary and encouraged her artistic talent, paying for her lessons with a noted Newcastle artist (though he held back from letting her study under Henry Sass in London, as she desired) and taking a keen interest in her work. At home they would sit side by side, he reading, she painting. Mary's daughter Elizabeth wrote: 'Her devotion to her father and his to her were constant and deep.'[18] Yet these moments of homely intimacy were all too rare.

Richard had inherited the extensive landed property of his father, Sir Thomas Burdon, when the latter died in 1826. It was this fact that brought the Burdon Sandersons to Northumberland, when Mary was in her first year, and Richard found he had many worldly activities with which to busy himself. He owned and managed the Wallsend Colliery near Jesmond, served as a Justice of the Peace, and was obliged to rebuild the unstable Manor House, constructing in its place the imposingly Gothic West Jesmond—though not before Mary and her siblings had gone through the frightening experience of being shut into the cellar of the old house in punishment for disrespecting Bradley the butler, 'whose self-importance aggravated us'.[19] It was a glimpse of things to come.

The practical occupations of their father and the birth of a younger brother, John (later Sir John Scott Burdon Sanderson, FRS), were the initial reasons for Mary and Jane's relative isolation from their parents. Following John's arrival, the two girls were placed under a governess, the cruel disciplinarian Miss Taylor, who had an apartment in a house adjoining that in which the family lived during the building of West Jesmond. They would spend twelve hours of every day with her. Jane was considered delicate, having had scarlet fever, and therefore avoided some of the more inhuman punishments inflicted by Miss Taylor, a favourite of which was to shut the culprit—or should that be victim?—in a room for a whole day, with only bread and water for sustenance. Mary could never forget being locked 'in a room never opened in a so-called haunted house which my father had taken for the shooting season. I remember to this hour the sound of the closing heavy door.'[20]

For one Sunday misdemeanour, Mary was forced to learn the twenty-four verses of Psalm 139, which ends, 'Search me, O God, and know my heart: try me, and know my thoughts: / And see if there be any wicked way in me, and lead me in the way everlasting.'[21] Its results were not salutary: 'I was often kept awake by the thought of the sinfulness of my nature and with the sense that at any moment judgment might be passed upon me.'[22] Each morning, after a night spent on mattresses of straw resting upon hard pinewood cross-bars without springs, Mary and Jane were woken by their nurses, taken hold of, and plunged to full immersion in a bath of cold water. 'The rule of life was Spartan', wrote Mary characteristically, 'but I do not regret it.'[23]

What she did regret, however, was her father's decision, when preparing the new foundation stone for West Jesmond, to have only her elder brother Richard's name inscribed upon it: 'From that time forward the fact of being merely a daughter rankled in my mind, and during my childhood, and for years afterwards, I used to feel as if I was nothing to anybody.'[24] The feminist instincts that Mary developed later in life are surely connected to this definitive experience of her girlhood.

These early years were spent in rigorous study. The practice of reading began at three years old. Before the age of six, grammar rules were mastered by heart, alongside French verbs, multiplication tables, and reams of poetry. The classroom looked more like a torture chamber than a place of learning. The girls' feet were placed in stocks—wooden boards to secure the legs, designed for criminals as a form of corporal punishment and public humiliation—and their backs were forced into uprightness by wooden devices, known as backboards, placed behind them. The boards had protruding horizontal ends on either side around which the girls' arms were hooked to avoid slouching. The seats were so narrow that they only just held their slender forms. When the hours of regurgitating information were at an end, there were none of the usual recreations that were open to boys of their class. Mary desperately wanted to play cricket and ride to hounds, but these activities were forbidden and there was no alternative entertainment on offer. In later teenage years, there was the exception of musical performance. Mary's younger brother, John, played the violin and she would accompany him on the piano in works by Mozart, Haydn, or Dussek. However, as Mary wrote, 'Woe betide me if I played a false note; his quick ear detected it immediately, and he and his violin nearly jumped off the ground.'[25]

Other gaps in the clouds appeared from time to time, when the family would take a house in a neighbouring vicinity for a period. On one such occasion, Elizabeth took over the education of her daughters, much to their relief. She was a born educator, drawing maps of different countries and telling the girls all about their mountains and towns, and not just their names as they were used to learning. This was a time of excitement. It was 1832, the year of the Great Reform Act—the announcement of which Mary, aged seven, heard as the Chevy Chase coach from Newcastle to Edinburgh passed their gate—and the year when the first devastating cholera pandemic hit Britain, having already killed off an estimated fifty million people across the globe in the previous fourteen years.[26] For Mary and Jane, the danger of the disease also meant a daily dose of port wine to fortify their systems against a possible attack—'a treatment to which we did not object'.[27]

But by now a new governess was on the scene, Miss Forster, an extreme evangelical and another terrifying disciplinarian. Of course, as Mary reminds us, it was standard practice for children to be treated with severity. Judging by the literature and stories of the time, children were not generally viewed, as we commonly view them today, as naturally innocent and mouldable, but as unruly and amoral. They were to be handled with stern discipline to inculcate a more serious attitude. In line with this, Mary remembered a cousin returning from his school in Yorkshire black and blue from the cane (a school fellow of his apparently lasted three days up a chimney: the safest place he could find to escape the terrifying teacher). Another girl cousin spent days on end locked in a barn for her so-called offences, fed—like the chastised Mary—on bread and water and forced by night to sleep in the maid's room. This same cousin was later present at the Siege of Cawnpore in India, where she was hacked to pieces along with her husband and child and thrown down a well. Mary writes: 'Possibly her early training was useful to her in the terrible times she had to pass through.'[28] This comment tells us more about Mary, perhaps, than the difficulties of a Georgian childhood.

Still, according to her own account, it was not the physical deprivations that affected Mary the most, but the fanaticism of the introspective religious atmosphere promoted by Miss Forster. Mary remained profoundly religious her whole life, but she steadily shed all vestiges of extremism and was, in the end, without illusion when it came to the dangers of dogmatism: 'Religion has too often been the wedge of torture, and to sensitive natures an engine of cruelty. One is thankful that the days have passed when such despotism is excited in the name of religion.'[29] There was something nightmarish, even Orwellian, in the system that prevailed in her youth. The girls were under constant surveillance, and what they said or did was often twisted to mean its opposite and reported back to their parents. There was no mercy, no compassion: 'Prayers were directed *at* us by our governess.'[30] The thought of her sinfulness dogged Mary wherever she went.

Matters were not helped by her repeated illnesses, which the spartan conditions aggravated and, in some cases, prompted. One Christmas, when Mary was fourteen, she and Jane were bathed in the open air in a bath so cold that the inch-thick ice had to be broken with sledgehammers. The activity, we're told, amused the girls, but it brought on a severe bout of rheumatism in Mary. Eventually, the country doctor was called. It took him a long time to get there, as he had to make his way across the endless wintry expanse of moorland which led to Otterburn Dene, where the family was staying. 'He appeared in my room attired in a bright green coat with brilliant brass buttons, corduroy trousers, and top-boots, a stout riding-whip in his hand', she recalled. 'Wud ye like to be bluided?' he asked. Mary was glad at the prospect of relief and consented. The doctor wrapped a garter-like material around her arm to make the veins show. At first, he was unsuccessful in drawing blood. He can't have reassured his teenage patient when he said, 'I see the artery; we must be careful.' After another unsuccessful attempt, he found what he was looking for and filled a basin with blood, stopping the bleeding only with some difficulty. Though relieved, Mary was left exhausted, and probably weaker than she was before.[31]

Richard and Elizabeth thought a change of scene would do Mary good, and organised a trip to Edinburgh for the purpose. It would be her first visit to the place she would later make her home with Robert Haldane (though she never quite felt 'at home' there; that distinction was reserved for Cloan). Her memories of arrival in Scotland tell us much about the land across the Border at the time. At Fushiebridge

Inn, outside Edinburgh, they encountered the supposed original of Meg Dods, the eccentric old-world landlady of Sir Walter Scott's *Saint Ronan's Well* (Scott had died only a few years before, in the momentous 1832). The uncouth and forcible language of this infamous innkeeper, affronted by Richard's complaint over the poor quality of her post-horses, provided Mary with her first experience of Scottish hospitality. When they arrived in Edinburgh itself, they found their intended hotel on St Andrew Square fully booked. They took lodgings nearby, but it was a fast day—and in Scotland this went with strict observance. It was a long time before food could be found for the tired and hungry travellers.

Mary marvelled at the character of the place, struck by the inequalities of class that were everywhere in evidence. Edinburgh's New Town, that symbol of wealth and elegance, was still in the process of construction. Its occupants, free of the rank and crowded streets of the Old Town, could be found gliding effortlessly through the wide streets on sedan chairs—the rich literally being carried around by the poor. Mary noted that even in lodgings of good repute a serving maid went shoeless and without stockings. What she didn't see were some of the even more distressing signs of poverty in the city. The *Reports on the Sanitary Condition of the Labouring Population of Scotland* of 1842, published three years after Mary's visit, comment on Edinburgh's many one-room dwellings:

> A few of the lowest poor have a bedstead, but by far the larger portion have none; these make up a kind of bed on the floor with straw, on which a whole family are huddled together, some naked and the others in the same clothes they have worn during the day.[32]

One minister who moved to Edinburgh to administer to the needy observed, 'I never knew what destitution was, among the poor in the country, I never saw a case of destitution that I could not relieve before the sun went down; but here there are thousands of cases that you cannot relieve.'[33] Conditions had not altered drastically by the time Mary joined her husband in Edinburgh, and they were to make a significant impact on her children growing up there. 'Could it be right', wrote her daughter Elizabeth, 'that there should be in existence these miserable objects whom we saw when our father took us to see the historic closes and vennels of Edinburgh in order that we might learn about the famous robberies and murders?'[34] The acute social conscience of Mary's children stems, in part, from these early sights of deprivation. For Mary, too, Edinburgh seems to have provided her with her first bitter taste of the injustices prevalent within British society.

From this time on, Richard and Elizabeth were themselves becoming ever more absorbed in religious matters. The writing and publishing of pamphlets became their chief concern. Richard had been much influenced by an encounter with the Honourable Paul Methuen, who had joined the strict Christian sect known as the Plymouth Brethren. Methuen had visited Richard in the North to make a personal appeal for Richard to attend the Brethren's approaching conference. Later, Richard would tell people with amusement that Methuen's first words to him were: 'As I approached your house I heard the unholy barking of dogs!' He may have been amused, but he was also evidently moved by the force of argument that Methuen brought with him, for Richard had a sudden change in outlook. He sold all his beloved dogs and horses, ceased going into society, and finally bought two chapels, one in Newcastle and the other between the city and Jesmond, where he and his eldest son held regular services.[35] Mary records rather bleakly: 'When our parents became more exclusively religious and devoted to religious efforts, excellent in themselves, it withdrew them much from the society of their children.'[36] When they did communicate with them, it was on a plane that was hardly accessible to the younger members of the family. Richard wrote to his youngest son, John, on his tenth birthday:

> I am glad the Lord speaks so graciously out of His Word, telling you no more to consider yourself a child; and I hope you remember the apostolic commentary on that subject, 'Nevertheless, in malice be you children, but in understanding be men.'... I pray God to keep you humble and teachable, that you may not be exalted with the abundance of the revelation, nor yet shut your ears to the voice of His Spirit.[37]

The girls now spent even more time with their governess. This was particularly distressing for Mary, who was practically an invalid for her remaining teenage years. She suffered at various times from pleurisy, jaundice, and headaches. It wasn't that she was bed-bound very often, but she was denied the chance to go with her brothers and sister on outings. She remained alone, with no opportunities for a change of scene. Her own memoirs of her childhood, which narrate the sunny beginnings with which she entered the world, end with the harrowing words: 'I had not the physical energy to do very much. Weakness of body is apt to lead to a condition of mind that makes all our surroundings look dark.'[38]

* * *

Mary's hardships were real and shouldn't be belittled, but they should also be seen in proportion to the backdrop of national hardship that the sights of inequality in Edinburgh typified. The palatial West Jesmond was worlds away from the single-room dwellings that could be found in Scotland's capital with an average size of 14 by 11.5 feet.[39] Mary and Jane may have had straw mattresses, but they had their own room, and they were sheltered from death and decay in a way that was impossible for children at the other end of the social spectrum. They knew nothing of what Glasgow's Medical Officer of Health, Dr J. B. Russell, reported on the death of children living in poverty within that city:

> Their little bodies are laid on a table or on a dresser so as to be somewhat out of the way of their brothers and sisters, who play and sleep and eat in their ghastly company... One in ten of all who are born there [the Glasgow tenements] never see the end of their first year.[40]

Mary and her sister may have been educated as if in chains and in an old-fashioned manner, but they were educated. It was not uncommon for children in Britain to enter employment at nine years of age and be engaged in work that was more degrading in its environment than the stocks and backboards of Mary's schoolroom. Until the Mines Act of 1842, many boys and girls as young as seven and eight were drawing tubs of coal in the darkness and the dirt for fourteen hours a day.[41]

Mary and her cousin may only have received bread and water when in solitary confinement for some supposed offence, but they ate proper plates of food at other times. Meanwhile, in Ireland, 3 million people lived off nothing but potatoes.[42] And when the potato famine struck there between 1845 and 1850, there were 1.1 million deaths by starvation.[43] Mary experienced cold winters, and the water jug in her room would be frozen over in the morning, but she was always sufficiently dressed. Again, in Ireland in 1841, when Mary was sixteen, there were reports of boys of twelve running about literally naked.[44] Mary was exiled to some extent from her parents, but they remained present on the fringes of her life and there were those rare, glorious moments together, walking, reading, or painting. Yet in the workhouses—where impoverished men, women, and children went as a last resort to find shelter and food in return for the most menial of jobs—the separation of child from mother was automatic. The conditions there were almost unimaginable.[45]

It will become clear in later chapters just how important Mary's children were when it came to putting some of these injustices right. At this stage, we simply need to recognise that her own suffering was part of a much wider national condition, which in many cases far exceeded even the terrible discomforts that she herself faced. Mary was still a girl of privilege, and she knew it. It is predictable that once she was free from her so-called carers, who forbade novel reading, Charles Dickens became her favourite author, 'owing to the good work he had done for the poor, and for ill-treated children'.[46] But her own experience of hardship was genuine and profound. Moreover, according to her daughter, 'she was so extremely sensitive, [that] what her sister took in a matter-of-fact way, and not too seriously, to her meant acute pain'.[47] These two facts of her life—a deep sense of her early suffering and a simultaneous recognition of her social advantages—lay at the bedrock of what she would instil in her children and how she would instil it. For she had empathy in abundance, coupled with a keen awareness of the responsibilities that come with wealth. The idea of service to others in need was integral to her being. Her religious upbringing had less to do with this than we might think. On the contrary, Mary's brother John believed it 'centred their thoughts while still children… too exclusively on their own feelings in relation to God and a future life'.[48] Mary's compassion had far more to do with her own hard-won recognition, gained through her childhood trials, of what human beings owe to each other. She knew what neglect was; she knew what it was to lack freedom. She had a hunger for liberation, both physical and mental. Her daughter wrote of 'the extraordinary isolation' in which her mother had lived as a child. Elizabeth continues:

> it could not possibly have been wise to separate the young people so entirely from those of their own ages or station in life. It was a singular experience, she remarks, and might, but for their deeply religious training, have had disastrous effects. In some ways it may have strengthened their characters and made them independent of outside influences and amusements, but it was also calculated to make them morbid. Their own good sense alone prevented this from happening.[49]

Elizabeth's words nevertheless gloss over some deeper complications. Their 'religious training' was part of the problem, even if it at times came to their aid. And it's not clear at all that Mary escaped morbidness. Could the closing words of her memoir be written by someone free from a morbid outlook? I quote them again: 'Weakness of body is apt to lead to a condition of mind that makes all our surroundings look dark.'[50]

Indeed, Mary's memoirs, penned in her nineties, are clearly written by a woman struggling to come to terms with her upbringing and sorely conflicted about those aspects of her early life most dear to her—her parents and her religion. The culpability of her parents is never admitted, but it lurks at the edge of every page and hides behind every jab at her governesses, whose guilt was naturally less problematic. She never quite gets to the stage of dealing properly with her parents' responsibility for the presence and ubiquity of these women of torment. At times, when writing of the manner in which she was brought up, she is of that old-fashioned school which says 'it didn't do me any harm'; at others, she writes with brutal honesty about the pain of it all. This perhaps explains some of the contradictions that her own children experienced. As we'll see, some of the very things of which she complained were implemented in the life of her children—though their father's influence and the social milieu of the time shouldn't be discounted in this. But she did seek to put certain things right. She said of education: 'I... rejoice to see our boys and girls brought up in the light of day with the full glare of public opinion blazing on the work of their education. It is their own fault if they are not independent thinkers.'[51] And as Elizabeth observed of her mother's views of religion: 'With her own children she had the utmost dread of dealing with religious things in a personal way or of encouraging them to express themselves in an unnatural fashion.'[52] Even with her grandchildren, she promoted liberty. When the young Naomi Haldane was locked in a battle with her prospective Mitchison in-laws over her unwillingness to get married in a church, it was her acutely religious grandmother who backed her up, 'If you're acting according to your conscience.'[53]

More positively, Mary was indebted to her parents, despite the religious strictures, for the high value they put on intellectual pursuits and the development of an enriching culture. Veneration of such things was to run through the family. She was intensely proud of her remarkable ancestry, her father's glory at Oxford, and her mother's powerful intelligence. But, again, there was conflict here. For she was also proud of the self-sacrifice shown by her father in renouncing his career, and until her very last days she was exhorting others to 'follow Him [Christ] in spirit and in action who made Himself of no reputation in order to fulfil that work which His Father in heaven had given Him to do'.[54] These tensions are reflected in her very worldly ambitions for her children (while her eldest child Richard was still in his crib, she thought him destined for the Lord Chancellor's seat on the Woolsack, a desire which he fulfilled in 1912), together with her tranquil acceptance and even encouragement of their moments of humiliation. When Richard lost that long-desired seat in 1915 for his supposed German sympathies, she wrote to him: 'you have... done more by your action in giving up the woolsack than you could have done otherwise. All self-sacrifice tells, and it also warns others to go and do likewise when called upon to sit and suffer.'[55]

* * *

The famous serenity and poise of Mary's later years were rooted in a childhood of distress and disquiet. They may even have masked a supressed personal conflict about her past with which she never fully came to terms. What we cannot doubt is that her early years profoundly shaped the upbringing she gave to her own children, and indeed the way she supported them throughout their lives. The depth, the learning, the care for others which were hers, and which she passed on to her children, all sprang from an early experience comprising both privilege and hardship. But what she gave to her children can never be neatly separated from that other source of influence in their lives: their Haldane inheritance. Our next chapter explores what it meant to marry into such a family and, for Mary's children, what it meant to be part of that ancient lineage. The task is not always easy. The person of Mary Haldane stands out from the pages of history with an astonishing clarity; not so Robert Haldane of Cloan. If Mary was her parents' 'sunny child', she was also a bright light for all who knew her in adult life; so bright, in fact, that her husband seems almost to disappear. We must do what we can to pull him from the shadows.

2

FAMILY MATTERS

In the summer of 1797, a young man in his twenty-ninth year wearing a blue and braided greatcoat, his long hair powdered and tied back, rode into a crowd of villagers standing expectantly on the banks of the River Deveron in the north-east of Scotland. He had come to preach the Word of God, but he was clearly no ordained minister. His outfit and bearing were those of a gentleman of independent means. He dismounted, gave his horse into the charge of another gentleman, and opened his well-thumbed Bible to Luke 13.3: 'except ye repent, ye shall all likewise perish'.

In the crowd stood a little girl, transfixed. Over half a century later, now a minister's wife well past middle age, she recalled the riverbank sermon to the preacher's eldest son:

> I can never forget the impressions which fell on my young heart, as your father, in a distinct, clear, and manly tone, began to address the thoughtless multitude that had been attracted to hear him. His powerful appeals to the conscience, couched in such simple phrase, at the distance of more than fifty years are still vividly remembered, and were so terrifying at the time, that I never closed an eye nor even retired to rest that night.[1]

It was her first and only encounter with James Alexander Haldane.

James Alexander, as he was commonly known, took the Bible very seriously indeed. Such was his obedience to the command 'be fruitful and multiply' that he fathered fifteen children across two marriages. His third and last son by his first wife was Robert Haldane, born in 1805 and the man who would eventually marry Mary Burdon Sanderson in 1853. Robert was devoted to his father and strove to emulate him. Though a lawyer by profession, he had a loft in the outbuildings at Cloan converted into a small chapel where locals would gather every fortnight during the summer and autumn to hear him preach 'the Word of God in all its strictness'.[2] He was not an itinerant preacher by his father's standards, but on alternate Sundays he would travel to remote settlements within a day's ride of Cloan so that there, too, the Bible might be opened and the gospel heard, however intimidating it might be.

In seeking to understand Robert, who would establish the Haldanes of Cloan as a distinct line within the family, first we have to understand the monumental paternal presence of James Alexander Haldane in Robert's life. For Robert's father was far more than a religious firebrand; he engendered the deepest loyalty and love in his children and friends. Indeed, he became something of a legend to his grandchildren, a guiding light in what it means to fight for the Truth. By the time the grandchildren were committed to their own campaigns, the content of that truth had shifted in the family's eyes and the word had lost its capital letter, but the certainty and conviction of their grandfather had in no way slackened. If anything, it was tightened to degrees that would have scandalised James Alexander. As one family friend of Robert and Mary's children jokingly put it, 'The Haldanes are so frightfully *un*-humble, they back their opinion against God's any day.'[3]

* * *

James Alexander (1768–1851) and his older brother Robert Haldane of Airthrey (1764–1842)—after whom Robert Haldane of Cloan was named—lived in an age of religious revivals and have been called 'the Wesleys of Scotland'.[4] Their fraternal mission in evangelism certainly recalled the joint work of John Wesley (1703–1791) and his brother Charles (1707–1788) in the cause of Methodism, particularly their emphasis on itinerant preaching irrespective of ordination or ecclesiastical sanction. Just as the Wesleys spread a new religious movement across England, so too the Haldanes—while not exactly founders of their causes—introduced Congregationalism into Scotland (congregations having complete charge over their own governance, that is), and, from 1808, they played a leading role in embedding Baptist views north of the Tweed. As you might expect, there were revealing differences doctrinally between these two sets of brothers. The Englishmen championed the possibility of human perfection in this life and the belief that Christ's death and resurrection opened the possibility of salvation to all people. The Scotsmen were resolute in their grim Calvinistic convictions about the 'total depravity' of human beings and the limited nature of the atonement. In the Haldanes' view, Christ died only for the predestined elect, amongst whom they were confident to be counted.

The impact of the Haldanes' evangelism is rather hard to assess. Robert reportedly invested over £70,000 into their work, which is over £9 million in today's money. This was made possible by selling his estate at Airthrey in 1798—a remarkable sacrifice. The magnificent castellated house at its centre had been designed by Robert Adam in 1790 at Robert Haldane's request. The latter had also commissioned a pupil of Capability Brown to design the landscaping of the grounds, which included the creation of a 23-acre man-made loch to complete the splendour of the outlook. (The house and grounds now form part of the University of Stirling.) Despite giving up all this, Robert and his brother's venture largely fizzled out within a decade, dying away 'amongst its own domestic quarrels', 'marred by bitterness of speech, obscurantism and fanaticism'.[5] Yet in its day, the movement—under the auspices of the newly formed Society for Propagating the Gospel at Home (SPGH)—provoked a significant public response. Vast crowds, often totalling over 3,000, would flock to hear James Alexander proclaim the gospel as he made his way across Scotland on one of his extended preaching tours. In 1799, the General Assembly of the Church of Scotland, fearful of the apparent threat to the established church order, was even forced to issue a Pastoral Admonition to its congregations, which denounced the itinerant preaching of the SPGH. Despite the forcefulness of James Alexander's message and the fears it aroused, he appears to have won for himself 'a more universal affection' than his brother, whose own brief foray into preaching ended rather painfully.[6] As a companion of Robert's recalled: 'with his characteristic vehemence and energy, he spoke so loud and so frequently, that he ruptured a blood-vessel, which made it necessary for him to desist'.[7] Robert sensibly stuck to writing thereafter and to financing the growing expenses of their activities, particularly the founding of preaching centres or 'Tabernacles' (a name adopted from the Wesleys' colleague, George Whitefield, in England) in Scotland's principal cities and seminaries to train their missionaries. James Alexander became the pastor of the Edinburgh Tabernacle, and gradually drew his lengthy tours to an end. Robert took no official leadership role, but such was his financial grip on all matters relating to their mission that he wielded immense powers in decision-making, so much so that one erstwhile colleague referred to him as 'the POPE of independents'.[8] Later, Robert would cause a sensation on the Continent, particularly in Geneva—which he called 'a synagogue of Satan and a citadel of ignorance and darkness'—as he undertook to convert the divinity students back to the city's lost Calvinism.[9] 'The results of that Mission stretch into eternity', wrote his nephew Alexander, 'and will forever connect the name of Robert Haldane with the revival of the Gospel in France and Switzerland.'[10]

There was a time when the brothers had lived more worldly lives, with neither showing much enthusiasm for religion in their early years. Robert had been a midshipman in the Royal Navy and had been on the Grand Tour, while James Alexander served as a captain in the East India Company and showed a particular skill in getting into, and out of, tight scrapes. Notwithstanding his renunciation of pre-conversion life, the family evidently relished the tales of James Alexander quelling mutinies and fighting duels. His son Alexander (elder brother to Robert Haldane of Cloan), in the memoirs he wrote of his father and uncle, tells these stories with an especial filial pride. His narration of events leading up to a duel on a return voyage from India is telling:

> The ship was crowded with passengers; amongst these was a cavalry officer, who was returning home,—a notorious shot, a successful duellist, and much of a bully... In the course of the voyage he made himself very disagreeable, and was rather an object of dread. On one occasion some high words occurred between him and Mr. James Haldane, arising out of a proposal to make the latter a party to a paltry trick, designed to provoke an irritable invalid as he lay in his cot..., and was, in fact, actually dying. Mr. J. Haldane's indignant

refusal issued in this captain's taking an opportunity deliberately and publicly to insult him at the mess-table, when, in return for a somewhat contemptuous retort, the aggressor threw a glass of wine in Mr. Haldane's face. He little knew the spirit which he evoked. To rise from his seat and dash at the head of the assailant a heavy ship's tumbler was the work of an instant. Providentially the missile was pitched too high, pulverized against the beam of the cabin, and descended in a liquid shower upon the offending dragoon. A challenge ensued...

Alexander continues with mounting satisfaction at his father's bravery:

> The two antagonists were placed at twelve paces distant [the duel took place on St Helena], and were to fire together and by signal... The signal was given, and, as Mr J. Haldane raised his pistol, with strange inconsistency he breathed the secret prayer,—'Father, into thy hands I commend my spirit;'... With this in his heart, and... with his eye fixed on his antagonist, without a symptom of trepidation, he calmly drew the trigger, when his pistol burst, the contents flying upwards and a fragment of the barrel inflicting a wound on his face. The other pistol missed fire, and the challenger immediately intimated... that he was so well satisfied with the honourable conduct of Mr. Haldane, that he was willing that the affair should terminate.[11]

Judging from his portrait by Colvin Smith, the exploding barrel left lifelong scars upon James Alexander's chin—an ineradicable sign of a swashbuckling past, of which his pious children were clearly not ashamed. That is no surprise when we remember that duels were a matter of honour, not just of the men in question, but of their family names. We only need know very little about 'Mr. Haldane's' lineage to realise that no amount of pacific spirit would brook an attempt to dishonour that ancient name.

* * *

The Haldane brothers were the great-grandchildren of John 'Union Jack' Haldane (1660–1721), the 14th—or possibly 16th[12]—Laird of Gleneagles, an ancient estate in the heart of Perthshire. John was proud to be able to trace his ancestry back along the direct male line for roughly half a millennium. One legend has it that the name Haldane came from an old name meaning 'half-Dane'—a detail of significance later in this book—while another claims its descent from a Danish chief called Haldanus.[13] More likely is its link to the lands of Haudene in the Scottish Borders, identified by today's hamlet of Hadden. These lands were once in the possession of Bernard fitz Brian (died c.1189), a man in the retinue of King William the Lion (1165–1214), whose descendants bore the name of Haudene or variants thereof; by the late eighteenth century, this had become Haldane. Traditionally, the Haldanes believed that it was Bernard's nephew, Roger, who settled at Gleneagles as early as the twelfth century, but there is little evidence for this. Nonetheless, there are enough clues in the historical records to link Bernard and his family with the emergence of the Haldanes of Gleneagles.[14] Centuries later, in 1769, Robert Haldane of Airthrey would become the senior male representative of the family, followed by James Alexander Haldane upon his brother's death in 1842. Neither, however, lived upon the ancestral estate.

Linking these generations was a remarkable array of public servants, politicians, soldiers, and sailors. In the fifteenth century, John Haldane held major posts under James III—a foreign ambassador, Master of the King's Household, Sheriff-Principal of Edinburgh, and Lord Justice General. Two other Johns, both Sirs, were to shed their blood across the following two centuries, at the battles of Flodden (1513) and Dunbar (1650). By the 1700s, 'Union Jack' Haldane was at the centre of political affairs as a member of the last Scottish and first Union parliaments. He would use all the nepotism he could muster to advance the prominence of his son Patrick, known as 'the Bear' within the family and 'the curse of Scotland' to the nation. It was never going to be an easy job to value and dispose of the estates forfeited by the Jacobites after 1715, but the task fell to Patrick, and he undertook it with pitiless efficiency. He may have had an easier time had he taken the route of his half-brother Robert, who became a commander of a ship in the East India Company. Not only was he the first Scotsman to do so, but he made the equivalent of £16 million in today's money in a single voyage.

The figure above all others whom James Alexander and Robert looked up to in the family was one they knew personally: their uncle, Admiral Adam Duncan (1731–1804). His famous victory over the Dutch at the Battle of Camperdown elevated him to the peerage as the 1st Viscount Duncan. It was under the Admiral's watchful eye that the Haldane brothers were raised as children, their own father dying before James Alexander was born. Duncan taught the boys to recite poetry, especially a well-known speech made by Cassius in Joseph Addison's tragedy *Cato*, which begins:

> My voice is still for war!
> What! Can a Roman senate long debate
> Which of the two to choose,—slavery or death?

When the young James Alexander found himself bed-bound with fever and his uncle entered the room to check on his progress, the delirious little boy would jump up and declaim with feeling, 'My voice is still for war!'[15] The boys most certainly believed that heroism was in the blood.

* * *

These stories already tell us much of what it must have been like for James Alexander's son, Robert Haldane, to have been born into such a family. There could have been no escaping the central importance of Calvinistic Christianity; the emphasis on the duty of preaching the Truth, irrespective of public opinion; the innately proud family spirit; the high regard for tradition; the tendency towards adventure. But none of this tells us much about Robert Haldane's early home life. For that, we need to dig deeper into the memoirs mentioned above.

Alexander, Robert's brother, writes of their father and their mother, Mary (née Joass, niece of Sir Robert Abercromby, Lieutenant-Governor of Bombay and Commander-in-Chief of the Indian Army), in terms that suggest not just great love for their children and each other but also tension in the marital relationship:

> [N]o man was more exemplary in all the private relations of domestic life. With his children he was playful as if himself a child, yet without losing sight, for a moment, of the reverence and authority due to a parent. With an increasing family, his affectionate wife could not but feel the discomfort of the protracted tours

of a husband so much beloved, and of the dangers, real and imaginary, with which they were associated... nor did she feel altogether reassured by the compliment paid to her own amiable qualities, when told, by some of her relations, that regard for her feelings had been a shield both to her husband and his brother. Still she endeavoured to console herself by the thought of the service in which he was engaged, and by reflecting on the necessity of patience and self-denial.[16]

James Alexander's long periods of absence and the ill-feeling he aroused in certain quarters evidently took their toll on his wife Mary. Though his preaching tours had drawn to a close by the time Robert was born in 1805, the evangelist could never quite get free of polemic: there was always a new heresy to combat and destroy. 'Even fellow Evangelicals and Dissenters were taken to task for errors', one historian observes of the brothers: 'this eagerness to criticize the doctrinal shortcomings of others conveys an impression... of an outlook essentially sectarian'.[17] It cannot have been easy living with a man so willing to make enemies.

James Alexander's love for his children expressed itself above all in his concern for their spiritual welfare. After the death in June 1802 of his six-year-old daughter, Catherine, he published a slim volume entitled, *Early Instruction recommended, in a Narrative of Catherine Haldane, with an Address to Parents on the Importance of Religion*, which ended up running through eleven or twelve editions. While there may be, as his son Alexander claimed, 'touches in it which indicate the tenderness of the fond parent', it is likely to repel most modern readers. James Alexander writes with evident pride that the six-year-old's confidence in her salvation 'did not arise from thinking all children went to heaven. In order to ascertain this, I one day asked her if she thought her elder sister would go to heaven if she died immediately. Catherine replied she did not know.'[18] We also learn that her favourite hymn verses were these from William Cowper:

> There is a fountain filled with blood,
> Drawn from Immanuel's veins;
> And sinners, plunged beneath that flood,
> Lose all their guilty stains.

Her father describes the lines as 'beautiful'.[19]

But if his son Alexander is to be believed, the reciprocal devotion between James Alexander and his children was deep and sincere. The following extract is perhaps the most revealing of them all:

> There [his family home] all his affections were centered... Great was the joy which reigned through the house whenever it was announced that... he was to remain at home on a Lord's-day evening. His children gathered round his chair, whilst he examined them as to their knowledge of the Bible, listened to the hymns or portions of Scripture which they repeated, or interested them by the recital of stories after the manner of the parables, in which the imagination was gratified, whilst truth was imprinted on their hearts... With prayer he parted with any of his family on going to a distance; with prayer and thanksgiving he welcomed them on their return...[20]

There were, then, significant parallels between the upbringings of Robert and the woman he would marry as his second wife, Mary Burdon Sanderson. For both, the father figure reigned supreme and religion dominated all concerns. There is not, however, the lurking sense of parental neglect in the picture just painted, as there is in Mary's childhood recollections. James Alexander was a more straightforward presence in the life of his children, not the psychologically disturbing presence-in-absence of Richard Burdon Sanderson.

* * *

It was the strong religious convictions of their fathers that lay at the origins of Robert and Mary's marriage. The two men inhabited a select religious world, where those holding to the same strict interpretations of Scripture inevitably banded together and sought intermarriage for their children. In fact, Robert's younger half-sister, Isabella, married Mary's eldest brother, Richard, in 1848, five years before their own marriage. James Alexander clearly had enormous respect for his Northumbrian counterpart, writing to a daughter-in-law after his first visit to the newlyweds in West Jesmond: 'We have much to be thankful that Isabella is so comfortably situated, and has become connected with a family in which the power of religion is more manifested than in most which I have witnessed.' But in this case, the Scotsman seems to have been more impressed by the elder Richard's architectural skill than anything else:

> I was much astonished to find that his house, which is very beautiful, in the Gothic style, was planned and built without any architect or estimate, but entirely by days' wages, under his own direction... This greatly surprised me, and I asked him how he had acquired so much knowledge of architecture. He told me he wrote a poem, which carried the [Newdigate] prize, upon the temple of Minerva at Athens, *The Parthenon*, when he found it necessary to study the Grecian architecture, which afterwards induced him to study the Gothic.[21]

James Alexander would have been even more surprised had he known that a second child of his was to marry another of the architectural wizard's children. He did not live to see it, and at the time of his death in February 1851 his son Robert was happily married to Jane Makgill, and the two were imminently expecting the arrival of their sixth child. That month of February, however, proved to be one of the darkest in Robert's life.

* * *

Until that time, the course of Robert's life—with one major exception—had been a smooth and conventional one and there is not much material to furnish an arresting narrative. He had been to Edinburgh's famous High School and University, as his father and uncle had done before him, with an interlude for study in Geneva (clearly the family no longer viewed the city as a 'synagogue of Satan'). Choosing the law as his profession, Robert became a Writer to the Signet, a Scottish term for those who have responsibilities similar to those of an English solicitor, and who also oversee financial matters for their clients. It was common at that time for clients to be relations, and Robert spent many of his working hours dealing with matters concerning the lands owned by his extended family. His nephew, General Sir Aylmer Haldane (1862–1950), once described him as 'a shrewd, clever, and successful man of business'.[22] Even in this, however, Robert sought to honour his father. 'It was said of him', wrote the General, 'that having once determined upon the right and proper course to be followed by a client, he never hesitated to advise him accordingly, even if by doing so he should be acting contrary to his own [financial and social] interests.'[23]

Judging from the two photographs that we have of Robert, probably taken when he was in his late forties, there was something quite handsome about him, even though his lips appear thin and his nose large. (In his granddaughter's novel, *The Bull Calves*, there is the rather wonderful line: 'Well, well, if yon's no' the first time that the Haldane nose has been compared with a turnip!')[24] There is an assurance and a dignity in his look, accentuated by the high Victorian collar. As a young man he can't have been a bad catch, particularly given his family connections. In 1841, Robert married Jane Makgill, daughter of John Makgill of Kemback, a man with many titles—8th Baronet of Makgill, *de jure* 8th Viscount of Oxfuird, and 8th Lord Makgill of Cousland. It was a classic match of the Scottish gentry and was swiftly fruitful. Jane gave birth every year between 1842 and 1844, and again in 1847 and 1848. The children bore the usual family names. In order of age, they were Elizabeth Joanna, Mary Abercromby, James Alexander (the eldest boy being named after Robert's father), Margaret Isabella, and Robert Camperdown.

With the family rapidly expanding, Robert bought a large family townhouse on the exclusive Charlotte Square in Edinburgh—designed by Robert Adam and now a UNESCO World Heritage Site—where he conducted much of his business. But his heart was in the country, and he eventually acquired Cloan in 1851, a small Perthshire estate of roughly 300 acres close to Gleneagles. It was not grand by the standards of the time, the main house being little more than a small farmhouse. It would be a further fifteen years before Cloan became a mansion house of some note, with Robert adding a large turreted extension to the west wing in 1866, giving the house a stately and baronial appearance. His son Richard—who inherited Cloan rather than his eldest half-brother James for reasons which remain mysterious—added to the east wing in 1904 and made the house what it remains today.[25] When Robert first bought it, Cloan was a thin rectangular building on two levels with attic rooms above. Some extensions of no pretention had been added to the sides and back, and a shaded veranda, hung with creepers, ran along its front. The house was (and is) north-west-facing, so there was not an abundance of natural light. To give a touch of warmth— or cold, depending on the time of year—a little conservatory was attached to the gable of the west extension. At Cloan, Robert could indulge his fondness for country sports and riding. To him, 'all animals were intimate friends… pigeons lit on his shoulders when he went out to feed them after breakfast, and the horses and ponies nosed his pockets for the bread which he carried for them.'[26] Cloan meant tranquillity to Robert and a retreat into the things he loved. At the time of buying it he needed a retreat more than ever.

* * *

The February of 1851 began with an emotion that is not contrary to tranquillity, the sadness associated with the loss of a beloved but aged father. James Alexander's death at eighty-two was full of peace and proclaimed his child-like assurance in his own place amongst the company of the elect. No one in attendance at the funeral would have been able to tell that he had made many enemies across his lifetime. Six hundred ministers, elders, and members of various denominations turned out to pay their respects. *The Scotsman* reported that such an honour had 'rarely been paid to any private individual'.[27] The family must have found considerable comfort in the fact that the venerable patriarch had lived a full and long life of service to his creed and in perceiving that such a fact was now receiving the recognition they believed it deserved. For Robert, the comfort was to be short-lived.

Within sixteen days of his father's last breath, his beloved wife Jane, mother to his five young children, and the girl she had borne within her for nine months were dead. As was so often the case then, complications in childbirth were responsible. Robert, in his grief, named the little girl after her mother, and the two Janes were laid to rest in the same grave. We do not have any first-hand accounts of the tragedy. But we do have a letter from Richard Burdon Sanderson, who within a few years would become Robert's new father-in-law, to one of Robert's sisters, which begins:

> Your letter shocked, but did not altogether surprise me. I scarcely dared to hope, and yet I *did* hope that the Lord would spare the mother for the children's sakes, to say nothing of the bereaved hus-

band. I *do*, however, think of him, and what is more, I believe that God thinks of him also, and, perhaps, will do him more good by the day of his wife's death than by the day of her espousals. It is, indeed, to her the marriage supper of the Lamb, and the Bride hath made herself ready...[28]

Could Robert have seen things this way? It seems incredible to think so. And yet, he had a model in religious resignation to turn to within his memory. For there was indeed an exception to the smooth course of Robert's life up until 1851, and that was the loss of his own mother, Mary Haldane, in February 1819, when Robert was just fourteen.

Robert's brother describes the night of their mother's death in vivid detail. It must have etched upon Robert's mind an immovable impression of what it meant to face the reality of suffering as a man of God:

> The moment that any danger became imminent, he [James Alexander] gathered all his children together, and kneeling down in the midst of them, offered up a prayer never to be forgotten, in which the most pathetic and earnest supplications for her recovery, if consistent with the Lord's will, were mingled with expressions of unreserved confidence in the love of God, and submission to the Divine pleasure... It was a night much to be remembered. It exhibited the struggle and the triumph of faith, contending with the fondest earthly affection, the tenderest and deepest feelings of the husband and the father controlled by the resignation of the believer, enabled to say, 'Though he slay me, yet will I trust in him.'[29]

It is likely that Robert faced the death of his own wife and child in the spirit of his father.[30] The astonishing description of Robert's reaction to a later loss, which we will come to in Chapter 3, supports this judgement. The stern acceptance of his lot may account for the speed at which he sought a new bride. More likely, it was the fact that Robert was forty-six with five children under the age of ten. Could he find someone brave or foolish enough to take them on? Could he, perhaps, tap into the vulnerabilities of youth, piety, and a broken heart?

* * *

At the time of Jane Haldane's death in 1851, Mary Burdon Sanderson was twenty-five years old and had renounced the prospect of marriage. Her heart had been broken by a dashing young man who had 'paid his addresses to her, and, indeed, fell passionately in love with her'. It is not that he eventually rejected her; far from it. It was Mary who rejected her suitor. Many years later, she described him to her own children as 'one of the most attractive men she ever met'. They were entirely in tune with one another, sharing a love of art and literature and a spirit of adventure. It was not enough. According to Mary's daughter Elizabeth, 'The young man was morally correct in every way, but he was not religious in the view of our grandparents, and our mother herself did not feel sure of his being a Child of God.' Mary had been influenced by a sentence from a Puritan divine, given to her by her father before she made the final decision as to whether or not to accept his hand: 'Take Christ for your Husband and He will provide one to his own liking.' It may have settled her decision, but it did not settle her soul: 'It was a bitter trial that our mother passed through when she rejected her lover, and one that left an effect upon her all through her long life.' As was typical for Mary, her mental condition manifested itself physically and she became severely ill. She was diagnosed with heart disease and her parents feared for her life.[31]

Mary eventually recovered, and in 1848 she moved with her parents to Devonshire in the common Victorian bid to find better air. The change of scene proved momentous. For it was here, in Plymouth, that she met the recently widowed Robert Haldane, down from Scotland on a visit to one of his sisters. Richard Burdon Sanderson was delighted to meet a son of his old friend, James Alexander, and a brother of his daughter-in-law, but Mary must have thought him ancient. He was twenty years older than her and had already lived through so much. Robert, however, found exactly what he was looking for. She may not have been attractive by conventional standards, but Mary's pronounced cheekbones, her slight pout, and her penetrating gaze must have given her a certain allure. Moreover, her youth, though blighted by repeated illness, is likely to have reassured Robert that she would be capable of handling the demands of his boisterous children. Most importantly of all, she belonged to that select religious circle which, to Robert's mind, guaranteed the soundness of the match in God's eyes.

FAMILY MATTERS

By November 1852, Robert had made it clear to Richard that he sought the hand of his daughter. She rejected the idea outright. What was one of his age and experience doing proposing to one as young and inexperienced as herself? Robert was not repulsed at the first setback. He sought a meeting with her and made his appeal in person. Still she thought the notion impossible, but she allowed him to write to her. 'He was a determined suitor', wrote their daughter, 'and kept up a correspondence which breathed a spiritual atmosphere that gradually inspired her with the conviction that this and no other was the path opened up to her, and that it was her mission to care for the motherless children.'[32] It is hard to escape the conclusion that this was less a marriage of love than of duty.

Mary's mother was wary. The sheer number of Robert's children made the whole thing unadvisable. She had envisaged something quite different for her daughter. It brought matters to a standstill for almost a year. Until her mother consented to attend the wedding, Mary refused to accept the possibility of marriage to Robert. Finally, maternal consent having been given, Mary and Robert were married on 27 July 1853 at Plymstock. Dressed in 'a beautiful silver-grey moiré silk gown with a Honiton lace cape and a veil of the same', the bride was made to walk a full mile to the chapel.[33] The whole way was strewn with summer flowers, thrown by friends and the local Sunday school children. After the ceremony, Mary witnessed a thing she had never seen before and she felt a sudden flash of sadness: her father, Richard, shed a tear.

* * *

A honeymoon on the Isle of Wight and in Paris—where the couple glimpsed another newlywed, Eugénie de Montijo, wife of Napoleon III and last empress of the French—was the final hurrah of excitement before the cold, hard reality of married life in Scotland set in. Not only were there five children to tend and bond with, but she had to deal with an extended Haldane family whose religiosity was peculiarly Scottish and particularly trying to the young Englishwoman. They were 'forcible' and 'rather narrow' and lived by unwritten rules of propriety which Mary, in her innocence and gentleness, found difficult to navigate.[34]

On one occasion, Mary was moved by the case of a married woman who had been condemned to death for killing her husband's mistress, and who cried out from the dock in distress for her children, 'My weans, my weans, what will they do?' Mary was expecting a child by this time, and such was her compassion for the mother that she sent a message to her expressing her anguish at her plight. The note eventually found its way into the press and caused a scandal amongst her Haldane relations. Given Mary's social standing, the Haldanes considered her actions an 'unforgiveable offence'. Mary struggled to understand their lack of compassion. How could they think themselves Christians if they believed that it was only 'the good people who should be cared for'? To Mary, Christianity and compassion were inseparable, and in her eyes 'all men were the same and she was ready to help all equally'.[35] In fact, Mary was also practising an early form of feminism. As her daughter observed, 'She sorrowed with all that sorrowed, good and bad, and to the horror of the North Country relatives went amongst those women who were termed "fallen" and dared to say that there were those of the other sex who had "fallen" with them.'[36]

Her suffering in Scotland was heightened when, on 24 March 1855, she lost her first child, a boy, who had been born just three days before. This sad fact is passed over with little comment in the family records of her marriage (the child's gravestone in the churchyard of St Cuthbert's, Edinburgh, bears a remarkable three-word biblical inscription from 2 Kings 4.26: 'It is well'), and the first major event that gains recognition is the birth, on 30 July 1856, of Richard Burdon Haldane. In Mary's view, it was 'sunshine after clouds' and 'one of the bright days of my life'. She liked to remember in her letters to her eldest son that he was born at precisely 3 o'clock in the afternoon. Mary's parents were by her side and 'many special prayers ascended for you which have been answered'. The new-born Richard 'looked prematurely wise as he lay in his bassinette of pink silk & lace, his grandfather's gift'. Fifty years later, just after Richard entered government for the first time, she wrote: 'Still I little guessed that I had a future minister of state for war.'[37] The dynasty had begun.

Mary bore a child every two years thereafter until 1864: George Abercromby (Geordie) on 27 May 1858, John Scott

(Johnnie) on 2 May 1860, Elizabeth Sanderson (Bay) on 27 May 1862, and William Stowell (Willie) on 19 August 1864. But what about her stepchildren?

The eldest of them was fourteen and the youngest eight when Richard was born. By the time Willie arrived, those ages were twenty-two and sixteen. The few appearances these siblings make in Mary's children's later memoirs would have one believe that all was harmonious in their relations. But a dig around the National Library of Scotland's Haldane Papers reveals significant tensions between the two sides of the family, as financial concerns pressed upon them in the wake of Robert Haldane's death in 1877.[38] At one point, Richard writes to Mary of his half-siblings, 'There is certainly something amiss with the mental composition of the three elder ones.'[39] Indeed, there is one earlier letter in the archives, from about 1864, in which Robert's eldest son, James, writes home to his father from Lausanne, and in doing so reveals a personality of almost Bertie Wooster proportions: 'Every day is so much like another that what may be extracted from my last letter home is my present mode of life, a jolly do nothing lazy sort of a life it is, to wh.[ich] I am becoming much attached.'[40] None of James's half-siblings could ever have written such a sentence.

The descendants of Robert's first marriage also form an intriguing group, ranging from the arch-Conservative Germanophobe, Sir George Makgill, to the extremely versatile administrator, Lieutenant Colonel Maldwyn Makgill Haldane, MI5's first recruit, who became one of its most senior members. That's not even to mention Robert Haldane Makgill, who is remembered as 'one of the architects of New Zealand's public health system in the twentieth century'.[41] Nevertheless, the strong creative drive and original streak in Mary's children and those who came after them is not so easily discernible in Mary's stepchildren and their families. While we cannot be sure of the genetic element in this, the deduction is clear: Mary was the game-changer.

3

THE WORLD IN BLACK AND WHITE

1860s AND 1870s

Robert and Mary's children—Richard, Geordie, Johnnie, Bay, and Willie (who we'll call in this chapter 'the Haldane children')—were acutely conscious of the differences between themselves and their older half-siblings. But this was just one of many stark contrasts in their early lives. Theirs was a black-and-white world, distinctly lacking in nuance. Reality was everywhere rent in two; wherever they turned, they found themselves on one side of an unbridgeable divide. Elizabeth's (Bay's) memoirs of their childhood are revelatory of this chasmic world.

There were, first and foremost, the saved and the damned. 'Religion permeated our lives', remembered Elizabeth, 'and the sense of sin and its consequences seemed to dog our footsteps when we remembered what it meant.'[1] Willie put it this way: 'One lived in an atmosphere of "fear" of God in dread reality, far distant from his love for his created.'[2] This was not simply the result of family tradition or their father's strict preaching in the chapel at Cloan. Church ministers in Scotland at that time continued to follow the old custom of rebuking 'sinners' from the pulpit.[3] The seriousness of sin was a public matter. Fear was in the culture. According to Elizabeth, 'There was still a Puritan dread of pleasure—even artistic pleasure—unless it were to lead to something useful to mankind. Could we use it for the service of God or of our fellows? Otherwise it might draw us into evil ways.'[4]

Working hours were particularly sacrosanct, as one would expect in a country so deeply infused with the Protestant work ethic.[5] Woe betide the Haldane child found reading a book of a non-instructive kind during the working day. Their God may have been a God of grace, but there was to be no testing of that generous doctrine. Scotland, in Victoria's reign, was a perfect exemplar of that strange paradox: wherever Luther's belief in 'justification by faith alone' is preached, there you find a pervasive obsession with the rights and wrongs of people's behaviour. It was quite natural for the young Willie Haldane, seeing a man smoking a pipe in the street one Sunday, to exclaim to his mother, 'That man is going to hell.' His mother's response exposed her origins south of the Border: 'You must not say that Willie: it is not for us to judge.' The effect on the small boy was lasting and profound: 'Did his mother really believe what he had been told, or was she not honest or truthful—she in whom he had implicitly believed? It was long before he got over that horrid alternative and was able to trust his mother again.'[6]

Mary also refused to participate in the common practice, enjoyed by the Haldanes and their pious friends, of riding in a carriage through deprived areas of the country, throwing religious texts 'at the heads' of the sick, and casting 'terrifying' tracts at the doors of workers' cottages.[7] There was an obvious implication in such condescending behaviour: those high in their carriages clearly did not think that they themselves were in any need of saving. Elizabeth herself admitted, 'I suppose we really thought that working people had morals more easily upset than those of the well-to-do.'[8] Although the Haldane children 'were taught that there were only two alternatives set before [them], and that it was a matter of infinite importance to decide which way should be chosen—one leading to eternal bliss and the other to eternal damnation', the Haldanes as a family didn't seem to be in much doubt about their final destination.[9] Looking back on her father's upbringing, Johnnie's daughter, Naomi, asked the question (knowing full well the answer): 'Did the Haldane family, without thinking about it too much, automatically consider themselves as the elect?'[10] Elizabeth's words are revealing on this point: 'we were brought up to remember that death was an essential part of life, and must be faced without fear'.[11] Surely only those confident in their own salvation can do such a thing.

Another glaring divide in their early lives was that between rich and poor. The opening chapter has already outlined some of the horrendous disparities within nineteenth-century Britain. Elizabeth's memoirs show her conscience-racked awareness of the prevailing conditions, pointing out that children of Scottish labourers began to work as young as nine, 'going to school just as they could, trying to avoid the days when fees were paid to the schoolmaster'.[12] The first census on Scottish housing in 1861 showed that 34 per cent of all houses had only one room; 1 per cent of the population even lived in houses without any windows. A staggering 64 per cent of the entire population lived in one- or two-roomed dwellings.[13]

Not only would Robert Haldane take his children on tours through the wretched environs of Edinburgh's Old Town, but they were also continuously reminded by their nurse, Betsey Ferguson (affectionately known as Baba), of the world from which she had escaped and into which they were never to fall. Baba was the daughter of a widow left with a large family to bring up, and she knew what it was to fear being without the necessities that make life human:

> We were told about working people and their struggles by our nurse, and urged to benefit from, and be grateful for, our advantages in having plenty of food and clothing. In those days the credit was always given to 'your Papa, who is doing all those good things for you'.

Elizabeth continues: 'Personally I felt that it was a case of marvellous beneficence on his part to clothe and feed us, and therefore that we must absolutely act on his smallest wishes.'[14]

The children were also free to read their mother's beloved Dickens: the one exemption from the blanket ban on novels imposed by their parents. It was important for Mary, nursing her own painful memories of childhood, that her children should know of the many evils inflicted upon the most vulnerable within society. Their yearly trips to London to visit relatives impressed on the children the reality of Dickens's world. 'I can never forget... the effect upon me', wrote Elizabeth.[15] Nothing could have been more remote from the genteel Charlotte Square and baronial Cloan than the London slums. It was an experience that would plant the seeds of the children's later work. And yet, while their religious upbringing certainly emphasised the need to serve the poor, there was 'no idea of abolishing class distinctions or bringing about equality economically'.[16] The chasm within society was a given.

The same could be said of the divide between masters and servants. It is true that Baba seemed to blur the boundary somewhat. Having left school at the age of ten, she was a true autodidact, and she 'guided our thoughts and deeds much more than did others of our seniors. She was one in a thousand, and even our tutor trembled at her word.'[17] Elizabeth went so far as to call her 'a second mother to all [Mary's] children'.[18] Baba's very closeness to her charges, however, was a sign of her lowly birth. The remoteness of parents was part and parcel of what it meant to function as a well-to-do family:

> In my wildest fancy I could not imagine my mother bathing or dressing me, and she never thought of such a thing. To my mind she was always as she appeared in the nursery near bedtime, a lovely figure in a beautiful moiré silk gown so widely spread out that when the boys' tutor came into the room unexpectedly she simply floated her frock over bath and child together, forming for the latter a delightful tent.[19]

Baba's constant presence was a practical necessity. Mothers of the upper classes simply did not mother their children in a hands-on way. Mary did take care of her children, but it was done, as it were, from a distance. As Richard recalled:

> She taught us children the Bible, the contents of which she had under great command, and she watched closely over our welfare... Our mother was gentle in her relations to us. She was always trying to bring about what she believed to be best for us, and we were devoted to her.[20]

But the nitty-gritty of mothering—changing nappies, bathing, clothing, putting to bed—was reserved for Baba. That said, her purpose was greater than this. In Mary's eyes, Baba was a 'good woman' and that was all-important. 'The influence of a good man or woman has a profound effect on a child when their principles are carried out in practice', observed Mary: 'A parent can only guide at a distance by supplying other channels of good influence so as to reach her children.'[21]

It is shocking to find Elizabeth saying that nurses, 'once they had embarked on their career, had to make up their minds to see no more of their relatives, for holidays there were none'.[22] Later, she rather naively writes of the family's servants: 'I have always wondered at their selfless devotion, sacrificing as they did their private lives for those of their employers.'[23] The truth, of course, was that hard and often dire economic circumstances forced people into such roles. The welfare state was still a thing of the future, and the most basic financial security remained, for many, a dream. Despite her apparent naivety, Elizabeth would devote much of her later energy to reversing these conditions, especially for women.

Then there was the divide between adults and children, one perfectly reflected in the interior design of 17 Charlotte Square, the family's house throughout winter and spring: 'I can never forget the ugliness of our schoolroom in Edinburgh,' wrote Elizabeth. It was right at the top of the five-storey house, and 'it seemed as if the refuse had gone upstairs'. While the rest of the house was exquisitely presented—'good rosewood and Utrecht velvet furniture in the drawing-room and rather beautiful marble mantelpieces and glass-drop chandeliers'—everything in the schoolroom spoke of a total lack of regard for the children's surroundings. A horrible smell hung in the air of the dingy room, emanating from the nasty brown cardboard slabs which held their atlases. The dim crimson carpet was unrelieved by the crimson rep of the single armchair, reserved for the tutor.[24]

The tutor of their early years was a young medical student, who had fought hard to gain himself an education and was planning a career as a missionary. He was a good teacher, but more importantly, he was able 'to climb a tree like a monkey and to leap over crevasses without fear'.[25] This made him an unquestionable hit with the children, and this despite his conviction concerning the merits of corporal punishment. He was comparatively lenient with Elizabeth, who received a smack upon the hand—a 'palmy'—if she made three mistakes in spelling. For the boys, he reserved the 'tawse', a leather strip split into tails. Elizabeth attributed her ability to spell to these old-fashioned methods: 'We bore no resentment excepting when through grown-up interference undeserved punishment was given.'[26] Fortunately, unlike their mother's childhood experiences, this was rarely an issue. The Haldane children considered themselves lucky to be treated 'as reasonable beings'.[27]

Still, they were not to be seen downstairs, with the exception of an airing in the dining room while the grown-ups ate their dessert. Elizabeth writes pathetically that the ceremony 'brought little pleasure, though we were given part of an orange or apple and were allowed to look at pictures afterwards in the drawing room'. Their 'real lives' were lived upstairs, where—despite the shabbiness—they lived in a kind of freedom. A feeling of warmth and closeness with their parents was not a feeling they knew at this stage: 'We loved our parents, but the love was mingled with awe till the time when we knew them better.'[28]

Though the children were treated as 'reasonable beings', nothing would change the fact of Elizabeth's sex, and here again the world was a black-and-white one—though change was afoot. The 'mildly Whig' household was largely old-fashioned in its practices and its views; even their mother Mary, who cared so much about the prevention of injustice, was too engrossed in religious matters and, at this stage, too much a lady of her time to voice advanced views on women's rights:[29]

> Our mother was somehow on a higher and more spiritual level, in which material things did not count in the same way. She no doubt ordered the dinner, but 'the books' were examined and paid by our father, who also paid wages. And yet she had money of her own, though she never received it except through her husband.[30]

Robert seemed oblivious to gender inequality; as with his wife, religion took up the entire field of vision. And yet, nationally in the early 1870s, debate raged over whether women medical students ought to be granted admission to university with a view to graduation. Encouraged by their tutor's hostility to the idea, Richard, Geordie, and Johnnie were all 'violently against women coming into universities'.[31]

Bay, aged only nine, took a different stand, penning a paper titled *Fair Play or a few words for the Lady Doctors*. It is a remarkable, courageous, and beautifully written document, still in the family's possession. Addressed to 'Gentlemen', it starts: 'I am going to say a few words for the lady doctors who, I think, are illtreated. What right have the men not to let ladies be whatever profession they choose?' Bay continues: 'When people get accustomed to lady doctors I am almost sure they would like them, they could talk to them, and they are so gentle, while men have got such hard hands (and hard hearts).' It concludes stirringly:

> But I am sure men should not call women effeminate when they are trying to work, and the men won't let them. As if women were effeminate. 'No.' They are not that, but I shall not mind. The women are determined to get to the top of the hill, and they shall.
>
> I remain
>
> keeper of woman's rights
>
> Elizabeth Sanderson Haldane[32]

The 1872 Education (Scotland) Act was one of the first momentous steps for women's rights in the country. 'Women were about to be recognized as sapient creatures', was Elizabeth's wry comment. Approximately 1,000 locally elected school boards were established as a result of the Act, with the authority to manage the existing parish and burgh schools. Crucially, women could stand as candidates for the boards. The first election in Edinburgh took place in 1873. Once again, Bay, now aged eleven, joined the fray, seeking to support the candidacy of Miss Flora Stevenson—a well-respected but progressive member of Edinburgh society. Bay knew that householders had the same number of votes as there were candidates, and it struck her that gaining just one of those votes in Miss Stevenson's favour would be a significant victory. Looking back, she described her tactics thus:

> At that time my father was suffering from headache and he liked me to sit by him and stroke his hair to set him to sleep. I waited till he was not quite asleep but, as I thought, in a peaceful state of mind, and then I screwed up my courage and said, 'Papa, do you think you would mind giving one of your votes to Miss Stevenson?' I can still remember the start of the peaceful papa, right out of his chair. 'What is this child speaking of?' he exclaimed in amazement. The world to him was evidently turning upside down, and so in fact it was.[33]

Even with these new avenues opening up, the prospect for Bay's own future looked bleak. Baba, in keeping with her mistress's wishes, had instilled in the children the requirement that they ought to give their lives 'to helping other people', but Bay was conscious of the gulf that lay between herself and her brothers when it came to the possibilities for achieving this. To her, 'what I could do did not seem to me very clear beyond possibly serving as a prop to those doing more important work'. In everything she did she tried to keep up with the boys, and before the onset of puberty, she largely had the freedom and the ability to do so. But she was convinced that in the long run it would prove futile:

> I broke my dolls to see what was inside, played cricket and climbed trees, and altogether was conscious of the impossibility of ever attaining to any social success. I wanted to do for myself and not just to be the helper of others who were doing—a quite unbiblical ideal for any woman to have.

It was not just a question of scriptural interpretation; society had its rules and they bent to no one: 'The "must nots" of propriety soon cast their net over the girl and she was directed to find her happiness where it did not exist.'[34] Bay, chafing under the weight of convention, was well aware of where her happiness lay: 'How one longed to be a boy and able to adventure!'[35]

* * *

Other societal divides were important, though less drastically stark. That between the educated and uneducated was, in Scotland at least, one that could be overcome, provided the young student had the brains, a supportive family, a capacity for hard work, and a certain amount of luck. In the 1860s, Scotland had one university place for every 1,000 people, whereas in England the ratio was one for every 5,800.[36] It could also boast that 23 per cent of those admitted to the arts faculties of the Scottish universities were the children of manual workers.[37] Indeed, Scotland was famous for what George Davie called its 'democratic intellect' thanks to the system instituted by John Knox, where education was the duty of each parish through its church.[38] Even the great High School of Edinburgh was a place where 'men of the highest and lowest rank of society send their children to be educated together'.[39] Yet these advantages should not be overplayed. As T. C. Smout has observed, 'considered as a whole, Scottish education at mid-century was extremely inegalitarian, mainly because economic pressures on the great mass of the population put anything apart from the acquisition of the most basic literary skills far beyond their reach'.[40] And as Elizabeth Haldane pointed out, by and large, 'school buildings were hovels, teachers were scandalously paid, and it was only the real keen interest in learning which seemed to be born in a Scot that prevented absolute collapse'.[41]

This interest in learning, coursing through Scotland's blood, was to prove critical for the Haldane children. But in their case, it was not to be developed in any hovel. Mary took control of their education, sending the boys—including her stepsons—once they reached the age of ten to the Edinburgh Academy, a handsome if restrained neoclassical building situated on the edge of the New Town. Compared to the High School, dating from 1128, this was a new institution, having been established as recently as 1824. Mary's choice may have been influenced by her English background, for the Academy was making an unashamed attempt to compete with the great public schools south of the Border by offering a more rigorous education in Latin and Greek than its ancient competitor in the capital. But, as one alumnus (Oxford's Professor of Poetry, John Campbell Shairp) said of the early history of the school, 'In vain you would look there for the green "Playing-fields" of Eton... or even for the green Close of Rugby with its venerable elm-trees... These things the Academy did not affect. But it aimed at and affected careful grounding, sound learning, and a most laborious work.'[42]

Breaking with national tradition, it was not a democratic institution. The school's intake was largely from the middle and upper-middle classes, and it had a clear intention to produce 'gentlemen' and citizens of the British Empire. To Mary, there was nothing suspect in that last ambition; it was laudable. In her eighties, she could speak of 'the Empire which I was training my sons to serve'.[43] Even the Academy's lack of religious affiliation was to its advantage. After her own early experiences, she was reluctant to mix religion too intimately with education.

Moreover, as Mary considered her options, former Academy pupils were beginning to make their mark in the wider world. Two of the most prestigious Professorships at Edinburgh were held by Academicals: William Young Sellar in Latin and Peter Guthrie Tait in natural philosophy, who became two of Richard Haldane's favourite teachers when he progressed to the University. Tait's school friend James Clerk Maxwell was Professor of Natural Philosophy at King's College, London, and was soon to be made the first Cavendish Professor of Physics at Cambridge (he would eventually be known as the 'father of modern physics'). By 1868, another Academical, Archibald Campbell Tait, was sitting on the Archbishop's throne at Canterbury.[44] Mary's veneration for her family's glittering academic tradition is likely to have steered her in the direction of an institution that—with enough hard work—could promise her sons similar triumphs.

It was a prudent choice. In Johnnie's class alone, as his friend and classmate Professor Sir D'Arcy Wentworth Thompson remembered in a letter to *The Times*, 'was one boy who won the Victoria Cross, one with a seat in the Cabinet, one Royal Academician, and four Fellows of the Royal Society'.[45] Johnnie himself, though later an FRS, was never quite at the top of the class. In fact, his daughter Naomi would write of his time at school: 'My father seemed to recollect it mostly for the pleasure of the running war with the town boys.'[46] When his brother Richard visited the Academy again in 1909, while serving as Secretary of State for War, he picked up on the same theme and the spartan conditions of the time, telling the assembled pupils, teachers, and dignitaries:

> Everybody was content with very little then. I recall how we used to fight for a currant-bun or half an Albert [cake] across the bar of the Janitor's window. In those days, the only drinking-water we had was to be got in a trough which was the centre of a mass of boys fighting to get their luncheon. You dipped down as well as you could and got a jugful of water—and crumbs. That slaked your thirst for the day... It was hard to get home in the afternoon without a fight, because there was an opposing enemy whom we always encountered somewhere about Church Lane. It developed habits of self-reliance, and the boy was very much looked down upon in those days who went skulking home round by the other side of the Water of Leith... in order to avoid a fight.[47]

Lessons themselves could be rather dry, and focused mainly on the classical languages, but for Johnnie at least, there was intellectual excitement to be had in the company of his friends. They formed a group known as the Eureka Club, which would spend its Saturdays 'botanising throughout the countryside, howking fossils in quarry-pools at Wardie, or searching the jetsam of Newhaven fishing boats'.[48] It was this select gang that produced the four members of the Royal Society.[49] Surprisingly, given the future careers of the Haldane brothers, it was the youngest of Mary's children, Willie, who prospered most at the Academy. Writing to his mother in July 1881, Richard notes: 'I am very glad to hear that Willie has come out second in the general mathematical examination. After all he has distinguished himself more at school than any of us.'[50]

Bay's education began at home with the boys' tutor. She was fearful at first, her brothers having teased her about the horrors in store for her, but she came to love her lessons. She relished, too, their 11 o'clock lunch, which consisted of bread and butter sprinkled with sugar. What she didn't appreciate was the apparently arbitrary nature of the curriculum. She could not understand why she had to write on topics such as 'Procrastination', which held no interest or relevance to her, or why she had to learn lists of capes and peninsulas without even knowing where they were on the map. Bay was hungry for real knowledge. The tutor 'marvelled when I asked for longer lessons because I liked them'.[51]

Eventually the children's beloved tutor left them for the mission field and was replaced by a succession of young men studying for the ministry. Each of them was desperately shy and they failed to push Bay in her learning:

> One of them confided to me that he thought it nonsense to teach girls Latin, as my mother directed, when they should be learning to bake; so I made him an enormous cake and presented it to him, to his great embarrassment, since he did not know how most conveniently to get rid of it.[52]

Even so, she got something of an education from these hours in the schoolroom. The same could not be said of the classes for girls which she began to attend in Edinburgh's Moray Place around the age of twelve: a situation brought about under the pressure of elderly relatives, who thought Bay 'too boyish... and not to have learned the technique of young ladyhood'.[53]

The classes were an embarrassment. In Bay's view, 'we were learning practically nothing... but just learned our day's lesson as it came, regardless of what preceded or succeeded'. She chiefly remembered the experience for the viciousness of the admonishments that she and the other girls received for acts which could hardly pass as malicious, like accidentally knocking over an ink-pot: 'Scoldings were formidable things such as I had never before experienced. They lasted about ten minutes and... I used to wonder how words were found for them—or indeed the time.' The one thing Bay was adamant about was that she would not cry. She 'hated' it when she saw other girls doing so.[54]

* * *

The Haldane children—especially Richard, Johnnie, and Bay—would make it their life ambition to chip away at the mortar of these seemingly unscalable divides in their early lives. The philosophical positions they developed broke down the religious barriers that sustained centuries-long ill-feeling, and took fear out of the equation; their political, legal, and scientific work combatted society's systemic inequalities between rich and poor, masters and servants, male and female; their educational endeavours granted a new sense of dignity to childhood and made a life of learning accessible to thousands of young men and women who had been denied such liberation in the past. But there was one divide in their lives which belonged to a different order of things and between which they went back and forth: the divide between town and country.

There was no doubt where their hearts lay. Cloan—or Cloanden as it was known from Mary's marriage into the family until 1904—meant space, freedom, and joy. By 1866 a substantial extension and elevation to the west wing had transformed the property into a turreted baronial home proportionate to the Haldanes' status within the county. Robert and Mary decided to make it the family's summer and autumn residence each year, the children's education carrying on under the watchful eye of their tutor.

The difference between Cloan and Edinburgh was profound. Elizabeth wrote of her mother, 'Edinburgh she never cared for; the society seemed to her stiff and cold, and she found her greatest pleasure in getting to the country and being with her children.'[55] Elizabeth herself called their time at Cloan 'the wonderful part' of the year.[56] Gone was the reek and dullness of their attic school-room. Here everything was

> sweet and fresh, and even as one entered the house there was a fresh scent such as I like to think of still, but which I cannot describe. Clean chintzes covered the chairs, and we had home-made scones instead of baker's bread and plenty of milk in old-fashioned white jugs adorned with raised ferns.[57]

The land, too, had undergone a makeover. Robert and Mary took the keenest pleasure in having it planted and drained, and they ordered paths to be created through the woods. The children loved to climb the trees around the house, a special favourite being a large lime tree close to the walled garden, where each child—and their descendants since—carved their initials into the bark. It is still known within the family as the 'Initial Tree'. There were louder activities than this, of course. The boys received their first guns when they turned twelve, and Richard, Geordie, and Willie rejoiced in their possession. Richard remembered 'rising before daybreak to stalk the grouse and black-game which visited the stubble fields'.[58] Johnnie and Bay had other ideas. Not caring for killing, the two set off with vasculums (flattened cylindrical cases for collecting plants) on their backs and hunted for rare ferns in the glens.

Walking was a passion. Robert Haldane led the family expeditions into the surrounding Ochil Hills and, somewhat unexpectedly, took great pleasure in showing a total disregard for signs stating 'Trespassers will be prosecuted'. They would take tea with shepherds in their high dwellings or bring a picnic with them in their bags. Mary was in her element, but made no sartorial concessions to the conditions. Her daughter records:

> I never remember her dressed otherwise than in her full Victorian skirts—very likely of silk—reaching to the feet, and voluminous petticoats, as well as a Victorian bonnet: never a hat. This did not impede her progress at all, and she continued to walk till well over seventy. In her youth she was reputed to have sent her English friends home in invalid carriages![59]

In later years, Mary's boys prided themselves on their durability on foot. A walk from Cloan to the top of the 4,000-foot Ben Lawers in the Grampians and back, totalling 73 miles, was not uncommon. Once, they completed it within 23 hours, having left the house at 2 o'clock in the morning. Even more startling was the brothers' walk of 30 hours and 50 minutes from Ballater in Aberdeenshire to Cloan: a cool 101 miles. (Richard had to pull out part-way, due to either blisters or his solitary lunchtime in-take of champagne.) Going the 40 miles from Edinburgh to Cloan on foot was to them a mere hop, skip, and a jump.

Inside the house, life was kept simple. For breakfast, there was the inevitable porridge—which, following a little-known Scottish tradition, the children ate standing—and bread and butter. Lunch, or dinner as they called it, usually consisted of mutton and plain puddings. For tea, toast and butter were on offer. Reading occupied a great portion of the children's time, or else they were with their tutor at their lessons. 'As to indoor games', Elizabeth adds, 'playing-cards were absolutely tabooed, and such cards were not even allowed to be in the house.'[60] An absence of indoor entertainment may have been trying when the weather was bad, but it certainly intensified the calibre of their conversations. As an older man, Richard would consider the British obsession with bridge to have 'done more to destroy the intellectual life of England than any other cause'.[61]

Much emphasis was placed on family tradition, and Cloan's proximity to Gleneagles only heightened this:

> We had, we considered, a wonderful ancestry, and though the element of piety was only developed a couple of generations before, it was very real to us. And through the many generations previous to this, in the country in which we dwelt there was at least a history of good living or what we deemed to be such.[62]

This sense of ancestry had a tangible impact. Elizabeth believed that 'the religion which had made our forebears give up lands and money for the cause of God's service' was what made the family care about public events.[63] They were looking to serve God, and not just in the sacrifices demanded by family life; they felt obliged and driven to serve on a large scale. As we will see, however, the meaning of 'God' and 'service' were to change. One thing was certain, whatever interpretations they offered: service was not going to mean joining the ranks of the man or woman on the street. It was always going to be highbrow, laced with the remote air of the intellectual life. As Elizabeth said of their later passion for philosophy:

> Possibly this intense interest in such matters resulted in a certain aloofness from the interests and amusements of everyday life, and this, with our exceptional devotion to home, may have caused a certain separation from one's fellows. If so, it resulted really from our family upbringing and traditions, which caused us to concentrate on things speculative rather than on those of everyday life. But it made us happy...[64]

As we'll discover, cold, hard reality was not going to evade them forever.

* * *

But first, Richard had to come to terms with his speculative ghosts. Slowly, the religious world of his Haldane inheritance began to crumble around him. He had entered the arts course at Edinburgh University in the spring of 1872, aged sixteen. Unlike students enrolled in today's university courses in Britain, he ranged wide across the field of learning, attending classes in Latin, Greek, English literature, and even Physics. Serious-minded and well-connected, he was taken under the wing of his professors, particularly William Young Sellar, who introduced him to some of the leading intellectual lights of the day, notably Matthew Arnold and Benjamin Jowett (Master of Balliol). Their broad sympathies and searching intellects were in obvious contrast with his father's religious obsessions. So, too, were the debates that delighted the Students' Philosophical Society, of which Richard was a member. Ideas emanating from Oxford and the pen of T. H. Green (later Whyte's Professor of Moral Philosophy) were seeping north of the Border. Green's suggestion that a fulfilling religion could be found not so much in immutable and unprovable doctrines as in a certain type of citizenship, was both exciting and unsettling to these young Scotsmen reared on Calvin. Richard was starting to glimpse a wider, more humane world. He was starting to doubt, too, whether the religion of his parents was based on reliable foundations. These he considered to be emotional foundations, and the more he read the more he found the feelings at the root of their Christianity to be baseless. To abandon them would mean letting go of all his family held dear and the certainties which gave security to his existence. Given how tight-knit and wedded to certainty the Haldanes were, Richard faced a terrifying prospect.

It was not uncommon for men of Richard's background and education to use a Scottish university as a stepping stone to Oxford or Cambridge. Balliol College, Oxford, was often first choice, and Mary and Robert considered carefully whether this ought to be the next step for their eldest son. But Oxford was Anglican through and through, and, oblivious to the troubles he was already battling, they worried for Richard's faith in such an environment. Through the intervention of Edinburgh's Professor of Greek, John Stuart Blackie, it was decided instead—with what Violet Markham called 'the curious and illogical faith in the unknown that parents sometimes betray'[65]—that Richard ought to spend the spring term of 1874 in Göttingen before completing his studies at Edinburgh. It was a momentous decision for Richard and for his family too. What he learnt and experienced there not only changed Richard's life forever, but also shaped by osmosis the interests and careers of his brother John, his sister Elizabeth, and his nephew Graeme.

Göttingen at that time was a small but famous university town, with one professor for every ten students. The place reeked of tanning from the local leather-producing factories, and the only place for the young men to bathe was the dirty Leine river. The atmosphere seemed shockingly laid back to the diligent Richard, who was the youngest undergraduate by two years. Although the students were well-informed and highly educated, they were in the habit of skipping lectures—sometimes delivered in Latin, sometimes in German—and preferred a leisurely drink and smoke in one another's company. That's not to say there weren't moments of high excitement. The duels that took place amongst members of Richard's *Verbindung* ('a sort of second rate students' corps', which met for weekly drinking sessions) could be violent affairs—'the wounds were sometimes formidable, and I have seen blood spurting an inch high from a vein'.[66] But such sights cannot have prepared him for what he witnessed in his lodgings a few weeks after his arrival in Göttingen. As he wrote to his mother:

> I have just witnessed the most horrible spectacle I ever hope to. This morning, a short time ago, I heard a pistol shot above me, and on running upstairs met another student, a German, with whom I went up. On the top landing of the stair stood a half open door. I looked in, and saw close before me a ghastly mass of brains, blood, and matted hair attached to the body of a young lieutenant in the army of about 25 years of age who was our fellow lodger. Presently the police came & took possession of a letter which was lying open on the table, and which explained that he had committed suicide. I did not hear why. There was also a letter to his mother; the corpse look [sic] horrible, the head being shattered to pieces… When his family comes it will be dreadful, as they will hardly recognise him.[67]

The impression left by this experience was nothing compared to that left by his encounter with Professor Hermann Lotze. Upon matriculation, gripping in his seventeen-year-old hand Blackie's letter of introduction (written in Greek!), Richard made his way to the door of the man he considered to be 'the greatest living metaphysician'.[68] Today's *Stanford Encyclopedia of Philosophy* agrees with Richard, calling Lotze, in his heyday, 'the single most influential philosopher in Germany, perhaps even the world'.[69] Lotze's philosophical positions do not concern us here, since they were not positions to which Richard subscribed. His importance is for other, less technical reasons. Firstly, Lotze provided Richard with a reading list that would transform his outlook from one of religious depression to philosophic optimism. In reading Johann Gottlieb Fichte, George Berkeley, and Immanuel Kant, Richard discovered that there could be wider meanings to the words 'God' and 'immortality' than those given to them by his parents. These authors showed him that happiness could be found not so much in a settled assortment of dogmas but more in an attitude of inquiry. Richard, moreover, felt convinced and liberated by Berkeley's insistence on the all-embracing power of the human mind to form reality for itself. Such a view meant empowerment; he could now cast off the shackles of the religious authorities of his youth and their constant demands for subservience.

Secondly, in Lotze—this 'slight and fragile figure' whose 'great head looked as though the mind that tenanted it had been dedicated to thought and to nothing else'—Richard found the embodiment of scholarship and the life of the mind.[70] Far from being a mere helpful accessory, Lotze's philosophy was his vocation. In Richard's eyes, he was a 'great man', worthy of 'hero worship'.[71] He inspired in Richard a desire to live for thinking. Thereafter, whatever he said or did was to be anchored in solid thought. Whenever he spoke in later life of the importance of a university education—something he did almost without ceasing—it was this encounter with an inspirational figure, committed to the search for truth, that Richard had in mind.

Richard was struck, too, by where the emphasis lay in German university life. As he told his mother admiringly:

> There are no such things as examinations in the classes, and much less anything as contemptible in the German eye as prizes—a great improvement upon us and I think this accounts for the fact that the Germans are so much better informed, since they do not cram things as with us, but really learn them.[72]

The utilitarian preoccupations of his native land—where every activity seemed orientated towards some practical (and usually money-generating) utility—now appeared a measly thing. Upon his return to Scotland, he wrote back to a German friend: 'I actually dislike my own country now. The people seem to think of nothing but how to make money and never how to attain to a high culture.'[73]

That culture was not only to be found amongst members of the university. Richard's German tutor in Göttingen, Helene Schlote, was a highly intelligent and well-read woman, with whom he kept up a lifetime's correspondence and to whom he provided financial aid after post-war hyperinflation swallowed her savings. She had been the headmistress of a respected girls' school and she 'knew her Goethe as only a scholar could'. On top of this, 'she had a wide acquaintance with English literature'.[74] To these early meetings with the venerable Fräulein can be traced Richard's passion for 'the Great Goethe' and his progressive views on the educational rights of women.[75]

In his autobiography, Richard writes: 'When I returned to Scotland it was in much better spirits, and with the first steps taken towards the attainment of something like a settled outlook, which was as time went on to mean much to me.'[76] The next chapter will look more closely at what constituted this 'settled outlook', as we unpick a published essay of 1883, encompassing both philosophy and science, written jointly by Richard and his brother John. In doing so, we'll see how Richard and John were able to leave the religion of their parents behind without negating it—a remarkable feat, which convinced Mary that all was still well with their souls. At present, it is sufficient to say that Richard's time in Germany provided him with some of the essential resources he needed, both to overcome the many binaries of his childhood and to face life's ups and downs. It gave him what he called a 'larger outlook', a bird's-eye view of human affairs.[77] Little did Richard know just how soon the hard realities of the world would try and pull him back to earth.

* * *

The first blow was struck in March 1875, less than a year after Richard's return. His brother Geordie was then sixteen and his closest companion. Geordie was the real animating spirit amongst Mary's five children. He was 'a beautiful child, very fair and with large expressive dark blue eyes'.[78] While his four full siblings were serious, questioning, and lacking in artistic talent, Geordie was a boy of constant merriment, a brilliant mimic, happy to accept simple Bible teaching, and possessed of quite exceptional musical ability. This gift became apparent at little more than a year old. He could rhythmically tap out the time of any tune, and passers-by would stop to listen as he hummed loudly along. Once he had graduated to the piano, he could play most songs simply from memory. As Richard recorded, 'His touch on the piano, and his power of expressing the deep feeling of the best music, were remarkable.'[79] In old age Willie wrote: 'I can see him too in memory, playing on a large piano in the Edinburgh drawing-room as from his very soul, his eyes entranced.'[80] A career as a professional musician was a genuine prospect.[81] He was clever, too, and was supposed to be the genius of the family, with a highly practical intelligence that expressed itself in a passion for railway engines and new building methods. It was an intelligence balanced by innocence and goodness. 'I used to marvel at the little hold that any evil had upon him', wrote Mary, 'and even wondered that he was my son, he seemed so much in advance of me.'[82] 'He could not bear to see the weak oppressed by poverty or bodily infirmity of any kind, and did all in his power to help them', she reminisced.[83] But he wouldn't let such sights stymie his lust for life. Geordie was the leavening element in a household prone to dourness. When he entered the room, all oppressive feelings lifted and the moment could be enjoyed.

When, that February, Geordie took to his bed feeling unwell, no one in the family was concerned; it would pass. But after four days there was no improvement and then a worrying sign showed itself: he turned the colour of copper. Mary was grateful to have at hand the speedy assistance of her husband's half-brother, Dr Daniel Rutherford Haldane, who lived just a few houses along on Charlotte Square. His assessment was stark. Turning gravely to Mary, he spoke the words no mother wants to hear: 'He is thoroughly and completely possessed.' It was diphtheria, a highly contagious bacterial infection which poisons the healthy tissue in the respiratory system. The dead tissue forms a thick, grey coating that can build up in the throat, making breathing very difficult. Geordie could hardly catch his breath and his temperature rocketed. With Mary and Baba risking their own health to be by his side, the other children were told to keep well clear of the sickroom. There was no hope. Eventually, on 10 March, the doctor asked Richard to summon his father, now that the end was approaching. He found Robert sitting alone in his room. Softly, Richard broke the news. Robert didn't move, but an expression of 'profound sorrow' passed over his face. Then, 'in a tone of deep solemnity', Robert uttered words that would have made his own father proud: 'Before the foundations of the world were laid it was so ordained.'[84]

The family, stunned by grief, removed themselves from the house in which Geordie's memory was everywhere present. Cloan was no option, of course. They went, instead, to Low Wood on the banks of Windermere in the Lake District. Unbeknown to her children (it would have terrified them had they known), Mary had contracted diphtheria herself. Baba had thankfully escaped it and was able to nurse her mistress back to health. The beautiful surroundings, made famous by Wordsworth's verse, did much to revive the family. But there was to be little respite.

In January 1876, Mary's elder brother, Richard Burdon Sanderson, was en route from Newcastle to London by train in the company of his wife Isabella (Robert Haldane's half-sister), his two adult daughters, and his only son, a law student. The weather was appalling, and the snow fell heavily. A couple of hours north of its destination, the train collided with a coal train. Richard's eldest daughter was locked into her seat by a twisted part of the carriage, though not badly injured. As her brother sought to release her, another train, bound for Leeds, crashed into the already mutilated carriage. The impact killed her immediately. In dismay and panic, her brother then went to look for his other sister and found her in an entanglement of iron, complaining that she could no longer feel anything below her waist. A few moments later she was dead. Their father and mother were both hurt, but it did not seem life-threatening. Richard's leg was broken and his right arm and collarbone were fractured. The shock was far worse. After three months in intensive care, Mary's brother died.[85]

The third blow came in June 1877. Robert Haldane was now seventy-two, but he had lived through enough griefs for many lifetimes. His health had slowly been deteriorating as a result of his diabetes. His death came, unlike Geordie's, 'in the established order of things'.[86] There are, therefore, few details of the event itself. His son Richard simply states: 'He passed away as he had lived, full of faith in what for him were eternal verities.'[87] But his death afforded a fresh appreciation of his character. Upon reflection, Richard saw him as 'much the best of the whole family of my grandfather'.[88] A letter of 1881 suggests that such a judgement was in contrast to the prevailing view amongst Edinburgh society. Responding to his mother, Richard comments:

> What you say about the non-appreciation of my father I very much sympathise with. He was an individual whom it took a clever man properly to understand & appreciate… People were apt to lay hold of the most attackable sides of his character, & take these to be the whole man when they lay only upon the surface. He had a sterling metal in him, & the world which is generally right, saw this although individuals did not.[89]

With Robert gone, new responsibilities fell on Mary, still only fifty-two (she had another forty-eight years ahead of her!). It was a daunting prospect, for she was, as her daughter pointed out, 'without practical experience of managing land or money and with a family of boys of great individuality to bring up and start in the world'.[90] The question of money was a particular problem, as her husband had organised, in the event of his death, for the payment of substantial capital provisions to or for the five children of his first marriage.[91] The fact that Robert left his wife in relatively straitened circumstances is a strange one. It remains unclear how Robert, a sensible Victorian professional, could have let this happen. Uncertain how to handle her new responsibilities, Mary turned to her eldest son, who had just embarked on a legal career after carrying everything before him at Edinburgh University (first-class honours, the Bruce of Grangehill Medal in Philosophy, the Gray Scholarship, and the Ferguson Scholarship in Philosophy, open to students of all four Scottish universities). A letter from his mother of 1911, looking back to the events of 1877, describes the role Richard played at this time, and we read it with the final comments of Chapter 2 in mind:

> You have never failed me, and helped me through many things that looked very formidable at the time… You have never forgotten the first family either, who seem to have been left by their father almost to hang upon you. None of them had force of character to be able to help themselves.[92]

The practicalities of providing for the family, of managing money and property, were as nothing compared to the challenge of dealing emotionally with the losses they had sustained. Six months after Robert's death and with Richard now relocated to London, he wrote to Mary: 'Our home has indeed been laid desolate and broken up, never to be restored again in this world. A wide gap seems to have presented itself between what we were as a family and what we now are; first Geordie and then our father.'[93] Geordie's death in particular left a raw wound that never quite healed for any of them. Willie believed that it 'bound us all in a common devotion for years to come'.[94] As Johnnie's daughter Naomi remembered, 'long afterwards my father spoke of his brother Geordie in words of love and loss'.[95] Even in the late 1890s he was still dreaming of him, as was Richard, who told his mother: 'Yes. Like Johnnie, I often dream of Geordie as back again—& he is strangely vivid in these dreams. The impression of him is as fresh as it was twenty one years ago.'[96] It is possible that Johnnie's scientific career stemmed from what he experienced as a boy of fifteen. His biographer reflects:

> He only heard the panic of short and forced breathing, and the final silence that followed... It is hard to know when a boy might decide to become a doctor, to give his life to investigating the passage of air through human lungs, to understanding the workings of oxygen on the human body and finding ways to administer it. John... heard his brother dying of diphtheria... His life had changed.[97]

Every anniversary of Geordie's death is marked in the correspondence between Richard and Mary, which lasted unbroken from Richard's move to London in 1877 until Mary's own death, aged one hundred, in 1925. Across all these years, the sorrow never diminished. Initially, Richard could find little sense in what had happened: 'the thought seems at times too hard, too bitter, too piercing for weak creatures like us to endure... there come at times moments when one's heart feels as though it would break under the pressure'.[98] But it soon became possible for the loss to be seen in terms of the 'larger outlook' that Richard's philosophy afforded and the providential views that Mary's religion granted, though the pain remained for both. In 1878, Richard already considers that 'the very sadness is good for us; it teaches that the things of time are passing away, and that life has a deeper meaning than that which is apparent on its surface'.[99] In 1913—by which time Richard was Lord Chancellor, having already served as Secretary of State for War and done much to smooth relations between Britain and Germany—Mary sees Geordie's death as an act of God which opened the way to her eldest son's achievements:

> But it was our heavenly Father's will that through his death you were prepared for a very remarkable life work. Had it not been for it, I do not believe you would have been where you are, nor would you have stood before Emperors & Kings to testify to the Truth. It opened the way through death to a very remarkable life.[100]

This was all very well for a man like Richard, with every educational and social advantage a man of privilege could expect. But what about a woman like Elizabeth? What openings were possible for her now that her mother was left widowed? Mary, for all her kindliness and compassion, was not going to make the possibilities numerous.

* * *

Elizabeth's hunger for knowledge had in no way abated by the time her father died (she was then fifteen). If anything, it had increased. It must have made her proud to witness the intellectual flourishing of John and Richard, but it must have been painful, too. She knew she was every bit as bright as them. In fact, the tutor of their teenage years, Peter Hume Brown (Richard's university friend and, from 1908, Historiographer Royal for Scotland), was once asked which Haldane he considered 'the most brilliant' out of Richard, John, and Elizabeth—to which he replied, 'I think Elizabeth's mind was the most remarkable of the three.'[101] But the net of Victorian propriety was closing in:

> My first conviction [after her father's death] was that I was not educated, and I thought of how this could be put right. I should have loved going to college, but college in those days was unusual for girls, and the idea was not encouraged. It was also expensive. For an only daughter to leave a widowed mother was indeed considered to be quite out of the question, and no one made the plan seem feasible.[102]

Her role was simply to be her mother's helper. Elizabeth found this deeply depressing, a situation exacerbated by being denied any form of financial freedom and the fact that Mary took no action to put the matter right:

> If ordinary wants of food and clothing were supplied, nothing else was thought necessary [for a young woman], and all through one's young life this was a quite unnecessary drawback in a case where money was not unobtainable. Probably it resulted from our mother carrying on the tradition in which she was brought up.[103]

Elizabeth was trapped, and the mother she loved so much appeared to do nothing about it.

There was one glimmer of light. For the winter of 1879–80, Mary, Elizabeth, and Baba decamped to Paris for a change of scene

(Johnnie and Willie remaining in Edinburgh to continue their education). They found the city dazzling in a blanket of snow and the Seine frozen hard. The shops and picture galleries offered feasts for the senses, and vestiges of the Revolution were still to be seen, exciting the historian in Elizabeth. Without her husband's restricting influence, Mary felt a flush of artistic freedom, sitting for hours in the Louvre copying the works of old masters (she would eventually exhibit some of her original paintings at the Scottish Academy). Elizabeth took painting lessons herself, and some in music. Not even dancing lessons were prohibited.

Balls were out of the question, of course, but parties at the homes of their Parisian acquaintances were acceptable. In her lifetime, Elizabeth was never famed for her beauty, but there was something fresh and even distinguished about her, and she evidently made quite an impression in her first long evening dress. To her 'dismay', a young man paid his compliments to her at one such party, and even called round to the Haldanes' lodgings with the offer of tickets to see a show. Mary's reaction spoke clearly of the possessiveness that was beginning to pain Elizabeth: 'my mother said she would see him and she did so, firmly and decisively!' That was the end of that. At least when her brothers visited in the new year there was the chance to go to the Grand Opera, where they saw *Faust*, 'an occasion never to be forgotten'.[104] One can only imagine what Robert Haldane would have made of his children delighting in such entertainments.

On the whole, Paris was a liberating experience for Elizabeth. But it was all too brief. They returned to life in Scotland with a bump. With money tight, it was decided that they ought to relocate to Cloan permanently, letting go of Charlotte Square. In fact, it was even suggested that Cloan ought to be sold. There was an immediate outcry, not least from Richard, who showed a rare glimpse of social vanity: 'I am all against the idea of parting with Cloanden. We should lose status to an extent which we cannot while we possess it realise.'[105] The idea did not last long, but economies had to be made, and, with the exception of Mary and Elizabeth's annual three-month stay with Richard in London, a quiet country life was now all that was on offer for Elizabeth.

How was she to fill her time? Correspondence courses—what we would today call 'distance learning', but carried out by mail—were just beginning, and Elizabeth joined in one scheme that involved reading Edward Gibbon's *The History of the Decline and Fall of the Roman Empire* and James Bryce's *The Holy Roman Empire*, amongst other weighty tomes. She profited from her mother's proficiency in Italian, and would read texts with her in that language. In the evenings, Mary made the daring move to part with the early family strictures on novel reading and, while Elizabeth spun wool or carved wood, she would read aloud from Walter Scott, Dickens, George Eliot, Jane Austen, and the Brontës. Apart from these activities, life was bleak. There were no cars or bicycles yet ('No young woman of the present day realizes the sudden sense of emancipation that it [the bicycle] gave'), so even a visit to a countryside neighbour was difficult.[106] As Elizabeth wrote in her memoirs, 'Altogether until towards the beginning of the eighties things looked black and grim... It seems to me, on looking back, that this is the only time in my life that I suffered from what is now called frustration, the disease which is supposed to attack unmarried women.'[107]

She had little choice but to acquiesce in the situation, and it was only through Richard's growing wealth and reputation that, in later years, she was able to find springboards into new, exciting lands. It makes one wonder if what her friends termed as the 'sacrifice' she made for her mother was really a sacrifice at all; she had no alternatives. But that's a question of semantics. It's clear the experience of these years left an indelible impression upon her, and, if her confidante Violet Markham is to be believed, it formed part of what made her so lovable:

> She was pure gold through and through, one of the most selfless people I have ever known.... I always suspected that love and marriage had been laid on the altar of her mother and of Richard to whom she was no less attached. Sacrifice had wrought in her a very noble quality of life and character. No woman was ever more beloved and honoured by her friends.[108]

* * *

Meanwhile, Johnnie—or John as we might now call him, having left his childhood behind—exploited the opportunities open to young Victorian men with brains and money. Like Richard, he proceeded from school to the arts course at Edinburgh University, during which time, 'owing mainly to my brother's influence, my chief interest was in philosophy'.[109] John duly obtained a first-class degree in 1879, with merits in moral philosophy, logic and metaphysics, and Greek. What he learnt under the Professor of Logic and Metaphysics, Alexander Campbell Fraser, about the fundamental mysteriousness of life remained with him for the rest of his days. John would never see scientific advancements as making inroads into mystery. Years later, delivering the prestigious Gifford Lectures at Glasgow University (twenty-three years after Richard delivered his own Gifford Lectures at St Andrews), he would say: 'It appears to me to be little better than unthinking credulity to believe that the mystery has become less deep through scientific advance.'[110] Campbell Fraser, who had edited the complete works of Berkeley, also reinforced in John the influence of the Irish philosopher. The sense of Berkeley's importance left another lifelong impression, and even in his eighth decade John was conducting experiments into the vision of brightness and colour to provide 'an experimental basis for Berkeleyan idealism'.[111]

It is no surprise that the next step in John's education was a term at a Germany university. Instead of Göttingen, in the spring of 1879 he made his way to Jena, with its many associations with Hegel and Goethe. Here he could keep up his philosophy and begin to lay the foundations for his intended medical degree by attending lectures in comparative anatomy. He could start to flex his more technical scientific skills as well, enjoying a course in botany and impressing his lecturer with his versatile use of the microscope. In each of his fields of interest there were professors of outstanding talent—the evolutionist Ernst Haeckel, who first coined the word 'ecology'; the physiologist William Thierry Preyer, a pioneer in the new field of child psychology and a friend of John's uncle, John Burdon Sanderson; and the botanist Eduard Strasburger, whose many achievements included the elucidation of the process of nuclear division in the plant kingdom. Echoing Richard after his encounter with Lotze, John would write: 'German Universities are infinitely ahead of us… [A] student there has, as a rule, the chance, if he likes to use it, of coming into real contact with men who are making the scientific history of their time.'[112]

John, along with Richard and Elizabeth, would make history, too. But to do so would mean breaking off the remnants of their childhood shackles. Richard's and John's were fewer and less visible than Elizabeth's, but all three were held in bonds of tradition, affection, religion, and social norms that kept them from their goals. Now they faced the hard struggle for freedom. They would have to learn new skills, live in new worlds, and take courageous action to reach it; and yet their past would come to their aid. Their family's history and achievements gave them the confidence to pursue their dreams, while their closeness to their mother anchored them in homely security as they cast themselves adrift into public and academic life. Even their early religion roused their commitment to acting in accordance with conscience and their willingness to stand at a remove from the ever-changing waves of public sentiment. There was a lot they were dependent on in their fight for independence.

4

THE DECLARATION OF INDEPENDENCE

1880s AND 1890s

The 1880s got off to a bad start for Mary's eldest three children. Richard had been called to the English Bar in 1879, but briefs were unforthcoming. With money getting tighter for the family back in Scotland, he felt the pressure of his new role keenly. He had few of the obvious qualities to make a successful London barrister: his networks were limited to the academic sphere and a handful of southern relatives, he knew no solicitors, he struggled in certain social settings, and his voice was high-pitched and reedy.[1] His romantic life was also in turmoil; he had fallen desperately in love with the sister of a school friend, only to find that it was unrequited. Richard plunged into black despair. 'The one thing is to occupy every moment with work', he told his mother.[2] All this was compounded by poor health, as rheumatism dogged his steps. There was one advantage of his frequent illnesses, and that was their ability to keep a check on his expanding girth. 'You would be amused with the vision of my once fat legs', he wrote to Mary after a particularly bad attack in the autumn of 1881 'they are about half the thickness of Elizabeth's arm. My boots envelope my feet like snowshoes.'[3]

While Richard sought to overcome these adversities, John was busy doing his best in Edinburgh to understand medicine, but also to fail his medical degree: 'I purposely paid little attention to any of the lectures of my examiners, as I consider that the present system of working for examinations by students is one which is doing a great deal of harm in every way.'[4] When he eventually sat his final examinations in 1883, John paid the price for his dismissive attitude and was failed in midwifery, which prevented him from graduating MD. But the streak of Haldane self-confidence ran strong within him:

> It seems scarcely worthwhile to waste another of the best years of my life because a man of the intellectual capacity of Professor Simpson [the man who marked the midwifery exam, son of Sir James Young Simpson, the discoverer of chloroform] is not of the opinion that I am sufficiently qualified as regards his department of medicine... Of my ultimate success at medicine I feel little doubt.[5]

To John's mind, it all pointed to the poverty of a university education in Britain when compared to Germany. He knew he'd find an understanding ear in Richard when he wrote: 'The intellectual degradation involved in cramming up notes on, say, Prof Simpson's lectures is... a good deal more than I could stand.'[6] So outraged was John, that he took the matter before the whole body of the Edinburgh professors and appealed the decision—unsuccessfully. His words to his mother as he considered such a move set the tone for this chapter:

> I am not sorry that circumstances have made it incumbent on me to bring up the matter here in Edinburgh. Intellectual freedom used to prevail in the Edinburgh School of Medicine; and I hope that before long it may do so again. I have both the money, and I think, the ability to stand against any number of professors on this matter, and probably my reputation, such as it is, in philosophy will be of use to me.[7]

Elizabeth no doubt wished she had the luxury of standing up to just a single professor. By this time, Cloan, which had meant freedom and joy to her as a child, had become a place of captivity. Her physical isolation was the visible sign of her inward struggle, as her intellect raged against the confines of Victorian womanhood. Thankfully, her brothers' devotion to their country home and their family brought them back whenever they could throughout the year, infecting Elizabeth with something of the buzz of two busy and intelligent men's lives. She wrote of these days: 'When we were at Cloan together, there seemed no end to the subjects we had to discuss, between politics, science and philosophy. One's life no doubt became what the Germans call *zersplittert* [fragmented], but if that does not make for efficiency (and it does not), it makes for great happiness.'[8]

Their animated philosophical discussions caused Mary some concern. Where did her children stand on the basic doctrines of Christianity? Did they still believe that Jesus was the Son of God and that salvation came through faith in him alone? Was this new word, 'idealism', compatible with the religion of their ancestors? A letter of reassurance from Richard to his mother, written in May 1883, is enlightening both as to her anxieties and as to the subtleties of Richard's handling of them:

> I read your letter carefully. It is difficult to express all one intends in a letter and I will not attempt it. But this I may say: You may rest assured that all your children (I do not speak for Willie whose interests and studies have been of a different character) think more or less continually of the subjects you mention. The problems and difficulties of the present day are altogether different from those of a generation ago and different criteria must be applied in judging. But the truth remains ever the same however different its form and I think you may take this as being so in our cases. As for Bay, she is probably going through a critical period and she must work it out for herself as best she can.[9]

At first blush, this seems somewhat disingenuous, particularly when we find Elizabeth writing: 'doctrines that meant so much to our forefathers, who had indeed spent their birthright in maintaining them, were to us empty words. Our interests were quite other. We were concerned faintly at first but in a growing way with the conditions of our fellow beings.'[10] Richard and John, while they would have agreed in large part with this assessment, would not have used the phrase 'empty words'. The brothers' joint essay of 1883, 'The Relation of Philosophy to Science', in a book titled *Essays in Philosophical Criticism* (edited by Richard along with the brothers' friend Andrew Seth, later Professor Seth Pringle-Pattison of St Andrews), gives a strong hint of how they could say, with all sincerity, 'the truth remains ever the same however different its form'. It demonstrates the first significant collaborative effort amongst Mary's children. Many other efforts would follow, critically advancing their respective missions to transform the world around them. In looking at the essay, we're not dealing with merely abstract points. The development of their philosophy coincided with the reversal of their personal fortunes. It gave them—and this includes Elizabeth, who shared their views—a new way to live.

* * *

Essays in Philosophical Criticism is dedicated to the memory of the Oxford philosopher T. H. Green, who had died in 1882, a year prior to the book's publication. Green was the driving force behind a potent reforming movement amongst the educated classes, predominantly young men fresh from Oxford, that considered selfless citizenship to be the most authentic form of human life. London settlements such as Toynbee Hall and Oxford House were a direct result of such thinking, and Green was equally instrumental in creating what Vernon Bogdanor has called the 'mandarin culture' in British politics, which, in contrast to classic liberalism, stressed the state's responsibilities in forming citizens.[11]

In the eyes of Green and his followers, to be a committed citizen, dedicated to the well-being of one's neighbour and community, was to be religious. In an age of doubt, Green provided the means to affirm the truths of Christianity in a new way, one that did not rely on dogmatic formulas but on a certain type of life. Richard's response to his anxious mother was textbook Green. In his famous 'Essay on Christian Dogma', Green had argued that Christian creeds were not final articulations of the truth but historically contingent forms of words responding to particular problems of the time.[12] As the problems shifted, so too did the forms of words that responded to them. Green was thereby able to protect the substance of Christian truth while granting licence to all manner of forms of its expression (so long as they were appropriate to their corresponding historical moment). It was this thinking that allowed Richard, John, and Elizabeth to reassure their mother that they had not abandoned her in her faith, even if they expressed their beliefs differently. So Richard could write to Mary in 1891: 'With what you said the other day about faith in God I completely agree. The form [of the words] is immaterial. In substance we are at one.'[13]

THE DECLARATION OF INDEPENDENCE

For the scientifically minded John, Green was particularly influential. Even at the end of his life, in the 1930s, he continued to feel a 'special obligation' to Green's thought.[14] This lifelong impact makes sense when we bear in mind the prevailing attitude within the British intellectual establishment towards the close of the nineteenth century. The churchman and academic Henry Scott Holland captured the change wrought by Green's thinking:

> [Before Green] Scientific Analysis held the key to the universe. Under this intellectual dominion we [Scott Holland and his Oxford contemporaries] had lost all touch with the Ideals of life in Community… We were frightened; we saw everything passing into the tyranny of rational abstract mechanism… Then at last, the walls began to break… mainly through the influence of T. H. Green… He released us from the fear of agnostic mechanism. He gave us back the language of self-sacrifice, and taught us how we belonged to one another in the one life of high idealism.[15]

It is this fight against 'abstract mechanism'—the view that the phenomena of life can be explained solely in physical and chemical terms—that Richard and John's essay engages in. Their respective hands are clear in its composition. The precise, scientific examples are evidently the product of John's pen. The more philosophical passages bear the marks of Richard's style, employing—just as Green had done—the tradition of the German idealists to advance his arguments. Kant is the main interlocutor, but the influence of Hegel is everywhere evident. The essential philosophical point the brothers make is summed up in the sentence: 'The fundamental fact beyond which we cannot get is the fact of self-consciousness.'[16] What did they mean by this and why is it significant? I will attempt to state the arguments as briefly as possible, but a certain amount of forbearance will be necessary. The words of one whimsical commentator on Richard's political oratory could just as well be applied to his philosophical writing: 'The lucidity of his mind is as conclusive as the fog in yours. The clearer he becomes to himself, the more hopeless is your bewilderment.'[17]

For Richard and John, whatever objects were 'out there' in the world beyond the mind (or self-consciousness), they only became objects for the mind because the mind had first made all sorts of abstractions and distinctions from the hugely complex and multifaceted world before it. Let's take a tree in a field as an example (the brothers' examples are far less straightforward!). They believed that you only see the tree as a tree because your mind has brought a host of general ideas about what constitutes a tree—that it has, for example, a trunk, branches, and leaves—into the process of perception and applied them accordingly. In the technical language of the essay, perception 'necessitates the isolation of definite relations presented by its object through the application to that object of a general conception'.[18] You'll not notice your mind doing this as it's practically instantaneous, but the brothers thought it made no sense to claim the entire passivity of the perceiver. Reality, for them, always has to emerge out of the interaction between subject (the perceiver) and object (in this case, the tree). And the mind or self-consciousness of the perceiver always has the priority, because the moment you start to talk about a tree or any object 'in itself', you've already presupposed the mind that is essential to making the object an object in the first place. As the brothers put it, 'only for mind do objects exist at all'.[19]

Despite appearances, this is not simply dry philosophy; this thinking took the brothers, with Hegel to help them, towards a radically reshaped way of conceiving that all-important presence in their family's life: God. Since they considered 'mind'—by which they meant not just individual human minds, but the mental processes of abstracting and judgement-making that we all share in—to be the Subject to which all objective reality was referable, mind could never be considered another object in the world. Rather, it lay at the foundation of reality. Mind could therefore be considered infinite and all-powerful because, unlike objects, it could never be bound by any limiting factors. Thus mind became identical to what the brothers called 'God'. God, in their view, was no transcendent being beyond the world; no, God was completely immanent to the world as we know it, totally at one with it. The infinite God worked himself out (despite their occasional efforts to the contrary, the gendered language remained) through the multiplicity of finite human minds. When an individual mind acts in accordance with reason and shapes the world before it in a reasonable manner (e.g., does not, because of ill-health, drunkenness, or bloody-mindedness,

THE DECLARATION OF INDEPENDENCE

believe the tree to be a giant scarecrow), then that individual mind is a finite expression of the infinite reality of God. No two human minds will view the tree identically of course, but this plurality of perspective is indicative of God's infinity.

While a naturalist and a landscape painter will each see the tree quite differently, their views will be equally valid and will represent what the brothers and their fellow British Idealists called 'degrees' or 'categories' within knowledge. As the naturalist and painter examine the tree, they will be guided by their different purposes. Richard and John state: 'When we say of something that it is a cause or a substance, we are simply abstracting, for the purpose of clearness of individual knowledge, from its other relations. That which in one reference presents itself as cause or substance, in others presents itself as quantity or quality.'[20] The naturalist, then, will note the scientific components of the tree, the painter its shapes and colours. It would be a profound mistake for one or the other to claim their view as the only valid representation of the tree's reality. Both representations belong within a wider reality which is God's reality. It is here that we begin to see why the mechanistic worldview, of which Scott Holland spoke, riled the brothers so much. Many advocates for this worldview believed it held the capacity to explain all aspects of reality. The religious viewpoint, the aesthetic, the moral—these were either redundant or very much in second place.

For Richard and John, each of these ways of approaching the world was not just valid but essential to the activity by which God brings himself to realisation. In their essay, they make their point by limiting themselves to the sphere of John's specialisation, showing the way in which organisms resist all human attempts to reduce them to mechanistic machines; without the category of 'life', you cannot do justice to the reality of the organism. Here, John's voice becomes evident:

> [T]he parts of an organism cannot be considered simply as so many independent units, which happen to be aggregated in a system in which each determines the other. It is on the contrary the essential feature of each part that it is a member of an ideal whole, which can only be defined by saying that it realises itself in its parts, and that the parts are only what they are in so far as they realise it. In

fine the relations of life are not capable of reduction to the relations of mechanism.[21]

Such an argument had both private and public consequences for the brothers. In their private lives, it meant that the religious world of their mother could be upheld as valid, if incomplete. Green's point about the creeds was part of this, but the understanding of knowledge as presented in their essay also showed that the religious perspective had a place just as much as any other. Richard made the point concisely in his later Gifford Lectures, when he said:

> The true view of experience would seem to be that it is for us what it is in all its complexity as the result of habitual reflection at many and different standpoints—scientific, ethical, aesthetic, religious, etc., at each of which abstraction... take[s] place under different conceptions and categories, adopted because of the purpose or end to be realised in each case.[22]

Indeed, the religious person had a particularly important role to play in his or her capacity to see beyond the surface of things: 'The artist, the poet, the moral being, the religious man—they... touch a higher level; it seems as if they could comprehend at a higher plane of intelligence, and thereby they show us how even finite beings can approach near to God.'[23] The brothers' essay of 1883 does not speak as openly of God as this, but the essential elements of such a view are there to be seen. It showed, obliquely, that Mary had no cause for concern. God was the foundation of her sons' lives.

As for their public lives, the scientific analysis that John offers in the essay sheds an important light on the relation between the individual and the community: 'When we have reached a standpoint from which we refuse to separate the individual organism from its surroundings and from its relation to other individuals, we see how the species may itself be looked upon as a compound organism, or as a member of which each individual attains its true significance.'[24] The influence of Green is discernible. If society is like an organism, we as individuals have duties and obligations to the societies in which we live. We must give of ourselves for the good of the whole, just as we can expect to receive back from the whole for the good of ourselves. When John writes that an organism 'realises itself in its parts, and... the parts are only what they are in so far as they realise it', he is also speaking of the reciprocal relationship between the community and the individual (and perhaps even between God and the individual).

This view allows the brothers to criticise those who become enslaved to an understanding of the state as 'a mere aggregate of isolated individuals'. They write:

> A less abstract category would prove more adequate to the facts in embracing, in the conception of the individual, his determination by the social organism of which he is a member. And in the light of such a conception the shortcomings of the abstractedly individualistic doctrines of the Manchester school in political economy [those who sought free enterprise capitalism] become apparent.[25]

Although neither brother ever embraced socialism in its entirety, this early essay exposes the groundwork of their lifelong commitment to a form of politics that pressed for state intervention on the one hand and engaged citizenship on the other, for the purpose of equalising society and benefiting the individual. In Richard's case, it was this thinking that drove him towards an active political career on the progressive wing. In John's, it meant seeking a 'profession which would... assuredly bring me into close and living contact with my fellow-man'.[26] He would even write: 'In losing our individual lives we find our true life, and in no part of human activity is this losing of the individual self more clearly realized than in scientific work.'[27] Was it a coincidence, one wonders, that their scientific and philosophical thinking—on appearance, light years from the Calvinism of their youth—coalesced so closely with the family tradition of service and its constant injunction from their seniors in childhood?

A final point is worth noting before we move back to our story. The brothers conclude their essay with a provocative observation:

> [S]cience and philosophy can no longer be kept wholly apart from one another. The inquirer who is to do anything more than simply observe and record, who desires to systematise his results and to generalise from them, must have assimilated the philosophical theory of experience. The philosopher, on the other hand, must... have the problems which arise within experience before him as they can only come before the scientific observer. But science is a wide

subject, and philosophy... is a narrow one. It would therefore seem that the work of philosophy in the near future must pass into the hands of specialists in science who are at the same time masters of philosophical criticism.[28]

Their prophecy was partly fulfilled: philosophy was certainly usurped by science as the arbiter of knowledge in much of academia and in the public imagination, but philosophical mastery did not transfer so easily to the scientists. More interesting than their prophecy, however, is the fact that here we find the first public statement from the Haldanes of Cloan on the importance of polymathia and the synthesis of knowledge. All subsequent members of the family would take the basic point to heart. Whatever area of interest occupied their focus, it was always undergirded and informed by a profound culture and a wide reading beyond their speciality. John's son, J. B. S. Haldane, became famous as a geneticist, and yet his only non-honorary degrees were in mathematics and classics, with the latter steeping him in the philosophy of Plato and Aristotle. His sister, Naomi, was a renowned historical novelist, and yet her (uncompleted) undergraduate studies were in biology, and her first publication was co-authored with her brother and appeared in the *Journal of Genetics* under the title 'Reduplication in Mice'.[29] Of Naomi's grandson, the Cambridge mathematician and scientist Graeme Mitchison, the novelist Ian McEwan could say: 'Graeme's polymathia extended the definition of the word. Along with plant morphology and quantum computing, we should count in hospitality, the art of the piano, literary judgment, drawing and painting, paragliding, hiking and risky mountain scrambling.'[30] Such extraordinary breadth did not spring out of a vacuum; its roots were long and deep.

* * *

The impact of *Essays in Philosophical Criticism* was considerable. According to *The Scotsman*, the book was 'devoured by young philosophers when it appeared' and represented 'the climax of T. H. Green's influence in British philosophy'.[31] With Richard as editor and the brothers as contributors, it established them solidly within the movement known as 'British Idealism' and marked

1. John Scott, 1st Earl of Eldon (1751–1838) by Sir Thomas Lawrence. Eldon served as Lord Chancellor between 1801 and 1806 and again between 1807 and 1827. He was Mary Haldane's great-uncle and a high Tory. The advanced liberalism of Mary's children would have shocked him profoundly.

2. The itinerant preacher James Alexander Haldane (1768–1851) by George Zobel, after Colvin Smith stipple and line engraving, c. 1845. James Alexander was Robert Haldane of Cloan's father. He cemented the family's commitment to the truth at any cost.

3. (Sir) John Burdon Sanderson FRS (1828–1905), c. 1870s. John was Mary's younger brother and first Waynflete Professor of Physiology at Oxford. Through Mary, a further five Fellows of the Royal Society have entered the family.

4. Robert Haldane of Cloan, early 1850s, surrounded by the children of his first marriage, whose characters were strikingly different from their younger, more intellectually curious half-siblings.

5. A sketch of Cloan as it was in 1855, by Mary Haldane, two years after her marriage to Robert.

6. Cloan, from the back, shortly after the western extension in 1866, with Richard and Geordie on horseback in the foreground, watched over by the gamekeeper and their mother Mary.

7. and 8. 'A second mother to all [Mary's] children'. A young Richard Haldane in the arms of the family's beloved nurse, Betsy Ferguson (Baba), 1856. Mary Haldane (below), with her second son, Geordie, 1858.

9. John, Richard and Geordie Haldane, c. 1870. When Geordie died aged sixteen in 1875, his father solemnly stated, 'Before the foundations of the world were laid it was so ordained.'

THE "ΕΥΡΗΚΑ" CLUB, 1876

Back Row: James Douglas, W. A. Herdman (F.R.S.), A. H. Spens Black, P. C. Robertson, D. Noel Paton (F.R.S.).
Front Row: J. Balfour Kinnear, R. H. Wood, E. W. Clarke, R. Kettle Anderson, J. S. Haldane (F.R.S.).

10. John Haldane, seated far right, with fellow members of the Eureka Club, 1876. These budding scientists were all in the same class at the strictly classical Edinburgh Academy. Four of this select band, including (Sir) D'Arcy Wentworth Thompson (missing from photograph), went on to become Fellows of the Royal Society.

11. Mary and Robert's children, late 1870s. From left to right: John, Elizabeth, Willie and Richard.

12. Mary, surrounded by her three eldest children, Richard, John and Elizabeth, on the steps at Cloan, early 1880s.

their first significant contribution to the wider intellectual world. They were now armed with a 'settled outlook' (all subsequent philosophical works from their pens were essentially very extensive footnotes on their 1883 essay) and, in Elizabeth's eyes, the change was dramatic—for her just as much as for her brothers: 'In looking back it seems as if "the middle eighties"... signified a time of wonderful cheerfulness and hope.'[32] And yet, it would be wrong to downplay the suffering that accompanied their new outlook. For all their assurances to their mother, they could not simply carry on as before.

Their connection to the church of their upbringing was an obvious case in point. Richard's adult baptism at seventeen—where he rose dripping from the font and announced to the assembly that he had only allowed the ceremony to allay the anxiety of his parents and that he had, from that point on, 'no connection to the church, or its teaching'—was a theatrical example of the issue.[33] John's and Willie's departure from their early ecclesial allegiance was less public, but equally painful. In the same year that he and Richard published their essay, John wrote from the quiet of his desk, on his own and Willie's behalf, to the minister of the family's congregation in Edinburgh and explained their reasons for leaving the church (Willie would later overcome his doubts):

> To make religion depend on historical fact is, to my mind... to make the existence of God have no deeper significance than a mere physical fact. Both the world and the self are thus left outside of God in their own innate imperfection and sin, & the spiritual unity of all things in God becomes only a name... It is a difficulty which I know is not present to many men, but it is vividly so to me, and I cannot shut my eyes to it without being dishonest to myself... Respect has prevented me from writing in a less direct manner. In lives that are real there must always be pain as well as happiness.[34]

The pain Elizabeth felt at her own gradual separation from the past is expressed in her memoirs, as she recalls reading the works of Mark Rutherford (real name, William Hale White): 'His first books recorded the life of a dissenting minister, who had to leave the church and suffer much in doing so... for those who had in their own way to pass through equal difficulties, they were very moving.'

But, as she goes on to record, 'gradually we seemed to be able to see light shining through the darkness and to have some hope and certainty for the future'.[35] It's clear that her hopefulness was rooted in the same source as her brothers': 'We did not so much want to do "good" to our neighbour as to develop the sense of a concrete life in which we should all play our part. That is, we did not wish to exist as isolated units but as part of an organism which should develop in the right way.'[36] The stage was set, then, for a cohesive and collaborative attempt to meet the problems of the day, in which Richard, John, and Elizabeth would each play a part. Free from the 'denominationally religious or ascetic attitude of mind characteristic of the Church', the family ties that had once felt so restrictive were now transformed into a means by which they would seek to change the world.[37] A sketch of their subsequent achievements over the 1880s and 1890s shows their commitment to making that change.

* * *

Richard's political work alone was as voluminous as it was effective. Between 1880 and 1900, he founded and developed that engine of Liberal thinking, the Eighty Club; won for the Liberals, with an immense majority and against all expectation, the traditionally Conservative seat of Haddingtonshire in 1885 at the age of twenty-nine; created the intellectual basis of Liberal Imperialism; successfully amended the Irish Land Law Bill of 1887; sponsored three private members' bills on female suffrage in 1889, 1890, and 1892 (he was chairman of the Women's Industrial League by 1895); drafted with Sidney Webb the radical Local Authorities (Land Purchase) Bill of 1891 and 1892; explained and defended the Second Irish Home Rule Bill during its passage through the Commons in 1893; prepared, in committee, the Bill for the major expansion of death duties (inheritance tax) in 1894; sat on the select committee for the Land Transfer Bill in 1895; and converted, by means of a single Commons speech in June 1898, the hostile and indifferent opinion of his fellow Members of Parliament on the question of transforming the University of London into a real teaching university. Here, already, the twentieth century's preoccupations with the improvement of education, the expansion of the franchise, the importance of devolution, and the equitable distribution of land and property are prefigured. Richard, as politician, was pressing the door of the future. But this was only a small chunk of his activities.

In law, after the early years of painful waiting for his career to take off, Richard's success had sky-rocketed. His work 'devilling' for the renowned chancery counsel Horace Davey broke the spell of disappointment. Soon, with Davey urgently summoned to another, even more pressing hearing, Richard was standing bewigged before the Privy Council on behalf of the government of Quebec in a request for special leave to appeal against a judgement of the Canadian courts, which, if not granted, could have toppled the provincial government. Having stayed up almost the entire night to be prepared, the unknown and baggy-eyed twenty-seven-year-old convinced the judges of the point. Leave to appeal was granted. Lucrative briefs began to pour in for cases on constitutional matters before the Privy Council and for appeals before the House of Lords. The expertise gained was enormous. Richard was laying the foundations for his later monumental contributions to the constitutional law of the Empire, especially that of Canada, as president of the Judicial Committee of the Privy Council in the 1910s.

He was fast becoming a rich man too, but even before this he was generous both with his time and his money. It was characteristic of him to write in 1882 to his mother, 'I have had to spend more money than I liked this year in relieving people I knew about from destitution. This however is money one cannot regret.'[38] At this stage, legal briefs were still scant and he offered himself as a lecturer at the Working Men's College and elsewhere, no doubt half-bemusing, half-inspiring his audience with his philosophical discourses. As his earnings increased, so did his productivity and his largesse. By 1890—a year of extremes, in which he became the youngest QC in a generation at thirty-three, but also entered into his doomed engagement to the beautiful but complex (and possibly lesbian) Val Munro-Ferguson—he had translated three volumes of Schopenhauer and written a life of Adam Smith. And by 1892, as he considered the necessity of sacking an old Cloan servant for various misdemeanours, he could assure Mary: 'I will pay his wife a pension of, say, £25 a year [£3,250 in today's terms], until the sons grow up... I can easily manage the pension—as one which I have been paying for someone else for the last three years falls in this year.'[39] There was also a price to pay for being in demand. There can have been few busier men in London, as this letter of 1891, again to his mother, suggests:

> I had a night of it last night—left court at 1 read a brief and prepared my speech and addressed 3000 people at Bradford at 7.30:—caught the 9.45 train, read two briefs with the aid of a candle—reached Members Mansions [his London home at the time] at 3.30 am to find an urgent invitation that I must read up my papers which were sent down—get up at 7.30 to read a new batch which were coming—be at the Courts at 9.45 and deliver an elaborate argument at 10.30. However I did it & am not a bit tired...[40]

Richard's growing prominence as politician and lawyer soon found him making friends with the great and the good. There were of course his political friendships, especially with H. H. Asquith, Sir Edward Grey, and the Conservative Arthur Balfour.[41] These were supplemented by his social connections which, in these early years, already ranged from the writer George Meredith (whom he first met in 1882 while walking with the 'Sunday Tramps', a group formed by Leslie Stephen, father of Virginia Woolf) to the financier Lord Rothschild and his wife Emma. He even made two visits to the incarcerated Oscar Wilde in 1895 and provided him with the books and writing materials that led to *The Ballad of Reading Gaol*. Significantly, Richard also attended an occasional gathering of the Souls, a cultured elite at the pinnacle of London society. Their 'High Priestess' was Frances Horner, the striking and forthright muse of the Pre-Raphaelite painter Edward Burne-Jones, and wife of John Horner of Mells.[42] Richard and Frances's initial encounter in 1893 was electric, with sparks flying over their shared love of Goethe, and led to a relationship at once profound and, as far as we know, chaste.

After the dramas and failures of his previous romances, the married Frances offered a safe harbour of acceptance, even adoration, without the pressures—or, indeed, pleasures—of sex. Much has been written recently on this relationship, which was to last unbroken until Richard's death in 1928, and this is not the place to repeat its details.[43] What must be stressed, however, is the fact that

THE DECLARATION OF INDEPENDENCE

Richard's political activities were closely intertwined with his romantic friendship with Frances; he shared everything with her, she guided his steps, she warned him of pitfalls (though he did not always heed her), and ultimately she convinced him of his duty to join the famous Campbell-Bannerman administration of December 1905. He was far from the bachelor politician most people thought him to be. In 1897 he could write to Frances: 'Yes indeed—what is there to compare with your record—nothing! I owe the best I have to you & and am bound by every real tie—by the ties I love to be bound by.'[44]

All this time, Richard's passion for education intensified, culminating in his assistance to Sidney Webb in laying the legal and financial foundations of the London School of Economics and his role, again with Webb, in overhauling the University of London from being a purely degree-giving body into a real teaching university. The former required all the intellectual subtlety Richard could muster, the latter a full measure of his political and social know-how.[45] Historians have shown a fair amount of attention to both, but it's interesting to reflect on how Richard's grand projects were given more intimate dimensions in the life of his brother John. While these developments in London (including Richard's later brainchild, Imperial College) were intended to create centres of knowledge and cutting-edge science that would be of benefit to society, John sought to put his own brand of cutting-edge science into practice for the public good. And while Richard operated at the institutional level in order to create the necessary structures that would make possible the all-decisive encounter with a great teacher (his early meeting with Lotze was never far from his mind), John operated at the human level, seeking to incarnate the spirit of the great teacher in himself.

One above others whom John looked to emulate was his namesake and uncle, John Scott Burdon Sanderson. The elder John's path-breaking research on the causes of infectious diseases had earned him election to the Royal Society in 1867, and his subsequent career was a remarkable example of what was possible within a single lifetime's dedication to science. Amongst many notable achievements, he paved the way for the acceptance of germ theory in Great Britain; he was instrumental in founding the discipline of

89

experimental pathology as an accepted field of scientific inquiry; at Charles Darwin's request, he conducted research into, and confirmed the presence of, electrical excitation in the leaf of the Venus flytrap; from 1882, after his election to Oxford's new Waynflete Chair of Physiology, he played an important part in founding the university's medical school and in establishing the first Chair in Human Anatomy; he was eventually appointed to the Regius Chair of Medicine in Oxford in 1895; and in 1899 he was created a baronet, becoming Sir John Burdon Sanderson.

Two aspects that made Burdon Sanderson stand out were his insistence on practical experimental work and his skill 'in devising or modifying the sophisticated measuring and recording apparatus that characterized the developing field of electrophysiology'.[46] In this respect his nephew was most certainly cut from the same cloth. As a medical student, John Haldane considered the litmus test for an effective lecture to be whether he and his companions 'had the opportunity of verifying for ourselves [through experiment] the facts and theories we were learning, and of understanding their real bearing'.[47] Practical work became the hallmark of his scientific approach, and eventually of his teaching. What distinguished John from his uncle, however, was his willingness to experiment even on himself. As early as May 1884 (he would resit and pass his medical degree the same year), John was recording his ingestion of a nineteenth-century medicine against diphtheria and scarlet fever named sulpho-carbolate of soda: 'It... seems to pass through the body almost unaltered in the normal condition.'[48] Curiosity alone did not drive him to such unusual behaviour. Every scientific endeavour was orientated towards the common good. His later colleague, C. G. Douglas, noted:

> to him the welfare of mankind was the fulfilment of the growth of knowledge. He was not the man to experiment simply for experiment's sake: he did not draw a bow at a venture in the vain hope that the arrow might hit some unseen mark. Few will have known what an amount of thought he gave to his work, for the spirit of inquiry was inherent in him and his mind was never at rest.[49]

Over time, his lungs and heart would bear the long-term consequences of his quest for first-hand scientific knowledge, pushing him

THE DECLARATION OF INDEPENDENCE

to the point when, at the turn of the century, a doctor declared him unfit for active work—an opinion John confidently brushed aside, surging on with further rounds of punishing research. The habit for self-experimentation would become one of the most noticeable trends within the next generation of Haldanes.

John also took his uncle's inventive streak to new levels. By the end of his life, he had designed a 'Haldane box' that allowed canaries to accompany miners down the pit and register, by means of their consciousness or lack thereof, the presence or absence of gases before they became life-threatening to humans; breathing equipment that allowed rescue teams to make their way into pits in the event of an explosion; the Haldane gas analysis apparatus, which could assess the precise mixture of gases; the 'Haldane Haemoglobinometer', which became the go-to commercial instrument for the measurement of blood gases; a coffin-like contraption that accurately recorded the amount of air a human being breathed; diving tables to help prevent the onset of 'the bends' in divers returning to the water's surface; the first effective, if improvised, gas mask for soldiers fighting in the trenches of the First World War; and even a prototype spacesuit, which became 'the early model for the spacesuits worn by astronauts on Extra Vehicular Activity'.[50]

Like his uncle, John resisted narrow specialisation in a single scientific area. His son, J. B. S. Haldane, once wrote of him: 'his work covered a field almost as wide as that of Darwin or Pasteur, and almost as difficult for others to understand or to imitate'.[51] John's career throughout the 1880s and 1890s showed his willingness to diversify. In 1884 he investigated the chemical pathology of fevers in Oxford and London, and spent six months as House Physician at the Edinburgh Royal Infirmary. He then moved to University College, Dundee, where, together with Professor Thomas Carnelley and Dundee's Medical Officer of Health, A. M. Anderson, he examined the air quality of the city's schools and slums—the latter by means of unannounced nocturnal visits to impoverished dwellings (the air was worst at night and the investigators didn't want the inhabitants to ventilate the rooms on their account before their arrival). In 1886, he and Carnelley were creeping the sewers beneath the Palace of Westminster to determine the origins of the so-called 'bad air' that was said to plague Parliament, an activity they went on to repeat beneath the streets of Bristol and Dundee. Their findings across these different locations and settings provided further evidence, to the joy of John's uncle, whose own research pushed in such directions, that microorganisms (germs), and not the supposed 'miasma' of foul-smelling air, were responsible for poor public hygiene[52]—a view that many eminent scientists of the time refused to accept, as, in the words of one detractor, they 'would have to put aside all the teachings of sanitary science and all past experience as to the spread of disease and fevers'.[53] History has judged the two Johns to be on the winning side of the debate.

That same year, 1886, John worked for a term in the Pathological Institute at the University of Berlin, where the Professor of Medical Chemistry hailed the young Scotsman's approach to experimental research as 'the height of science'.[54] From there it was back to Oxford for John to take on the post of Demonstrator in Physiology in January 1887, under the watchful eye of his uncle. This was where John could come into his own as a teacher. Those who studied under him remembered how 'his teaching was characterised by his efforts to make the students observe and think for themselves'. They considered him to be blessed with 'a unique power of encouraging the faculty for research'. One friend recalled his 'force and charm of character' which secured for him 'the attachment of his pupils'.[55] John was moulding himself into the hero of learning of whom his brother Richard so often spoke.

Knowing what a difference such inspiration could have, John now had the confidence and the position to write a scathing attack on the Edinburgh Medical School, published in 1890 as *A Letter to Edinburgh Professors*. Though the authorship was anonymised, his run-in with the professors seven years earlier made it obvious who bore the pen. His judgement on his teachers was damning: 'They influenced me little more than the reading of a dictionary might have done.' Even a number of his fellow students he found 'intellectually dead'. The greatest problem with his alma mater was its obsession with assessments: 'We were all hurrying on from one examination to the next; we had to take as it came all that was taught us, without stopping to inquire as to its significance, and far less as to its truth.'[56]

Real inspiration could still be found in other universities, and in December 1893 John and his colleague James Lorrain Smith travelled to Copenhagen to visit the laboratory of the physiologist Christian Bohr, father of the future Nobel laureate Niels Bohr. Here, momentous advances in the study of respiration were taking place. The two Scotsmen enjoyed more than just the science, spending Christmas with the Bohr family, and revelled in the spectacle of their renowned host lighting up a cigar, which he'd been given as a present, only to discover that it was in fact an oversized pencil with an extremely flammable celluloid top. Their trip was crowned by a New Year's Eve game of golf on the King's deer park—the very first game of golf on Danish soil.[57] When, in later years, John returned to Denmark in the company of Niels Bohr, another game was pursued. According to John's daughter, Naomi (whose utterances sometimes require a salt cellar near to hand), one of the scientists hit his ball over the palace walls, so they decided to climb over. Noting the clubbed trespassers, the King stepped forth from the palace and, instead of calling his guards, asked to join in the game.[58]

* * *

John's face was all nose and moustache, he was alarmingly absent-minded, and he had an intensity that could make social chit-chat difficult. But the opposite sex was not immune to him, and he was not immune to romance either. In 1883, while still in Edinburgh, he had met briefly a beautiful young woman whose family was interested in renting 17 Charlotte Square from Mary, and his interest was piqued. Her name was Louisa Kathleen Trotter (known as Kathleen), but John didn't leave the best first impression. When the letting agent led Kathleen and her mother into the dining room, they found John sprawled on the floor in front of the fireplace, open books scattered about him. Despite John's claim to be 'working', Kathleen knew he had been enjoying a good nap. When John then proceeded to follow the viewing party round the rest of the house, she couldn't help but feel his lack of tact—it was not exactly his place to listen in to the strangers' questions about things as delicate as the house's sanitary arrangements.[59]

If such a first encounter was inauspicious, neither did the differing political outlooks of John and Kathleen's respective families bode well. Kathleen was a fierce Tory and Imperialist of the old school, with a strong sense of hierarchy within society. She certainly couldn't warm to John's politician brother, finding 'his omniscience, his self-satisfaction and his sneers at the ideas and loyalties of people who disagreed with him' repulsive, though not quite as repulsive as 'the harm that he and his party were doing to the country'.[60] Richard, for his part, tried his best to be balanced, but he struggled. As he told his mother:

> I have called on Kathleen & also... Mrs T[rotter], so I have done my duty. I own that I find I have been making an effort. Commend me for narrowness to provincial Toryism. I feel much as my grandfather Sanderson might if you had married a Church of England clergyman. However all passed smoothly and pleasantly last night & it is done. I do not doubt that on my side I am narrow too, but then politics are my very life.[61]

Kathleen was not predictably Tory in every particular. She had ambitions to be a doctor and she loathed the idea that a wedding involved the bride being 'given away'. Later, she supported the first Oxford birth control clinic. Her individualistic, even feminist, streak must have appealed to John. As for her other, less palatable views, John was convinced that silence (mainly his own) would work its magic and resolve any tensions. But it took eight years and two rejections before Kathleen finally accepted his proposal of marriage. Was she just running out of other options? She was certainly impressed by his integrity and intelligence, but it is hard to know how far her affections went. Reflecting on their early letters to each other, John's biographer notes: 'From [John] Haldane we hear of love, from Kathleen mostly of respect.'[62] When Kathleen reached old age and looked back on their wedding in 1891, she did little to hide her feelings about the match: 'We had a big reception to show the wedding presents and to drink healths. I tried to make it something of a festive occasion for my cousins... but it was no good; they were as depressed as I was.'[63]

Nevertheless, with the couple settled in Oxford, the 1890s brought a new generation of children into the family. The arrival of John and Kathleen's first child in 1892 was greeted by fireworks—it was 5 November, Guy Fawkes Day. Named John Burdon Sanderson

Haldane after his great-uncle, it was clear from the start that this was a life that would cause a bang. At seven months, his father gave Mary the following update: 'Kathleen & Squawks [their onomatopoeic nickname for the baby] are both very well. The latter is growing fast, & is becoming much more amenable to reason in all sorts of ways.'[64] This amenability would be prodigious. Before he could walk, he was handling objects 'with a precocious and scientific expression'.[65] His mother taught him to read at three, not so much to encourage his learning but to stop him asking so many questions. His vocabulary already contained the words 'oxyhaemoglobin' and 'carboxyhaemoglobin'. Even more impressively, he knew in which context to use them. The toddler was well accustomed to having his chubby arms punctured by a needle, as his father saw no issue with involving him in his experiments with blood. At thirty-six and four years old respectively, father and son were also investigating the atmosphere within the Metropolitan Underground, the former opening carriage windows and collecting 'air samples in glass bottles from which he sucked the air with a rubber tube', the latter watching in rapt admiration.[66] It was quite within the little boy's abilities by the time he was five to read aloud in front of his maternal grandfather *The Times*'s reports of the British Association for the Advancement of Science. His family may have felt less pride when they discovered the five-year-old's handwritten notes left scattered around the house, each one simply stating: 'I hate you.' When his sister, Naomi Mary Margaret Haldane, was born on 1 November 1897, it was clear whose shadow she would be living in for the rest of her childhood.

The presence of young children did nothing to deter the rise of John Haldane's scientific eminence, and the year of Naomi's arrival was the year of his election to the Royal Society. He had been promoted to the position of lecturer within the physiology department at Oxford in 1894, though he was unsuccessful the following year in his application for the professorial chair his uncle had vacated for the chair of medicine—a 'failure' more due to Burdon Sanderson's fear of accusations over nepotism than John's lack of ability, and which led to tensions between the two. But more important to John than titles and income was the discovery of knowledge, as Naomi remembered: 'What mattered was never measured by money standards; it was an idea spreading out to new conclusions... It was a saving and bettering of human life.'[67] John was convinced of the origins of such an outlook: 'A sane and whole man or woman wants to do a man's or woman's work, and not exist simply for the benefit of his or her health, or for the sake of making money. That is a piece of psychology which I learned from my mother and my old Scotch nurse.'[68] Amongst much important work for the good of others, the 1890s saw the beginning of John's investigations into mining disasters—their causes and preventions—which were to make his name.

Medical opinion was divided regarding the cause of death in colliery explosions. Did those who died from the poisonous 'after damp', which John believed was more lethal than the explosion itself, die because of carbon monoxide or because of suffocation from the lack of oxygen in the air? Could clarity on this question save lives? Though he could learn a certain amount within his Oxford laboratory by inhaling carbon monoxide himself at different concentrations in the air—a truly horrible self-experiment that brought him to a state of unconsciousness on at least one occasion—John needed to be at the epicentre of tragedy if he was to make real strides. His visits to South Wales in the immediate aftermath of disaster at the Albion Colliery in 1894 and Tylorstown in 1896 were brutally enlightening. John was called to the latter at the request of the Home Secretary, and his round-the-clock autopsies of men and horses, both above and beneath ground—employing test tubes, spirit burners, scalpels, needles, and hacksaws to gather the raw evidence—showed beyond doubt that carbon monoxide was the principal killer, not the explosion as was commonly thought nor a lack of oxygen. More importantly, John, in his subsequent report, was able to advise on ways in which those not within the immediate zone of an explosion could be saved. His message was simple but contrary to intuition:

> At the least warning of approaching flame or disturbance a man should at once fall flat. In this way both burning and violence may be partly or completely avoided. Moreover the air along the floor will be cooler and contain less after-damp, and when fresh air comes it will come first along the floor. Any exertion will... hasten the action of the after damp. For a man near the shaft, the best plan would probably be to lie still. For a man in a road, far in, the most

hopeful way of escape, if consciousness remained, would be towards a return air-way, or towards the face.[69]

If a small animal could be present with the miners at their work, that would save lives too, because their high relative metabolism would mean that they'd be affected by the carbon monoxide far faster than any man. Canaries have since been in use in pits around the world (they were very often held in a 'Haldane box' which resuscitated them once they became unconscious), and were only phased out in Britain in 1987, replaced by digital devices. As John's Royal Society obituary says: 'This remarkable report clarified a situation which was frankly obscure and it was translated into several foreign languages; it was of fundamental importance in the development of means for combating the dangers arising from explosions in mines or from underground fires.'[70] With impact like this, it is not surprising that by the end of the century John was named one of three Metropolitan Gas Referees, increasing his prestige, supplementing his university income, and expanding his responsibilities.

* * *

Back in Scotland, John's sister Elizabeth sought to transform her role in life from that of observer to that of participant. In some respects, she still relied on her brothers to make this happen. She became a leading campaigner for Richard as he continued to fight over subsequent elections for his seat in Haddingtonshire (later renamed East Lothian) and became treasurer of the Scottish Women's Liberal Association. Through John, she was able to develop her scientific knowledge and experience, overseeing his Cloan-based experiments on carbonic acid in the outside air while he was away in Oxford. As she explains:

> The experiments were done amongst the evergreens, both at midday and midnight and in winter time, so that this entailed going out amongst the bushes with my apparatus and then weighing the tubes, through which the air had been drawn by an aspirator outside, in a laboratory which we rigged up in an attic inside the house. In snowy weather the task was none too easy, as the aspirator froze; but it was great fun, for one felt that something practical was being done, and

though I had no experience of such work I gradually learned how to do it moderately well.[71]

Later, on a trip to Italy with her mother in 1898, she enjoyed surprising her fellow tourists by doing on-the-spot air quality experiments in tunnels and capturing samples of the gas that was famous for killing small animals, especially dogs, in the Grotta del Cane near Naples. She had been trained well: 'John was infinitely patient and as he explained everything carefully he was delightful to work with.' Elizabeth continues:

> I don't think anyone can have had brothers as kind and helpful as I had, for the elders were always advising me with my philosophical work [she was becoming a translator and author in her own right by the 1880s] and discussing its bearings, whereas the youngest [Willie, the lawyer, of whom more later] looked after my temporal affairs, so that hitherto they have never troubled me.[72]

There were other situations in which Elizabeth struck out on her own. A meeting in 1884 with the social reformer Octavia Hill (1838–1912) proved decisive. Hill was already well known as 'the friendly face of "landlordism"' in London, fostering communities within housing schemes where fair rents, good conditions, and access to culture and nature became the norm.[73] A movement in Scotland, known as the Social Union, wanted to know Hill's magic formula and sent a deputation to meet with her to discuss what improvements could be made north of the Border. It just so happened that the day of the deputation's visit coincided with the day that Elizabeth, through the introduction of an aunt, went to see the great woman: 'Miss Hill told the deputation that she would have to train the lady who might start work in Edinburgh. They were nonplussed until Miss Hill turned to me and asked if I would help. I was rather taken aback, as I was young, about twenty-one, and had no experience.'[74] It was just the kind of opportunity for which Elizabeth had longed, and by accepting she put her future on a new footing—one that was both exciting and disturbing.

She had seen something of Edinburgh's poverty in her childhood, but the work now demanded of her required her regular presence amongst the most marginalised in Scotland's capital: 'Where I worked there was much sweated labour and families were living in small single rooms where the man did tailoring, while the woman bore her children, sewed and cooked and tended her little ones.'[75] Very often, the meagre rents couldn't be paid. Worse still, in the older buildings bug infestations were rife and no amount of poison seemed to make a difference. The extent of the challenges was so vast that Elizabeth came to see government assistance on a national level as the only answer. In this she parted ways—intellectually speaking—with Hill, who felt that state interference would only undermine the importance of self-reliance amongst the poor.

Elizabeth's new-found convictions tied in, of course, with the kind of thinking about the constitution of the state that Richard and John had exemplified in their 1883 essay; but one wonders if Elizabeth's first-hand experience of such living conditions—before Richard even became a Member of Parliament—in turn shaped her eldest brother's political focus. Three areas of particular dominance in Richard's early speeches were the extension of university education, women's suffrage, and—importantly—housing. For Richard, moreover, it was essential that the state got its hands dirty in dealing with this last question. Leaving it to churches, philanthropists, and charitable endeavours would never provide lasting change. If Elizabeth did influence her brother in this regard, it was a significant moment of power-reversal.

Elizabeth's next steps showed her growing confidence. In 1890, no doubt to Hill's approval, she co-founded the Scottish Women's Benefit Society. By means of members' small monthly in-payments, the Society provided various forms of insurance in cases of misfortune or need, and encouraged both thrift and what Elizabeth called 'a moral element'. She explained what she meant in an article for *The National Review* in 1896: 'members are directed "to seek their own good through the good of others," to discard for the time being all social distinctions and party feeling, taking as their motto, "each for all and all for each"'.[76] Hill would have perhaps been less pleased when in 1912 the Society—by then part of the Ancient Order of Foresters—became involved in the state system of national insurance in the wake of Lloyd George's radical National Insurance Act the previous year. Like her brothers, Elizabeth was ahead of the trend.

There were also cultural needs that Elizabeth felt were pressing. The village of Auchterarder, over which Cloan keeps watch, was the perfect setting for Elizabeth's new ambition to set up a public library. Initially, it was a case of raising enough money through bazaars to buy a small collection of books—mostly fairly highbrow, which was uncommon for lending libraries at the time—and to provide courses of related lectures. It was something of an eye-opener, for it showed the intellectual thirst that existed amongst a number of the working men in the district, one of whom read through all three volumes of Schopenhauer's *World as Will and Idea*, which Richard had translated. Not all the books on the shelves were welcome. The Free Church Minister had no time for George Eliot (a set of whose works had been donated by John Haldane), considering her 'an atheist, and other things unmentionable'. But, as Elizabeth records, 'After his denunciation from the pulpit, I asked the librarian what was the result. He said "all the Elders came to borrow the novels in order to see what the pernicious books were like!"—so that the good man's end was apparently not attained'.[77]

What started as a very small venture grew into a significant library, with its own building and institute. This growth was largely due to the assistance of none other than Andrew Carnegie, an occasional neighbour to the Haldanes of Cloan and a great admirer of Mary. When he opened the new buildings in 1896, he rode the mile from Cloan to Auchterarder in a carriage with Mary, and Elizabeth, now secretary of the Institute, formally presented him with a gold key to open the doors. Richard was present, too, and five years later was asked by Carnegie to join the first trustees of the Carnegie Trust for the Universities of Scotland. When the philanthropist established the Carnegie United Kingdom Trust in 1913, it was Elizabeth's turn to be asked; the only woman at that time to be so.

* * *

Where did the youngest brother Willie fit into all this? Like his father, he trod a more conventional professional course. From the Edinburgh Academy, he progressed in 1881 to the city's University and chose the law as his profession, becoming a Writer to the Signet in 1888. He was thickset and moustachioed, and he hated wasting time. In fact, he was inexorably practical and shared little of his siblings' enthusiasm for long hours lost amongst philosophy books.

THE DECLARATION OF INDEPENDENCE

Willie initially intended to join the firm in which his father had been a partner, but due to difficulties amongst the existing partners, he chose to strike out on his own after his apprenticeship, founding his own firm, W. & F. Haldane (F. for Frank, a cousin). Willie was evidently talented and built up a significant reputation for his knowledge and reliability. Such was his standing that he was considered an acceptable suitor to Edith Stuart Nelson, daughter of the famous (and very wealthy) Edinburgh publisher Thomas Nelson. The couple married in June 1892, but not without a hint of concern from Mary and Richard, with the latter writing to his mother: 'I think as you do that their danger will be the tendency to grow like Edinburgh Society. Still this is a minor evil.'[78]

Edith's granddaughter, Jennifer Halsey, describes her as 'shy and retiring', with Willie very much the dominant and controlling force in the relationship.[79] Another grandchild has said of Edith that 'she obviously worked on the principle that it was easier to give in than to fight'.[80] Edith bore her first child, Robert Patrick (known as Pat), the year after the wedding; a daughter, Mary Elizabeth (known as Elsie), in 1894; and another son, Thomas Graeme Nelson (known as Graeme), in December 1897. That year, Willie—a true countryman with a passion for agriculture—had bought the Foswell estate, directly adjacent to Cloan, and the development of these lands would become his main interest. Most importantly, after Richard's initial oversight in the wake of their father's death, Willie took on the role of family caretaker, tending to all their financial and legal needs. It was not exactly an exciting part to play, but it proved crucial. It helped free Richard and Elizabeth (John ran his own affairs) to turn their attention outwards and give their time to causes of national importance. That said, Willie's relationships with his siblings were not all conducted like business transactions. The spirit of their childhood was still discernible. A letter of Richard's to his mother from 1898, after attending a wedding in Aberdeen with his youngest brother, almost sounds like the confession of a naughty schoolboy: 'Willie and I slipped away during the reception—got hold of bath towels & had a swim in the Don—leaving our wedding garments on the bank—with umbrellas over them to keep off rain & cows.'[81]

Willie also relieved Mary from concern over her temporal needs, giving her time and energy to tend to the spiritual needs of her children. She was their pole star in all things. Whatever they did, no matter how remarkable, it always came second place to their mother. Richard's words to her in 1889 are representative: 'You must not think of me & my future in your consideration of yourself. My first and most binding tie is to my old mother, and anything which conflicts with this shall certainly so far as I'm concerned, go by the board.'[82] It was Mary's presence at Cloan more than anything else that made their Scottish home so special to them. Again, Richard says it all: 'It was a very happy week at Cloanden & I look back on it much. I love the being near you, & the library… & the atmosphere, physical & moral of the whole place.'[83]

The demands on the time and abilities of Mary's children would only increase as the new century rolled in, but they always made space for Cloan. This was the centre of the love that sustained them in their various activities. Mary, looking on at her children's growing achievements, sometimes worried that she hadn't used her life quite as she should have. They reassured her that, without her constant support, none of their successes would have been possible. In this she took solace. As she told her eldest son soon after her seventy-second birthday in 1897:

> I cannot tell you how precious your words are to me, and how they make me feel that, after all, my life has not been a failure, as I am sometimes apt to think when I see my children doing so much that I cannot do. 'Love is the fulfilling of the law.' And love must fulfil what is lacking in the powers.[84]

Little did she know that she had twenty-eight years of love left to give. With armies to reform, lives to save, and injustices to fight, her children would definitely need it.

5

A NEW CENTURY

1900–1905

The station at Auchterarder was cold after the warmth of the train, with its iron foot-warmers filled with boiling water. The Oxford Haldanes—John, Kathleen, Jack and Naomi—tumbled out of their cosy compartment after a long night's journey north in pursuit of a holiday. Waiting for them stood a coachman and carriage, with two horses stamping and tossing their heads in the bright morning light. Clambering in, the family were met by an intense smell of straw, spiced with a whiff of horse dung. They trotted out of the station yard and bumped along the rutted country road. Half an hour later, as they crossed a small stone bridge and started to climb the hill towards their destination, the fustiness of the carriage gave way to fresher smells. Gradually, the air became rich with the scent of pine needles and beech leaves. The horses slowed down as the incline steepened, and at last they turned through a pair of rounded gate-posts, topped proudly with mock cannonballs.

The young Naomi Haldane (known to the family as Nou), five or so at the time, pulled down the window to enjoy the sound of the hooves and wheels churning up the gravel drive with a satisfying crunch. Above her the wind rustled in the leaves, and near, unseen, a burn cascaded and tumbled. It was an assault on the senses, quite different from the sights and sounds of urbanised Oxford. Having curved past a dense wall of shrubbery, Cloan loomed before them in its cloak of jasmine, the high turreted tower dominating attention. Out shot a pair of dogs from the front door, one large, one small, tails aflutter, barking welcomes of delight. Following them, with a matron's bustle and with opening arms, came Elizabeth, now almost forty years old. Her heavy eyelids—set above the bulbous Haldane nose, and flanked by two oversized ears—seemed to pull her eyes down at the sides, lending her an aura of endearment. Richard, recently home from London, appeared on the steps moments later. He wore an impish grin on his round, pale face, while his curled forelock and spherical body gave him an almost Napoleonic air. John's smile lit up as he saw his siblings. Naomi jumped out of the halting carriage and ran towards them. A reserved Jack eyed his Uncle Richard, wondering at what point he'd be offered his usual golden half sovereign.[1]

Inside, the low-ceilinged hall—with its wooden panels, its large table solid beneath a mass of learned journals, its fire popping and snapping in the grate—spoke not of opulence but of homeliness. Gas lamps sent arcs of light into the corners of this windowless cavern. There was no grand staircase to be seen, but the visitors could hear, off to the right behind them, the grunts of Richard's German butler as he wrestled their cases around the corkscrew turns of the narrow stairs that spiralled up the tower towards the bedrooms. Elizabeth, feeling the hard-won heat escape, quickly closed the small door that led to the stairs and took the new arrivals through the much more stately doorway next to it.

They were now in the vast drawing room, part of Robert Haldane's additions of 1866, where an almost comically high ceiling and an expanse of windows seemed to mock the dark, diminutive hall. Mary Haldane, in her seventy-eighth year, beamed up at them from her fireside chair, too frail to stand. Beside her lay an open copy of Johann Winckelmann's *History of Ancient Art*. Flowers were in profusion on every surface, and an almost tropical smell of plants came floating from the little conservatory at the far end of the room. With the usual babble of greetings, kisses were exchanged, the journey was discussed, and news was shared. It was a happy reunion. Meanwhile, the perspiring butler returned quietly to arrange for refreshments, and a submissive parlour maid scurried off to the kitchen with orders. The family settled into their chairs and rubbed the heads of the panting, encircling dogs. They could now look forward to a long holiday in the quiet of the Perthshire hills. All was as it should be. All was right with the world.

* * *

A NEW CENTURY

But, of course, this wasn't the case. Those nameless, background figures of the story—the waiting coachman, the German butler, the obliging parlour maid—remind us that this was still a world of marked inequalities of power. It was 1903 or thereabouts, the opening of the Edwardian era, the golden age of the country house. That sense of a golden age accounts, perhaps, for the tendency to idealise the scene of the Oxford Haldanes' arrival at Cloan, the details of which are taken partly from Naomi's own memoirs. We'll come to discover how catastrophic the 1914–18 war was for Naomi and her generation, and with this in mind it's understandable if her recollections of the early twentieth century have a faint prelapsarian feel. Even in writing about it now, there's an almost irresistible pull towards romanticisation, stemming from a national tendency to view Edwardian Britain as a land of milk and honey, a place of endless tea parties on verdant, canopied lawns. There may have been an abundance of tea parties for the privileged few while Edward was on the throne, but the reality for the many was not noticeably different from the poverty and lack of opportunity of earlier eras. Access to good healthcare and education—principal concerns of Mary Haldane's children—remained a challenge for the majority of the population. Women still didn't have the vote. Significant changes in welfare would start appearing by 1906, as the Liberal governments' social reforms began to take life. But the opening of the century was hardly a time of contentment and peace.

The earth-shattering convulsions of the so-called Great War can easily blind us to the fact that the century began with a bloody war in South Africa. If we find our patriotism stirred by thoughts of later images bearing Kitchener's bushy moustache and pointed finger, it may also cloud our recognition that this earlier conflict, known as the Second Boer War (October 1899 to May 1902), largely originated in the British Empire's hunger for money and prestige, and that the man responsible for its greatest injustices was Kitchener himself. The war claimed the lives of 28,000 soldiers and 46,000 civilians. The civilian losses comprised 26,000 Boers and 20,000 Black Africans interred in British-run concentration camps, established as a way of 'concentrating' into one place those made homeless by Kitchener's decision, as Chief of Staff, to adopt a 'scorched earth' policy: razing to the ground, with growing indiscrimination, the homesteads of any family that might possibly harbour Boer guerrilla fighters and their supplies. Three-quarters of all those who died in the camps were children. Henry Campbell-Bannerman, then leader of the Opposition in the Commons, famously called Kitchener's tactics 'methods of barbarism'.

If war abroad and disparities of power at home were two of the most pressing issues of the new century, then the Haldanes of Cloan were right in the thick of them, sometimes pushing them to fresh conclusions they might otherwise not have reached. They were not the only shunters and shifters of history, but they put their backs into the task as much as any family could.

* * *

John's role in redressing the worst elements of the South African concentration camps is a notable case in point. In 1900, the welfare campaigner Emily Hobhouse (sister of the political theorist L. T. Hobhouse, who'd studied briefly under John at Oxford and to whose book, *The Labour Movement,* Richard had contributed a foreword in 1893) had been sent by the government to investigate conditions in the camps. Her subsequent report confirmed the deadly scarcity of soap, water, fuel, and food. In such a context, lethal outbreaks of measles, bronchitis, dysentery, pneumonia, and typhoid were inevitable. Hobhouse recorded: 'I call this camp system a wholesale cruelty… To keep these Camps going is murder to the children.'[2] John's aggressively Tory wife, Kathleen, continued to insist that the camps were just another instance of the Empire's graciousness and Christian example, insofar as they diverted to non-colonials money and resources that belonged by right to the Empire. She couldn't understand John's reaction: 'It seemed as if he were deliberately closing his mind to any reasoning on that matter, and could only talk about "inhumanity" and "starving women and children".'[3]

Having read with horror Hobhouse's report, John fired off letters to newspapers detailing the necessary food requirements that would begin to make a dent on the death rate. He even offered to go to South Africa himself, to see through implementation. Feeling ignored, he turned to his brother Richard, who arranged a private conversation between John and the colonial secretary, Joseph Chamberlain. The consequences were momentous. Chamberlain effected changes based on John's recommendations that reduced the death rate to a tenth of what it had been.[4] According to Admiral Jacky Fisher, well-known for a punchy statement, John 'had done more to save human lives than... the whole of the medical profession put together'.[5]

Richard's own attitude to the conflict and the camps was less progressive than his brother's, despite his openness to playing the mediator with Chamberlain. Richard and his fellow Liberal Imperialists largely supported, as 'the least of two terrible evils', the unpalatable policies of the Marquess of Salisbury's Conservative administration, the British generals, and the controversial High Commissioner for Southern Africa, Sir Alfred Milner.[6] He did speak out tentatively against the appalling conditions in the camps, but there was little firmness in his utterances. Perhaps he would have seen matters differently had the pressure of his legal work not forced him to decline an offer to chair a governmental committee of inquiry into the conflict in 1900. But Richard still felt he could do something towards the war effort.

During the course of a brief train journey in 1900 in the company of Lord Lansdowne, then Secretary of State for War, Richard expounded on the need for a committee to examine the improvement of explosives. This was a key way, Richard thought, of remedying the military's defects in the opening year of combat. Lansdowne, astonished at the level of Richard's knowledge, not only agreed to establish such a committee, but also offered Richard the chair. Richard declined, convinced he was too inexperienced and that only a very great scientist would do the job properly. Instead, he suggested Lord Rayleigh, Professor of Natural Philosophy at the Royal Institution, who accepted the position. Nine years later, having by then won the Nobel Prize for Physics, Rayleigh would prove a very able president of the Advisory Committee for Aeronautics, established by a successor of Lansdowne as Secretary of State for War: Richard Burdon Haldane.

Richard gained much experience for that Secretaryship sitting on the Explosives Committee between 1901 and 1904. It is hard to know how he found the time for it. Between the turn of the century and his entry into government in December 1905, Richard's place within the law was almost unsurpassed; he acted as counsel in some of the most high-profile cases of the era, including the Taff Vale and 'Wee Frees' cases. His loss of the former for the unions led to the historic Trade Disputes Act of 1906, granting total immunity to trade unions from being sued, while Richard considered the latter case, which caused extensive ecclesiastical disruption in Scotland, 'probably the greatest litigation of its particular kind which ever occurred in our history'.[7] Somehow, besides all this, he was able to raise the funds for and, with Sidney Webb, bring into being what would become Imperial College London in 1907, a project heavily indebted to Richard's 1901 visit to the Technische Hochschule at Charlottenburg in Germany. Extraordinarily, he also found the time to prepare and deliver the Gifford Lectures at the University of St Andrews over two academic years, between 1902 and 1904, which became his two-volume book *The Pathway to Reality*—'an extremely brilliant exposition of Hegelianism pure and simple', as one review put it.[8] Such was its strength that Richard was offered informally the Chair of Moral Philosophy at St Andrews. He knew he could be of more use elsewhere, however, and turned it down. This may also have had something to do with the fact that he was, by this stage, earning today's equivalent of over £2 million a year at the Bar.

Shortly after his first set of lectures in 1902, Richard was made a Privy Counsellor. To his annoyance, this barred him from leading the major case he'd prepared on behalf of University College Liverpool before a committee of the Privy Council, with Liverpool seeking independence from its examining body, Victoria University in Manchester. Instead, he arranged to be called as Liverpool's principal witness before the committee. His wide-ranging answers and suggestions contributed towards a resounding victory for Liverpool, which set a precedent for the speedy expansion of the 'civic' or 'red-brick' universities across England. Soon, Liverpool, Manchester, Leeds, and Bristol (where Richard became Vice-Chancellor in 1912) all had their own royal charters, with Sheffield and Reading following after. Higher education had never been so accessible. When, in 1904, Richard was asked to chair a Treasury committee to review the state grant system for England's university colleges, he was able to take a further extraordinary step. It was this committee's report that first suggested what became the University Grants Committee, the government's main advisory body on British university funding from 1919 until 1989.

What was it that made Richard capable of such multifaceted achievements? A diary entry of January 1905 by H. H. Asquith's wife, Margot, shines a light on this question, and much else. It has not, to my knowledge, appeared in any other biography of Richard, and is worth quoting at length:

> R. B. Haldane... is one of the rare men of my life time. He is everything that a man sd. be xcept [sic] a sportsman... He has more friends than anyone... He feels death & rarer still he feels life... Having suffered a... love tragedy himself & lost much that he has loved he is never unhappy or out of touch with the happy[;] he is never unkind with all his wit... Whether he has 2 hours in bed or 7 is all the same to him. He never thinks of himself at all tho [sic] he has a strong individuality & very individual opinions. He is impervious against any touchiness or smallness & gives the very best he has got to every body & every subject. He has an unhandy & not particularly attractive physique about wh.[ich] he has no illusions. He is both simple[,] subtle & suppleminded. Every one nearly tells him everything... He can not only keep a secret but he can recognise one... He is called a wirepuller & an intriguer. Daresay he is, but... being the confidant of people in cottages[,] castles[,] villas[,] rectorys [sic][,] barracks & universities, & realising what widely different arguments appeal to each of them I prefer to call him a strategist... He is chivalrous, temperate & fearless. He is not exactly a good speaker but everyone likes to listen to what he says.[9]

Few pen-portraits could present a rounder, more sympathetic picture of the man.

* * *

Returning to John, his intervention in South Africa was certainly remarkable but it was of a piece with his other scientific work during the early part of the century. In the same year (1901) that he was elected to a Fellowship at New College, Oxford, John was appointed to a departmental committee of the Home Office on the ventilation of factories and workshops, and he co-founded the *Journal of Hygiene*, which is still running to this day under the title *Epidemiology and Infection*. His son, J. B. S. Haldane (whom we'll call hereafter JBS when in adulthood, and Jack when a child), recorded:

> In its first volume he explained the red colour of salted meat as due to NO-haemochromogen, which, unlike NO-haemoglobin, is heat stable. He was very fond of cold ham, and would discourse on it at breakfast. My mother had made a rule that no physiology 'below the diaphragm' was to be discussed at meals, but ham did not come under this prohibition.[10]

Another of JBS's stories concerning this time shines as much light on the son as it does on the father. In 1901, European governments were anxious that ships arriving from plague-torn India should not bring infected rats into their countries. John Haldane was asked by the British government to report on the measures that France had taken to combat the arrival of such creatures, which consisted in gassing the rats in the holds with sulphur dioxide when ships entered French docks. Ever conscious of where fun might be had, John brought his wife and eight-year-old son with him to Dunkirk where his investigations were to be carried out and where a member of the Institut Pasteur met the family. JBS continues the story, writing from his home in India in 1961:

> My father's French was readily fatigued, and after a few minutes' conversation he found himself saying '*Ach mein lieber Kollege*.' The gas was turned on from a barge. On opening the holds a number of dead rats were seen. The crew [from India], being Muslims, had no reverence for rats, and I joined in their competition as to who could collect most dead rats on entering the forecastle with breath held... The ship was guarded by a very fat gendarme with a sword. I eluded him and got down a dry dock. He stood on the edge saying, '*Ventre du diable*.' These were the first words of French which I heard on French soil. I have liked French and Indians ever since.[11]

JBS adds the following aside: 'Rats with plague were reported in the Central Hotel, Glasgow, and for some years my father always stayed there when passing through that city in the vain hope of seeing a rat die of plague in his bedroom.'[12]

A NEW CENTURY

In 1902, the Home Secretary once again called on John's knowledge of the mining industry and asked him to investigate an outbreak of anaemia amongst Cornish tin miners. John discovered that the tropical conditions down the mines were causing an epidemic of a hookworm disease known as ancylostomiasis. The worms' eggs were passing out in the miners' faeces and producing larvae that could penetrate human skin. Having entered the bloodstream, the larvae could create holes in lung capillaries and even reach the duodenum (the first part of the intestine). The infection can lead to chronic blood loss, hence iron deficiency anaemia; in other words, the blood lacks adequate healthy red blood cells. While in a place such as Puerto Rico this did at one point account for 20 per cent of all deaths, it was not in fact very deadly amongst the Cornish miners. Drastic measures had been taken in Germany to eradicate a similar outbreak, costing vast sums of money and numerous dismissals. To stop the spread of the worms' eggs, the German miners were fed extracts of male-fern, with some suffering the side-effect of temporary or permanent loss of sight. John took a saner approach, as JBS explains:

> My father concluded that a few worms did no particular harm, and drastic measures would merely cause infected men to disperse. With the cooperation of… the manager of Dolcoath mine, and of the local trade union leaders, sanitary accommodation was provided underground, and men were persuaded to use it, the sick were treated with thymol, which did not blind them, and the epidemic died down… [M]y father… came back [to Oxford] convinced that German authoritarianism was dangerous and inefficient.[13]

Dolcoath mine became the site for further experiments. Here John could examine the physiological effects of high temperature, and he could also prove that changes in barometric pressures did not disturb the constancy of the partial pressure of carbon dioxide within the air pockets of the lungs (the alveolar air). This latter investigation was part of his wider research across 1903 and 1904 with J. G. Priestley into the regulation of breathing, leading to a paper of 1905, which John considered his most important contribution to physiology. Along with descending mines and ascending mountains, the two physiologists submitted their bodies to a host of variables to work out what actually regulated the respiratory system. Experiments showed the body's exceptional ability to offset changes in the external and internal environment: a further disproof, John thought, that the body was more or less a machine. He and Priestley eventually discovered that it was the pressure of carbon dioxide in the alveolar air that regulated breathing under normal conditions. As one contemporary commentator explains:

> A very small rise in alveolar carbon dioxide produces a large increase in breathing, which consequently tends to flush away excess carbon dioxide. The same increase in pulmonary [i.e., lung] ventilation makes a more plentiful supply of oxygen available to the body. Such an arrangement clearly benefits the organism: any increase in metabolic activity demands a greater supply of oxygen, but it also produces the excess carbon dioxide which stimulates an increase in breathing rate.[14]

As John's Royal Society obituary remarked: 'The importance of these conclusions can hardly be exaggerated, for with the help of his subsequent work they were to revolutionize physiology.'[15]

The 1905 paper had established a relation between the activity of the respiratory centre and the mass of carbon dioxide produced by the body, and offered an explanation of the natural changes in breathing which occur with changes in bodily activity. It also gave the first insights into the correlations between chemical changes in the blood and the activities of different parts of the body. Again, as John's obituary stated:

> The implications of these conclusions were far reaching, for the identification of the chemical coordination of the breathing naturally suggested that this might be but a specific instance of a principle that was applicable throughout the body, and that in the living body quantitative chemical correlation may play just as important a part as nervous correlation.[16]

As science progressed, there were less cheering developments for the Haldanes of Cloan, both personally and nationally. On 23 November 1905, Mary's remarkable brother, Sir John Burdon Sanderson, died, having resigned the Regius Chair of Medicine at Oxford two years previously on the grounds of ill-health. His accolades were legion, not least the distinctions awarded to him by the Royal Society (the Royal Medal, and Croonian Lecturer on three occasions) and his numerous honorary degrees—distinctions echoed throughout the following generations of his sister's family. Mary was deeply affected by the loss. 'I know what this means to you', wrote Richard the day after his death, 'but you have your children still. Geordie is gone before—but we are by you.'[17] Elizabeth records in her diary the 'striking' scene of the funeral at Magdalen College, where the 'crowded' chapel was moved to hear Chopin's Funeral March and the slow chanting of the choir as it swayed in procession in front of the coffin.[18]

* * *

On a national level, there was also reason to be sombre. JBS's earlier comments about his father's disdain for 'German authoritarianism' reflected a wider concern in Britain at that time about the intentions of Kaiser Wilhelm II and his advisors. A growing German navy was a particular cause for worry. In the same year that John first visited Dolcoath, the First Lord of the Admiralty, Lord Selborne, could write: 'I am convinced that the great new German navy is being carefully built up from the point of view of a war with us.'[19] John and his siblings began to feel a certain ambivalence about Germany, the most formative country of their youth next to Scotland. On the one hand, they were enormous admirers of their educational and scientific developments, which were increasingly undermining Britain's industrial and commercial dominance. Richard seemed to give endless political speeches on the lessons Britain had to learn from his beloved land across the Channel. But he was as anxious as his brother about a rising authoritarian and militaristic spirit, and he would soon be at the very forefront of seeking, as a government minister, to meet possible threats from that direction, while also seeking to foster more cordial relations between the two nations.

Richard's capacity to play a leading role in these matters was in doubt right until the eve of the formation of Campbell-Bannerman's Liberal administration in December 1905. Predicting in the autumn that the Conservative and Unionist Party did not have long in power, Richard and his two closest political allies, Edward Grey and

Asquith, determined that they would essentially force C-B (as their 'leader' was known) into taking a seat in the House of Lords, from where he would lead the new government more by name than by action. Their intention has since become known as the Relugas Compact (based on the name of the fishing lodge on the River Findhorn that Grey had rented for the autumn). The country was in the midst of a tariff reform crisis, and the three Liberal Imperialist friends thought C-B lacked the strength to lead a free trade ministry with the full confidence of the public, especially when faced with the arch-protectionist and highly persuasive Joseph Chamberlain on the Opposition benches.

Knowing that C-B needed their energy and ideas (well, he certainly wanted those of Asquith and Grey; he cared less for Richard), their plan was for all three to refuse to join the cabinet unless they were each offered their desired places: Richard as Lord Chancellor, Grey as Foreign Secretary, and Asquith as Chancellor of the Exchequer and leader in the Commons (the man with the real power). Richard, who was already on friendly terms with Edward VII, hurried off to Balmoral to seek the King's approval for their scheme, which was duly granted. When C-B refused to be moved, Asquith quickly rescinded his pledge and agreed to go to the Exchequer even if the wishes of his friends weren't fulfilled. Grey was still offered the Foreign Office, but C-B wished to allocate the Lord Chancellorship elsewhere and could not be persuaded otherwise. The War Office, which had had a habit in recent years of ending the political careers of its incumbents, was still up for grabs, however. The King felt it was the right post for Richard's reforming talents, and C-B relished the prospect of Richard going to this, the most torturous of departments. In confusion over what to do next (and with the ever-reliable Grey not budging from his side of the original pact), Richard turned to his beloved Frances Horner. It was she who told him in no uncertain terms that he and Grey would be letting down King and country if they refused to join. Thus sobered, Richard made his way to C-B and offered to take charge of the country's military defences. C-B's response afterwards was as cynical as it was Scottish: 'We shall now see how Schopenhauer gets on in the Kailyard.'[20]

* * *

A NEW CENTURY

Before we come, in the next two chapters, to those crucial years between 1906 and the outbreak of war, in which the careers of each of Mary Haldane's children reached their apotheoses, it should not be forgotten that the coming of the twentieth century also coincided with considerable successes on the part of Elizabeth and Willie. Their mother provides us with a wonderful snapshot of her youngest son during these years, writing to Richard in 1901:

> He [Willie] reminds me thoroughly of your father when he has his children about him. He took Pat [his eldest son] to Leith the other day, and showed him all the things there… Yesterday Willie was wading through the snow cutting trees and looking after drains etc. and lastly shooting partridges. He is always busy, and never seems to suffer from exposure to wet. Certainly these farms [at Foswell] have been the greatest benefit to him… It is odd how a family differs in taste and in habit. He & Johnny seem at opposite poles and yet they had the same family.[21]

Willie's industry was also part of his professional success, but he needed the odd stroke of good fortune as well.

The Cowden estate lies nestled in the Ochil Hills, about 10 miles south of Cloan. Since 1865 it had belonged to the Christies, family friends of the Haldanes. The two Christie daughters—one of whom was the extraordinary Ella Christie, the first Western woman to meet the Dalai Lama and creator of the renowned Japanese Garden at Cowden—were expected to inherit the estate upon the death of their father. When he died in 1902, they discovered that he had left the entire estate to an orphanage that he had established without their knowledge. The sisters contested the will in the belief that their father must have been mentally defective at the point of making such a decision. With their family legal agents thinking the case hopeless, the Christies called upon their lawyer friend Willie Haldane to get them out of their predicament. Initially, there was no way to prove their father's deficient mental state, as every action or statement of Mr Christie's that could be pointed to could be made to look reasonable. But Willie gradually noticed that when certain events or occasions involving Mr Christie, which looked explicable in isolation, were placed in contrast, the soundness of his mind became much more debatable. Willie set to the task of examining

Mr Christie's past actions 'with great zeal', but no amount of zeal could achieve what then happened. As Willie related in old age:

> A crucial point was evidence of the Testator's condition in an illness when he was served by a valet who had served him devotedly before and after it. But he had left years before, and no trace could be discovered unless that he was believed to have taken a situation as valet in some block or blocks of apartments somewhere in St. James's London. The only method left for his possible discovery was a search through all such blocks for trace of him, and such I undertook day by day, only to discover how numerous these were, almost hopelessly so. After my first day at this, and I had at last given up the quest and was about to cross the end of Pall Mall towards St. James's Park, a man passed along the pavement, crossing my route like other passers-by, and some strange impulse made me stop him and ask the same question as I had been asking all day. No, he said, I am not he but I am his brother. I nearly dropped,—through ecstasy,—this enabling me to secure a witness of extreme value for the Case. I have often wondered what led me to accost that man whom I had never seen at any time before...[22]

Willie's subsequent success in the case made his name professionally. As for the Christie sisters, they settled to share the estate with the orphanage, and so it was that Ella had the land on which to start working in 1908 with the garden designer Taki Handa to create what has been called 'The most important Japanese Garden in the Western World'.[23] It is, moreover, 'the first and only garden of its size and scale to be designed by a woman'.[24]

If Willie's professional ascent had something to do with luck, it also had to do with his powerful eldest brother, who, just nine days after entering government in December 1905, could inform Mary: 'There is good news about Willie. The Crown Agency is the blue ribbon of the W. S. profession—besides very lucrative. He owes much to Asquith who did for me what I could not do myself. But it is to merit, & the good opinion of the Lord Advocate that he owes the position.'[25] Willie, as Crown Agent, thereby became the principal legal advisor to Scotland's Lord Advocate. His new position automatically made him one of three Prison Commissioners for Scotland, vastly extending his workload. The commissioners were responsible for maintaining all prisons, appointing prison staff, inspecting prison buildings, and monitoring the condition of inmates. Willie would hold this role, along with the Crown Agency, until 1917.

Elizabeth, meanwhile, was ever more advancing the prominence of what Richard called 'the female force in life'.[26] Sharing her elder brothers' concern for public health and education, she was elected to the board of the Edinburgh Royal Infirmary in 1901, and to the Auchterarder school board in 1903. Such was her experience that, in the following year, she was called to give evidence before the departmental committee appointed by the local government board for Scotland to inquire into the system of poor law medical relief, where she spoke especially on the administration of Scottish poorhouses. In 1905—the same year in which she published her acclaimed *Descartes: His Life and Times*, earning the first honorary LLD to be awarded to a woman by St Andrews—Elizabeth was helping, when in London, to run the recently established Westminster Health Society. According to its current incarnation, the London Early Years Foundation, the Society in 'a time of poverty and shockingly high mortality… helped to introduce the first health visiting programme in London. This included health education and training, clinics for maternal and child welfare and training in domestic skills.'[27] Like John, Elizabeth was always willing to roll up her sleeves in order to counter unacceptable mortality rates, especially amongst women and children.

But unlike her brothers, Elizabeth could not live her life wholly at her own will. There was always her aging mother to think about, and the domestic arrangements at Cloan. Disruption to their orderly home life came in 1904, when electrical wiring and a second large extension were added to the house (with them came a gradual reversion to the original name of Cloan after the 'Cloanden' years), which required Mary and Elizabeth to move to a neighbour's house for nearly six months. For Richard, who financed the project but remained happily occupied in London, it was entirely worth it. Now, whenever he returned to Scotland, the wealthy barrister and soon-to-be statesman could have a suite to himself, consisting of bedroom, bathroom, and study, on the second floor in the new east wing. The study was a glorious book-lined room, with three large windows looking out over the 'Highland line', a huge sweep of the Grampians to the north and west. Here, lost in a mist of cigar smoke and metaphysics, with a faithful dog weaving between his legs, Richard would come to hatch his plans for the transformation of the country. For visiting nephews and nieces the hallowed study remained a definite no-go area. The heady aroma of tobacco, leather, and dog that wafted from underneath the doorway made it all the more intriguing.

* * *

This reminds us that the lives of the Haldane children were progressing all this time, while the elders made their names. Willie and Edith's four were children of the countryside to the tips of their stockinged feet. Though schooled in Edinburgh, they always resented their time in the city (much like the previous generation) and longed for the streams and hills of Perthshire to which they returned every Christmas, Easter, and summer. For Pat and Archie especially (Archibald Richard Burdon Haldane, Willie's youngest son, had been born in November 1901), fishing was their all-consuming boyhood passion. The interests of John and Kathleen's children, Jack and Naomi, were rather more eccentric, and made all the more so by the unusual responses of their father—or 'Uffer', as they called him—to their displays of enthusiasm. At the age of seven, Jack made a collection of seashells and asked his father for help with finding out their various names. John turned to the shelves of his study in their Oxford home and pulled down a two-volume textbook of zoology, handing it to the little boy. Jack had his work cut out. It was written in German.[28]

Jack clearly had the urge to classify. A summer holiday diary of 1904 (when he was aged 11) recounts: 'I got some fairly good specimens of *Planoribus corneus, Paludina vivipara, Limnaea auriculata,* & *Anodonta anatina*. N.B. This year I am going to make Naomi write all the botany, as she is far better at it than I am.'[29] This says a lot about his sister, who was only six at the time. As Naomi remembered, 'My brother was five years older than me but I tried so hard to keep up and often succeeded.'[30] It helped that when she reached school age she was granted permission to join the all-boys Dragon

School in Oxford, where her brother had already blazed a trail—with his intelligence, his sense of superiority, and his furious temper. One master put it thus: 'His mind like his body is powerful, but neither at present under his control.'[31] Tormented one day in the playground, Jack hauled from the ground with its roots a large sapling and assailed the culprit with 'massive sweeps of the weapon'. When the bell rang for the end of break, Jack cast the sapling from him and returned to the classroom, booming out the words: 'I wish I could kill. I wish I could KILL.'[32] This was also the boy who topped the class lists in Latin, arithmetic, and geometry, well before he'd even reached the top form of the school. His school fellows put it down to the fractured skull he received from falling from his father's bicycle, but Jack's natural intellect had been on show since his earliest years. Indeed, it is possible that his remarkable personality, with all its positive and negative sides, could have been due to him having high-functioning Asperger syndrome.[33] This is at least the view of his great-niece, the psychiatrist Sally Mitchison, who sees a strong streak of neurodiversity running through the family.[34] It is worth bearing this fact in mind as our story progresses.

Jack's intelligence was also fostered by his father, who 'consistently treated me as an adult'. John would practise his lectures on the young boy, so that 'I learned of Emil Fischer's work on the stereochemistry of the sugars before I learned that silver chloride is insoluble in water, that hydrogen burns in oxygen, and so on.'[35] It was almost natural that, in 1904, Jack should get the First Scholarship to Eton—the only school good enough to satisfy Kathleen's snobbery. There was some worry when he announced that he hadn't completed the scholarship paper in mathematics, though he said he'd answered the last question. When asked to confirm that he hadn't completed the paper, Jack responded: 'No more I did. It was much too long. Oh I did not touch the first questions. They were marked too low to be worth doing. I began with the last.'[36]

It can't have been an easy act for Naomi to follow. And Jack could be cruel, too. As Naomi recalled:

> [He] did testing things sometimes like making the water in the basin live-off the ordinary house electricity when we finally got it –and putting in pennies for me to snatch. Often he teased me till my

temper went and I stamped and screamed, feeling furiously helpless. I hated him for minutes and then suddenly it was all over.[37]

The little Naomi had enough on her plate, filled as she was with anxieties, usually about the mysteries of non-living things: 'What I was afraid of was not alive. It was what lay behind the apparent silence and stillness of inanimate objects, including bed knobs, roof finials and the pigeon house—not the pigeons.'[38] For her, her father was not so much the intellectual torchbearer, as he was for Jack, but the ultimate source of comfort and security:

> nothing could get at me if I curled up on my father's lap, holding on to his ear with one thumb tucked into it. He had a big brown moustache and a wide Haldane nose with a small lump on it which I liked. When he kissed me it was rough and tickly. Across his front was a gold watch chain with a big tick-tock watch on the end... All about him was safe.[39]

Things were different when it came to their mother, Kathleen, whom they called Maya. When Naomi, at the age of four, had failed to graduate to reading four-letter words, having mastered those with three, Maya was infuriated: 'She spanked me hard and I was put into my cot, the nursery curtains were drawn and I was left to think it over as soon as I had stopped howling.'[40] What Naomi and Jack appreciated about their mother in these early days was her political fervour; they attended rallies with her in support of the Empire's causes and dominance. It was only later that her right-wing slogans started to feel unreal and unjust. In time, the siblings would come to embody diametrically opposite views from the blue-blooded Maya.

When visiting Cloan, Naomi also had the combined terrors of her brother and cousins to deal with. One memory from Willie's son, Graeme, tells us something of the boys' antics:

> Jack, in his very early years, certainly enjoyed his Christmas visits to Cloan and as a small boy I can well remember certain rather dubious, and I fear ruthless, activities with him—rat hunting in the piggery and exciting the huge St Bernards [sic] dog to attack rats, cats and other dogs.[41]

A NEW CENTURY

Neither did Jack and the Foswell boys hold back when it came to Naomi. Cloan has always had a history of ghosts, and Elizabeth had added to the pantheon of shadows by inventing for her nephews and nieces what she called the Gorgonzola, a terrifying creature who haunted the tower room at the top of the spiral stairs. Jack and the Foswell boys would lead Naomi up there, feeding her all sorts of information about the horrors in wait for her, delighting in her anguish (except for Graeme, who was equally afraid but only admitted the fact in adulthood). The spectre of this monster would appear in Naomi's dreams until her very last years, and she even ascended the ninety-five steps to the tower room (and a further seven steps to the roof) in her ninety-sixth year to exorcise the demons. But as a child, her fear of the Gorgonzola didn't match the fright she got when she pulled back her bedcovers one night and found a dummy's head waiting for her: 'I screamed so loud and long that everyone was concerned, including my brother. He certainly hadn't meant it to be like that.'[42]

Naomi's greatest torturer, however, was her own imagination, which could play all sorts of tricks on her and which made the line between fact and fiction difficult to distinguish. But as she herself later admitted, 'without it I would have no wings'.[43] It was a faculty that was unusual in the Haldanes of Cloan, and it was the faculty that made Naomi's career. As a girl, looking on at her father and his siblings, and at Jack, she knew she would have to do something special to stand out. After 1905, that task got even harder.

6

THE HALDANE MISSIONS, PART ONE

1906–1914

It is easy to forget that the roots of the major social developments that emerged out of the First World War—the passing of the Representation of the People Act in 1918, for instance, or the formation of the first Labour government in 1924—went deeper back into history than 1914. It was 1911 when the Parliament Act abolished the absolute veto of the House of Lords, a seismic shift of power away from the peers towards the Commons. That shift was triggered by the misplaced retaliation of an Upper House faced with the radical proposals of Lloyd George's 'People's Budget' of 1909. To the ears of the privileged and ennobled, a 'supertax' on the highest earners to fund old-age pensions sounded like socialism pure and simple. Pensions were just one aspect of a wide range of progressive reforms inaugurated by the pre-war Liberal governments. From 1906 onwards, under the premierships of Sir Henry Campbell-Bannerman and H. H. Asquith, the financial burden of secondary education was removed, free school meals were provided, young offenders were offered alternatives to prison, labour exchanges were established, and unemployment insurance and minimum wages were introduced, as were sick pay and compulsory health insurance for low-income workers. These measures had their limitations, of course. The fact remains: they all took place before the war.

There are those who would go further and argue that the years 1914–18, far from accelerating change, temporarily halted it, especially when it came to devolution and the emancipation of women.

In Roy Hattersley's opinion, 'The war, so often said to have made Irish Home Rule and Votes for Women irresistible, postponed, not promoted, both reforms. The arguments were won in Edwardian Britain.'[1] We might contest this, but these were certainly well-worn debates even in Victoria's reign.

It is also tempting to think of the years prior to 1914 as the years of the British Empire's pre-eminence. That is pretty well true, but we ought to be aware that the economy in Britain was struggling to keep pace with the growing world powers of Germany and the USA. In absolute terms, Britain was becoming richer. Relative to its principal competitors, it was on a downward track. Thanks to exceptional scientific and educational advances in Germany, products that had once been the cornerstone of the British market were being produced more cheaply and more plentifully across the Channel. The puffed-out industrial chest of Britain was slowly being deflated.

Meanwhile, the British navy, the Empire's protectress and greatest boast, felt threatened by the shipbuilding programmes underway in the German dockyards. And with a German standing army, fed by conscription, of 600,000 soldiers by 1905, it is understandable that Britain felt vulnerable. An atmosphere of suspicion and jealousy pervaded the British Foreign Office. Germany's apparent desire for commercial, naval, and military supremacy radically endangered what many felt to be Britain's 'rightful' supremacy on the world stage. When Anglo-German relations deteriorated further after the Agadir Crisis of 1911, talk of a preventative war became rife on both sides of the Channel. The fact that the German Emperor, Wilhelm II, was Queen Victoria's grandson, Edward VII's nephew, and George V's cousin did little to help promote cordial relations; if anything, his close links to Britain, complicated by envy and wild mood swings, exacerbated the tensions.

And yet, after India, Germany was Britain's second-largest customer by 1914, and on Britain's part it relied on Germany for everything from dye-stuffs (how else could it kit out its army with those fetching khaki uniforms?) to beet-produced sugar.[2] By the time war came, 60,000 German nationals had settled in Britain, a small band of whom had made or expanded their fortunes as British citizens. German-born millionaires such as Sir Ernest Cassel, Sir Julius

Wernher, and Alfred Beit left vast financial legacies to their adopted country that are still felt today, especially in education. Indeed, a number of Britain's most successful businesses were founded by Germans—think of Reuters or the General Electric Company.

The Haldanes of Cloan, as ever, refused to watch these developments unfold from afar. Their respective missions to change the world became even more focused and ambitious in the years directly preceding the war, and the power they had to make a difference dramatically increased. What they achieved in these years still reverberates today.

* * *

Richard was mainly preoccupied with the mammoth task of army reform over his first seven years in political office, but he still had a part to play in the social reforms that were to make the pre-war Liberal governments famous. He was extensively consulted in the preparation for the Education (Scotland) Bill of 1908, for example, and spoke at length on its behalf in the Commons. Why? Because, as he explained to his fellow MPs:

> If we cannot see that our future rests with the children and that the future of the child rests upon securing adequate training in early life—and it cannot be adequate unless it is carried beyond the elementary school, with the chance of the University or technical school—if we cannot see that, we have not realised what is the extent of our duty with regard to education. It is because I believe that this problem is one of the most important and pressing of social problems that I am proud to be associated even in a minor capacity with the Bill as a first step in realising an educational ideal short to which we cannot afford to halt.[3]

Richard also made critical Commons interventions on land and inheritance taxation throughout 1909, and on the passage of the Parliament Bill thereafter. He even wrote the preamble for the Bill in his own hand, 'and converted the Cabinet to it'.[4] Indeed, in March 1911 he was elevated to the Lords precisely to see the Bill pass through the Upper House, before it finally became the epoch-making Act by which that year is defined.

But the army was his number one political priority. The Boer War had made it painfully clear just how unfit for purpose it was. The question of how to remedy the situation was a point of contention amongst the generals and the politicians, and too often the latter imposed their plans to the strong disapproval of the former. Richard wanted to do things differently. His philosophical training had assured him of the wisdom of getting clear principles in place before action was undertaken. With the constant aid of Lord Esher—confidant of the King and chairman of the 1904 Esher Committee, which had recommended various steps to improve defence—Richard sought out the best military minds to help him establish both the precise purpose of the army and the means to achieve that purpose. Again, his philosophical approach gave him an openness to views that appeared divergent and the skills with which, in many cases, to reconcile them. He got on close terms with generals of widely different opinions and, principally through his friendship with the Conservative leader A. J. Balfour, won broad cross-party support for his proposed measures of reform—though not without making a number of highly placed enemies along the way. His detractors would watch for the right moment to wreck his name.

Reform was all the more pressing in January 1906, when Grey started to inquire of Richard what military capacities Britain had if war were to break out on the Continent—a prospect that was looking increasingly likely as tensions grew between France and Germany. Given the Entente Cordiale and Grey's own French sympathies, the Foreign Secretary felt Britain could be obliged to aid France should Germany make an unprovoked attack upon its neighbour. Could British support make a significant difference? Did it have the capacity to support France in the first place? Richard had to bear these questions in mind (even making the controversial decision with Grey to allow private military talks to take place between the British and French generals) as he considered the direction of travel, along with a host of questions about the army's ability to defend the outposts of Empire. The issue was complicated further by financial considerations. Whatever reorganisation looked like, it had to remain within a reasonable budget to keep the Liberal heartland happy. It also had to increase military effectiveness (and thus appeal to the Tories), which usually meant an increase in costs. Richard had long campaigned as a Liberal Imperialist backbencher for a programme of 'National Efficiency'. This was his chance to show exactly what that meant.

The plan that emerged was a radical one, but it was practical too. It based itself on the assumption that the purpose of the army was war overseas, as the Royal Navy could cover home defence. The army's ability to mobilise rapidly would thus be crucial. What was needed was a small, highly trained, and fully equipped Expeditionary Force, which could travel at speed. This would be composed of six infantry divisions and a cavalry division. To ensure numbers did not fall if losses were incurred, and to avoid conscription, Richard envisaged a second line of support coming from non-professional, partly trained soldiers, who would be called up in the event of a sustained conflict. This second line would be called the Territorial Force, and its numbers would come from repurposing the existing auxiliary forces (Militia, Volunteers, and Yeomanry), as well as an exhaustive recruitment campaign. The Force would need all the accompanying services of the regulars: field artillery, engineers, medical relief, and so on. To redress a shortage in officers in both regulars and reserves, there would also be an Officers' Training Corps in the public schools and universities. Undergirding all this, there was to be a body of intelligent men, relieved of all administrative duties and dedicated to thinking, who would oversee and guide matters. This would be based on the model in Germany and called the General Staff.

It was one thing coming up with these proposals and keeping them within budget (both of which Richard did collaboratively); it was quite another thing to get those measures that needed parliamentary approval through the Commons and to secure the backing of the public. Sensitive and authoritative statesmanship was all-important, and it is in this respect that Richard proved himself to be one of the greatest war secretaries in British history.

One by one the proposals became reality. The passing of the Territorial and Reserve Forces Act of 1907 is, perhaps, Richard's crowning political achievement. Some plans had to be altered, as one would expect. A Special Reserve was formed to accommodate Militiamen unwilling to join the Territorials, for instance, and the

Territorials themselves had to be accounted for as home defence in order to appease those radicals to whom the thought of expeditionary activity was deeply discomforting (of course, when war came, the Territorial Army, as it became known, served abroad as originally intended). Richard's willingness to make concessions when faced with the realities of political and military obstacles, while still being guided by a fundamental idealism, was just one of the many factors contributing to his success. We might also mention his mastery of the relevant data; his endless explanatory speeches in the Commons, full of courtesy and reassurance to both sides of the House; his pruning of unnecessary expenditure to divert funds into essential resources; his travels the length and breadth of the country to give Territorial recruitment speeches; his powers of persuasion when meeting the important figures who would have to be brought round to make his scheme work; his ability to connect with the King and eventually win his approval; his coolness in the face of threats from those colleagues within cabinet who demanded further budget reductions (Lloyd George and Churchill were notable but temporary enemies); his unwillingness to succumb to the National Service League's cry for conscription, headed by the country's most revered soldier, Lord Roberts; and finally his delight in the task itself.[5]

Richard put Cloan at the service of the army, too. Colonel Ellison, his private secretary, was his guest over his first Christmas in office, and the two thrashed out the essential shape of reform from the comfort of Richard's study. For a whole week at the beginning of July 1907, the fields in front of the house were occupied by the tents of 1,000 soldiers on manoeuvres, along with their 500 horses. That autumn, the house resounded to the clanking spurs of three German Staff Officers, sent to Scotland for their edification and entertainment. There was entertainment all right. One morning, Richard's young, but very large, St Bernard dog, with the controversial name of Kaiser, bounded up to the guests and their aides as they stood discussing the day's work on the lawn before the house. Somehow, Kaiser managed to prise from a hand the Orders of the Day and make a quick exit with the document clenched between his teeth. Richard and Elizabeth watched on with a mixture of alarm and amusement as the visiting soldiers turned and ran in hot pursuit of the dog.

THE HALDANE MISSIONS, PART ONE

This visit was also the occasion of the sole recorded trip to Cloan made by Douglas Haig, then Director of Military Training and a close colleague of Richard's. Sir John French, who would serve before Haig as Commander-in-Chief of the British Expeditionary Force (BEF) during the early stages of the war, likewise visited Cloan in these pre-war years and was a regular guest between 1906 and 1913. Even Lord Roberts, Richard's arch-nemesis when it came to the conscription debate, visited in 1906. Old Mary Haldane, widowed now for decades, was in her element whenever military men were around. As a young girl living in West Jesmond, she had experienced the fizz of excitement when cavalry officers, stationed in nearby Newcastle, turned up at her parents' dinner parties wearing their ornate and close-fitting mess uniforms.[6]

Richard loved military company as well. He called the generals 'angels—no other name is good enough for these simple, honourable, souls'. Indeed, he considered his job to be 'the best of fun'.[7] But the workload was staggering and undoubtedly to the detriment of his health. He developed iritis in his eyes, and by 1910 he was forced to his bed for weeks. There is at least one photograph of him, having emerged back into public, wearing shaded goggles. At about this time, his doctors discovered he was suffering from diabetes—the disorder that had killed his father. Winston Churchill wrote to him with his sympathies, but told him bluntly that he worked too hard.[8] When we remember that these years also saw, under Richard's direction, the instigation of Robert Baden-Powell's Boy Scouts movement and the Army Class at LSE, as well as the creation of the Imperial General Staff, the Secret Service Bureau (today's MI5 and MI6), the Advisory Committee for Aeronautics, and the Royal Flying Corps (today's Royal Air Force), then we might be surprised that the repercussions on Richard's health were not more severe.

Richard was one of those rare figures for whom time seemed to expand. He was fond of quoting Goethe's words, 'Die Zeit ist unendlich lang' (time is infinitely long), and he made the line ring true. For, simultaneously with his responsibilities at the War Office, Richard was at one time or another—and I hope you will forgive another list; his life seems to demand it—Lord Rector of Edinburgh University; a Fellow of the Royal Society; president of the Royal

Economic Society and the Aristotelian Society; co-founder of Imperial College London (securing major funding from those German-born British businessmen, Wernher and Beit) and the Academic Committee of the Royal Society of Literature; vice president of the London Library; the author of two books; chairman of the Royal Commission on University Education in London; and a member of the Judicial Committee of the Privy Council. It is tiring just to read this list, let alone to have lived it.

* * *

Once again, John's work tied in with that of his older brother. Even before Richard had entered government, John had been asked by the Admiralty to advise them on the ventilation of submarines and battleships. He faced a problem, however, when they invited him to join a submarine trial run. As was often the case, his son Jack (whom the family often simply called 'Boy') proved to be the solution. Kathleen later recounted:

> One difficulty, [John] said, was that this was secret work, and he would need someone to look after the soda-lime. 'I can't just take any laboratory man.' Jack was standing on one foot, then on the other, as he did when he got really excited… Then when John had got thoroughly worried about the laboratory man, I said casually, 'Why not take Boy?'… his father said, 'Eh, what? Is he old enough?' and then suddenly, 'What's the formula for soda-lime?' Jack drew a deep breath and rapped out the formula. His father said, 'Well, that would simplify matters, but remember, you mustn't even *look* as if you knew anything about it.'[9]

Clearly John impressed and Jack kept schtum, for the Admiralty then asked him for advice on the best methods to ensure their divers could dive safely and effectively in deep water, and how they could better counteract the dangers associated with decompression during resurfacing. John's initial experiments dealt with issues surrounding the respiratory difficulties that deep-water divers experienced as the pressure of carbon dioxide built up within their helmets. He was quick to realise that this could be overcome if it were possible to increase a diver's air supply in direct proportion

THE HALDANE MISSIONS, PART ONE

to the increase in absolute pressure. One way to move in that direction was to alter the pumps that were supplying divers with air, so that they no longer leaked. Another was to add within a diver's helmet a canister capable of absorbing the unwanted gas. With these two easy fixes, John was already able to increase dramatically a diver's time and capacity for work under water. This was only the start of his interventions.

Decompression sickness—commonly called 'the bends'—is caused when bodily tissue, which has become saturated with nitrogen as pressure mounts on the body, releases nitrogen in bubbles during decompression. These bubbles can lead to a blockage of circulation and, in some cases, death. The Admiralty's attempts to ensure their divers avoided such eventualities were badly in need of improvement. Looking back at the state of affairs before his father became involved, JBS commented: 'The ignorance of the physiological principles involved in diving at that time was only equalled by the confidence with which "experts" recommended foolish and dangerous procedures, and the failure to test apparatus in use.'[10] One of the big issues was the snail's pace (5 feet per minute) at which divers were being lowered and raised from the water, losing precious time in which to carry out their actual missions.

To put matters right, John began with a deduction. It was known that it was safe to decompress a diver very quickly from two atmospheres absolute of pressure to one. John reasoned that it would also be safe, therefore, to decompress from four to two, from eight to four, and so on, with breaks of increasing length for the diver in-between. (The process has similarities to what we do when we very slowly let the gas out of a bottle by unscrewing the cap at intervals.) It was called stage decompression, and John arranged for it to be tested by his colleague, A. E. Boycott, together with two naval divers, Lieutenant Damant and Gunner Catto, at the Lister Institute in London. (Again, they had a German-born British millionaire to thank, for it was the chemist and industrialist Ludwig Mond, FRS, who supplied the Institute with the decompression chamber in which these experiments took place.) At first, Boycott used goats. Eventually, Damant and Catto entered the chamber, as John's predictions proved accurate. John could now start to create tables to show the necessary timings for stage decompression, depending not only on the depth and length of the dives but also on the fact that different parts of the body's tissues release nitrogen at different rates. The next step was to put these tables to the test in nature's own laboratory.

In August 1906, the Oxford Haldanes travelled to the Kyles of Bute in the west of Scotland, where Damant and Catto were now attempting a series of deep-diving records from the nobly named HMS *Spanker*. As well as trialling his tables, this was the ideal setting for John to assess what tasks could be performed by divers at the new depths that were being attempted, and for how long. The divers proceeded to break numerous world records, many of which were their own, with their deepest dive taking them to 210 feet below the surface: 20 feet deeper than the record set by Greek and Swedish divers two years earlier. There was the odd moment of panic. On one dive, Catto's safety line became tangled with the lines of the *Spanker*, leaving him caught on the bed of Loch Ridden, frantically pulling at his rope. Thankfully, his colleagues were able to disentangle the lines in time, and Catto was diving again the next day.

In calmer moments, under John's directions, the divers were able to demonstrate that they could carry out demanding physical tasks—such as pulling on ropes attached to weights—at these new depths for considerable periods of time. The improvement of their air supply was a big part of this, but the real game changer in terms of time-saving was the use of stage decompression, as this allowed for an extremely rapid ascent in the early stages of resurfacing. John's job would have been a lot harder, however, had his son Jack not been on hand.

The elder Haldane realised he had forgotten the tables and graphs that showed the rate at which nitrogen entered and left various tissues by diffusion. The younger Haldane, though only thirteen, had just the kind of brain to work them out afresh, even without the logarithms that would normally guide such calculations. Jack relished the paternal challenge, and set to work in the hotel at Colintraive, where he and Naomi were staying with their mother. Jack had never failed a test in his life, and he was not about to start a new habit now. As a reward for producing the necessary data, John promised to let his son dive.[11]

THE HALDANE MISSIONS, PART ONE

Jack was accustomed to being put into hazardous situations by his father. Two years previously, when the two were down a coal mine, he had been used to demonstrate to the accompanying party that gas was lighter than air. Having crawled along an abandoned 'road', the group reached a place in which it was possible to stand and a safety lamp was raised to the ceiling. A blue flame appeared inside the lamp and then went out with a pop. Had it been a candle, the whole group would have likely perished. Evidently, the air near the roof contained firedamp (methane) but it was safe to remain near the floor. Knowing that Jack would only be in danger of asphyxia if he stood up, John asked him to rise and recite Marc Antony's famous 'Friends, Romans, countrymen' speech from Shakespeare's *Julius Caesar*. Jack got to the end of the fifth line, but after the words 'The noble Brutus', fell flat upon the floor, unconscious. His father, showing no anxiety, simply waited for the floor-level air to do its revitalising work.[12]

When it came to diving, John could not make such assured predictions. It is true that he himself went down into the depths before his son—a remarkable fact, given that John had never learnt to swim—and found nothing to suggest his son wouldn't manage, too. Yet he hadn't envisaged that the cuffs of Jack's diving suit wouldn't grip his teenage wrists. Water began to seep in as Jack made his rapid descent to 40 feet. He was determined to have his full allocated time of half an hour, and to ignore the fact that his ears felt as if they were about to burst. Instead, he focused on the marvels of the natural life creeping along the loch bed, while using his suit's valves to keep the water from rising far above his waist. When he finally re-emerged, he was shaking with cold. The Scotsmen on board knew the perfect remedy for the laddie: whisky, then bed. Naomi, hearing of these adventures second-hand, was filled with envy. Her holiday diary says it all: 'I wish I were a boy.'[13] It was a childhood desire once shared by her grandmother and her aunt, as we know. On this front, nothing much had changed for three-quarters of a century.

The report which John and his colleagues submitted to the Admiralty in 1907 was to transform the face of diving.[14] The following year, all naval divers were ordered to adopt the use of the diving tables first published there. In 1912, the US Navy gave similar orders, an arrangement that was to last until 1956. In fact, even today, almost all international diving tables, including those which govern the multibillion-dollar diving tourism industry, are based on John's originals.

* * *

The year 1907 brought other excitements. John was promoted to Reader within the physiology department at Oxford, and served upon a Royal Commission on health and safety in mines. He and Kathleen also built a new home for the family on a large tract of land at the end of Linton Road in Oxford. It was named Cherwell, after the river that ran past it, and John had the Haldane motto, 'Suffer', inscribed above the fireplace in the hall. This was particularly appropriate, as John eventually constructed his own laboratory at Cherwell where he carried out some of his most punishing self-experiments. He added to it over the years, and his laboratory came to have two rooms, growing like a jointed limb off the side of his study. The larger outer room contained airtight chambers for gas and pressure experiments, along with 'sinks and fume cupboards, glassware and balances and labelled bottles'.[15] The inner lab contained even more bottles, row upon row of them, and Jack and Naomi delighted in the sensation of falling among stars after they'd fished out the chloroform and given each other a dose.

A less pleasant experience was the broken ribs and leg and dislocated neck that Naomi suffered after a riding accident on her tenth birthday. When this was followed by an operation to remove a neck gland harbouring tuberculosis, Kathleen decided to consign her daughter to the maternal bedroom for recuperation. Even once she was better, it was understood that Naomi was not to return to her own room. In fact, she slept in a bed beside her mother's for the rest of her adolescence—an arrangement that she suspected had more to do with Kathleen's desire to keep John out of the marriage bed than anything else. He had a bedroom of his own on the other side of the hall, small and reeking of pipe tobacco, and it was there he would have to stay.

Naomi's lack of independence became even more pronounced when, in 1911, at the first sight of blood in her underwear, she was removed without explanation from the Dragon School. Except for the knee-high black stockings, an inhuman mathematics master, and the skin lining the top of her daily milk, Naomi had loved everything about the school—its smell, her friends, her inspiring headmaster Mr Lynam (who insisted on being called Skipper), and the examinations which played to her quick, fierce intellect. She had been absolutely at home in its intensely masculine atmosphere: 'I felt I was a boy who unfairly was not allowed to play rugger.'[16] For Kathleen, the onset of her daughter's period made the whole thing suddenly out of the question. Naomi now found herself with four other girls in the schoolroom at the top of Cherwell, under the care of a governess named Miss Blockey (quickly turned into Blockywox). Naomi was full of resentment, but with tales of public-school brutality filtering back from Jack at Eton, she realised that things were not all merry for the opposite sex.

Jack's misery at Eton is typified by the predicament he faced during his Uncle Richard's official visit to the school as a government minister. When the War Secretary asked to see his nephew, he waited and waited for his appearance. The boy never came. Unbeknownst to Richard, Jack had been forcibly trapped beneath an upturned desk, while his peers proceeded to pile it with sandbags.

The bullies may have been motivated by Jack's failure to hide his sense of intellectual superiority when around his contemporaries. His teachers could find him trying, too. Two reports of 1910 from his German and History master paint an entertaining picture. That Lent term, his report read:

> What with losing his books and his wits, not turning up till after the last moment or if he does arrive in time, being so exhausted by the victory as to be incapable of further effort, beginning an Essay and dropping it in the middle to start another which in turn is to be prematurely abandoned, half remembering things by an exertion of intelligence instead of quite learning them out of a book like an ordinary mortal, he does not give his great capacity a chance. Only two essays out of seven were finished and these were both brought at the wrong time. His grammar is very shaky, though it might just as well have been word-perfect. Prose and imitative sentences rather better, reading aloud respectable. In this he shows a turn for

language which makes it all the more deplorable that no way should yet have been discovered of combing him out straight.[17]

For the summer term, the exasperated master continued the theme: 'Haldane, in spite of his undoubtedly great powers, is suffering from diffuseness... If only he could learn a little method, a little tidiness, a little punctuality! I like him very much and am always glad to have him about, but he defeats me.'[18]

Yet even before his final year, Jack was topping the school in mathematics, physics, biology, and chemistry. As early as 1908, he had been predicted a 'brilliant first' in classics, should he go on to study that at university.[19] Indeed, when his much-loathed classics tutor told him that he could only get off doing Latin verse if he passed Smalls (the obligatory Latin examination that all Oxford undergraduates had to sit the year before graduation), Jack wired home to his mother, 'Long leave (date) please arrange for me to see the pageant and pass Smalls.' Jack thus returned to Cherwell, donned the stipulated Oxford dress required for the exam, and passed the test with ease. The tedium of schoolboy Latin verse composition was no more.

By 1911, he was Captain of the School, the title reserved for the school's brightest pupil. In this capacity, he received and addressed King George V on his first visit to Eton after his accession. Jack's afflictions at school had instilled in him a deep resentment for all forms and figures of authority, so the visit gave him little pleasure (it hadn't helped that he'd gashed his chin with a razor that morning after a particularly vigorous shave). A more important feature of his final year was his election to 'Pop', the exclusive group of prefects that almost all younger boys wished to join—for their social cachet, their blue-ribboned canes, and the carnations in their buttonholes. It was a startling reversal of roles for this former outsider. His sister even conjectured, 'He probably enjoyed beating the younger ones, too—that was part of the game.'[20]

Jack was conscious of his desire to be a man of power. He wrote in his diary:

> I intend to do some good to mankind, and having this ideal before me, can make it overcome other cravings. I do not expect any special reward, here or hereafter. I look for ambition to be its own

reward... I am probably right in saying that I am boundlessly, quite boundlessly ambitious.[21]

The first two sentences could have been written by any Haldane of Cloan of his father's generation. The final sentence, even if it had been felt by his elders, was a new voice. It marked a subtle shift in direction for the family: a shift towards total, uncompromising honesty about the will to succeed. In the 1930s, Naomi would write words that her Aunt Bay could never have committed to paper: 'I have had this devil of personal ambition biting at me, and I know I haven't got him down yet. I like power, and I know only too well that while I am using it I am apt to forget that I must not use it for my own satisfaction.'[22]

7

THE HALDANE MISSIONS, PART TWO

1906–1914

Naomi's aunt, Elizabeth Haldane, certainly wielded tremendous power for a woman in Edwardian Britain. Take education. In 1909, she was appointed to the Privy Council's Scottish Universities Committee, granting her a say on all proposed amendments to the statutes of the four ancient Scottish universities. And yet, it was not until 1940 that a woman actually held a professorial chair in Scotland. It's doubtful that Elizabeth herself would have wanted such a position, but Cambridge University Press made her scholarly credentials unmistakable by publishing, in two volumes across 1911 and 1912, the translation that she and a colleague had completed of *The Philosophical Works of Descartes*.

Through Richard, Elizabeth also worked on establishing the Territorial Force Nursing Service and the Voluntary Aid Detachment, which were to play such distinguished roles in serving the war-wounded in the coming years. The plan to organise a nursing service within the Territorials was made excessively difficult by Queen Alexandra, who was reluctant to dissolve or even impinge upon the existing Nursing Reserve. Even after a compromise was suggested that would have allowed their coexistence, she remained unmoved. Her intractability led Richard, at the height of his frustration, to write—with uncharacteristic vehemence—to his sister: 'The Queen… wants one organisation. This we cannot consent to. They must be separate. We had better dispense with Royalty… She is (the Q) about the stupidest woman in England.'[1]

Once Alexandra's assent was finally obtained for the new service, she still made issues over uniforms, insisting on a hideous khaki outfit, despised by Elizabeth and the nurses themselves. It was a long time before she agreed to a far more becoming uniform, grey with touches of red. No doubt Richard was able to leave his old frustrations behind when, in 1910, the newly widowed Queen, remembering her husband's affection for his War Secretary, invited Richard to join her alone in the bedchamber where Edward's body lay. Richard wrote to his mother at Cloan: 'I kissed her hand & promised that I would never forget him or her.'[2]

Elizabeth was also able to play a part in the historic social changes connected to Lloyd George's National Insurance Act of 1911. Although she had to decline the Chancellor's offer for her to become a Commissioner for Scotland, on the grounds that she would have to leave her mother for lengthy periods (it was essentially a full-time Civil Service post), she was able to accept a place on the Advisory Committee for Insurance in England in 1912. In this capacity, Elizabeth made real inroads, pleading directly and successfully to Lloyd George that certain provisions regarding maternity benefits be implemented, principally the right to call a doctor as one of the claims on the maternity fund.

When, again in 1912, she served as the only woman on an Interdepartmental Committee on outdoor staff to be appointed under the Insurance Act, she championed the equal pay of women— this time unsuccessfully. She faced similar resistance as one of only two female members of the Royal Commission on the Civil Service (1912–15), and it depressed her to find that the few female civil servants there were were segregated from the men. Nonetheless, Elizabeth urged improved pay and greater possibilities for women's advancement; she could not have guessed that it would take a war to creak the doors open. And yet here she was, a woman herself, sitting on a Royal Commission in 1912. It helped to have powerful brothers, but had she not been highly intelligent, well-informed, and effective in bringing about change, there is little chance she would have found herself in such a remarkable position.

Willie Haldane was also beginning to have a UK-wide influence. He had been instrumental south of the Border since 1910 in his role as a member of the Rural Development Commission, a permanent

Royal Commission to advise and administer the Development Fund voted annually by Parliament to benefit the rural economy of England. Willie's name even featured on the proposed list of four hundred Liberal peers that George V may have been forced to create had the House of Lords rejected the Parliament Bill in 1911. In 1912 a title was added to Willie's name, when he received a knighthood for his services as Crown Agent. His sister-in-law, Kathleen, probably out of jealousy, believed the origins of this honour lay elsewhere, telling one correspondent: 'When John's brother William—known by the nickname of "Wheedle"—was knighted for his political services (chiefly in cash), or for his relationship to the Lord Chancellor, the amusement which the event caused in Scotland was enormous. I have seldom come across so much derisive enjoyment.'[3] When Kathleen wrote 'Scotland', we ought to read 'Scottish Tory newspapers'.

To reduce Willie to a cash machine or a beneficiary of nepotism was more than unjust. In fact, in 1913 his knowledge of land law was of especial use to Lloyd George in his campaign for land reform. The two were in close touch, though Richard sometimes played intermediary. Richard was proud to tell his mother of the 'wise counsel' his youngest brother was showing to the Chancellor of the Exchequer, adding that 'Willie has had much to do in putting Ll G's plans into proper shape.'[4] A diary entry from Elizabeth around the same time records: 'L.G.... occupied with Land policy. Willie's scheme he calls it. W's scheme is pretty well adopted though L.G. did not make it clear in his first speech.'[5] In a letter to Lloyd George, Willie summed up his contribution thus:

> It seems to me that an underlying principle must be to make land a much more fluid form of Capital than our present land system has it so that it may be possible to constantly adapt it to the changing needs of the times, so making it more valuable to all classes of the community.[6]

Even if Willie was the odd one out of Mary's children, he was clearly still a Haldane through and through.

* * *

Richard's intercessions for his brothers were far more constructive than trying to secure them public honours. Organising the diplomatic arrangements with the USA for John's 1911 mission to Pikes Peak in Colorado was characteristic, however. This mission has been hailed as 'the most important high altitude expedition in the early 20th century'.[7] While the *New York Times* called John 'the moving genius in the work',[8] he was joined by his Oxford colleague C. G. Douglas, the Yale physiologist Yandell Henderson, and biologist E. C. Schneider from Colorado College. John also included the remarkable Mabel Purefoy FitzGerald on the team, though she only visited the summit itself on one occasion for five hours. She and John had worked together at Oxford and had published a joint paper in 1905. At John's suggestion, FitzGerald's role in the expedition was to travel amongst the mining communities of the Rockies and record the effects of different barometric levels on the human body. But more on FitzGerald in a moment.

Pikes Peak, which stands at 14,115 feet above sea level, is the highest summit of the southern front range of the Rocky Mountains. It was chosen as the site for the team's investigations into the physiological impact of high altitude due to its ease of access (the world's highest cog railroad could carry the team and its equipment all the way to the top) and the small hotel that stood at its summit at the time. John wanted to work on 'a nice, comfortable mountain'. A place such as the Capanna Margherita on one of the peaks of the Monte Rosa in the Alps did not quite fit the bill, for, as John explained to Henderson, 'one must climb several thousand feet over snow and ice... the climate is arctic even in midsummer... worst of all the investigator must cook for himself'. He could not quite trust the results of previous studies there as it was 'open to question whether the effects observed were due to the barometric pressure... or bad cooking'.[9]

The superior gastronomy of Pikes Peak could have done nothing against—in fact it could positively have worsened—the initial shock to the system that John and his colleagues faced when they reached the top. Along with blue lips and shortness of breath, the investigators experienced headaches, nausea, and stomach cramps over the first forty-eight hours. They were not the only ones. As their official report relates, 'the scene in the restaurant and on the platform outside can only be likened to that on the deck or in the cabin of a cross-channel steamer during rough weather. The walkers straggled in one by one, looking blue, cold, exhausted and miserable, often hurrying out again to vomit.'[10] After a few days of acclimatisation, life for John and his team became not just scientifically concentrated, but almost luxurious. A recent writer has called their working space 'a combination of a laboratory and a gentlemen's club'.[11] As FitzGerald wrote to her sister after her summit visit:

> They are having all the delicacies of the season to eat. Canteloupes in the morning etc. They have many amusing experiences with the trippers. They have a barbed wire door which they call the portcullis which they put across as soon as the train comes... Some lady came in, asked a question, & finally asked if she might leave her hat in the laboratory[,] a huge one with trailing ostrich feathers. She thanked them for the 'accommodation' when she fetched it. We could just contain our laughter till she had gone... J. S. Haldane seems very interested in everything and very amused at all the incidents. He also seems to like the ice cream soda fountains![12]

The work itself was anything but luxurious, especially John's daily intake of carbon monoxide from inside an airtight gas chamber. As the team put it in a statement in a local newspaper, 'The subject registers his sensations up to the limit of human endurance.'[13] These particular experiments were part of an indirect way of measuring the arterial partial pressure of oxygen. Unfortunately, they turned out to produce what proved to be erroneous results. Not conscious of any error, John thought the data gave evidence for his theory of oxygen secretion by the lung—a theory that was important for John in his crusade against mechanistic understandings of the human body. It did not take long for others, outraged by these findings, to produce counter-data to upset his claims.

Despite this mistake, the other results from the five weeks spent on top of the mountain were extremely useful for the progress of physiology, and indeed for practical medicine. The team's investigations settled an old debate and proved conclusively that low oxygen, not low carbon dioxide, was the cause of mountain sickness, and the paper detailing their expedition was one of the first to suggest oxygen treatment as an appropriate cure. John's additional recommendations to use pressurised chambers to increase oxygen levels, or to breathe small amounts of carbon dioxide to stimulate ventilation, 'saw him well on route for pioneering successful deep oxygen treatment'.[14] Other beneficial findings included the discovery that the oxygen cost of a given work level at high altitude was the same cost as at sea level; that oxygen treatment could also abolish periodic breathing; that there was an increase in haemoglobin concentration in the blood over the course of their stay on the summit; and that the initial rapid increase was caused by a reduction of blood volume. Such was the professionalism of their approach and the contribution of their results, the expedition went on to have 'an enormous influence on later high-altitude studies'.[15] In fact, one recent historian of science, commenting on later attempts to ascend Everest, has said, 'The Pikes Peak publications… produced theories and technologies which were central to (at least the British) expeditions.'[16] And, as Martin Goodman has pointed out, 'the Pikes Peak findings paved the way for the aeronautical achievements of the First World War'.[17] Not a bad outcome for a mixture of a laboratory and a gentlemen's club.

That description should not blind us to what has been called John's 'relatively ungendered view of science'.[18] It is unclear why Mabel FitzGerald did not join the main party on the summit. One suggestion is that the lack of a chaperone made it inappropriate; another is that it would have made the living arrangements too complicated. This may appear rather backward, but it was astonishing that John instead suggested that she travel throughout the mining communities in the Colorado Rockies to measure alveolar gas concentrations and haemoglobin levels in the blood. As Professor John West recently put it, 'She did this accompanied only by a mule and indeed it would be very difficult to think of a more hazardous situation for a single woman than that.'[19] John Haldane expressed it more positively when he wrote to her afterwards, 'Your work has been much more adventurous than ours!'[20]

Using John's air analysis apparatus, FitzGerald measured the partial pressure of carbon dioxide in the alveolar air of scores of people living at altitudes between 6,000 and 12,500 feet. Her measurements were so accurate and extensive that they are still cited today, well over a hundred years later. She was also the first person to record the differences between the sexes when it came to the body's reaction to acclimatisation. As for the issue of where and under whose name her findings ought to be published, John went against the expectations of his fellow team members and insisted that FitzGerald's work should not be subsumed within the Royal Society paper that would outline the Pikes Peak experiments. As Douglas noted, 'it was Haldane who suggested to me when on the Peak that this was not fair to her, as she was doing a great work in which we had no real part: we had no right to take any of the credit due to her'.[21] Instead, FitzGerald's methods and results were given prominence in a separate Royal Society paper with her as sole author.[22] In 1913, the same year in which that paper was read, John moved a resolution in favour of admitting women to membership of the Society; it was carried by a small majority.

A modern champion of FitzGerald's work, Robert Torrance, believes her work even outshines the discoveries made at the summit. In 2001, he wrote:

> Haldane and his colleagues on Pikes Peak showed for one altitude… that the time required for the full resetting [of carbon dioxide levels] to occur was about one or two weeks. But it was FitzGerald who showed the sensitive, lasting, and overwhelming role for oxygen in breathing. She revolutionized our ideas of how breathing is controlled lifelong.[23]

As recently as 2019, the Nobel Prize-winner Professor Sir Peter Ratcliffe, FRS, delivering Oxford's inaugural J. S. Haldane Lecture, hailed FitzGerald as the real hero of the 1911 investigations. When FitzGerald noted in her paper that 'a very small difference in the oxygen pressure in the arterial blood has a great effect on the breathing and on the percentage quantity of haemoglobin', Ratcliffe believes she gave 'the first description… of oxygen sensing' in the history of science.[24] Everything suggests that had John been present at the lecture and known what we now know, he would have been the first to signal his agreement.

The remaining years before the war were a mixture of achievement and disappointment for John. He sat on yet another Royal Commission, this time on metalliferous mines and quarries, and was made director of the Doncaster Mining Research Laboratory.

Initially, he filled this post in addition to his Readership at Oxford, but in 1913 he resigned from his department after failing again to secure the Waynflete Chair of Physiology once occupied by his uncle. Bitterly disappointed, he now ploughed his energies into extending and improving his private laboratory at Cherwell. Little did he know, he was building up the resources for life-saving war work of the first order.

* * *

If Pikes Peak can be described as the crowning 'mission' of John's pre-war scientific career, Richard's diplomatic visit to Berlin the following year, known to historians as 'the Haldane Mission', can be similarly described in his life of statesmanship. It was February 1912, and Richard was nearing the end of his time at the War Office. He was by now Viscount Haldane of Cloan, having been elevated to the Lords in March 1911. The mission can rightly be considered as one of Britain's most significant attempts to improve relations with Germany, which had fallen to a new low after the Agadir Crisis. The decision to send Richard to speak with Wilhelm II and his ministers in Berlin was rooted not just in Richard's linguistic capacities and his familiarity with the country, but also in the relationships he had already formed with the key players in Germany.

He had visited Berlin in 1906, when he met the Kaiser and toured the German War Office. Richard and Wilhelm met again the following year, during the latter's state visit. It was on this occasion that Richard sat in on a meeting of the Kaiser and his ministers at Windsor. He subsequently described himself as 'the only Englishman who has ever been a member of the German Cabinet'.[25] (Upper-class Scotsmen at that time had a strange habit of calling themselves English; that said, his mother was English.) New levels of intimacy were struck when, during another visit to England in 1911, the Kaiser invited himself to a lunch that he heard Richard was giving to the German generals at his London home. Only men attended. Elizabeth was at the top of the house in Richard's study with Asquith's nine-year-old son, Anthony, known as Puffin. Wilhelm insisted on climbing the steep stairs to talk with them. Elizabeth reflected in her diary:

> He has a most attractive personality so keen and fascinating that it is difficult to remember that he is an Emperor and not simply a most interesting human being with whom one would like to converse for a long time. He admired Puffin much and kissed him twice—a cherub he called him.[26]

Richard later wrote that Wilhelm 'used to chaff me about the size of 28 Queen Anne's Gate, which he called my "Dolls' House"'.[27] When the property went up for sale in 2017 for £19.5 million, *The Times* ran an article with the title, 'A Palace in Westminster'.[28] It's all relative, I suppose.

The 1912 Berlin Mission would not just involve the Kaiser and his Chancellor, Theobald von Bethmann Hollweg, both of whom Richard found easy to talk to; he was also going to meet the German Naval Minister, Admiral von Tirpitz, whose fork-pronged beard seemed to proclaim his leadership of the rising militaristic spirit in Germany. Richard was there to scope out what kind of arrangement between the two countries might be possible—preferably one that secured a reduction in Germany's planned naval expansion—then report back to his cabinet. Nothing was to be official, and no treaty was to be negotiated during the talks. It was felt that the British public ought to be kept in the dark at this stage of inquiries, so a cover story went out that Richard was simply going to speak with eminent biologists in the German capital as part of his duties as chairman of the Royal Committee on University Education in London. Alongside his ever-reliable butler-cum-valet, Pusey, he was joined by John, acting as his 'Private Secretary', to lend authenticity to the fabrication. The presence in the travelling party of a German-born financier with connections to the Kaiser, Sir Ernest Cassel, suggested other matters were envisaged.

The newspapers were having none of the cover story. On 12 February, the *Daily Chronicle* reported:

> Yesterday some credence was attached to the statement that the War Minister's visit was of a purely private character, or connected with the University Commission, of which he is president. To-day there is a general disposition to regard it as epoch-making, and to regard Lord Haldane himself as the High Plenipotentiary of the British Empire on a mission fraught with immense and far-reaching possibilities. The truth probably lies between these views.[29]

SERIOUS MINDS

The *Daily Mail* captured the German perspective:

> Germans are astonished to find a War Minister without sword, spurs, and helmet. He looks, they say, more like a good-natured country parson than the Secretary for War of the mighty British Empire. His arrival is the dominating topic of the hour. It has utterly obliterated interest in the opening of the Reichstag.[30]

Richard found his discussions with Bethmann Hollweg promising, as the Chancellor was clearly intent on maintaining peace, and on their second meeting the two even drew up a draft of what each considered to be a reasonable agreement, with both sides making major concessions. But Tirpitz, whom Richard saw separately with the Kaiser, wouldn't give an inch on his desire to go ahead with their new Fleet Law. Wilhelm was initially caught between the two opposing factions in his own camp, though he gave Richard reason to believe he might be inching towards his Chancellor. This at least gave signs of hope. One newspaper, knowing nothing of the content of the discussion, could still proclaim confidently that 'almost in a night the breath of a higher and purer atmosphere is over the land',[31] and it was in this state of optimism that Richard left Berlin. In the end, however, Tirpitz won the Kaiser over to the view that nothing short of unconditional neutrality on Britain's part—an impossible request, in light of Britain's treaty obligations to France and Russia—should stop the rapid enlargement of the German fleet. As Germany appeared to have no valid reason, other than war, for their intended fleet size, it was an ominous sign.

What is perhaps even more interesting for us is the light that the whole affair throws on Richard's reliance on his mother in the midst of such an internationally momentous occasion. His letters back to Cloan also show a man for whom the greatest moments in life, as for so many Haldanes before him, demanded the invocation of an omnipotent God. He seems to speak more with the voice of his grandfather than of Hegel.

On the midnight before his departure, and having come straight from a conversation with King George V, Richard wrote to Mary of the mission:

> I have a deep sense of... the tremendous responsibilities which rest on me. I put my trust in God, & this I know you look upon as the

first thing, & it is the first thing. Given this, success or failure matter little. Still, to feel that much of the future of this country may turn on the work of the next week is to feel that one needs all one has, and more than any man can possess in his own strength. I know you are thinking of me & praying for me.[32]

On his return journey, he concluded a lengthy letter detailing the tone and character of his conversations with the words:

It is a solemn call this, & come what may I shall feel that the effort has been one to do God's work. Please seal up & keep this letter when you have done with it. Later on what I have written will belong to the past, & it will not matter. For the present I am sending for your eye the secrets of Europe.[33]

Signing the letter 'H of C' for 'Haldane of Cloan', he added in the third person, 'He is thankful for his mother's prayers.' Four days later he wrote exultingly:

There is at least the chance of the greatest event there has been for some time in the history of the world. I feel that I was borne through my task in Berlin & over its difficulties by a power greater than myself. I never was left for a moment with a doubt what to say, or of my capacity to face the formidable personages with whom I was wrestling.[34]

By 7 March, however, he noted with dismay that 'the Admirals are getting the better of the good chancellor, & are increasing the fleet'.[35] Mary, as ever, returned his thoughts to the divine realm and the peace that she was confident would prevail in the end. For all the philosophical bulwarks he had built for himself, Richard needed these maternal reminders. As he told her, 'There is a sense of harmony which comes to me after reading your daily letters, & makes other things easy.'[36]

Richard had advanced ideas of what good international relationships should be. His 1913 address in Montreal to the special joint meeting of the American Bar Association and the Bar Association of Canada (which Richard attended with Elizabeth) was a remarkable statement of cooperation, based not on legal or written treatises but on shared ethical standards. It was a philosophically informed view of what he termed 'Higher Nationality', and his address of that title still merits reading today in the fractious context of European, and even UK, politics.[37]

By the time of the Montreal visit—which involved travelling from New York up the Hudson in J. P. Morgan Jr's private yacht to inspect the largest ever military parade put on by the US Military Academy at West Point—Richard was Lord High Chancellor of Great Britain, having received the Great Seal from King George V in June 1912. This new, long longed-for position saw Richard once again intervene in areas well beyond his cabinet remit. He needed to draw ever further on his time-stretching skills to make this possible, given that his official duties included overseeing the judiciary in England and Wales, the speakership of the House of Lords, and—Richard's favourite responsibility—the presidency of the Judicial Committee of the Privy Council. It was this presidency that was to have such lasting consequences for Canada, as Richard implemented a radical reinterpretation of the country's constitution in favour of provincial over federal power. But that is another story, and well told elsewhere.[38]

How Richard found time to chair the Royal Commission on University Education in London between 1909 and 1913—with the vast reading it required, alongside seventy-two evidence hearings, deliberative meetings (another seventy-two of them!), and report writing—is hard to fathom. It's also hard to detect the Commission's impact, as the war followed so swiftly upon the publication of its report. It is certainly true that London University's eventual decision in 1927 to move to its now iconic Bloomsbury site had its origins in the commissioners' recommendations, as did important changes in the teaching of medicine and the structure of the university's medical departments. Perhaps of greater influence was a separate cabinet committee on education that Richard chaired between 1912 and 1913, which laid much of the groundwork for H. A. L. Fisher's transformative Education Act of 1918.[39] In fact, when Fisher became president of the Board of Education in December 1916, he only took the role because he knew Richard would not be asked, even though Fisher considered him 'much the best man for the purpose'.[40]

* * *

THE HALDANE MISSIONS, PART TWO

Richard's time in government brought with it a corresponding blossoming of Cloan, and these pre-war years represent the house's heyday. The country's leading thinkers and doers seemed to flock to the Perthshire retreat when the courts and Parliament were in recess between August and October. To an astonishing variety of people—spanning the intellectual, scientific, literary, military, and ecclesiastical worlds—Cloan opened its doors. There was an exception when it came to politicians; Cloan was an escape from Westminster. A flick through the visitors' book from that era, which the family still possesses, shows the signatures of many who continue to feature in the public consciousness, from John Buchan to Robert Baden-Powell. Two regulars were the archbishops of York and Canterbury, who quickly learnt not to wear their customary silk stockings, after the boisterous Kaiser laddered them one too many times with his welcoming paws.

Men of the cloth faced other hazards, too. On one occasion, Richard took the Archbishop of Canterbury, Randall Davidson, on a walk through a steep ravine, only for the two to find themselves on a path that was crumbling beneath their feet and petering out to nothing. 'Which helped the other it was difficult to ascertain', wrote Elizabeth, 'for both claimed to have done so, but on the whole the palm was given to the Archbishop. We all speculated on the sensation it would have made in the Press if the Archbishop of Canterbury and the Lord Chancellor had been found lying together at the foot of a Scottish glen!'[41]

A Cloan constant in the autumn was Peter Hume Brown, Professor of Ancient (Scottish) History and Palaeography at Edinburgh University and, from 1908, Historiographer Royal for Scotland. This highly lovable scholar, adored by all the children, had once been a university classmate of Richard's and a tutor to his younger siblings. He shared with Richard a passion for Goethe, and across every Easter holiday from 1898 to 1912 the two would make a pilgrimage to Germany to follow in the sage's footsteps. At Cloan, Hume Brown went by the simple title 'the Professor', and there he had his own room kept especially for him, and his own armchair in the library. The dogs became particularly attached to their bearded guest. Even today in the dogs' cemetery at Cloan, which can be found beyond the formal gardens amongst clipped yew hedges and moss roses, one can still make out an inscription on the tombstone for little Culie, who died in April 1914. It reads simply, 'The Professor's Friend', because, according to Elizabeth, 'when dying of old age, he managed to creep up to Professor Hume Brown's room at the dawn. He heard him, opened the door and the dog who loved him lay down and died at his feet.'[42]

Naomi's memoirs offer a fascinating glimpse of Cloan at this time from a child's perspective. With her powerful imagination, there's need for caution before believing everything she says. We know, for instance, that Einstein, although he stayed with Richard in London, never visited Cloan. That didn't stop Naomi from telling others that he did, and that she found him wondering lost in the woods. 'I know I remember things that never happened', Naomi said late in life.[43] JBS saw it this way: 'I think she sometimes remembers "with advantages", as Shakespeare put it.'[44] What Naomi's words do offer, however, is a novelist's descriptive power that makes tangible those remote times. As Lesley A. Hall says of Naomi's novel writing, 'She had enormous skills in evocative world-building.'[45] The almost erotic sensuousness of the following passage tells us far more than any photo album could:

> Year after year I ran out and bit off the tips of the tropaeolum flowers that shone in brilliant scarlet on the dark holly leaves of the big hedge, and sucked the honey... In late April I picked the tiny delicate flowers of the wood sorrel, white penciled with white, touched them with fingers and tongue, at last ate them. In summer I ate half-ripe plums and green apples, the last, late, slug-nibbled strawberries... Tremendous sunsets flamed over the hills on the far side of the strath... In sparkling brightness after a shower I saw in a single raindrop hanging from a rhododendron leaf the whole thing reflected as in an eye and it threw me into a turmoil of pleasure.[46]

Place, people, and power are all conjured in Naomi's writings about Cloan. We're pulled through corridors and landings where monochrome prints of old masters hang in the gloom; we stride between a panoply of irreverent *Punch* cartoons of her Uncle Richard as we make our way along the passage to the smoking room, where we find John Haldane puffing away at his pipe as he peers over his latest scientific paper. Here comes Richard now dressed for dinner in a velvet

THE HALDANE MISSIONS, PART TWO

smoking jacket that speaks of decadent luxury. At dinner, we taste the sweetness of the fresh broad beans, picked that day from the walled garden, and the small bunches of hothouse grapes, delicately cut by the butler. If it's tea, we can see Naomi chomping through homemade oatcakes with comb honey, and can watch with intrigue as the Lord Chancellor shoots a chubby hand towards the little snacks prepared specially for him of red herring and other German delicacies. On Sundays, at lunch, the smells are less appetising. On the table lies the singed sheep's head in its barley sauce. We wait for the moment Uncle Richard teasingly offers an eyeball.

From what Naomi tells us, we know that family prayers that evening will be 'very flavoursome'.[47] Again, the gong resounds through the house, a game of draughts is abandoned, and into the drawing room come the purple plush benches to seat the servants, who now enter in order of precedence, like actors taking the stage for the bow. There's Mrs Cook in dark satin, followed by the butler, and here's Burser the head housemaid, who's tugged Naomi's hair into shape that evening. On it goes until the youngest kitchen maid closes the door behind her. Out of courtesy, the Methodist chauffeur is also there, wearing his smart Sunday suit. He's been entertaining the locals, having rigged up the horn on Richard's Daimler to play the opening notes of 'Lead Kindly Light'. The prayers are serious, though somewhat compromised by a rogue cairn terrier belonging to Mary Haldane alighting upon a kneeling back and making its way along the row of servants. Neck and ears receive the obligatory sniff. When it gets to the teenage kitchen maid, the silent heaving of her shoulders sends Naomi into a convulsion of giggles. John Haldane unwittingly injects a touch of humour on those occasions when canine entertainment is lacking. He refuses to follow tradition and give an improvised prayer in best Presbyterian style; instead, he takes a written one, but reads it with such a surprised voice that it sounds improvised.

Long walks were of course a feature of the holidays. The main expedition was up Ben Vorlich, which required the chauffeur's services to ferry the walking party across the strath to the foot of the mountain. One year, when the Stracheys were visiting, Naomi was seized with jealousy as Jack asked Amabel Strachey, cousin of Lytton, to accompany him on the ascent. Her rage was perhaps the first hint that her burning fraternal love could bleed over into the sexual realm.

There were calmer moments, too. The autumn shoots brought picnics high up at 'the edge of the moor above Foswell, all females hatted against the sun, the men large in tweeds, keepers and gillies discreetly eating, and doubtless drinking, in the background, and an exquisite tiny burn over-hung by miniature cliffs over which grass of Parnassus and bell heather hung from moss beds'. Naomi remembers her little cousin, Archie, catching trout by hand from the burn, when 'Uncle Richard had some specially important guest and none had been caught with rod and line.' Naomi couldn't quite click with Archie in these early years, but found his older sister, Elsie, an inspiration. Her diary states: 'One of the horses bolted for a mile with Archie but Elsie managed to get beside and stop him.' In another entry we discover that 'Elsie is an expert motorist now and she drove us to Dunblane the other day.'[48]

These down-to-earth competencies of the Foswell cousins (the 'Fossils', as Jack and Naomi called them) brought Naomi's own imaginative contortions into sharp relief. As she herself acknowledged, 'they were the ones who knew and understood the real, factual place, who knew where to find the birds and the fish, who were aware of exact growth and change'.[49] Yet they had their own romantic streak. When Archie, as A. R. B. Haldane, wrote his tales of boyhood fishing adventures in later life, Naomi read them and discovered to her surprise 'the same passionate feeling as mine for certain aspects of natural beauty'.[50] That is true, though Archie's works are more deeply imbued with elegy, with a longing for a lost innocence that he found reflected in the tranquillity of river, stream, and loch. The source of this evocative melancholy is a question we must reserve for later.

Archie's works also offer a snapshot of Cloan from this time. Foswell was closed up over the winter, so Christmas holidays for Willie and his family were spent as guests of Mary, Richard, and Elizabeth. *The Path by the Water*, written towards the end of the Second World War, contains a chapter titled 'Town and Country' which almost matches Naomi's writing for sheer descriptive power:

> In the big Red bedroom near the top of the house where we slept was a huge four-poster bed with canopy and side curtains of red

repp covered with a pattern of white *fleur de lys*. Lost in its wide expanse, I would lie awake watching the light of the wood fire make flickering patterns on the ceiling, fading and then brightening as a charred stick burst into momentary flame, to die again to a glow and then at last to soft grey ash as I slept. In the schoolroom where we had our meals, the cups and plates had a pattern of twisted green dragons on the thick china, a pattern which at this moment recalls the scene vividly to my mind, and especially a tall narrow strip of a cupboard let into a corner of the wall from which my grandmother's maid, who ruled the schoolroom, produced exciting tins, and a delicious brand of thick biscuit peculiar to the local baker.[51]

Other details emerge, like the ghost stories that Richard wove for the children as he relaxed in front of the drawing-room fire after dinner, stories 'made more vivid by the wind in the trees outside, and the thought of the dark passages upstairs which we must soon face'; the image of John caught transfixed 'in a land of thought and contemplation', an absorption that would come on suddenly 'while sitting at table, while walking outside, or even while standing in the front hall, the carriage or the car waiting to take him to catch a train'; the insight into Elizabeth's 'tireless energy', focused not so much on 'ultimate principles of law, science and philosophy, but rather people, their lives and their thoughts'.[52]

In Archie's and indeed the entire family's view, the most important room in the whole house was the bedroom above the drawing room. Here, from 1911 until her death in her centenary year in 1925, Mary Haldane—or Granniema, as she was known to all the grandchildren—was permanently to be found. Sitting up in her bed, with a veil of white lace covering her frail white hair, surrounded by an ordered abundance of flowers, books, and letters, she looked in her dignity like a queen, in her piety like a saint. Often, the bed would be placed before the large bay window, so that she might watch the play of light upon the fields and far-off hills, and see, if only for a moment, the departing train from Auchterarder as it bore her children away to their missions in the South. For them, the room up the spiral stairs became 'the still point of a turning world'. She was their 'mainspring', their 'source of strength'.[53] She gathered up and united in herself the thoughts and interests of her family and her many friends, and, from her room, 'she maintained to the very last a wide and lively interest in the outside world'. Archie continues:

> She had in a degree unequalled in the experience of any who knew her the power of projecting herself into the interests and activities of others. No interest was too obscure, too divergent, or too trivial for her understanding and sympathy. I believe that this was given no more readily and freely to those who came to her room to talk of great matters of Religion, State, Science, or Politics, than to us when as children we came to tell her of our walks and our fishing, of the birds and the animals and the wild flowers, while we sat by her nibbling the little coffee-flavoured chocolate beans which she kept for us in the silver-topped box at her bedside.[54]

* * *

In these pre-war years, the family needed Mary's reassurance more than they ever had. Conflict was still far from certain, but things were looking grave in the Balkans. It was a trying time for Richard politically, as international concerns were matched at home by the problems over the government of Ireland. Willie and his wife Edith were surely unsettled, too, as their middle son, Graeme, was now in training at the naval colleges of Osborne and Dartmouth. In hopes that peace would prevail and that Graeme would develop the family's love of Germany, a German boy was invited to stay at Cloan and provide language lessons for the sailor-in-training while he was on leave over the Christmas of 1913. It was a relatively quiet party that year, with only Elsie and Naomi making up the other youthful guests, but the atmosphere exuded warmth and unity. Towards the end of her life, Elizabeth remembered that last Christmas before the war and wrote: 'One looked at the young ones dancing, German and English together, and never thought that in a few months they would, some of them, be fighting for their lives, trying to kill one another, and that all the matters that seemed so important to us would be as nought.'[55]

Graeme's awareness of coming conflict was made inescapable when, in June 1914, he was woken after 10 pm from his Dartmouth dormitory bed and told that the First Lord of the Admiralty, Winston Churchill, who was visiting the college, wanted to see him—immediately—on board the Admiralty yacht, *Enchantress*. Graeme later recorded in his memoirs:

> On arrival I was taken at once to the main saloon where Churchill, after a good dinner, was smoking a large cigar. After a brief apology for not getting me on board in time for dinner, he waved me (and I think a couple of other arrivals) into chairs and started to talk at considerable length. The theme... was what would happen... if the Country went to war. He told us all about the mobilization procedure and all he said duly came to pass a little later.[56]

It didn't take much for the sixteen-year-old Cadet Haldane to guess that he had Churchill's cabinet colleague, the Lord Chancellor, to thank for the experience. No doubt Graeme wrote home about the encounter, and it's likely his parents felt ever more anxious about Churchill's talk of mobilisation. They could not have known that Graeme would come through the following years physically unharmed (the same could not be said for him emotionally and psychologically) and that tragedy awaited them elsewhere.

Their eldest son Pat was by this time at Oxford, reading modern history at Balliol, and enjoying the intensities of life as a college rower and a member of the Officers' Training Corps, founded by his uncle. His cousin Jack was also rowing and in the university OTC, having gone up to New College with a mathematical scholarship in the autumn of 1911. Jack's first-class in Mathematical Moderations within a year was almost boringly predictable. Less predictable was his decision then to switch to classics, not the sciences, achieving another first a year ahead of schedule in the summer of 1914. Perhaps he was influenced by the disparaging comments he had heard his father make about 'mere mathematicians'.[57] Unsurprisingly for a Haldane, Jack loved the philosophical side of the degree, and he absorbed by heart the great poems of the ancients. He would spend his life impressing, intimidating, and annoying others as he poured forth torrents of Homer or Lucretius in their original languages. A favoured drunken party trick, we might add, was to speak exclusively in blank verse of a Shakespearean kind.

The tedium of Naomi's studies at home was considerably offset by her brother's return to Oxford and the social world into which she was now catapulted. This was largely made up of Old Etonians, some of whose names are still well known. The grandsons of 'Darwin's Bulldog', T. H. Huxley—the brothers Julian, Trev, and Aldous Huxley, and their cousin Gervas—were prominent among the group. Jack had been Julian's fag (errand-boy) in his first year at school. To the newcomer, Julian had offered a rare ray of compassion. He was now a Demonstrator in Oxford's department of zoology and comparative anatomy. It was perhaps because of this that Jack decided to take a term off from his Latin and Greek and study zoology instead: the only nugget of an official university science education he ever received. Still, this didn't stop him co-publishing a paper with his father and C. G. Douglas in 1912, with the catchy title, 'The Laws of Combination of Haemoglobin with Carbon Monoxide and Oxygen'.[58]

Aldous was two years Jack's junior at Eton, but Jack admired his scientific curiosity and intelligence. Such was their friendship that he came to live with the Haldanes at Cherwell in 1913, shortly before going up to Balliol as a scholar that autumn. He was still recovering from his traumatic loss of sight two years earlier. The fifteen-year-old Naomi was attracted by Aldous's vulnerability and wit, and sought to make the lanky, piano-playing invalid her lover. She found herself gently rebuffed. No such attempt appears to have been made on his brother, Trev—'a rock-climber, blond, outgoing, well-liked'.[59] He was then a postgraduate at the university, after shocking his high-achieving family, and painfully disappointing himself, by 'only' managing a second-class degree in classics. Despite the personal difficulties that were dogging his life, including an affair with his father's housemaid, Trev would accompany Naomi for regular walks out into the Oxfordshire countryside, walks full of 'endless interest and conversation, Huxley jokes and limericks'.[60] According to Naomi, 'the Huxleys were so nearly counted as kin that chaperonage was not considered necessary'.[61] As she picked and munched her way through the berries growing from the sides of the paths, Trev would stop her and direct her attention to the birds. Could she differentiate between them by their song? A good ear was, alas, one of the gifts denied to Naomi.

Back at Cherwell, Aldous was busy observing the peculiarities of his hosts, some of which would make amusing, and occasionally barbed, reappearances in his later novels. The character of

Shearwater in *Antic Hay* (1923) is unmistakably Jack at his most eccentrically scientific and, when it comes to love, pathetic. Lord Tantamount in *Point Counter Point* (1928), with his passion for phosphorus and nocturnal experiments in his home laboratory, is a clear evocation of John.

Others on the scene in Oxford included Lewis Gielgud (older brother of the actor John) and an intelligent, empathetic young man named Gilbert Richard Mitchison, known as Dick. If Naomi was not busy in the Cherwell garden breeding and monitoring guinea pigs for the genetic experiments she and Jack were patiently conducting, she was cajoling her new friends into performing her plays or marshalling them into punts for afternoon jaunts down the river. Looking back, the summer of 1914 was wonderfully idyllic. Gervas Huxley—intentionally forgetting, perhaps, that both Julian and Trev were battling nervous breakdowns that year—wrote over half a century later:

> In retrospect it seems as if the sun must always have been shining that summer… I fancied myself in love with Naomi: it was a pleasantly mild and undemanding form of love… and was satisfied by enjoying the presence of its object. An especially happy and hilarious farewell evening river picnic followed the play's final performance [Naomi's *Saunes Bairos, A Study in Recurrence*]. It was the end of term, and poling our punts back in the warm moonlight we planned further play acting for the next summer and bade each other goodbye until we should meet again in October.[62]

As Naomi's biographer poignantly writes, 'For some it was a very long goodbye.'[63] Before the first British casualties of war had fallen, Trev Huxley hanged himself in a Surrey wood. It was an act unconnected to international events, but it signalled for Naomi and her companions the start of four long years of horror.

8

THE MOTTO COMES TRUE

1914–1918

If things felt rosy for Jack and Naomi in Oxford in the first half of 1914, it was not a recognisable feeling on the national stage. In fact, to their elders and to many others, it looked as if something in the nature of an apocalypse was approaching. It had little to do with troubles in the Balkans or between the Great Powers on the Continent. No, the danger appeared to lie elsewhere: Ireland. The slow-growing tensions between those who supported some form of Irish self-government through Home Rule and those who emphatically resisted the removal of power from Westminster had now reached fever pitch. Elizabeth Haldane's memoirs paint a frightening scene:

> [T]here was the feeling of a nightmare. Peers, elderly Dons and great soldiers like Lord Roberts signed the 'British Covenant', declaring that any action to counter a [Home Rule] Bill they disliked was justified... Militant suffragism was rampant: beautiful and famous pictures were destroyed and a case of porcelain in the British Museum smashed. In April there was gun-running in Ulster and the coast guard was destroyed. Rifles and cartridges were bought from Germany, and this was enough to make her [Germany] think civil war was imminent. When at the end of May the Home Rule Bill received its third reading, Sir Edward Carson went to Belfast 'to make arrangements for the final scene.'[1]

Elizabeth even remembered a Downing Street garden party on 23 July, less than two weeks before the outbreak of war, where 'no one seemed to think of anything but Ireland'.[2] On that same day Austria delivered its ultimatum to Serbia.

The following afternoon, Elizabeth sat in 28 Queen Anne's Gate sipping tea in the company of Richard's former private secretary—the young, dashing, and one-legged Lord Lucas, known to his friends as Bron. The two were deep in talk about the failure of the recent Irish Peace Conference at Buckingham Palace when Richard entered, looking tired and pessimistic, having come straight from a cabinet meeting. Ireland was no longer the source of anxiety. The PM and his ministers had been discussing the possibility of imminent European war. As with the dancing at Cloan the previous Christmas, for Elizabeth this was a snapshot moment that remained with her for the rest of her life: 'I cannot forget the scene in the Queen Anne drawing-room, with "Bron", so handsome and adored by his friends, sitting at tea: and suddenly having a vision of what might be in front of one. Poor "Bron" was to lose his life with the rest.'[3]

Other Haldanes too had their defining eve-of-war moments. The tragedy of Elizabeth's vision was matched by the surrealness of her nephew JBS's. Around 1 am on 29 June, sleeping out amongst the heather in the Surrey countryside as part of his signalling training with the OTC, he awoke to the roar of an engine. It was an Austrian stranger, named Sobotka, pulling up on his motorbike, 'attempting to interest me in various new radio devices and also announcing the murder of Archduke Franz Ferdinand and the probability of a war between Austria-Hungary and Serbia'. JBS continues: 'We had not envisaged the possibility that the Angel of Death should arrive on a motor cycle, not only announcing the death of many of us signallers but the death of the culture into which we had been born.'[4]

Naomi's defining memory, recalled in her very old age (and so perhaps to be placed amongst some of her other questionable recollections), was of being at her uncle's London home and witnessing the moment when Richard turned to Edward Grey—the Foreign Secretary was living with the Lord Chancellor at the time—in the knowledge that war was inevitable: 'I suddenly saw two people who were struck to the heart with what was happening; I could see it in their faces.'[5]

Whatever the truth of Naomi's presence at this most heartbreaking of moments shared between two men who were directly involved in Britain's decision to go to war, it is undoubtedly true that they shared such a moment together—Richard's and Elizabeth's memoirs confirm it. It was made all the more bitter by the contrasting reaction of Asquith, a reaction that was not included in the published records of the Haldane siblings, but which Elizabeth noted in her personal diary. This is what Richard wrote in the official retelling of the story in 1928, the year of his death:

> [A despatch] box was brought in, while we [Richard, Grey, and Lord Crewe] were dining together, with a telegram to the effect that the German Army was about to invade Belgium... Grey asked me what my prescription was. My answer was 'Immediate Mobilisation'. He said that his view was the same. We decided to go without delay to see the Prime Minister. We found him with some company, and took him into another room... We expressed our view... Asquith agreed to it at once.[6]

This is what Elizabeth wrote in her diary six days after the actual events, having heard the full details from Richard on her return to London from Cloan:

> Then came the advance on Belgium, a friendly Power, whose rights we were bound as one of her guarantors to respect. To E.[dward] G.[rey]'s mind this settled matters. He went on Sunday 2nd August to Downing Street with R.[ichard] and Lord Crewe who had been dining at 28 [Queen Anne's Gate]. There he found the P.M. [Asquith] and ladies playing Bridge. Lord Crewe said it was like playing on the top of a coffin. They waited till they had finished—about an hour.[7]

It is hard to imagine what Richard and his colleagues thought as they were told that they would have to wait for the prime minister to emerge and give his opinion on the declaration of war because he was busy playing bridge![8]

Once Richard, Grey, and Crewe had secured Asquith's attention, things moved extremely quickly. Richard found himself at 11 am the next day back at the War Office at the PM's request (Asquith was temporarily War Secretary at this stage, as well as premier) to mobilise the army which he had created. Over the next two weeks the swift transportation of the BEF from Britain to France occurred without a hitch—a far cry from the two months that it would have taken in 1905. While the details of the transportation owed much to the hard work of Sir Henry Wilson (Director of Military Operations, 1910–14), Richard deserved a great deal of credit for establishing and reinforcing, from 1906 onwards, the fundamental principle of speedy mobilisation. Credit was the very opposite of what he received.

Richard was used to being the odd one out amongst British statesmen. Others may have had a spell at a German university, but Richard's enthusiasm for German culture and state organisation was unusual, as was his ability to speak the language fluently. John Buchan once said of him, 'he probably understood the German spirit better than any man in Britain'.[9] His continual reminders to his countrymen about German progress in education, science, and military thinking were not always accepted with tolerance in peacetime; in wartime, when his fellow Brits thought back to these suggestions of German superiority, they became anathema. On top of this, Richard's habit of looking as if he was deep in some form of intrigue, rather than simply helping with something behind the scenes, didn't do his reputation any favours. To the public, his 1912 mission to Berlin—still shrouded in mystery in 1914—was the supreme instance of this. When *The Times* then heard of a letter sent to Richard by the German shipping magnate, Albert Ballin, on the day before war was declared, and which Richard—for honourable reasons, it turned out—refused to make public, the floodgates opened.[10]

Two of the most persistent accusations were that the secret discussions in Berlin had been treacherous, and that Richard had been responsible for the decision not to dispatch immediately all six available divisions of the BEF when war was first declared. These accusations were not true, but they were at least believable, especially once the public discovered in December 1914 that Richard had told a German acquaintance in the years prior to the war that Germany was his 'spiritual home'. Of course, in a time of extreme anti-German sentiment and witch-hunting, the quote was pulled wildly out of context (Richard had been referring to the classroom of Professor Lotze), and it paved the way to yet wilder claims. Soon, rumours were circulating that Richard had a secret German wife; that he was Wilhelm II's illegitimate brother; and that the German government had told him of the intended war and he had withheld his knowledge from his cabinet colleagues. *The Times* and the *Daily Mail*, both owned by Alfred Harmsworth, Viscount Northcliffe, were particularly venomous. Northcliffe had held a grudge against Richard ever since he failed to persuade the War Secretary, back in 1909, to amass early forms of aircraft for military use. Richard had thought it more worthwhile to invest in aeronautical research before any significant purchases, and rebuffed Northcliffe's approaches. It is dangerous to refuse the pleas of a press baron.[11]

The clamour around the Lord Chancellor in 1914 and after might have abated had Asquith and Grey agreed to Richard's request that the reports on the Berlin Mission be made public, but they didn't want to stir any further controversy in time of war. They left their friend to deal with the consequences. One of those consequences—alongside an unprecedented level of hate mail—was that Richard's place in the cabinet came under increasing pressure. By May 1915, the Liberals had lost the confidence of the public, and it was clear that a Liberal–Conservative coalition government would need to be formed—though with Asquith still at the head. One of the Conservatives' non-negotiables was that Richard should no longer remain in office, either because of the furore in the press or because of animosity towards him within their own ranks. Asquith made a sad capitulation to their demands and failed to write to his oldest political friend once the final decision was taken to leave Richard out of the government. Their relationship never quite recovered.

Richard was heart-broken and ill, but did his very best to hide it. Perhaps he didn't want others to think his famous philosophical serenity was abandoning him just at the moment he needed it most. In fact, the pressure of his vilification had been affecting him for months. Back in March, Elizabeth had noted in her diary:

> R. came down [to Cloan] on Saturday very depressed... R. felt he had been a failure as Cabinet Minister; no good in council as a body, better with one or two, and has no voice for assemblies, nor able to push forward... Work based so much on German ideals and all broken to pieces, education impossible etc... Really tired, and more hits at him.[12]

Receiving the Order of Merit from King George V on 26 May, the day after the formation of the new government, did little to cheer him. He travelled back to Cloan for eight days of recovery in the beautiful late spring weather. He went fishing with his thirteen-year-old nephew, Archie, and 'read immensely'. It was also an opportunity to think back with frankness—perhaps even bitterness—on the shortfalls of his former colleagues in cabinet. Once again, Elizabeth's diary tells the inside story from Richard's perspective, not just on Asquith, but also on Lloyd George, the Chancellor of the Exchequer, who was now intent on taking Asquith's place as prime minister. According to Elizabeth, Richard ruminated on

> [the] P. M.'s lack of passion and industry and initiative... amusement an obsession with him, Bridge and women and girls. In 1911 [Richard] thinks [he] began to lose touch with him, especially when in H.[ouse] of L.[ords] holding Chancellorship, & would not see him... L.[loyd] G.[eorge] evidently making for premiership. Cunning peasant but illiterate, though wonderfully clever and fine intentions. He and R. would have been admirable rolled into one, R. says... Wonder whether A.[squith] really did 'fight for him in spite of his tears.' Never got a line or message after seeing him till saw announcement in papers. Surely ought to have had it.[13]

Richard still felt his own apparent faults, particularly around his time as Lord Chancellor. The objective truth merited a far more positive assessment. The real property and conveyancing bills he introduced in 1913 and 1914 laid the bedrock for Lord Birkenhead's and Lord Cave's revolutionary Acts of the 1920s. In 1925, the *Columbia Law Review* would claim: 'It is probable that if the War had not intervened, Lord Haldane's bills would have been enacted and real property reform set forward ten years.'[14] In addition, Richard greatly strengthened the judicial tribunals of the House of Lords and the Privy Council, by passing an Act which added two new paid Law Lords to their service. As president of the Judicial Committee of the Privy Council, he had also started to make a major impact on developing the scope of independent powers of the provinces in Canada.

Beyond the legal sphere, Richard even managed to put a memorandum before his cabinet colleagues in April 1915, only a month before leaving government, that contained the first outlines for the idea of a League of Nations. According to Robert Joseph Gowen, 'Not only was Haldane the first to bring the League idea before the cabinet, but in doing so he unveiled most of its essential features.'[15] At the time, Elizabeth noted in her diary that Richard believed it 'better to consider this matter even now though will be thought premature; will sink into people's minds. War so likely to break out again and must do everything to prevent it.'[16] It wasn't until 1971 that his foresight was recognised amongst historians of the League. Gowen hailed him then as the 'Neglected Apostle of the League of Nations'.

* * *

The months of April, May, and June 1915 were quite extraordinary for the family more widely. When, on 22 April, the Germans first utilised gas as a weapon against Allied forces during the Second Battle of Ypres, Lord Kitchener, by now War Secretary, immediately dialled through to Britain's premier respiratory physiologist: John Haldane at Cherwell. The next morning John was standing in front of Kitchener at the War Office discussing what the British scientific response ought to be, only to be broken off by the arrival of Winston Churchill. The First Lord of the Admiralty thought he had just the answer to their problems. 'Oh, what you want is what we have in the Navy', said Churchill, 'smoke helmets or smoke pads, and you make them out of cotton wool or something. You'd better get the *Daily Mail* to organize the making of a million of them.'[17] An example was brought for John to look at; it amounted to a piece of lint, held over the mouth by a piece of string. It was completely useless.

The following day, John and a chemist from Imperial College, Professor H. Brereton Baker, travelled to the British army's general headquarters in Saint-Omer, France. From there they drove to the town of Bailleul to examine the bodies of the dead. Their inflamed lungs, and the fluid filling their air spaces, confirmed that the gas had been chlorine, as did the green colour of their brass buttons. Survivors, breathing with difficulty, were blue in the face from want of oxygen. Clearly, some form of respirator had to be developed, and quickly. Once that was achieved, a way of administering oxygen treatment to casualties would also have to be provided. Adequate laboratory space was not exactly easy to find at the Front, so for John it meant going back across the Channel to Cherwell—his bag harbouring a dead man's lung—for a week of gruesome self-experiments in his home laboratory. He also made time to write up his findings for Kitchener, which were then printed in *The Times* on 29 April: 'the first official report of the unleashing of chemical warfare on the modern world'.[18] According to the historian of science Jon Agar, 'newspaper editors at first played down the attacks, but as soon as the physiologist John Scott Haldane submitted an official report... confirming the lethality of the gas, the editorials and letters pages filled with accusations of atrocity'.[19] This 'holier than thou' stance could only be maintained for so long. By September that year, the British were also unleashing chlorine on their enemies.

On his return to England, John was outraged to discover that *The Times* was also being used as a platform for a public campaign of monumental stupidity. An article bearing the headline 'RESPIRATORS WANTED' was calling for the women of Britain to make thousands of masks for their men abroad, based largely on the design advocated by Churchill, and known by John to be useless. John went straight from Dover to the War Office, where his anger was met by reassurance from the Director-General of the Army Medical Services and Haldane family friend, Sir Alfred Keogh, who told John it was sheer propaganda to give hope to those at home. None of these pointless devices would be sent to France. In fact, 90,000 of them found their way there. There is no evidence any lives were saved as a result; if anything, they increased the death toll.[20]

John was convinced something effective could be produced. Fighting against the clock, he and a small group of Oxford companions set to work with a will. The sights and sounds at Cherwell were extraordinary. Not even Aldous Huxley, who was staying with the Haldanes again, was spared from the scientists' endeavours, as Naomi remembered:

> The house reeked of chlorine, the noise of coughing and retching was continuous from the study and beyond. Everything that would make into a mask was seized upon—stockings, vests, Aldous'

woolly scarf, my knitted cap... then there was the violent telephoning to the War Office. Aldous did most of the necessary typewriting. I remember my father, cut off, shouting at the operator: 'Damn you, I'm the Lord Chancellor!'[21]

By Monday 3 May, John was off to France once more, this time clutching a prototype mask which amounted to a pad of cotton waste, wrapped in black gauze and moistened with a solution of sodium hyposulphate, sodium carbonate, glycerine, and water.[22] Unlike Churchill's recommended device, it covered the nose as well as the mouth. The mask became known as the 'Black Veil', since the gauze could also be pulled up over the eyes to provide some protection from tear gases.

It must be admitted that this first gas mask, often attributed solely to John, was more the brain-child of his colleague, Professor Baker, who had seen a similar German model.[23] What John and his Oxford team did was to establish the concentration levels of chlorine that the Germans were using, by inflicting various measures on themselves, and then to test and refine the proposed mask in light of this information. It is fair, then, to see the first British gas mask as a work of collaboration: John's biographer is right to call it the Baker/Haldane respirator. John also ruled out all sorts of other suggestions for protection, and devised further models that could be formed out of the kinds of materials available in the trenches. A bottomless beer bottle, its neck filled with cotton wool, the rest with loose earth, was one such ingenious creation that made its way into an official military pamphlet. But the front runner for effectiveness and speedy mass production, before more complex box respirators could be developed, was the 'Black Veil'. Further testing was still required, so it was back on the ferry for John.

John would need a gas chamber once he reached France. A small glass-fronted room in the school-turned-hospital at Saint-Omer would do the job nicely. He would also need help with his trials, so the War Office called back some friendly faces at his request. C. G. Douglas, John's Pikes Peak colleague, was soon there, as was J. Ivon Graham, a former collaborator from the Doncaster Mining Research Laboratory. Finally, John's son, JBS, arrived, fresh—well, that's hardly the word—from the trenches. Going by the nickname 'Bomber Haldane', he had been leading the explosives unit of the 1st Battalion of the Black Watch, a job which made him, he claimed, blissfully happy.[24] Douglas Haig called JBS 'the bravest and dirtiest officer in my Army'.[25] The experiments he would now conduct with his father would leave no doubt about his courage.

To test the levels of physical exertion that were possible while wearing, or not wearing, a respirator in gas conditions, John ordered a wheel to be constructed within the glass-fronted room. Each of the men went in, one after the other, sometimes with a mask, sometimes without, and turned the wheel, while known quantities of chlorine were released into the air. Brief 50-yard sprints once outside the chamber, still wearing their respirators, were par for the course, as attempts were made to replicate actions that might take place in the context of combat. 'None of us was much the worse for the gas, or in any real danger, as we knew where to stop', JBS later wrote. He couldn't help adding, 'but some had to go to bed for a few days, and I was very short of breath and incapable of running for a few months or so'.[26] As we'll soon discover, JBS's incapacity had other causes too.

According to biographer Ronald Clark, these few days of experiments in early May 1915 'saved many thousands of Allied lives and helped blunt the cutting edge of what might have been a decisive German weapon'.[27] The scientists had shown that the Black Veil could be effective for about five minutes when faced with a normal concentration of chlorine. John was back in England on 9 May—'very choky over fume of chlorine', as Elizabeth wrote in her diary.[28] Within eleven days of his return, the War Office had begun to issue the Baker/Haldane mask to British troops. It had many drawbacks and limitations, as soldiers soon learnt, but it was enough to be a suitable stopgap defence until more sophisticated contraptions were available.

John had already warned Kitchener that box-type respirators would be needed, and, thanks to the remarkable work of the chemist Edward Harrison, these became standard by 1917. John was to have no official role in their development; his brother Richard was just too suspect in the public eye. Already, on 16 May 1915, as items of hate mail in their hundreds poured through the letterbox of 28 Queen Anne's Gate, Elizabeth was recording that 'even Johnnie is accused of selling secrets to the enemy!'[29] Thankfully,

John's protégé, C. G. Douglas, did make it onto the government's chemical defence committee, so there was still a chance to influence proceedings, if indirectly.

This at least gave John time for other endeavours and accolades—delivering the Silliman Lectures at Yale in 1916, for example, in front of an audience which included ex-President Taft (who'd also heard Richard lecture in Montreal in 1913), and winning the Royal Society Medal the same year. Nor did he forget the necessity of finding the appropriate way to deliver oxygen treatment to gas attack survivors. Professor Philip B. James claimed, in 2015, that it was John who 'designed the first tight-fitting oronasal mask to cover both the mouth and nose, and fitted it with a reservoir bag to allow storage of sufficient oxygen for each breath'. He also 'taught medical orderlies at the battlefront how to use the equipment, and a colleague later commented that nurses could be trained to use the equipment in just three minutes. This was the first time that pure oxygen was systematically used as a *treatment*, rather than simply as a supplement.'[30] John's determination and success in finding a way of delivering 100 per cent oxygen, and the logical reasoning he had for doing so (made clear in a paper of 1917), establish him as 'the father of oxygen treatment'.[31]

No doubt he was helped by further discussions with his son, who had returned to Cherwell to convalesce, but not from chlorine poisoning. On the same day that John had embarked for England, the young Black Watch bombing officer had been heading back to join his brigade, who were then in the thick of battle near Richebourg-Saint-Vaast. Amid the unstoppable thunderclaps of the German and Allied shelling, which produced in him a kind of exaltation, JBS forged on towards his troops. Before he could reach them, a shell erupted in front of him, spinning him round and knocking him to the earth. At first, he wasn't aware of any major injury, but he felt an aching in his head and chest and he worried for his memory. Passing soldiers pointed out that his right sleeve was covered in blood. He managed to make it to a nearby medical station, where a doctor dressed his arm and torso wounds.

The station, from its first floor, provided a horrifying panorama of the battle in which JBS's friends were engaged. He watched on through a pair of binoculars, and years later remembered the scene vividly: 'Then our barrage lifted and the Black Watch went forward. Sometimes a whole line would lie down suddenly. It was difficult to realize that they were not obeying an order, that in fact all of them had been wounded and most of them killed.'[32]

JBS's day got stranger yet. He made his way to another dressing station at Le Touret, where he hoped to get a lift in an ambulance to the hospital in Béthune. He found the ambulances full, and a fellow officer flagged down a passing car. The driver, seeing JBS's distinctive burly frame edge its way onto the seat next to him, recognised him immediately, despite the bandages and mud-encrusted kilt. 'Oh it's you,' said the driver. JBS looked up. It was the Prince of Wales. They had met in Oxford the year before. The two sped off to Béthune, and before he knew it, JBS was falling asleep in a hospital bed to the sound of wailing men and the boom of guns.

He believed that his experience that May resulted in 'a genuine case of shell-shock'.[33] The next step, after a brief spell of recuperation at home, was to volunteer to organise a bombing school—obviously. This he did, at Nigg in the north of Scotland, with characteristic panache:

> I began by lecturing on the anatomy of hand grenades, and made each pupil attach a detonator to a fuze with his teeth. Should the detonator explode in the mouth, I explained that the mouth would be considerably enlarged, though the victim might be so unfortunate as to survive with rather little face. Pupils who did not show alacrity when confronted with this and similar tests were returned to duty, as unlikely to become efficient instructors.[34]

JBS managed to get himself close to being court-martialled, but it was not for any antics with bombs and teeth; appalling drunkenness in Inverness, brought on by boredom, was the issue. After October 1916, JBS's war became more interesting. He found himself leading a band of Black Watch snipers in Mesopotamia, learning Hindustani, suffering an accidental bomb wound, and recuperating in India. In time, he was running a bombing school in Mhow. Jaundice intervened, and he was sent as an invalid to the Himalayas. In total, JBS spent a year and a half in India; it left a deep impression. It confirmed his liking for its peoples and culture, and undermined the vestiges of colonial arrogance that still clung to him from his mother's rhetoric. As his recent biographer, Samanth Subramanian, has written: 'he could only feel truly close to another human being when they could both presume to be equal to the other. In the relationship between colonizer and subject, that kind of equality was impossible.'[35] JBS had always been a rebel. India taught him to be a radical.

If JBS had been bored in Scotland in 1915, it was a feeling other soldiers, living on the brink of their own destruction, would have envied. JBS's cousin and fellow Black Watch officer, Pat Haldane, was one of them.

* * *

Like JBS, but without the academic glitter, Pat had graduated from Oxford in the summer of 1914. His plan was to return to Scotland to study for the law, join his father's firm, and become a Writer to the Signet—the third across three generations of the family. It was not to be. On the outbreak of war, he joined the Auchterarder company of the 6th Battalion (Territorial) of the Black Watch, as 2nd Lieutenant, receiving his commission on 12 August. The battalion remained in Scotland for eight months. From Queensferry, Pat wrote to Graeme: 'I wish we were all at home. There are a great many partridges and no one to shoot them.'[36] The Cloan visitors' book shows that Pat saw in the New Year with his family. Shortly after this he was promoted to Lieutenant. It must have felt like a terrible waiting game. Overshadowing all his activities was the knowledge that embarkation to France must eventually come. And come it did, in that eventful spring of 1915. On 16 April, the 6th Battalion left Scotland from Dundee and travelled down to Bedford to join the 2nd Highland Brigade of the Highland Division. There they would prepare for imminent entrainment for the Front.

Waving them off at Dundee station were Pat's parents, Willie and Edith, and his youngest brother, Archie, who was then thirteen years old. Archie hero-worshipped Pat and modelled himself on his eldest brother in every way. The two shared a passion for trout fishing, and for Archie, no adventure up into the hill burns surrounding Foswell was complete without Pat's company. In a diary composed in 1917—just long enough, perhaps, after the event for emotions to have settled—Edith captured the prosaic and intimate details of the scene at Dundee:

> We lunched together at a Hotel and did a little shopping and then Pat had to go back... to duty. We went to the station with him and saw him off. I can see him yet leaning out of the carriage window and waving his hand to us. It was the final goodbye between Pat and Archie. They never saw each other again.[37]

For Willie and Edith, there was one more chance to say farewell. Bedford was easily reached from London, where Willie was often called for work, and Pat arranged rooms for his parents on the eve of his departure for France. The party of three tried to enjoy themselves for the few brief hours they could now spend together; Pat even hired a canoe and took his mother up the Great Ouse. We can only imagine the sense of foreboding as mother and son glided along the river that afternoon, 27 April. Everything since the autumn before told them that the chances of a young officer returning from the Front were slim.

Edith's diary continues:

> We [Edith and Willie] had to go to the station to catch our train for London. We were a few minutes too soon and Pat and I walked up and down the platform together. It was impossible to realize that this was 'goodbye'[.] I remember so well the feeling of why why should I being [sic] going home in peace and safety and Pat be going to face the German guns. Pat spoke so bravely about it all and so humbly about trying to do his best... I shall never forget those few minutes—our last together. Then the train came up and we had to get in and with a kiss and a wave of his hand the party was over.[38]

By 2 May, Pat was in France. On the afternoon of 12 June, he returned to the trenches near Festubert. The next day, a Sunday, he was wounded during 'a specially violent bombardment in that bit of the line', and taken to a field hospital at Locon, 4 miles north of Béthune (where JBS had been the month before). Six hours later Pat died. He was buried the following day, 14 June, in the small British military cemetery in Locon.

Back in Perthshire, on the morning of Tuesday 15 June, Edith and her sister-in-law Elizabeth—oblivious to the news—were attending a Patriotic Society Meeting, where the subject was the war work women could do in agriculture and gardening. It was serious stuff, but there was the odd chuckle. One old gentleman stood up and told the gathering that women were all right so long as they were 'kept under glass'. A woman in a greenhouse was fine, he thought, but put her in a field and who knew what havoc she might wreak.

That evening, just after 6 pm, Willie returned from his work in Edinburgh, with two new letters from Pat stowed away in his briefcase. He was met at Auchterarder station by his daughter Elsie (home for a short break from her nursing activities in the capital), who drove him up to Cloan to meet his wife and sister. Entering the low hallway, Willie immediately showed the letters to Edith, who recalled that

> one was a very short note written on the Saturday, just before he went on duty with a bombing party and I think he wrote it really to say 'Goodbye'[.] I think he hardly expected to come back safely it was such a dangerous job. As a matter of fact it was his very last letter to us.[39]

Edith handed the letters to her daughter, who ran up the spiral stairs to show them to her grandmother. Willie, meanwhile, settled down in the conservatory to enjoy a large tea—a rigid requirement of any day for this particular Crown Agent of Scotland. Edith and Elizabeth (who was known to the Foswell Haldanes as Elsa) came and sat with him, chatting away as he munched through his scones. But the homely scene was about to be disrupted.

Edith remembered the exact details:

> [I]t would be about 6.40 P. M. when Fraser the butler came and said to Elsa that she was wanted on the telephone. She rose to go but asked as she did so who wanted her and Fraser replied 'Foswell'. 'Then it is not for me but for [Edith] Lady Haldane?' she said—but Fraser replied with marked emphasis 'No Miss it is you who are wanted.' Something told me then that it was bad news... She hurried to the telephone and I followed her and in another minute got the awful news that Pat had died of wounds. Willie came hurrying to the telephone too... I called Elsie down from Mrs Haldane's room and told her and then we telephoned to Foswell for Archie to

come down at once to Cloan... I started to meet him and met him just at the Rose Garden.[40]

Edith's heartbreak is evident in every line. An insight into Willie's grief is provided in a letter from Richard, then in London, to his mother two days later: 'For Willie the blow is staggering. He writes to me truly that Pat was more than a son.'[41] For Archie, who was suffering from whooping cough at the time, the loss was catastrophic. His own unpublished memoirs pick up the story from his mother's narrative:

> I can still recall the exact spot on the path beside the Cloan garden where I met my parents overcome by the news which had just reached them. That evening my father and Mother and I walked up the road past Bellshill [farm]. John Waddell who was at that time our gamekeeper was digging his garden. He had not heard the news. My father said to him 'Waddell, they have killed Mr Pat'. I shall never forget his deep and silent grief as he stood bare-headed in the garden.[42]

Archie went on to record that Pat's death 'certainly brought me face to face with the harshness and realities of life as nothing hitherto had done'.[43] It is quite likely that his later historical books, with their intense focus on the lost world of the past, and his fishing memoirs, with their exquisite descriptions of nature that carry the reader far from 'the harshness and realities of life', were born out of this tragic severance from his beloved brother. It was, for Archie, the end of innocence. He would spend the rest of his life trying to recapture what he'd lost.

* * *

The middle brother between Pat and Archie, Graeme Haldane, was then serving in the Aegean as a midshipman upon HMS *Doris*, a ship he described as 'uncomfortable, dirty, cockroach-infested'.[44] He was sixteen years old, and like his brothers, of diminutive build. He was also very shy, but set himself high standards both intellectually and morally. In November 1914, Willie spoke to Richard about the impression the war had already made on his son. Richard reported back to his mother: 'Willie is struck by Graeme's development, &

by his high point of view & deeply religious outlook.'⁴⁵ Perhaps that high point of view accounted for his early signs of gallantry. Just a day after his seventeenth birthday, as the *Doris* sailed up the Mediterranean coast, he and a fellow shipmate were sent to attack the Turkish trenches near Ashkelon. In an almost absurd spectacle, the two boys—for that is what they still were—were sent off 'armed with a revolver, cutlass and rifle' to conduct the raid.⁴⁶ They came under fire but responded in kind, and sent the Turks running from their trenches. By the following month, January 1915, his commanding officer was reporting back to headquarters on another landing party that Graeme had been involved in, this time with a mission to destroy a railway embankment and telegraph lines. Graeme's CO singled him out from the twenty-seven members of the landing party, reporting: 'Mr T. G. N. Haldane, Midshipman, exhibited perfect coolness under fire and was of great assistance to me.'⁴⁷

Graeme was going to need that coolness even more as the all-important spring of 1915 unfolded. It was then that the *Doris* was ordered to the Dardanelles. The cruiser's role was to take part in the naval bombardment of German and Turkish defences during the ill-fated attempt to land Allied troops on the Gallipoli peninsula and take control of the Turkish straits. Graeme simply called it a 'massacre'.⁴⁸

His memoirs, written towards the end of his life, focused less on the grand scheme of the Gallipoli campaign, and more on personal experiences and anxieties. His anxieties were well-founded:

> On one occasion, during a lull in firing, I had sent my gun-crew to get a much needed meal when we suddenly had again to open fire. I tried to reload the 6" gun myself but the shells weighed about 100lbs. and I was small. The shell slipped from my arms and fell [from] a considerable height onto its point. For a second or two I thought it bound to explode, but it didn't and with help I got it into the gun and fired.⁴⁹

This was not the only heart-stopping moment. For a time, Graeme was responsible for firing the forecastle 6-inch gun and setting the time fuses on the shrapnel shells. When Turkish soldiers coordinated a surprise attack on one of the landing parties, the fuse was set at a range that looked likely to threaten more than just the ambushing Turks; the shrapnel could pepper the very men whose lives Graeme was trying to save. But the shell was already in the gun and there was not enough time to take it out and reset the fuse. The landing party needed support fire then and there. Graeme had to make an instantaneous decision: should he fire and put at risk the lives of those on his own side or should he refrain and leave the ambushed men unassisted? He chose the former. The shell exploded exactly where he expected. To Graeme's immense relief the shrapnel landed almost entirely on Turkish troops. Only one Allied soldier was slightly wounded. 'For months afterwards this event remained a sort of nightmare to me', Graeme recalled.[50]

These events took place towards the end of April 1915. Graeme wouldn't have known that back home in Britain his parents were saying goodbye to Pat for the final time. When Willie's letter informing Graeme of Pat's death eventually arrived on board the *Doris* on 4 July, the ship's captain, Frank Larken, read it first and then broke the news to Graeme:

> For my close-knit family this was a terrible tragedy and its affect [sic] on me, far from home, would have been even more devastating than it was, had it not been for Captain Larken and the wonderful letters of comfort I received from home especially from my father, who perhaps suffered most of all.[51]

Judging by Graeme's letters back to his father, Willie was working hard to impress upon his second son the spirit of their religious forebears, encouraging Graeme to cast a positive light upon the loss. On 11 July, Graeme wrote:

> Like you I am really feeling now how close Pat is to us all and am much more cheerful than I felt before. It is so nice to feel that all that was best in Pat is living on with us and helping us to be less selfish and lead better and purer lives… I am sure I am more prepared than I was before for anything which may happen. After all it wouldn't be hard to die with Pat so close to one all the time and the thought of rejoining him, would it?[52]

Such an outlook may have helped Graeme the following year when he faced the prospect of the Battle of Jutland—what he later called the 'greatest-of-all naval action'—between the Royal Navy's

Grand Fleet and the Imperial German Navy's High Seas Fleet on 31 May and 1 June 1916.[53] Thankfully, Graeme managed to telephone home to say that he was safe before Willie and Edith had heard anything more than rumours of the devastation. Graeme was then serving on the new and very fast battleship HMS *Valiant*, stationed in Orkney's Scapa Flow (and, for a few days prior to battle, the Firth of Forth). Jutland had been unlike anything he had ever experienced. In old age he wrote, 'I still find it quite difficult to write about this horrifying experience, witnessed so fully from the Conning Tower of the *Valiant*.'[54] He could only watch on as one after the other the battle cruisers HMS *Queen Mary*, *Indefatigable*, and *Invincible* were struck and sank beneath the surface of the water, taking with them many of his teenage school friends from Dartmouth. When HMS *Defence* was hit, it was like some sick magic show: 'bright flashes spread along the whole length of the *Defence* and she disappeared in a vast column of black smoke. When that cleared there was just nothing to see.'[55] Graeme added: 'The long night after the main action, when we expected at any moment to meet German battleships at very close range, was perhaps worst of all, but the German fleet managed to avoid our Grand Fleet and got back to port never to come out again as a fighting force.'[56]

After his time on the HMS *Valiant*, Graeme was transferred to HMS *Tiger* and promoted to Sub Lieutenant. Starved of an education since 1914, his mind was restless and inquisitive, especially when it came to the complicated electrical equipment of the navy's bigger ships and their guns. Graeme already appeared to have something of his Uncle Johnnie's inventive streak, and he went about devising a new type of electrical range finder that used the whole length of the ship as the base. It was no childish fancy, and soon attracted the attention of the navy's top brass. Indeed, Admiral Sir David Beatty, Commander-in-Chief of the Grand Fleet since December 1916, even wrote him an official memorandum praising his work, as did the Admiralty, who remarked that 'Great credit is due to Sub Lieutenant Haldane for his ingenious proposals.'[57] Unfortunately, there were practical details that kept the proposals from becoming reality, and it was not long before radar methods superseded his idea. Nevertheless, Graeme had had a taste of what it was to think independently and gain recognition for it, and it left him wanting more.

* * *

Graeme's cousin Naomi Haldane, almost his exact contemporary, had always been hungry for recognition. The war would change forever her means of seeking it. The obliteration of her own generation left her bitter and angry at the generation before. As a result, Naomi took the inherent iconoclasm of the Haldanes of Cloan to new levels. The writing that made her name would be provocative, sometimes erotic, and often violent. She was determined to overcome the conventions and repressions of her elders and set new standards; not just for herself, but for her age.

When war began in 1914, the sixteen-year-old Naomi—for all her outspokenness and dissatisfaction at the lot of women—was still very much enmeshed in the social niceties and expectations of Edwardian ladyhood. She, like so many of her contemporaries, was excited by the prospect of war, and firm in the 'back-by-Christmas' mentality. She was being courted by one of the quieter members of her brother's Eton and Oxford set, Dick Mitchison, who was swift to find his way into the 2nd Dragoon Guards (Queen's Bays), a mounted regiment. Naomi's reaction was predictable: 'I was upset because I was "out of the fun", as I might have put it. Or my mother might have, at first.'[58] She was yet her mother's daughter. In the eyes of both, it was a glorious honour to fight for the Empire.

Naomi had embarked on a university course in the natural sciences at what later became St Anne's College, Oxford. She revelled in the dissection of animals, 'especially the elegant inside of a pithead frog', and in the botany sessions, where her father's old cut-throat razor did a beautiful job of cutting the plant materials.[59] If such implements would no longer be acceptable in a university laboratory, other elements of her student life as a young woman remain sadly familiar. 'I never got on well with physics and chemistry; one of the lecturers tried to kiss me, which I didn't like at all, yet probably giggled while dodging, which only led him on', she later recalled.[60]

Naomi was short and full of energy. Her strong brow, Haldane nose, and slightly drooping eyes reminiscent of her Aunt Bay's were

13. Elizabeth and Richard Haldane, possibly during the 1907 army manoeuvres at Cloan. Richard had been Secretary of State for War since December 1905. Elizabeth, meanwhile, assisted in the creation of the Territorial Force Nursing Service and the Voluntary Aid Detachment, both of which would distinguish themselves during the First World War.

14. The fields in front of Cloan were the home to 1,000 soldiers and 500 horses during the army manoeuvres of 1907.

15. Cloan, 1908, four years after it had been extended to the east to make space for the increasingly well-to-do Richard Haldane's suite of rooms.

16. The drawing room at Cloan, 1908. Unlike most country houses of the time, there are no card tables to be seen. In Richard Haldane's view, nothing had greater responsibility for debasing the intellectual life of the nation than the game of bridge.

17. Richard's new study at Cloan, 1908. The inscribed German words of Hegel are just discernible in the wood of the fireplace.

18. Frances Horner, c. 1910s. Richard kept this photograph in a folding travelling case and took it with him wherever he went.

19. Jack (JBS) and Naomi Haldane, 1911, when Jack was Captain of the School at Eton.

20. John Haldane (left) and his team during the Pikes Peak expedition, 1911. Before women were recognised in the world of science, John invited the pioneering Mabel Purefoy FitzGerald, who sits second from left, to join the team. Her high-altitude measurements were so accurate and extensive that they are still cited today. Her subsequent Royal Society paper gave the first description of oxygen sensing in the history of science.

21. Richard Haldane, by now Viscount Haldane of Cloan, as Lord Chancellor, 1912.

22. The cast of Naomi Haldane's play *Saunes Bairos* in the cloister of New College, Oxford, summer 1914. Naomi is seated sixth from the left in the second row, with her brother, JBS Haldane, two along on the right. Their mother, Kathleen, stands behind Naomi, with Lewis Gielgud to the left and Dick Mitchison, Naomi's future husband, beside him. The tall figure behind Kathleen is Aldous Huxley, with his brother Trevor on the right. Trevor's suicide just before the outbreak of war seemed to presage the coming doom.

23. Voluntary Aid Detachment nurses in the improvised hospital at Cloan, formerly Robert Haldane's chapel, 1911.

24. Belgian soldiers at Cloan, where they were sent to recuperate in 1914. Kaiser, Richard Haldane's St Bernard dog, was a favourite amongst the Belgian visitors.

25. and 26. JBS (left), otherwise known in the trenches as 'Bomber Haldane', 1914. Field Marshal Haig called him 'the bravest and dirtiest officer in my Army'. (Right) The 'Black Veil' respirator, created by John Haldane and Professor H. Brereton Baker, in 1915. This was the first gas mask to be used on the Front by British troops. It was just one of John's many ingenious inventions.

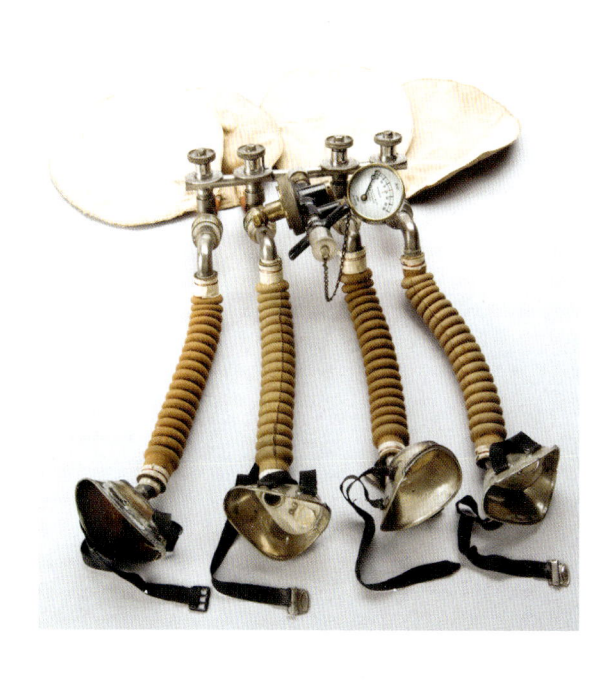

27. John Haldane is considered the father of oxygen therapy. The oxygen apparatus pictured here, developed by John during WWI, allowed four patients to receive oxygen at a pre-selected concentration at any one time, which was critical in the treatment of those suffering in the wake of a gas attack.

28. Pat Haldane, Willie's eldest child, 1915. He died of wounds received near Festubert in June 1915. His youngest brother, Archie (A. R. B. Haldane), was devoted to him, and spent the rest of his life seeking to reclaim the innocent youth he had shared with Pat as they fished amongst the streams in the hills behind Cloan and their home at Foswell.

29. A kneeling Sir William (Willie) Haldane and family, c. 1915. His youngest son, Archie, rests on his father's shoulder, with his older siblings Elsie and Graeme on the far side. Graeme saw action at Jutland and Gallipoli as an officer in the Royal Navy, while Elsie served as a nurse in France. Brodrick Chinnery-Haldane of Gleneagles stands in the middle of the photograph, with Willie's wife Lady (Edith) Haldane next to him.

30. Richard Haldane and Albert Einstein on the steps at Richard's London home, 28 Queen Anne's Gate, during Einstein's first visit to the country, 1921. After the dreadful war years, in which Richard was branded a traitor to his country for his German connections, it was a brave move to invite Einstein to Britain as his guest. Three years later, Richard was once again serving as Lord Chancellor, in the first ever Labour government.

31. Like father, like son. JBS Haldane in oxygen breathing equipment, possibly 1920s. JBS's investigations on behalf of the British Admiralty into underwater respiration during the Second World War mirrored his father's earlier efforts for the Admiralty before and after the First World War.

32. John Haldane (right) with son JBS (centre) and Australian physiologist Harold Whitridge Davies, in John's private laboratory at his Oxford home, Cherwell, 1920s. The sealed chamber for self-experiments with gas can be seen in the background. It was here that John and his team tested the first gas masks of the First World War. JBS joined them for further experiments near the Front.

33. Cherwell, the house built in 1907 by John and Kathleen Haldane, date unknown. Wolfson College, Oxford, now stands on the site.

34. Mary Haldane, 1924, the year before she died, aged 100. Her 'upper chamber' at Cloan was a hallowed spot for many a famous writer, politician and churchman.

35. The Haldane family, gathered on the occasion of Mary Haldane's 100th birthday, 1925. Front row, left to right: John, Richard, Bruce (the dog), Elizabeth and Willie. Middle row: JBS, Edith (Lady Haldane), Archie, Elsie, Graeme, Agnes Chinnery-Haldane, Brodrick Chinnery-Haldane and (James) Brodrick Chinnery-Haldane of Gleneagles. Back row: Guy Bullough, Marjorie Bullough (née Chinnery-Haldane), Gen. Sir Aylmer Haldane, Alex(ander) Chinnery-Haldane, Katherine Chinnery-Haldane.

36. Naomi and Dick Mitchison's three eldest boys, 1925. Left to right: Denny, Murdoch and Geoff. When Geoff died of spinal meningitis two years later, aged nine, it tore Naomi apart. Denny and Murdoch in adulthood were two of the most accomplished scientists of their time. They never spoke of their dead brother.

37. John, Elizabeth and Willie Haldane at the funeral of their brother Richard, 1928.

38. The Mitchison family, mid-1930s, at their London home, Rivercourt. Denny stands with his parents in the back row. Lois, Val, Av and Murdoch are seated left to right. By this stage, Naomi was renowned as one of the great historical novelists of her generation. By mutual consent, she and Dick had been pursuing other relationships outside of marriage for some years. This was of a piece with their left-wing politics, which was certainly radical but not quite as radical as that of JBS.

39. JBS Haldane in leather jacket, Spain, 1936. One fellow Republican fighter described him as 'A big shaggy bear enjoying a picnic'.

offset by her mischievous, even sensuous, mouth and impish blue eyes. She had a wicked sense of humour, prodigious memory, and searching intellect. Men found her a formidable force. The rivalry with her brother, JBS, only intensified her charisma. There were not many—were there any?—who could walk the 5 miles from Cherwell to Chilswell (to see Robert Bridges at home) in the company of JBS, and match him, across the entire one-and-a-half hours, in the recitation of poetry from memory. Their companion on that particular walk was stunned by their treasure-trove minds. They knew how to keep them well stocked. It had long been their habit, during their lengthy treks at Cloan, to 'cap' verse in each other's company: taking the last word of the line just recited and finding another line which included it. JBS was particularly strong on Milton and anything in Latin or Greek, but Naomi could outmatch him, eventually, on the modern poets.[61]

Certainly, if anyone was going to marry her, they would have to meet her brother's approval. Unlike some protective (possessive?) older brothers, JBS actually wanted his sister to marry one of his friends. That way he could be sure the groom was the right sort. In Dick Mitchison, Naomi did not find uncommonly good looks. She found a man to whom she could unburden herself, who met the disclosures of her strange inner world—with all its fear of inanimate objects, its strange rites and propitiations—not with alarm or judgement, but understanding. Dick didn't have the flair of some of the Eton set, but he had the brains and he had the money. His first in classics was taken for granted, as was the ease of life to which he was accustomed. His Mitchison forebears had worked up the social ladder from craftsmen in the early eighteenth century to 'gentlemen' by the mid-nineteenth. Through marriage into a slave-owning family, Dick's ancestor John Mitchison was able to purchase a silk warehouse and, in time, six manor houses. By the beginning of the twentieth century, the Mitchisons 'lived in great houses, entertained sumptuously, employed governesses and armies of servants, enjoyed the sport of kings and travelled widely'.[62] This was not the 'intellectual aristocracy' to which Naomi belonged, but it brought security and a set of social assumptions of which even her mother could approve.

And yet, when Dick proposed in the early days of the war, Naomi's response was not one born of deep thought or overwhelming passion: 'I am inclined to think now that I might have said yes to the first man (I beg your pardon: officer) in uniform who asked me to marry him in August 1914. It would have been "war work".'[63] Now she found herself face-to-face with the reality of a young man's physical expectations, a young man who had been almost entirely kept in the dark about the actual details of sex. Naomi, not yet seventeen, was nearly as clueless, and had little idea of how to react to Dick's advances:

> I couldn't explain that there were words and touches I didn't want. It had been somewhat of a shock to find that someone whom I had considered as another brother... had turned into something else. Perhaps if it had been possible to take the whole thing at a slower tempo I would have been able to respond. But there was a war on and nothing could wait.[64]

The wedding was the exception. That had to wait until February 1916. Now, Dick was off to France and, while he was away, Naomi hoped to extend her 'war work' beyond accepting the hand of an officer. At first, she remained in Oxford, where she completed her Red Cross first aid and home nursing exams (the first time she ever learnt how to make a bed), continued her studies in the sciences, staffed the university co-op shop with Aldous Huxley, and secretly attended meetings on guild socialism. These latter activities provided Naomi with not only her first taste of radical, left-wing politics, but also her first encounter with G. D. H. Cole, 'the dark and flashing Magdalen revolutionary'.[65] Douglas Cole, together with his wife Margaret, would come to play a pivotal role in the lives of Naomi and Dick.

Despite the new arousal of political excitement, Naomi was discontented. After much nagging, her parents allowed her to become a nurse with the Voluntary Aid Detachment, which her aunt had helped to establish. This brought a move to London and her first experience of a real hospital, St Thomas's. It was a shock to the system for the sheltered girl from Oxford. All of a sudden Naomi was cleaning lavatories, bed pans, floors, and lockers; polishing brasses and making beds. When told to prepare tea, it came as a surprise to her that it was made with boiling water. More alarming was the confrontation with exposed human bodies and the extremes of human pain. Her writing of the early 1920s, especially the suffering and the blood of her first novel, *The Conquered* (1923), was a way of externalising the experience, 'in order to get it out of my mind'.[66]

Her time as a VAD nurse lasted only a few months. Scarlet fever brought Naomi once more back to Oxford, where she would stay until settled in London with Dick after the war. Dick had returned, mind and limbs intact, in February 1916 for a week of leave from the Front, just enough time for a small registry wedding. During another brief spell of leave, they honeymooned in the west of Scotland, and resumed their bungled attempts at love-making. Naomi later thought that the physical side of their relationship never really recovered from these early disappointments, even after they'd discovered the tips and techniques of Marie Stopes's *Married Love* in 1918. But their tempers complemented each other, and there was an emotional bond of remarkable strength. It would need to be strong to withstand what the two would later throw at it.

The sadness of this early sexual failure only compounded the sadness, disillusionment, and grief that was mounting for Naomi, as, one after another, the letters home from friends on the Front dried up. One of those letters, which Naomi quotes in her memoirs, tells us something of the horror and loss that were experienced by the men of her generation, and, by extension, those who loved them. In 1915, Old Etonian Ned Grove wrote to Naomi:

> The regiment went into action about three weeks ago, leaving myself and four other officers in reserve… and when we arrived a week later we found that of the 360 men and ten officers 170 men and two officers remained. We found them in what was euphemistically called a rest camp which consisted of a large number of holes, some few hundred yards behind the trenches.[67]

Her whole life was subsequently overshadowed by the war. In her very final years, anger and grief still welled up when she spoke of it. It was not just her friends that she lost; the Dick that she had married was radically changed by the experience.

He had been hit by a French army car while riding a motorbike behind the lines and left for dead. He was found unconscious with a fractured skull. Hearing the news, Dick's father quickly pulled strings, enabling himself and Naomi to travel to France. Naomi was soon by Dick's bedside in the hospital at Le Tréport—a privilege which most wives were never afforded, but which she seems to have taken for granted. Dick was disconcertingly normal at first, but later visits revealed that all was not well with his brain. It would have been comic, had it not been real life:

> I reminded him of who I was, but he was politely incredulous, a little surprised at my wearing his wife's rings. 'Admit, nurse, that you have stolen them!' and utterly shocked—the picture of virtue!—at this strange nurse kissing him! 'My good girl, I've never met you before; I quite like you, but I wish you'd go away.'[68]

It was only a temporary loss of memory, but Dick took years to recover. Naomi even told a granddaughter that it was like having an entirely different person for a husband—more readily fatigued and prone to despondency; generally debilitated and often angry.[69] Some of these changes may have had other sources, too. In 1917, Dick's brother Willie was killed in action. His mother fell apart, turned to spiritualism, and her marriage to Dick's father was pushed near to breaking point.

No wonder Naomi felt she must do something in the face of war's madness. She started writing under pseudonyms for the *Oxford Times*, demanding some form of 'supernational authority', and before long, big names in Oxford intellectual life joined her campaign. She even served as the first secretary of the Oxford branch of the League of Nations Society, but this was short-lived. Naomi was pregnant. In February 1918, Geoffrey Mitchison was born, named after another lost friend. It had been a difficult birth, but new life implied hope. There would be a future beyond this war.

* * *

Naomi's aunt and uncle, Elizabeth and Richard, were busy trying to determine and influence that future. For the former Lord Chancellor, that meant committee work on a truly staggering scale, alongside his judicial work. He had been instrumental in getting governmental attention directed towards scientific and industrial research, and in July 1915—two months after his cabinet departure—Richard became a member of a Privy Council committee dedicated to its consideration. But he was at his best when in the chair, and this was clearly recognised. Between 1916 and 1918 Richard was appointed to, and oversaw, the Royal Commission on University Education in Wales; the subcommittees on education and coal conservation of Asquith's Reconstruction Committee; and, most importantly, the Machinery of Government Committee.

The report of the latter, issued in 1918, has been more responsible than anything else for the continued influence of the Haldane name in public life. It gave rise to the 'Haldane Principle', which ensures the freedom of government-funded research from political manipulation by leaving funding decisions to scientists, not politicians. It influences the activities of the British state in scientific research to this day. The farsightedness of the report, however, went well beyond the field of research. Its recommendations concerning the administration of justice, for instance, which included a politically independent supreme court, took over ninety years to materialise. Moreover, Richard could enthuse to Elizabeth about 'a splendid and full paragraph in the opening part of the Report, insisting on the Civil Service being thrown completely open to women & on them being fully employed even in the highest posts'.[70]

Interestingly, Elizabeth already felt the war was taking care of many of her pre-war battles. A diary entry of 9 November 1915 reads: 'In London last week for last meeting of Royal Commission [on the Civil Service]. Glad it is done with now. Discussions seem so futile; women's question e.g. has been settling itself.'[71] Her other activities can hardly have seemed futile. Well before the outbreak of war, she had transformed her father's long-neglected chapel at Cloan, opposite the stables, into a hospital ward for Voluntary Aid Detachment nurses. By late autumn 1914, it housed a small band of wounded Belgian soldiers. They enlivened the otherwise sombre atmosphere no end, and in April 1915 gave a Grand Belgium Concert in Auchterarder's Aytoun Hall to raise money for the Scottish Red Cross. Shortly afterwards, the authorities requested their transferral to London. Elizabeth's diary for 21 April records their departure: '7 Belgian convalescents left Cloan Hospital, very sad. Very emotional beings with great power of expression and affectionate ways... Kept assuring us they would return and left various bits of luggage.'[72] For her work, Elizabeth was mentioned in despatches and awarded Belgium's Queen Elisabeth Medal.

As with Richard, the list of Elizabeth's wartime contributions almost tires one to weariness—vice-chairman of the Advisory Council of the Territorial Force Nursing Association; first woman member of the Scottish War Savings Committee; deputy president of the Perthshire branch of the British Red Cross Society. Her diary records many visits to London—the train journey in these years could easily last fourteen hours—especially for Carnegie Trust meetings and the preparation of their 1917 report on the physical welfare of mothers and children.[73] When King George V founded the Order of the Companions of Honour in June 1917, to decorate those who had shown special service to the country in connection with the war, Elizabeth's name stood fourth in the inaugural list of seventeen. This was a major honour, and yet Elizabeth's diary shows a certain unease: 'Curious list and had bad press. New titles somehow do not seem serious, especially just now.'[74]

That diary, still unpublished, gives a remarkable glimpse into the characters who dominated the headlines during the war. We hear Churchill described, after a dinner of July 1915, as 'a curious faun-like being with his strange lisp; not British in character but with tremendous and overflowing vitality'.[75] After the disaster of the Dardanelles, the tone changes; he's now 'impetuous and overbearing'.[76] Asquith, in October 1915, is 'thinking of schemes and people, not how to beat the Germans'.[77] We hear that Lloyd George's modus operandi is 'to act first and then think'.[78] Edward Grey, visiting Cloan in 1917, confided in Elizabeth that he 'used to lie awake and listen to the tramp outside 28 Q. A. G. and think of the horrors that were coming on the world'.[79] Amidst the darkness, there is also humour. Almost inevitably, it's Churchill-related:

> [Richard] told us... [an] amusing tale of Winston when he had made speech in Park to King Edward's horror. Had to be turned back on way to Palace. R. says the King said in stentorian tone 'what was this?' R. said, 'Sir, things have altered and the ways of ministers change.' With this the King took up his chair and planted it down with his back to R. Later he turned and said his family was against the marriage [of Churchill's parents] and had it not been that he had interfered W. might never have been born, 'And... what is he now? A COWBOY!'[80]

THE MOTTO COMES TRUE

Laughter must have been much needed. Not just because it seemed 'as if all the lads we know will be killed or maimed'.[81] For almost the entire duration of the war, Richard remained the focus of a vile press campaign. In July 1915, the *Daily Express* even had a form in its pages, which readers were asked to fill out and post to the House of Lords, demanding that he never be readmitted to cabinet. The very next day, 2,600 forms arrived at Parliament. In August, Elizabeth writes: 'R. still getting anonymous letters... some hoping he might burn eternally and some so filthy he would not read me them.'[82] It's a good job that the censor was asked to keep quiet when, that very month, Richard was sent to Saint-Omer by Kitchener to talk over details of Territorial organisation with Sir John French—an eventful expedition which saw the British headquarters bombed by a German Taube, with Richard and the generals watching from the street as anti-aircraft guns fought off the attack. Richard also made time to pay his respects at Pat's grave at Locon, as he did again when he returned to France in October. On that occasion, he lunched with Douglas Haig and drove out to the British lines during the Battle of Loos. He reported back to his mother at Cloan: 'There was much activity. But no shells came near me, & it was too misty to see much.'[83] It seems as if Richard's life was in greater danger if he remained on British soil. In July 1916, Elizabeth noted: 'Many letters of all kinds; some threats of assassination etc.'[84] And a year after that: 'Whenever he speaks [in public, it] is followed by quantities of anonymous and abusive letters.'[85] It was not until January 1918 that Elizabeth could write: 'R. has had no disagreeable letters now but Morning Post etc. still attacks.'[86]

What made the whole thing so painfully ironic was that Richard's time as War Secretary had ensured that Britain was in a position to go to war on the Continent immediately in August 1914. The country was, of course, not prepared for the sheer scale and length of the conflict; it never could have been, given the political, social, and financial conditions that prevailed before the war. Within those conditions, however, what Richard achieved was just about as good a preparation as could have been hoped for. Most crucially, his reforms allowed Britain to send troops speedily to France's aid when war was declared, and in just a sufficient amount. Without the BEF's assistance, it is hard to see how Paris would not have fallen to the Germans in the autumn of 1914. The way would then have been open for the German occupation of the Channel ports and the invasion of Britain. When viewed in this light, it is understandable that Richard's successor at the War Office, Major General J. E. B. Seely, summed up his contribution to the war as follows: 'He saved the State.'[87] As we'll discover in the next chapter, the Commander-in-Chief of the BEF saw matters similarly.

* * *

The Haldanes of Cloan had certainly been made to feel the full force of their single-word motto, 'Suffer'. But what of Mary Haldane in all this, she who felt each member of the family's highs and lows with an unparalleled keenness, but was too old and frail to move from her bed at Cloan? The death of a grandson, or the vilification of her eldest child, or the chlorine-wracked lungs of her second son and his son, or the near total collapse of the old order that she had known for almost ninety years—did these cause her to succumb to the narrowness of perception and common resentments of old age? Not a bit of it. If anything, she grew in stature. As Richard said of her, 'her outlook and mental grasp were widening to the end steadily';[88] 'Of insularity she had not a trace.'[89] This was rooted in her profound faith in God. That she came through the war ennobled, not embittered, is unsurprising when we read the words she wrote to the Archbishop of York, Cosmo Lang, in the midst of those years of slaughter:

> In my quiet resting-place I can in my feebleness take hold of the Almighty power of our Father in Heaven to strengthen the arms, and I may add the brains of those who are bearing in one way or another the strain and weight of the awful struggle in which we are engaged. These are ever present with me, and night and day it seems as if we never could yet fix our thoughts on anything else in the world. But yet I feel unshaken in my confidence that the Lord Himself will be exalted and destroy the power of wickedness on the earth.[90]

9

CHANGING OF THE GUARD

1918–1930

'Peace! London to-day is a pandemonium of noise and revelry, soldiers, and flappers being most in evidence. Multitudes are making all the row they can, and in spite of depressing fog and steady rain, discords of sound and struggling, rushing beings and vehicles fill the streets.'[1] So begins Beatrice Webb's diary entry for 11 November 1918. That afternoon, amidst the rejoicing crowds, and protected by the black arcs of their umbrellas, members of the Houses of Parliament made their way to St Margaret's, Westminster, for a service of thanksgiving. The Archbishop of Canterbury presided, opening with the words of the hundredth psalm: 'Make a joyful noise unto the Lord, all ye lands.'

The next day, Richard Haldane reported back to his mother at Cloan: 'I attended the thanksgiving service yesterday afternoon. The Archbishop of York took me aside & said the minds of those who knew were turned to myself, who had saved the nation by years of forethought.' After all the calumnies against his name, it was a much-appreciated gesture. Things were to get even better that day for Richard: 'In the evening I dined to meet some of the American peace commission. They were equally enthusiastic & told me that the American Govt. had nearly asked me to be sent out to them to guide them in fashioning their Army. However there was not time.'[2]

* * *

Nor was there much time for Richard to be joyful. On 1 December, his dearest friend, 'the Professor', Peter Hume Brown, died suddenly. Richard wrote to Elizabeth: 'for both of us it was a friendship as perfect as it was intimate. He will haunt the rooms and the walks for us at Cloan. I cannot realise that I shall not see him again… I find it difficult to speak.'[3] It now fell to Richard to prepare for publication, and write the missing chapter of, Hume Brown's two-volume *Life of Goethe*. The biography appeared in 1920. One review called it 'the most dignified monument so far erected to Goethe in the English speaking world'.[4] It was typical of Richard to connect himself so willingly to the publication of a work on a German genius within two years of the war's end.

But signs started to appear suggesting that he did not need to fear adverse reactions from the public. On 19 December, Richard was out for a walk in central London and turned onto St James's Street, only to find himself caught up in something like 'a triumphal procession with the people'.[5] Unknown faces approached him from all directions, extending their hands or saluting in recognition of his work before the war. He had Field Marshal Haig, Commander-in-Chief of the BEF, largely to thank. In the summer before the armistice, Churchill confided in Richard that 'Haig is full of the Army Reform which [you] made, & says that he tells everyone that it saved England.'[6] Ten days after peace was declared (at which point Haig was a national hero and not yet the villain he would become in the public imagination), Haldane could tell his mother proudly:

> I have a remarkable letter from Sir Douglas Haig… He writes to thank me in the name of the Army for the great reforms of 1906–12. These he enumerates and says that to them he & the armies of today owe their victory, & he looks forward to the British Empire realising this.[7]

Haig sent a copy of the letter to the King, and in his public speeches he praised his former chief at the War Office as one to whom all should be grateful. Before long, others were joining in the chorus. Churchill, at a great gathering of Territorials, made sure that Richard was 'publicly thanked for the creation of the force'; Asquith proclaimed 'the genius of Lord Haldane' to his constituents in Fife; Major-General Sir Francis Bingham impressed upon the benchers at Lincoln's Inn that Richard 'not only made the old Army but mobilised it with much swiftness & no one had believed it would happen'; even Colonel House, President Wilson's spokesman in Europe, told those he met—with the humility of one representing the nation that ensured the final Allied victory—that the American government 'considered that the saving of the War' was due to Richard.[8]

The icing on the cake was the personal visit that Haig insisted on making, directly after leading the Victory March through London on 19 July 1919, to 28 Queen Anne's Gate, where Richard sat alone in his study. Haig was determined—despite suffering from a heavy cold and being exhausted from what was the greatest military procession in front of the largest crowds that London had ever seen—to tell Richard that 'he should have been present to share the cheers and gratitude of the people... for the work he had done for the Army which had never been properly recognised or even partially recognised'.[9] In December that year, the Field Marshal's sentiments were expressed succinctly in the inscription he penned within the copy of his *Despatches* which he gifted to Richard. It read:

> To Viscount Haldane of Cloan—the greatest Secretary of State for War England has ever had. In grateful remembrance of his successful efforts in organising the Military Forces for a War on the Continent, notwithstanding much opposition from the Army Council and the half-hearted support of his Parliamentary friends.[10]

When Richard then published *Before the War*, an account of his actions prior to 1914, on 15 January 1920, a lunch was given in his honour, at which both Asquith and Haig proposed his health. The former prime minister told the guests that Richard's name should be written 'in letters of gold', and the Commander-in-Chief expanded enthusiastically upon the words of his inscription. The door towards a new political career was edging open.

Sir Ernest Cassel was certainly in no doubt about his integrity. In 1918, he asked Richard to take charge of a newly formed committee of trustees, under the title of the Cassel Trust, to distribute £500,000 (£30 million in today's money) towards educational ventures, especially those that supported adult education, the higher education of women, and the teaching of commerce at university level. Few tasks could have given Richard greater delight, but in the past he would have looked to Germany for guidance on such matters. As the post-war reparation discussions got under way, he felt less assured.

Richard was known for his delicate perceptiveness when it came to how future events might pan out—think of his 1915 cabinet memorandum on the League of Nations. Nothing, however, quite matches his prediction to Frances Horner, in a letter of April 1919, concerning the consequences of (what would become) the Treaty of Versailles:

> From Paris I hear privately bad accounts. The French are backing the Poles. They want to cripple Germany permanently. There would be something to be said for it were it not that 45 million people cannot cripple 70 million. But they can lay the seeds of war in the future. I am apprehensive of what is likely to happen twenty years hereafter.[11]

Elizabeth Haldane's diary entry for the previous month fills out the context, and takes us to the heart of the international, national, and local situation:

> The developments of the last months are difficult to follow. Germany is in a welter… we are disputing as to feeding her and helping to bring defeat to Bolshevism thereby or not. The poor must be starving[,] infants die and profiteers flourish. The blockade not yet raised. Then our country has been in turmoil too over labour disputes[,] risings of troops dissatisfied with rate of demobilization etc. But here [Cloan] all is peaceful and the boys are coming back by driblets. It is good to see them on the street. It is difficult to get labour because of the unemployment benefit and women won't go to service… Wages are up immensely but so is the cost of living… The Coal Commission is sitting and we hope to escape a coal strike… Meantime the country has not dismantled its war expenditure and is borrowing still—when will it end?[12]

While Richard thought through the ways he might help shape matters for the better across the wide canvas of international politics, Elizabeth's response was characteristically local. She simply got on with the immediate tasks that confronted her in Auchterarder—though not without that domineering element to which she was susceptible: 'We are busy making up a Roll of Honour—serving and killed in the parish, I am Ch.[air] of the Committee. On Foswell and Cloan 12 have served and 3 have been killed. Pensions work take up a good deal of time. We have sub-Committee here (I am Chair.).'[13]

More and more, Elizabeth was justifying the title by which locals sometimes referred to her: 'The Queen of Perthshire'. In 1919 she was elected to the county's education authority, and served upon it for three years. The same year saw the passing of the Sex Disqualification (Removal) Act, and this paved the way for Elizabeth's appointment the following year as the first female Justice of the Peace in Scotland. To mark the occasion, the 1920 edition of the *Justices' Handbook* was dedicated to her name. The demands of her new duties were negligible—she was mainly concerned with licensing tradesmen, alehouses, and proprietors of one form or another within Perthshire—but the title carried prestige and brought Elizabeth ever further out from under her brothers' shadows.[14]

Yet she continued to long for their presence at Cloan. She craved their intellectual stimulus, something which her aged mother, despite her intelligence and wisdom, could not quite provide. When the family gathered together for the New Year celebrations of 1920—which culminated, as they did every year, in a circle around Mary's bed, where a male member of the family would address (lecture?) the Almighty about the doings in the past year of each of those present, and call down a blessing upon them for the twelve months ahead—the atmosphere was typically intense. Elizabeth wrote in her diary:

> John was here very busy with his book... and Jack and Graeme full of discussions about theory of Relativity. Graeme gave an excellent lecture in A.[uchterarder] on 'Science and Warfare' at which his Uncle [Richard] presided and spoke of early days of flying... R. is much interested in a book by a Miss Follett on Group System as a form of real democracy.[15]

This was Elizabeth's first reference to Mary Parker Follett, a pioneer in the field of organisational theory, the forerunner of today's management consultancy industry. Judging by her most readily found photograph, she looked every bit the old-world schoolmistress of the harsher variety—a carpet of plaited hair topped her long, sad face, while her rimless spectacles encircled sagging, disappointed eyes, set disarmingly close to each other. Her ideas were anything but sagging or sad. They were alight with optimism and hope for a society that might flourish through community cooperation. Richard was especially drawn to her conception of local group work as the foundation upon which the state could be built, and he wrote the foreword to the British edition of her book, *The New State*, in 1920. Her thinking was deeply in sympathy with his own judgements on the Judicial Committee of the Privy Council, upon which he still sat, as he sought to disperse ever more power away from central towards local governments.

From Follett's side, for all that she appreciated Richard's championing of her ideas, the personal connection with Elizabeth was equally important. When she visited Cloan in August 1926—where the 'conversation was unbrokenly of the highest brow order'—the two quickly established a bond that had, at least for Follett, a strong romantic edge.[16] In the Christmas of that year, remembering the loss of her closest female friend, Isobel Briggs, with whom she had lived, Follett wrote to Elizabeth from America:

> These days which I am passing through now are the hardest I have ever known, for these weeks a year ago were the last in which I had my beloved friend, and the loneliness is sharp and poignantly present. I miss her in two ways just because she was she, but also because she was a rare and noble soul, high-minded and single-minded to a degree which few people attain. What I wanted to say was that I feel a little less bereft at having that gone out of the world because in August I found these qualities in someone else. Please don't mind me saying this. We are so far apart and may never meet again so that it may never get expressed in any other way than in these words. I shall just carry the knowledge tucked away to warm me when life seems too sad.[17]

It remains on the level of speculation whether the feelings were mutual. It would not be altogether surprising to discover that Elizabeth was more physically attracted to women (especially high-achieving women) than to men. She certainly never showed a will to marry, though that may have been because she felt it her fate to dedicate her personal life to her mother and to Richard (she went as Richard's plus-one to the many gatherings in London that he was obliged to attend, and she ran his London household, alongside Cloan). And like Follett, though without the co-habitation, Elizabeth had her own fiercely loyal friendships with other single women. None of this, however, was unusual for the period.

What *was* unusual was the behaviour of the next generation of Haldanes.

* * *

By the summer of 1922, the twenty-four-year-old Naomi was already a mother to three boys. Following the arrival of Geoff in 1918, Denis (Denny) Anthony Mitchison was born on 6 September 1919 and John Murdoch Mitchison (known as Murdoch or Murdo) appeared on 11 June 1922. Despite the commitments of motherhood (considerably offset, it must be said, by a host of nannies and servants), Naomi was also well underway with her first novel, *The Conquered*—a book that attempted to illuminate contemporary troubles over British imperialist rule in Ireland through an exploration of power relations and conflicting loyalties during the time of Caesar's invasion of Gaul. Revealingly, the novel also shines light, in the siblings Fiommar and Meromic, on the complex feelings that Naomi harboured for her own brother, JBS, to whom she dedicated the book.

In later autobiographical writings, Naomi claimed that her novels were always 'tangled together' with her private life, especially her 'love relationships'.[18] The fact that the brother and sister idyll at the opening of *The Conquered* comes under threat from the Roman invasion, and that Fiommar, the sister, kills herself early in the story, surely tells us something. But what? Perhaps it's a reflection of the abrupt end to Naomi's experience and dreams of living like a boy, when the onset of puberty brought her immediate removal from the Dragon School, severing her forever from the masculine world of her brother. Perhaps it mirrored the end of innocence that was the onset of war, or the change that the conflict had wrought on JBS and its effect on his relationship with Naomi. A manuscript of Naomi's in the National Library of Scotland records that 'One or twice he talked to me about pain and terror and love. I had begun to write *The Conquered* and began the transmutation of present into past, fears and feelings into writing.'[19] Playing into it all was the fact that JBS wanted children very badly, and he looked on with jealousy as Naomi birthed child after child. Naomi later claimed that this caused a rift between them. But perhaps the narrative of *The Conquered* also tells us of a form of love that could never have been between Naomi and JBS.

Naomi's biographer, Jenni Calder, called JBS 'in some respects her most lasting love', and Naomi towards the end of her life confided in Calder, 'We were far too involved with one another for either to be totally themselves [*sic*] without the other.'[20] That being the case, what are we to make of the following passage from her memoir, *You May Well Ask*? It describes a moment shared between the two sometime in 1922, while JBS was a young Fellow of New College, Oxford, and the same year that Naomi gave birth to Murdoch:

> While I was writing *The Conquered* and *When the Bough Breaks* [a collection of short stories published in 1924] I was passionately eager to see the actual places, Gergovia and Alesia, to touch the stones, to feel the same sun and wind. So my brother and I went walking in the Auvergne… It was very hot. On those mountains covered with blaeberries three times the size and juiciness of Perthshire ones, I took off my thick tweed skirt and walked in black silk knickers… Once we came down hungry to a village, ate well, washed it down with red wine and staggered into an old quarry full of wildflowers to sleep it off. And turned dizzily towards one another. And suddenly Jack was shocked to his respectable Haldane soul. I wasn't. But that was all. The next year he had gone to Cambridge.[21]

Naomi is at her most teasing and intriguing in this passage. The whole thing is fantastically erotically charged. The appeal to the senses is unmistakable: the touching of the stones, the feel of sun and wind, the heat, the berries large and juicy. The reference to her state of undress and black silk knickers seems deliberately placed such that we go into the closing scene of the paragraph—somewhat against our will—with sex on the mind. We can almost see her impish grin as she then purposefully withholds the actual details of what passed between her and her brother. We cannot know if it became physical or, if it did, how far the physicality went, though the setting, with its wildflowers and hiddenness, seems intentionally to evoke a lover's bower. The scene is then subverted by humour and a childish one-upmanship—JBS would have been horrified to find himself described as 'respectable', and would have laughed in outrage at Naomi's claim to be the less susceptible to moral shock. The closing of the paragraph, with its swift attempt to brush the whole thing off, fails entirely in its purpose—a failure Naomi may well have intended. The final sentence is anything but explanatory. In fact, it seems to imply that, had it not been for JBS's departure to Cambridge, their sexual involvement would have continued. Does that mean there were more intimate encounters before he left for his new post? Naomi clearly delights in frustrating her readers.

Naomi once said that she was 'in the hands' of the books she was writing.[22] Flickering in the background of the early pages of *The Conquered* is a sense of almost illicit sibling closeness. ('Quickly she stooped and pulled the blanket right off him; on arms and body the thick golden down shone in the sunlight. He sat up, clasping one bare knee; Fiommar slid her hand down back and side, admiring the faint ripple of movement that followed her under the smooth skin.')[23] Was the attempt to experience the world of her book, as she sought to do through her holiday, pushed to new extremes in her dizzy moment with her brother? Perhaps it was another manifestation of the Haldane passion for self-experimentation. But Naomi also once said, 'I know I remember things that never happened.'[24] One can't help wondering if the moment in the quarry was one such event, with Naomi projecting a possible scene for her novel onto real life. But if her relations with JBS did become sexual, it would be of a piece with Naomi's post-war outlook and politics. She, like so many of her generation, was very definitely on a campaign to tear up the old rule book and rewrite the rules afresh.

The Conquered met with glowing reviews when it appeared in 1923. Naomi was admired for her capacity to recreate the world of the first century BC in a way that was both authentic and accessible—though later she would say, 'there's a lot that's badly wrong with it historically'.[25] Her language was the language of the present, but it rarely felt out of keeping with the past. She was assured, wrote H. C. Harwood in *Outlook*, 'of an especial position among modern novelists'.[26] E. M. Forster, in what was the start of a close friendship, wrote to her in appreciation, describing the book as 'moving and beautiful'.[27] Soon it was on the reading lists for Oxbridge classicists. A school edition was produced in 1926. One young school student wrote to her anonymously in gratitude—and in verse!—for bringing the classical period alive. He or she particularly liked the beatings. It was 'a real bedside book'.[28]

By writing historical fiction, Naomi was able to provide a gloss of respectability to the violence and simmering sexuality. As she inimitably put it, 'All forms of sexual loving become acceptable if the lovers wear togas or wolfskins.'[29] Her remaining stand-out publications of the 1920s—*When the Bough Breaks, Cloud Cuckoo Land, Black Sparta,* and *Barbarian Stories*—continued to prick the bubbles of convention under a historical veil. The voice of Phoebe, for instance, in a story from *When the Bough Breaks*, bursts with contemporary rage at the treatment of women. It is also the voice of a twelve-year-old Naomi, banished forever from an all-boys' world:

> It's so hard being a girl! Here I am, just the same as a man really, and no worse than my brother anyway... But just because of two or three silly little differences I have to be treated as if I was an animal, ordered about, not allowed to decide anything for myself! I'm shut up, I'm watched. I have to do what men tell me—nothing's my own, money or husband or religion—I have to take what they give me and say thankyou.[30]

Naomi, as an adult, was determined to have a different fate.

* * *

The timing was opportune to try a new pattern of living. This was partly a result of the war. As Samuel Hynes wrote of the 'Auden generation', to which Naomi in many ways belonged, 'they were like survivors of some primal disaster, cut off from the traditional supports of the past, and so dependent upon themselves for such meanings as their lives might acquire'.[31] This fuelled a willingness to experiment, as did the political events of the 1920s. After the Russian Revolutions of 1917 and the formation of the Communist International (Comintern) in 1919, the British establishment was living in fear of a Marxist world revolution. When the Communist Party of Great Britain (CPGB) formed in 1920, it took on the role of national agitator, stoking the fires of anger that were constantly flaring up over the appalling unemployment levels and falling wage rates of the time. The year 1921 saw the establishment of the National Unemployed Workers' (Committee) Movement (NUWM) and the unsuccessful coal miners' strike against wage reductions. The following year, Sir Eric Geddes released his reports on national expenditure, heralding spending cuts of devastating proportions. The situation worsened when Churchill restored the Gold Standard in 1925, resulting in the cost of British goods to foreign buyers shooting up by 10 per cent. The Wall Street Crash of 1929 brought matters to a resounding crescendo.

With the dark side of capitalism so insistently failing society, it's no wonder that socialism, to the intelligentsia and to many workers, looked as if it might bring order out of chaos. It is in this context that the first Labour government, under Ramsay MacDonald, appeared in 1924. Naomi found herself deeply sympathetic to Labour's opposition to a society governed by the principle of ownership, and enthused over its desire to grant equal rights to the dispossessed. She was not the only member of the Haldane family to feel this way.

Things seemed to be going in the right direction for women at least, but progress was hardly speedy, and the signs of resistance were everywhere. It was not until the Equal Franchise Act of 1928 that all women over twenty-one could vote, and, across the decade, the maximum number of female Members of Parliament at any one time was eight. Marie Stopes, who'd brought hope to Naomi and Dick's fledgling sex life, was busy advancing the cause of birth control amongst working-class women, especially through clinics in the East End of London. But it is telling that, in 1923, the film version of her book, *Married Love*, was refused a certificate from the Board of Film Censors. A certificate was only granted once all reference to birth control was removed and its central message was eliminated.

Predictably, Naomi ranged herself on Stopes's side—though, unlike Stopes, she supported the legalisation of abortion. Naomi and her friend Margery Spring Rice—who has been called a 'pioneer of women's health'—even opened their houses for illegal procedures to take place.[32] Both women, as well as Dick, were on the committee of the Stopes-inspired North Kensington Birth Control Clinic, opened in 1924. Naomi would occasionally help out on the premises. It was her first encounter with the plight of working-class women, bewildered and afraid at the many children they were not only rearing, but losing in infancy. One forty-two-year-old woman had lost six of her twelve children. It was an experience that drove Naomi—again with Margery and Dick—to join the Birth Control Research Committee in 1927. In pursuit of its mission to investigate new contraceptive methods, Naomi, in true Haldane style, put herself forward as a test subject.

Her mature views on the issue, which branch out into the larger question of what sort of life a woman ought to be able to live, receive thoughtful expression in her long article of 1930, 'Comments on Birth Control'. Here Naomi offers a profound insight into not only her personal desires, but also her unwillingness to overlook the practical difficulties that lay in the way of their fulfilment. Naomi took the old Haldane ability to combine idealism and realism and pressed it into the service of new ideas:

> Intelligent and truly feminist women want two things: they want to live as women, to have masses of children by the men they love and leisure to be tender and aware of both lovers and children; and they want to do their own work, whatever it might be… They insist—as I think they should—on having both worlds, not specializing like bees or machines: but they must give up something of both, not necessarily all the time, but sometimes the work and sometimes the full sex life. It is very unfortunate, but there seems to be no way out of it.[33]

Naomi was certainly taking steps towards her ideal. She and Dick—both sexually disappointed, and now advancing a politics that rejected ownership—agreed, in 1925, to an open marriage. The arrangement was only made possible by the fact that both of them had a willing someone in mind. In Dick's case, it was Margery Spring Rice. In Naomi's, it was Theodore Wade-Gery, or 'Widg', an Oxford classical scholar in his thirties, who had been helping deepen her understanding of the ancient Greek world about which she was then writing. Unlike Margery, Widg was unmarried. Naomi was not shy of advertising the fact that she had looked beyond her husband for sexual fulfilment. When *Cloud Cuckoo Land* appeared in

1925, it was dedicated 'To my lover'. (She completed the manuscript in an all-night writing session while at Cloan, and ran out to meet the dawn with the typescript beneath her arm: 'In one of the high fields among bracken and wild pansies I met the sun, I plunged into light, I showed it my finished book.')[34] The relationship with Widg brought its liberating elements, but inevitably it brought pain too. One of the conditions upon which they'd agreed before sleeping with each other was that each was free to fall in love with other people; jealousy was not allowed. Not for the last time, Naomi's designs for freedom suffered from naivety. By 1928, Widg was married to someone else, and his relationship with Naomi never recovered. Even in her nineties, Naomi could say: 'It is still swords sticking into me.'[35]

Open marriages were not unheard of amongst left-wing intellectuals of the interwar period, and Naomi and Dick had a dominant place within that band of society. The guest lists for their extravagant Boat Race parties at their enormous London home, Rivercourt, spoke volumes. Jenni Calder names the following figures as typical attendees: Douglas and Margaret Cole (Margaret and Dick later began sleeping with each other, and Douglas and Naomi were entangled for a while), John and Celia Strachey, E. M. Forster, W. H. Auden (whose poetic career Naomi helped to launch, and who briefly tutored Murdoch in Latin), Julian Huxley, Krishna Menon, Miss Nehru (Mrs Gandhi), Barbara Betts (Barbara Castle), and J. D. Bernal.[36] It was not lost on Naomi that her life was a cacophony of contradictions. The servants, the vast house with loggia and squash court, the luxurious holidays on the Continent, and, later, the children at public school—none of this sat easily with the Mitchisons' socialist principles. The refreshing thing was that Naomi recognised the hypocrisy, and knew that a certain amount of it was predictable in anyone who sought to do things differently.

* * *

Naomi's move to the Left was not exactly subtle. Her Uncle Richard drifted more gently in that direction, though he ended up one of Labour's most prominent voices. Haig's outspokenness had opened a route for him back to public life. Being Richard, he would have been influential had he remained behind the scenes, and in fact the 1920s rivalled any previous decade in terms of his backstage activities on behalf of the public good. Across these years, he had a hand in founding three major institutions: the Royal Institute of International Affairs (Chatham House), the British Institute of Adult Education (now the Learning and Work Institute), and the National Institute of Industrial Psychology. He was the first president of the Institute of Public Administration and the chairman of the Expert Committee appointed to unite the Church of Scotland and the United Free Church of Scotland. Alongside all of this, he published three tomes of philosophy. When *The Reign of Relativity* appeared in 1921, one of the most highly regarded idealist philosophers of the time, Bernard Bosanquet, thought it would 'produce a considerable effect on the course of philosophy in Europe'.[37]

It didn't. What did create genuine waves were the scientific ideas upon which Richard's philosophy was based. To make these better known in his own country, Richard initiated and hosted Einstein's first visit to Great Britain in June 1921. Other books have already told how Einstein and his wife, on their arrival, were intimidated at the sight of Richard's footman and butler; how statesman and scientist went together to lay a wreath at Isaac Newton's tomb; and how Richard then introduced his guest at a public lecture with the words, 'You are in the presence of the Newton of the twentieth century'—but a dig around Richard's archival papers yields other, more personal nuggets.[38] On 13 June, with Einstein still under his roof at Queen Anne's Gate, Richard wrote to his mother: 'Einstein has had [a photograph] done of myself to hang in his study at Berlin. He said to his wife "I loved Haldane from the first".'[39] Richard's words about Einstein, despite his enormous admiration, were not always so gracious: 'I have had framed the rather ugly picture Einstein gave me of himself, & have put it by the photograph... of the Great Dog [Kaiser, the St Bernard] in the drawing room. But the Great Dog looks as if he knew more about Relativity than Einstein, & generally eclipses him.'[40]

Einstein's first visit to Britain did much to improve Anglo-German relations, and in the years following, through their continued correspondence, Richard would channel back to the high places of British politics Einstein's ideas on further improvements.

CHANGING OF THE GUARD

But Richard was reluctant to come into the limelight, even as the governmental situation worsened. The Liberals were in the throes of their 'strange death'; Baldwin's Conservative administration, by late 1923, had fallen apart over their leader's stance on protectionism; and Ramsay MacDonald was in desperate need of an old political hand if he was to make his own potential minority government a viable option, as most candidates for a Labour cabinet would be novices. That old political hand turned out to be Richard. Not that he was a card-carrying Labour supporter; he remained aloof about certain aspects of their policy and was critical of their leaders. 'Labour has captured the heights from the Liberals', he would tell his nephew Graeme, 'and it is in the Labour movement that the real idealism is now to be found—if only their leaders were not so stupid!'[41] But Labour was the only party placing educational reform at the heart of its agenda, and there was no surer way to win Richard's admiration.

He didn't hide that admiration. So, by the time that a MacDonald government became likely, the world at Westminster had put his name down for office. The Conservatives were particularly anxious to have his experience on the Labour front bench. As Richard told Elizabeth, 'They lay great stress on my joining otherwise, they think, chaos.'[42] On 12 December 1923, he wrote to Mary:

> When I went into the H[ouse] of Lords yesterday the Lord Chancellor [Lord Cave] told me grandly that it was my duty to try and save the State by taking office, & all the officials I found expecting me to resume the Chancellorship. Later on Ramsay MacDonald telephoned urgently for a meeting. In the evening he offered me anything I chose, if I would help him; the Leadership at the House of Lords, the Chancellorship, Defence, Education, & the carrying out of my plans... it may be my duty to advise & help him, & be prominent in the Lords. But I shall remain independent. The Press is in full cry & Williams [the butler] is keeping them off.[43]

He was not independent for long. When MacDonald visited Cloan early in the New Year, he was talking 'as though he had begun to lean on' Richard.[44] What swayed Richard ultimately was the fact that MacDonald was willing to let him resume the Lord Chancellorship under the conditions of his 1918 Machinery of

Government report, which would leave him free of his daily judicial duties, and allow him, as he told Edmund Gosse, to devote 'my time to supervision of the whole machine along with R. M.'.[45] Not only would he lead the party in the House of Lords, but Richard would also chair the Committee of Imperial Defence, giving him oversight of his old love, the defence services. These were not the emphases of a dyed-in-the-wool socialist, but Richard did at least nod in this direction by offering to take only £6,000 from the Lord Chancellor's £10,000 salary. The remaining £4,000 went directly back to the Treasury.

No doubt Richard had grand ideals, but they would need time to bear fruit. Time was not on MacDonald's side. Having formed his government on 22 January 1924, he was back in Opposition by 4 November, unable to stem the tide of public distrust over Labour's possible links with the Bolsheviks (a distrust exacerbated, interestingly, by Richard's half-nephew, Sir George Makgill).[46] Richard wrote back to Cloan: 'Yesterday we resigned & I am in partial repose. I am very glad that I joined the Labour Govt. I have got masses of things through by not advertising them, so as to bring on attacks. But they are done and slowly they will come to light.'[47] Getting John Wheatley's Housing Bill through the Lords was one such achievement. This reversed the Chamberlain Act of the previous year, and reintroduced subsidies for council housing at a higher level than the Housing Act of 1919.

Richard also had a constant hand in the plans that were drawn up under Labour for the generation and supply of electricity across the entirety of the country, which Stanley Baldwin's Conservative government subsequently enshrined in the Electricity (Supply) Act of 1926. It was through Richard's connections with the great mind behind the Act, Charles Merz, that Graeme Haldane's career as an electrical engineer was launched. Richard was willing to pull strings for almost anyone who approached him with a just cause, but he had a special admiration for this particular nephew. In 1925, on the fiftieth anniversary of his brother's death, he told his mother: 'There is something in Graeme that reminds me much of Geordie—an integrity & simplicity of character.'[48] These characteristics and Graeme's quick, practical intelligence would speed him up the ladder with the consulting engineering firm Merz & McLellan. With them, Graeme would become deeply involved in the establishment of the National Grid: a resounding fulfilment of a recommendation for a 'national system of electric power supply' first laid out publicly by the wartime Coal Conservation Committee, of which his Uncle Richard had been chairman.[49]

* * *

After he'd left the navy at the end of the war, Graeme went up to Trinity College, Cambridge, in 1919, where he read physics and came into regular contact with some of the most renowned scientists of the day, notably J. J. Thomson and Ernest Rutherford. Having taken a double first, Graeme continued with graduate studies under Rutherford at the Cavendish Laboratory. Knowing the great Cambridge figures of the time may have prepared Graeme for his meeting with Einstein during the 1921 visit, and the two met again in Berlin in the summer of 1922. Einstein even gifted to Graeme an inscribed copy of *The Theory of Relativity*, which remains a prized possession of the family. In 1924, however, it was Einstein who was opening the pages of a Haldane book for illumination. The work was that of Graeme's cousin, JBS, whose slim volume *Daedalus; or, Science and the Future* not only added to the literature on Einstein ('the greatest Jew since Jesus', thought JBS), but lit the scientific imagination of a generation.[50]

The book's first incarnation was a talk to the Heretics Club at Cambridge, where JBS had been a Reader in Biochemistry since 1923. The famous Oxford personality Maurice Bowra was present at the time, and wrote forty-three years later, 'I have never heard anything so thrilling.'[51] Its thrills were manifold, full of the kind of perception-altering observations in which JBS excelled—'there is not a slum in the country which has a third of the infantile death-rate of the royal family in the middle ages'[52]—and prediction after prediction that has since become more or less true. JBS foresaw the exhaustion of coal and oil fields, the tapping of the wind and sunlight for energy (England would be 'covered with rows of metallic windmills'),[53] the development of the hydrogen fuel cell, and the ability to have children outside the context of sexual union. JBS was no longer alive to utter a satisfied 'I told you so' when the first 'test-tube baby' was born in 1978, but he was still very much around in 1932 to see his idea of 'ectogenesis' form the heart of his old friend Aldous Huxley's dystopian novel, *Brave New World*.

JBS got a number of predictions wrong, of course. His estimation that infectious diseases would be largely eradicated by the late 1950s will feel particularly naive to most of us today. More unsettling were his comments on eugenics. The question of JBS's relation to eugenic thinking has been admirably dealt with in Samanth Subramanian's biography, *A Dominant Character*, which sets JBS's views within the wider (and to us, shocking) political and scientific context of the times, without pardoning them. Nor does Subramanian reduce his views to a straw man. At some points, JBS called out eugenic fallacies; at others, he fell into them. JBS could write, 'Many of the deeds done in America in the name of eugenics are about as much justified by science as were the proceedings of the inquisition by the gospels.' But he could also say that, if the feeble-minded were to be segregated, 'it should be in their own interests, and because they are unfit to bring up a family, quite as much as on eugenical grounds'. Then again, he could reject as meaningless the notions of 'superiority' and 'inferiority' when comparing humans, as he knew full well that human capacities are shaped by environment as well as genes. Yet he could write of Aboriginal Australians, 'they huddle around fires in cold weather. But they never thought of making clothes from the skin of the animals they killed. I find it hard to believe that their descendants will produce a Watt or Edison.' By the end of JBS's life, he was impressing upon his readers the importance of human diversity for scientific advancement and social welfare. He had by then accepted that science could not demonstrate which precise human characteristics ought to be preserved in the interests of the future. And even if it could, he knew that it would not know how to breed them selectively.[54]

When Einstein read *Daedalus* it was not the comments on eugenics that interested him. According to Freeman Dyson, who later owned Einstein's copy, a single marginal pencil mark indicates that it was the book's ethical point that caught Einstein's attention. 'He evidently grasped at once', wrote Dyson, 'the main message of Haldane's book, the message that the progress of science is destined to bring enormous confusion and misery to mankind unless it is accompanied by progress in ethics.'[55] We do not need to rely on

Dyson, however; Einstein recorded his views in a letter to a German publisher as follows: 'Haldane reveals with a master's touch the harrowing contrast between technical and intellectual ability [on the one hand] and [on the other] the petty and malign passions to which human longing is bound.'[56] The importance of this contrast is one that we can well imagine JBS's father understanding, but the many other 'progressive' or subversive ideas contained within JBS's volume caused John considerable anguish. He was far more of a traditional moralist than even his children realised.

Until 1924, the father–son relationship had been one of exceptional closeness, and they worked together in Oxford from the end of the war up to JBS's appointment at Cambridge. (It was during this period that John set his son the challenge of finding out how the acidity of the blood affects respiration. JBS's self-experiments went to the extraordinary length of smuggling hydrochloric acid into his body by drinking a solution of ammonium chloride—though not without violent vomiting on the first attempt. On two separate later attempts, he was left short of breath for a whole week.) 'This must have been the happiest part of his life for my father', wrote Naomi.[57] An extract from a 1919 letter written by Richard at Cloan to Frances Horner captures something of the bond (and JBS's fierce intellect):

> I had a seven mile walk yesterday on the hills with John & his son Jack. The relation between them is extraordinary—They work together—John thinks & Jack brings the technical knowledge of mathematics & physics that are required for investigation, so it makes a well assorted partnership. Jack is fearfully full of conversation—During three hours we ranged from Inflammation to the Cantorian Aleph, Transfinite numbers, & the nature of logic.[58]

But by 1924, Richard was telling his sister: 'Yes. It would have been better had Jack not written "Daedalus". But, as you said, it is typical of the new youth to have done so. Poor Johnnie, who will be mixed up with this in the mind of the man in the street!'[59] According to Julian Huxley, 'Oxford was talking of nothing else [but *Daedalus*], and the family became the butt of donnish jokes and quips.' John's wife, Kathleen, felt compelled to write to Julian in warning, though not without humour:

> I find the S[enior] P[artner] is frightfully upset about *Daedalus*. Will you abstain altogether from poking fun at him on account of it? And if you can do so, keep people off the subject altogether when he is about?
>
> I knew he'd object, but had no idea till to-day how really unhappy he is—odd people these Liberals and no accounting for them![60]

For better or worse, *Daedalus* made JBS's name. Such was its reception that Bertrand Russell felt compelled to write *Icarus, or the Future of Science* in immediate response, combatting the hopefulness of JBS's outlook. It did little to dampen JBS's appeal. He now became the nation's leading voice in popular science, giving the subject a mass audience and relating its complexities and discoveries to the everyday world of working men and women in an understandable and exciting way. But the excitement of *Daedalus* overshadowed what was really of far more interest to the scientific community that year: the publication of JBS's first paper on the mathematical theory of evolution.

He had already made a significant contribution to evolutionary biology with a 1922 paper in the *Journal of Genetics*, which formulated what came to be known as 'Haldane's rule': that is, 'when in the offspring of two different animal races one sex is absent, rare, or sterile, that sex is the heterozygous sex' (i.e., the offspring is the sex in which the sex chromosomes are not the same, usually called the heterogametic sex).[61] JBS had an uncanny ability to make evolutionary observations of this kind, and those working in the biological sciences today will be well aware of 'Haldane's sieve' and 'Haldane's dilemma' (now proved incorrect), as well as his 'rule'. His 1924 paper offered more than an observation; along with a further nine papers from his pen over nine years and in conjunction with the work of Ronald Fisher and Sewall Wright, it invented a new discipline. The discipline is known as population genetics, which the journal *Nature* defines as 'the study of the genetic composition of populations, including distributions and changes in genotype and phenotype frequency in response to the processes of natural selection, genetic drift, mutation and gene flow'.[62]

What JBS, Fisher, and Wright were doing was showing a way beyond the impasse between Mendelians (those who followed the monk-scientist Gregor Mendel) and Darwinians that had come to a head in the 1920s. Though neither of these schools of thought doubted the power of natural selection, nor gave credence to Jean-Baptiste Lamarck's belief in the inheritance of acquired characteristics, Mendelians argued—based on some empirical observations—that species evolve by sudden adaptive jumps. Darwinians, on the other hand, were convinced that statistics and biometrics showed the process of evolution to be a painfully slow one, made up of accretions of small genetic variations. JBS's major contribution was his use of mathematics to prove that even small Darwinian variations, multiplied through the power of natural selection, could produce large Mendelian changes in a species.[63] This was a key step towards what we now know as the 'modern synthesis'. He made the step with characteristic thoroughness and liveliness, holding under the microscope of his remarkable intellect all sorts of factors that might influence the rate of change. What do cases of inbreeding do to the numbers? What happens when an offspring of a plant fertilises its parent? How do we factor in random mutations? His findings were summarised in (just about) layman's terms in his 1932 book *The Causes of Evolution*. Here, despite the hard-headed rationalism of its mathematics, the old Haldane concerns shine through: 'The world is full of mysteries. Life is one. The curious limitations of finite minds are another. It is not the business of an evolutionary theory to explain these mysteries.'[64] John Haldane must have beamed when he read these lines. Had JBS atoned for the sins of *Daedalus*?

If JBS used the microscope of his intellect, he didn't often use the microscope of the laboratory. He relied on the findings of others. This was as true of his evolutionary thinking as it was of his other major contribution to scientific thought in the mid-1920s: his collaboration with G. E. Briggs to derive the basic law of steady-state kinetics, known as the Briggs-Haldane equation, which continues to shape the design of enzyme experiments to this day. It was a highly original equation, but it was built on the technical manual work of others. JBS's reliance on such work, along with a bit of extra power and money, may have played into his decision to join the John Innes Horticultural Institution near Wimbledon on a part-time basis in 1927, splicing it with his work at Cambridge.

The appointment brought its own sagas, but it also highlighted an aspect of JBS's character that might too easily be lost amidst the bravado: his appreciation and support of women scientists. Just as his father had promoted the work of Mabel Purefoy FitzGerald, at John Innes JBS championed the experiments of Rose Scott-Moncrieff, Dorothea de Winton, and Alice Gairdner. Indeed, JBS 'found his closest colleagues among the women'.[65] While he may have initiated some of their work, he did not step on their toes nor patronise, but rejoiced in the incremental steps of discovery, and, when he could, turbocharged them with his own theories. Later in her life, when Scott-Moncrieff had made significant strides in our understanding of how genetic differences impact on the pigmentation of flowers, she wrote:

> All Haldane's enthusiasm and appreciation of the possibilities of a break-through were manifested throughout in his encouragement and contribution of ideas. He kept closely in touch with our work, much of which he supervised. Although at no time contributing any practical work, he congratulated himself with great vigour on having initiated this marriage of two disciplines [chemistry and genetics]. He lectured and published extensively and built theories on our findings.[66]

JBS himself put it this way: 'I regard her work as a model for future researches, and suspect that my initiation of it may have been my most important contribution to biochemistry.'[67]

His relations with women were not always so easy to follow. When JBS met and fell in love with the journalist Charlotte Burghes (née Franken)—a married mother of one, aflame with excitement at the new ideas leaping off the pages of *Daedalus*—the ensuing wish to release her from the bonds of her hopeless husband led to a series of convoluted, indeed laughable, events, involving the discovery of the lovers sharing a hotel room by a private detective (orchestrated in advance by the lovers themselves), followed by a bizarre denial of infidelity, and a refusal on JBS's part to step down from his Cambridge post under university pressure. Then came his dismissal at the hands of Cambridge's *sex viri* (a panel of six men with oversight of staff morals, whom JBS delighted in calling the 'Sex Weary') and an appeal at the panel's decision, in which John Haldane—still grating from the *Daedalus* experience—was called as a character witness for his son. Ultimately, the *sex viri*'s original decision was overturned, and a victorious JBS was reinstated to his Readership at the university.

JBS and Charlotte married in 1926. Shortly afterwards, Graeme Haldane was asked to visit his cousin and his cousin's new wife for the weekend. They had taken a cottage to the west of London and JBS offered to drive Graeme down. In some unpublished reflections entitled 'J. B. S. H', Graeme records:

> I don't think I have ever had a more dangerous drive which culminated in Jack trying to overtake a horse drawn cart when another car was approaching on a two-lane road. The consequence was that Jack had to pull in to the left forcing the car into a ditch. Instead of apologising, Jack upbraided the unfortunate car driver in the most violent terms while I sat in considerable embarrassment.

Such was the man that Charlotte had just married. He could be kind to children and younger colleagues, but his rudeness and fierce temper were famous. It was going to take a lot for Charlotte to manage relations with so difficult a character; if anyone could it was she. The daughter of German Jewish immigrants (much to Kathleen Haldane's distaste), Charlotte was intelligent, seductive, and politically engaged. She was also relentlessly hardworking and ambitious, not only for herself but for her husband too. If JBS provided the output that made him the most widely read scientist in the land, it was his wife who ensured that the newspapers and magazines were lining up expectantly. It helped that JBS's polymathic knowledge allowed him to contribute in areas well beyond his specialism in genetics, and with that spark of originality that made his work so persistently entertaining. Sometimes that originality was momentous. When *The Rationalist Annual*—a publication with a large public readership—appeared in 1929, his contribution would become 'a milestone in the history of ideas on the origin of life'.[68] In his article, JBS mused on the conditions that would have been necessary for life to have emerged on earth, and to his musings we owe the idea of the 'primordial soup'—though he himself used the words 'hot dilute soup'.[69] No one had used the word 'soup' quite like this before. It was typical of JBS to take a mundane substance we all know from our drab everyday world and connect it in our minds to one of the most fundamental questions posed by humankind. This ability was one of the keys to his popularity.

* * *

JBS was still in his thirties when this article appeared. But youth is no prerequisite for originality, as his father's career was proving. There was no letting up in the 1920s in John's capacity to conceive of, or do, something game-changing. After a series of pressure chamber experiments with Alexander Kellas (who died on the first British expedition to Everest in 1921, led by the ill-fated George Mallory) and JBS (who lost an hour of his memory from one of the experiments), it was John who first insisted that it was humanly possible to ascend Everest without supplemental oxygen—a conviction eventually borne out by Reinhold Messner and Peter Habeler in 1978.

John knew, of course, that beyond certain heights breathing apparatus would always be necessary, so when he came to write his 1921 book, *Respiration*, he did the natural thing—for John, that is—and designed a prototype spacesuit. This 'stratospheric suit', which became a reality with the support of the Royal Air Force and Philip Drinker, inventor of the iron lung, paved the way for high-altitude flights that would change the course of history. Sadly, according to Martin Goodman, this even stretches to the ascent of the Boeing B-29 Superfortress that dropped the bomb on Hiroshima on 6 August 1945. Goodman also connects John's suit to the development of the U-2 spy plane, and identifies his prototype as 'the early model for the spacesuits worn by astronauts on Extra Vehicular Activity'.[70] Had he lived to see these 'advances', anger undoubtedly would have mixed with pride.

It is unlikely that such ambiguities of feeling beset John in the 1920s. He had produced five book-length publications that decade, found himself elected to an Honorary Chair in Mining at Birmingham University in 1921—at last, he was a professor!—and added to his catalogue of accolades in 1924, with his appointment as a Gas Referee to the entirety of the United Kingdom and his election to the presidency of the Institution of Mining Engineers (a remarkable honour, given that he had no engineering qualifications whatsoever). He was Gifford Lecturer at Glasgow across the years 1927 and 1928, twenty-three years after Richard's series at St Andrews, and in 1929 he travelled to South Africa to speak at that year's meeting of the British Association for the Advancement of Science. His fellow speakers included his old school friend Professor D'Arcy Wentworth Thompson and Jan Smuts, the former prime minister of South Africa. Given his humility, John may not have worn the riband and badge of a Companion of Honour during the meeting, but he was entitled to do so, having joined his sister Elizabeth the previous year in that sovereign-appointed Order that cannot exceed sixty-five members at any one time. Between 1928 and 1936, the Order was over 3 per cent Haldane.

And what of Elizabeth? She, too, lengthened her already long list of public duties across the decade, with her role as governor on the board of Birkbeck College (where Richard was president) and her membership of the General Council of Nursing. She also occupied these years with a spate of writing to rival that of her brothers'. *The British Nurse in Peace and War* appeared in 1923, a record of her mother's life in 1925, and a biography of George Eliot in 1927, and she edited Richard's autobiography before its release in 1929. One little-known fact is that she also helped save London's Sadler's Wells Theatre and Ballet in 1928, by persuading her fellow trustees at the Carnegie Trust to inject money into it when it otherwise would have closed through penury. Today the Theatre is known as the world's number one venue dedicated to international dance. Haldane connections appear in the most unlikely of places.

* * *

Despite these achievements, the darker side of life could not be held at bay. By 1925, Mary Haldane had been in bed for fourteen years. In April, she turned one hundred. She had lived through the founding of the police force, the Great Reform Act, the abolition of slavery, the enfranchisement of women, and many more nation-shaking events, including the Crimean, Boer, and Great wars. She herself had become, in Richard's words, 'a national institution'.[71] She was, he thought, the secret of the family's success, and in his view, she eclipsed them all: 'You inspire your children, & lift them to a high level by what you say to them. You have grown of late in personality... & that is the secret of your influence. You have more personality than any of us.'[72]

On her centenary, telegrams and letters flooded in from all over the world. The King and Queen sent their congratulations, as did Queen Alexandra and the archbishops of Canterbury and York, plus hundreds more. When Edmund Gosse sent her as a gift her favourite plant, the Daphne, Mary responded, 'I do not deserve it—Why are people so overflowingly kind?'[73] That day, a broadcast went out from London about her life and her children, and this was followed by a supper and dance at Cloan—though Mary remained upstairs in her bed, listening to the jigs rise through the floorboards. Richard was not one for dancing and snuck away from the hurly-burly to write letters in the quiet of his study on the other side of the house. As he so often did, he reported back to Gosse on the activities of his Labrador, Bruce, the successor to Kaiser: 'The Black Dog was puzzled but after a little entered into the spirit of the proceedings wholeheartedly.'[74]

Then the festivities came to an end. By the beginning of May, Richard was compelled to travel back to Cloan to be by his mother's side for her final hours. Though physically very weak, she remained strong in other ways. 'The spiritual power and personality are striking. No metaphors—simply grasp', wrote Richard.[75] On 20 May, he penned the following words to Frances Horner:

> Darling,
>
> My old mother passed away five minutes after 1 this morning. I was by her. The end came quietly and peacefully. She was not conscious.
>
> The relationship with her was a very close and fine one. She had grown in stature & had become a remarkable personality. I feel that much has gone out of what remains of life for me. I must work while day is left.[76]

Again, the telegrams and letters came rushing in, five hundred of them. But if Mary's death brought sadness, it also brought much gratitude for a long and glorious life. This cannot be said for every death, of course. Naomi, scarred forever by the war, knew that only too well, and in 1927 she had the fact rammed home in the most brutal way. Her eldest son Geoff had turned nine that year (Naomi had given birth to her fourth child and first girl, Sonja Lois—always known as Lois—the year before). Geoff was a boy who showed huge promise, and no doubt Naomi felt the Haldane tradition was secure for another generation. When he developed a bacterial infection in the mastoid bone behind his ear, the family remained fairly relaxed. Naomi continued her hectic social and literary life, happy to let the children's nurse deal with much of the care, even as Geoff's condition worsened. The infection led to spinal meningitis, and with penicillin yet to be discovered, there was little that could be done. It was a horrible death.

Naomi reached out to various friends, describing the details in an attempt to work through them. One such friend was Aldous Huxley. It seems, however, that he listened with a novelist's more than a friend's ear, and without Naomi knowing, wove the details she had provided into his fiction. In *Point Counter Point*, published the following year, this is what we read of the character Elinor Quarles's experience during the final stages of her son's life:

> Next day, instead of whimpering with every return of pain, the child began to scream—cry after shrill cry, repeated with an almost clockwork regularity of recurrence for what seemed to Elinor an eternity of hours. Like the scream of a rabbit in a trap. But a thousand times worse; for it was a child that screamed, not an animal; *her* child, trapped and in agony.[77]

Naomi's relationship with Aldous took a long time to recover—if it ever did. There was certainly never any real recovery from the grief she felt for Geoff. Even in her nineties, she told her biographer: 'it leaves... a sort of stupid pain which inevitably just goes on and on forever and ever'.[78] The pain was intensified by JBS and Charlotte's reaction. She drove to see them at Roebuck House, their home just outside Cambridge, looking for comfort, but found only disapproval and blame. It was an unthinkable crime to Charlotte that Naomi had been absent for parts of Geoff's illness. Charlotte had, in fact, just published *Motherhood and its Enemies*, denouncing women who failed to prioritise their children. To JBS, who longed to have children of his own but (for some unknown reason) couldn't, Naomi's behaviour seemed to suggest that she took parenthood for granted, failing to prize it for the privilege that it was. With Naomi already racked with guilt prior to her visit, she left Roebuck in a state of almost complete breakdown. She had her seven-year-old, Denny, with her. It was only his presence in the car, she later claimed, that stopped her from a suicidal acceleration and turning of the wheel.

But Denny did suffer, as did his brother Murdoch, who was five at the time of Geoff's death. The loss made a lasting impact upon both of them. Their near total silence in later life about this brother and their complete lack of memories about him, even though they had slept together in the same room, suggest repression on a significant scale. According to their younger sister Lois's later account, Denny retreated into himself and Murdoch retreated into his head—and, indeed, in after years, Denny simply seemed to edit out inconvenient past events, while people were sometimes astonished at the level of detachment with which Murdoch could view human disaster and pain. His own daughter, Sally, believes Murdoch—like his uncle JBS—was capable of sympathy, but not of empathy, that key ability to feel how others feel on the inside.[79] To what extent this was genetic, part of the neurodiverse streak within the family, or a result of Geoff's death is hard to say. When it came to Denny's reaction, Naomi was convinced he was visibly damaged by the loss. To make matters worse, she did not quite hide the fact that she thought Denny less academically brilliant than Geoff.[80] In a family in which one already felt a certain pressure to achieve, Denny's life became yet more intense and stressful. It is notable that where Denny really did shine in later life—in his work on the treatment of tuberculosis—his focus was on a deadly infectious disease.

For Naomi, there was consolation when she gave birth to Nicholas Avrion (known as Av) in 1928 and Valentine Harriet Isobel Dione (known as Val) in 1930; but the deaths kept coming. At the beginning of the year in which Av was born, two of Naomi and Dick's servants were tragically drowned in the basement of Rivercourt when the Thames burst its banks. And by that summer, it was clear that time was running out for Richard Haldane. His health had never been great. Diabetes, rheumatism, and unceasing work had aged him prematurely. Indeed, doctors would nowadays regard the bout of iritis he had suffered in 1910 as a symptom of a more widespread autoimmune disease.[81] Watching his bent, shuffling figure on the British Pathé recording of the opening of the Law Courts in 1924, one would think him aged eighty rather than sixty-eight.

He worked up to the last, especially on the judicial bench and as Leader of the Opposition in the Lords. In June 1928 he was appointed Chancellor of the University of St Andrews, and in July he presided at the annual meeting of the London Library. That was his last public engagement. With his strength quickly ebbing away, he returned to Cloan, the place he always considered his real home, to see in his seventy-second birthday at the end of the month. He may well have known that he was dying. Certainly, he had given much thought to death, as those who had been with him in recent months testified. By 12 August, doctors were summoned, and a nurse from Glasgow. Their job, it seems, was simply to make him comfortable. On the morning of 19 August, he was able to dictate one final note to the woman who, next to his mother, he loved beyond all others—Frances Horner: 'Getting on. All well. Love. A little tired but going on quite smoothly. Hope to write soon. Ever yours R.' That afternoon, at 3.30 pm, Richard died. Elizabeth, Willie, Edith, Graeme, Archie, and Elsie were by his side.

When the obituaries hit the newspapers, hardly a word of the old recriminations was to be found—except regarding their stupidity and malignance. Praise followed praise. Richard was now publicly recognised as the man who had saved the nation by his forethought between 1905 and 1912. He was, in the words of *The Times*, 'one of the most powerful, subtle, and encyclopaedic intellects ever devoted to the public service of his country'.[82] The vindication was complete.

The story of the mile-long funeral procession led by sixty Territorials and four pipers, and of his internment at the family chapel at Gleneagles, has been poignantly described by Richard's biographer, John Campbell, and needs no repeating here.[83] What do bear repeating are the words written to Elizabeth three days after Richard's death by Frances, stranded in France and unable to attend the funeral:

> It is everything that he had little suffering & that he was able to work up to nearly his last days—& I feel happy too that he was at Cloan

wh[ich] he loved & that you were able to surround him with care & comfort. It will be terribly lonely for you. It seems hard that they should always go first: for 35 years now he has been the most perfect friend to me & mine—without desert—beyond requital—& I feel very proud that I sh[oul]d have had such a gift & been able to hold his love for so long: I have never doubted it & I don't now... Dearest I won't mourn too bitterly for him because one ought really to be full of pride & thankfulness, as I know you are—& you have had the great blessedness of being able to live beside him & to shelter him (as much as he w[oul]d ever allow shelter!)... Almost the last letter he wrote to me he said Elizabeth is perfect to me... Now goodbye. I could go on talking forever...[84]

10

LIVING TRADITION

1930–1945

With Mary and Richard gone, Cloan could loosen its metaphorical bow tie and slip into the more relaxed attire of the 1930s. Elizabeth now held sway, and an easy informality allowed Naomi to travel up every year with her young children in the knowledge that they could run free without the danger of knocking down a visiting dignitary. The grand old days were over. Elizabeth was getting old. The woman who had once given so much thought to the future turned to the past. She titled the books of her final years accordingly: *Mrs Gaskell and her Friends*, *The Scotland of our Fathers*, *Scots Gardens in Old Times*, *From One Century to Another*.

John would visit too, often with Naomi and his grandchildren. A life of self-experimentation had taken its toll. His ideas continued to stretch and rise into the future, with him even winning the Royal Society's Copley Medal in 1934, the Society's oldest and most prestigious award, joining the ranks of Einstein and Darwin. But his body was crippled and bent double, as if his large moustache had been yanked towards the ground by an overwhelming gravity. It was not uncommon for him to pop ten aspirins in a day. Naomi, as a girl, had once loved to sit upon her father's shoulders as he strode the paths through the glens behind Cloan. Now his cane edged forwards slowly on their walks, and his daughter silently grieved for the man he had been. In her own old age, she would relive those lost days of youthfulness in her poetry, writing 'The Glen Path' in memory of her father.

Naomi's mother wasn't much of a visitor to Cloan, but in Oxford she continued to rule the roost. 'Various people try vainly to look after her from time to time', wrote Naomi to her brother:

'[I]f she will treat her maids like dogs she must expect them to behave like bitches.'[1] Naomi's deteriorating relationship with Kathleen, largely due to ever-widening political differences, didn't stop her sending her four boys to live with her mother and father while they were at preparatory school in Oxford (predictably, Naomi had enrolled them at the Dragon). For boys with a scientific bent, Cherwell was an idyllic place to live, with its laboratories 'full of mouldering equipment', just waiting for pranks and explosions.[2] Murdoch remembered:

> I had heated nitrate and charcoal in a clay crucible to make a glowing fizz. Then why shouldn't I have the extra excitement of a smell? So, I added sulphur. Luckily I then left the room from which came a loud bang. The crucible had exploded because I had unwittingly made gunpowder.[3]

In Denny's memory the intention to explode things was very much conscious, and was unhindered by 'Uffer', their grandfather, who was fully aware of their experiments: 'Outside we mainly tried to create bombsites... We worked on how to make better and better explosives by, for instance, mixing sodium chlorate and sugar and a small bit of sulphuric acid—this would burst into flames very satisfactorily.'[4] When chemicals were deemed unusable, these were poured down a garden pit with the unfortunate name of 'Mrs Haldane's Hole'.[5]

The boys, unlike their mother, adored Kathleen (they knew her, with the rest of the family, as 'Maya'). They were aware of her passion for colonial domination and right-wing causes, but she was kind to them, reading to them from Rudyard Kipling after school, and instilling in them a lifelong interest in other countries. According to Av, Maya taught him that 'a man, particularly a Scotsman, had to "go East"—in other words, don't sit on your backside, travel the world!'[6] He would take the lesson to heart. When staying with Maya, Av would also come to know what his dead brother, Geoff, looked like. In an act of self-protection, Naomi had put away all signs of his existence at Rivercourt. At Cherwell, Maya let his photos stand proudly on display.

Maya's message about foreign travel chimed with, though it was not the same as, the internationalism of the Haldanes. Her arch-enemy Richard had often stressed the importance of the 'international mind' when it came to politics. But in the 1930s, Naomi and JBS were developing that 'mind' in a way that would have worried their uncle. It certainly horrified their mother.

* * *

As Elizabeth turned to the past, Naomi became ever more charged with hope for the future. In many ways, Naomi was her aunt's successor. Both had a deep desire to improve the quality of life for the downtrodden and for women in Britain, and ironically, both could display what Jenni Calder has called a 'benevolent paternalism' in their relationships with others.[7] That didn't stop Naomi taking issue with the mode of Elizabeth's attempt to make a difference. In one letter from this period, she wrote to her aunt:

> I don't think we can separate life up into 'inside' and 'outside' as you do. Women are not merely occupied with personal relationships and the conservation of means of life. That is an archaistic view... We have kept away from the 'outside' things very largely because we were forcibly kept out of them by our economic position.

Given Elizabeth's actual career, it's bizarre that Naomi thought her aunt held such views. When Naomi, in the same letter, expressed her own views on what politics meant, it was in fact remarkably close to what Elizabeth, in her own post-Christian way, clearly believed: 'The moral basis of politics goes down to our deepest roots, politics means danger and beauty, conversion and rebirth. It also means a lot of small, ordinary things—more dust-bins and bathrooms for people who haven't got them, more leisure and more education for people who need them desperately.'[8] Naomi would later title one of her non-fiction books *The Moral Basis of Politics* (1938) and expound upon these rousing sentiments. Amusingly, her lecturing to her aunt on this matter only reinforces the similarities between the two. But in some respects, Naomi was certainly different.

The political experiment going on in Russia would not have appealed to the older generation of Haldanes, whose pragmatism, hatred of bureaucracy, promotion of the entrepreneurial spirit, and belief in the sanctity of individual freedom (within the context of a mutually enriching community) sat uncomfortably with the spirit of communism and the USSR. Naomi and JBS imbibed many of these Haldane characteristics early in life, but both siblings shared a sense that something more radical was needed than the step-by-step constitutional approach that marked the progressiveness of the former generation of the family. Only a revolution would bring the change they wanted.

What they wanted differed. When JBS went with Charlotte to Russia in 1928, as guests of renowned Soviet plant biologist Nikolai Vavilov, the thing that really struck him was the prominent place science was given in public life and education. The state was endowing scientific endeavours on an unprecedented scale, and men of science were held in the highest regard. No wonder he longed for a similar regime in Britain, though he still had reservations at this stage, writing in 1931, 'I cannot accept the American and Communist ideals, because both are too exclusively economic.'[9] Naomi's concerns were quite other. Setting out in 1932 on the SS *Cooperazia* for her own tour of the USSR with a Fabian Society group (which included, amongst others, Hugh Dalton, a future Chancellor of the Exchequer, and her cousin Graeme Haldane), she wrote in her diary:

> I wonder what we all think we shall get in Russia, apart from technical things; I talked to Ridley, the architect, for a time, and I think he hopes to find what I hope for—that people will look at one differently, that there will be real happiness and freedom—not, presumably, political freedom, but a real liberte [sic] des moeurs [moral freedom].[10]

Naomi's naive yearning came from a place of deep personal insecurity, as she revealed on the next page of her diary: 'Why should I insist that my children should... be in high-brow professions that may make them feel as timid and valueless as I do?'[11] Her politics always had this definite subjective edge to it. Yes, she deplored the rise of fascism in Europe; yes, she objected to the lordship of capital over labour; yes, she condemned the economic, social, and sexual plight of women. But she did not fight against these conditions simply because they were objectively wrong. She felt tangled in these nets herself, especially those concerning women, and she also felt guilty for being free from some of the weightier nets that bound others of her sex—she had money of her own, a prosperous career, access to birth control, a measure of sexual freedom. (She even stood for Parliament after her Russian tour, as Labour candidate for the Scottish universities, but was unsuccessful, as was her husband Dick for King's Norton in 1931 and 1935.) Her daughter-in-law, Rosalind 'Rowy' Mitchison, would later write perceptively: 'Naomi's demand to express female experience in full, the approach which shocked publishers, reviewers and the respectable... came from her emancipation from formal career concerns.'[12] Naomi knew she was privileged, asking herself at the opening of her Russian diary, 'Am I—is anyone—sufficiently valuable to get all the things I've got?'[13] Her fascination with Russia can perhaps be explained by the fact that here, at last, she hoped to discover a general levelling of society that would make her question redundant.

Such high hopes could only ever be disappointed. Stalin's show trials and executions, which had begun in 1928, were not much on her radar at this point (by 1938, they very much were), but she could at least see that:

> for anyone who is not definitely in some kind of an organisation, for the children for whom there are not yet enough creches and kindergartens, for the quite unskilled worker, for the women who are not working, for old people who are not pensioned and not in rest homes, for people who used to do some kind of job which is now, in the present state of society valueless... they haven't enough to eat... some people are actually, now, dying of starvation.[14]

She felt the account book could still be balanced. For workers, there was job security, long holidays, excellent leisure facilities, cheap food. There was free healthcare, free education, state-funded museums and laboratories. More than that, 'they have solved, or nearly solved, the sex question which has preoccupied us for so many years, simply by giving women complete economic freedom and equality'.[15] Naomi could rejoice that 'The citizens of the Soviet Union are done with [sexual] "morality" and can put it away in a museum of horrors, where it properly belongs.'[16] The availability of birth control and legal abortions was, in Naomi's view, proof of this remarkable claim (the stomach-churning depiction of an abortion in her 1935 novel, *We Have Been Warned*, was based on what she had seen in a Moscow clinic, and offered a sideways critique of Russian methods). She could detect no trace of 'sexual shame or slander' in their society.[17] And yet she was not going to pull her punches: 'They cannot get rid of certain characteristics, especially the longing for power. There is terrible bureaucracy everywhere… They are inefficient, muddlers, dirty, unpunctual, to some extent liars.'[18]

Staying true to her Haldane roots, what she really couldn't stand was the total lack of nuance in the communist position: 'Communists hate Socialists, but lump Liberals and Conservatives together as Capitalists and really not so nasty, needing only to be destroyed, not to be hated and reviled.' She continued:

> Of course it may be necessary just now, but one is faintly shocked to find people regarding open-mindedness, seeing both sides, as a dead [sic] sin, something impossible to a good person. And of course they are awfully pleased with the intelligence of their children who realise at six years old that capitalism is a bad thing. Well, no doubt it is, but it is no credit to the children, who have never been allowed to think anything else… All one can say is, that it may be necessary so long as the rest of the world is against the USSR, but it is a damned dangerous policy for the life of a nation, and I am not prepared to swallow it.[19]

Naomi's own open-mindedness was never more on show than on this trip, guided and inspired by her then lover, John Pilley, to whom she wrote throughout her time away. A lecturer in the history of science at Bristol, Pilley was a committed member of the Communist Party of Great Britain, and a dominant and idealistic young man. He had contributed to a collection of progressive and controversial essays of which Naomi was editor, *An Outline for Boys and Girls and their Parents* (1932). She found him captivating, not least for the way he thought about sex. For Pilley, sex was an expression of comradeship. The body was meant to be shared freely, just as much as the mind. It was socialism in its most embodied form. Sex was a path to healing, a way of showing kindness.

Kindness, in this sense, became central within Naomi's vocabulary about this time, and she wanted to live it. She had already shown what she thought of the possibility of incest with JBS, but that seemed less a political statement or an act of kindness than an experiment bound up with competition and confused emotions. Sleeping with her cousin Graeme was another matter. Graeme, like Naomi, was now thirty-four, with strong sympathies towards socialism. But he was totally devoid of sexual experience, having lived in male-dominated environments most of his life. He was travelling to the Soviet Union to inspect their power stations and industrial developments. In Naomi's eyes, he was clearly repressed—even his small, refined handwriting, she said, betrayed his lack of experience between the sheets. Naomi took it upon herself to conduct the rites of initiation, though not without trepidation, as she wrote to Pilley:

> John, I am really rather frightened: you have landed me with being a priestess, when my individual self wants to be your lover and nothing else. I am very inexperienced and I am so afraid of doing something which will leave a bad memory for him (and, for that matter, for me).[20]

The year before, the same year in which she had joined the Labour Party, Naomi had published her most widely remembered and highly acclaimed book, *The Corn King and the Spring Queen* (or, as her friend W. H. Auden liked to call it, *The Prawn King and the String Queen*), in which the central protagonist Erif Der—'Red Fire' in reverse—has her own priestly functions to perform. This remarkable novel, set in mythic Marob and a tumultuous Sparta—a novel which led the author Winifred Holtby to assert that Naomi was 'of the calibre of which Nobel prize-winners are made'[21]—offers a profound meditation on the way in which self-giving or sacrifice can lead to healing and wholeness.[22] It suggests that a commitment to act as an individual, as opposed simply to being immersed in one's community, can allow for a new, heightened level of belonging in community, though the journey will be long and hard. Naomi's reflections to Pilley about sleeping with Graeme show her consciously playing the role of sacrificial victim, and—despite what she says about letting go of her individual desires—she is evidently preparing herself for a highly individualised act. As ever with Naomi, fact and fiction were allowed to intertwine. Thus she lay down with her cousin in a hotel bed in a Russian port city (both encouraged, perhaps, by the tradition of Haldane self-experimentation). Afterwards, in the dark, Naomi detected a 'deep happiness' in Graeme's voice. She felt 'he was out of prison'.[23]

This was a premeditated political act, devoid of passion and consequent commitment. Was there even something patronising in it? Naomi playing the saviour, the liberator? Probably. The self-appointed title of priestess was a typical inflation for Naomi. But in some ways, she looked up to Graeme, rather than down upon him. He was by this stage a well-respected engineer, who had already made a significant impact on his field by being the first person in the world to construct (at Foswell), monitor, and document the performance of a heat pump system for space heating—an idea that had its origins in a conversation he'd had with JBS (Graeme thought JBS was 'undoubtedly a genius of the first magnitude') and which subsequently revolutionised heating systems in the United States and beyond.[24] Even as I write in 2021, the heat pump is central to the UK government's plan to introduce low-carbon heating systems to Britain's homes in its fight against climate change. That Graeme could develop such advanced technology was certainly appealing to Naomi. He was a 'worker' in a way she was not. If sleeping with him wasn't motivated by physical attraction, there was certainly an element of admiration.

The episode left her wounded. She was unsure if she had done the right thing and was worried about telling Dick; she didn't for quite some time. For Graeme, there was gratitude, in the form of a thank-you note, but his future wife, Billee, would never know.[25] The very fact that Billee eventually came on the scene was, in Naomi's view, a justification of her actions. She had written to Graeme after their encounter telling him that she was feeling uneasy, but that such feelings would recede once he found 'someone nice to live with'. She added, 'You see, when that happens, I shall feel justified of my theory, and what more beautiful thing can ever happen to a Haldane?'[26] Of course, Naomi never let Billee in on the secret, but her reserve dropped after Graeme's death in 1981. That year, Naomi summoned Graeme and Billee's son, Dick, to Murdoch's house in East Lothian where she was recuperating after a hip replacement. Dick hardly knew Naomi at this stage. With evident pleasure, she disclosed the news that she had taken Graeme's virginity, revelling in Dick's shock. There have been three biographies of Naomi Mitchison. This is the first time the identity of her lover on her Russian tour has been revealed in print.

* * *

It was a decade for eventful travel amongst the Haldanes, with Naomi venturing into the midst of Austria's defeated Socialists in 1934, smuggling funds and papers to them in her thick woollen knickers, liaising there with a former lover and future Labour leader, Hugh Gaitskell, and lunching 'with a nice young Englishman called Philby'.[27] In 1935 she crossed the Atlantic to campaign against the shameful conditions under which sharecroppers were forced to work in the southern states of the US. In both cases, Naomi had passed from being observer (as she was in Russia) to participant—though not always with happy results. In the 1940s she would write, 'I want to be in danger, but not uselessly, not as a sight-see-er.'[28] The problem was, her involvement sometimes brought danger to others. When a Black leader of the Southern Tenant Farmers' Union introduced Naomi at a demonstration, he placed his hand upon her shoulder. White men later tracked him down and beat him.

Graeme's steady rise with Britain's leading firm of consulting electrical engineers, Merz & McLellan, his intense interest in scientific developments, and his quiet humility placed him in the position of something approaching a diplomat in his field. He was in Sweden in 1937 to investigate their political system and power organisation, and this brought lengthy conversations with the Swedish Prime Minister Per Albin Hansson and others of his cabinet. Hansson wryly remarked to Graeme 'that he was an admirer of Great Britain—she always did the right thing but equally always did it too late!'[29] The next year, Graeme found himself in discussions—over dinner and during a private one-to-one meeting—with President Franklin D. Roosevelt as part of a trip to the USA to inform the authorities there of Britain's energy plans in the event of another European war.

Alongside an extensive lecture tour and meetings with other senior American officials (including Louis Johnson, Assistant Secretary of War and Chairman of the National Defense Committee) and intellectuals (most notably the philosopher John Dewey, then eighty years old, and Heinrich Brüning, the exiled former Chancellor of Germany), Graeme also wanted to study the Tennessee Valley Authority and the Hoover Dam. He learnt much from these experiences, but the greatest lesson was the firmness of Roosevelt's attitude to the growing tension between democracy and totalitarianism in Europe. Upon his return to England (with an inscribed photograph of the president in his bag reading, 'For Graeme Haldane from his friend Franklin D. Roosevelt'), Graeme quickly put together a confidential memorandum for Chamberlain and his ministers and arranged for a private interview with Sir John Anderson, the Lord Privy Seal. His memo was full of fascinating insights. 'I have little doubt', wrote Graeme, 'the President would like to intervene in European and world problems and to co-operate with the democracies to a much greater extent than is politically expedient at the present moment.' Elsewhere, he states: 'Economically America may be able to exercise great pressure on Germany... For instance Dr. H. A. Morgan—Chairman of the Tennessee Valley Authority...—informed me that great pressure could have been brought to bear on Germany through the control of the export of phosphates, particularly from Florida.'[30] Ultimately, as he later wrote, Graeme wanted to convey the 'immense fund of American goodwill and support to democracies, such as ours, in the fight against totalitarian blackmail', as well as their expectation that Britain would 'pursue a determined policy of resistance'.[31] It was to no avail. Graeme could only watch on with dismay as Chamberlain followed the fated road of appeasement.

Graeme was exhausted by his trip to the United States, but he had ways to unwind. He found relaxation chiefly through fishing holidays with his brother Archie, whose own trips abroad revolved around trout rather than prime ministers or presidents. In the 1930s, the brothers were yet to marry and would holiday together each Easter and autumn, visiting some remote corner of Scotland where they could cast their rods in peace. This was one of the few similarities between them. Archie, in his memoirs, puts the difference succinctly: 'I have sometimes thought that one of the fundamental differences between Graeme and me is that he tends to live in the day after to-morrow whereas I think he might feel, and perhaps with much justice, that I incline to live in the days before yesterday.'[32]

Archie undoubtedly opted for the quiet life, bound by tradition, family loyalty, and fear of the new. Apart from two years at Winchester after the Edinburgh Academy, he followed the path of his eldest brother Pat as closely as he could—Balliol, Oxford, where he occupied Pat's old rooms; a modern history degree; rowing in the college eight; and a position as Writer to the Signet in his father's firm (as Pat would have been had he outlived the war), becoming partner in 1927. He did not particularly enjoy the law or office life (exacerbated by Willie's eccentricities, such as refusing to leave the office to catch the train to Perthshire until the very last second, earning him the nickname 'the Late Knight' at the station),[33] but it gave him long holidays in which to indulge his love of fishing, which was Pat's first love too. Archie wanted a world of safety, of predictability. His brother's death had ensured he would spend his life in search of an ungraspable past where happiness reigned.

Meanwhile, Archie and Graeme's sister, Elsie, showed a robustness that Archie lacked. After dedicated service as a VAD nurse in northern France during the First World War, she took an agricultural degree at Oxford, then returned to Foswell to run the estate with her father. Elsie was the apple of Willie's eye. She met his ideals of what a child of his should be more closely than Graeme or Archie ever could. It was not just agriculture that interested her. She was accomplished in all aspects of country life, even shooting, a sport which was not traditionally practised by women. In many ways, Willie was closer to his daughter than to his own wife, Edith. He must have felt bereft when, in 1931, she married Alec Campbell Fraser (grandson of Professor Campbell Fraser, who had taught philosophy to both Richard and John Haldane at Edinburgh) and moved with him to Yorkshire. Not only was she now physically distant, but there was a sense that she had married a little beneath her, as Alec's father was a 'mere' deacon in the Church of England. Elsie and Alec's son, Pat (born 1933), thinks that Elsie—a serious-minded person who idolised her Uncle Richard—would have liked to have had a more intellectual partner, but that, like so many women of her generation, she simply didn't have many men left to choose from after the first war. That said, Elsie and Alec had met prior to 1914 through family connections, and Alec quite literally left an impression. While he was erecting a wooden pole with a view to a game of 'Bumble Puppy' (similar to Swingball, I'm told), he managed to hit Elsie in the face with said pole, knocking her teeth out in the process. Still, it was a successful marriage. Alec was a land agent and so shared her interest in agriculture, and both of them hunted. It was a comfortable, upper-middle-class life, but unshowy.

* * *

Her cousin, JBS, took the opposite line. He rejected the trappings of upper-class life, but revelled in the limelight. Like Graeme, he found the British government's attitude to fascist dictators shameful. Unlike Graeme, JBS had a wide platform from which to voice his disagreements and make an impact on public opinion. He had been appointed to the Fullerian Professorship in Physiology at the Royal Institution in 1930, to a Visiting Professorship at the University of California, Berkeley, and a Fellowship of the Royal Society in 1932, and to the Chair of Genetics (later Biometry) at University College, London, in 1933. With a rapidity that was astonishing even for the Haldanes, JBS published ten books between 1932 and 1940, all with a wide readership, not least his children's book, *My Friend Mr Leakey*. So captivating were JBS's depictions of the ingenious magician Mr Leakey, with his household of octopus, dragon, and djinn, that the *New York Herald Tribune*'s review opened with the words: 'From now on and until further notice all modern fairy-tales, I think, should be written by Professor Haldane.'[34] His wife Charlotte later claimed that the book was a result of JBS's uncompromising competitive streak. When Ronnie Burghes, Charlotte's son by her previous marriage, wrote a fairy tale at the age of twelve, JBS felt he had to respond with a tale of his own.[35] With behaviour like this, it is little wonder that his marriage with Charlotte was breaking down at this stage. They were still unable to produce a child, Charlotte was seeking consolation elsewhere, and there was now a young and spirited PhD student in JBS's lab, Helen Spurway, who was more than catching his attention. Charlotte and JBS would divorce in 1945, and JBS and Helen would marry shortly after.

Where JBS really made an impact on the popular imagination was in his articles in the press. If you lived in Britain or the US they were almost unavoidable, popping up with freakish frequency in the *Daily Express*, the *Daily Mail*, the *Spectator*, the *Manchester Guardian*, *Harper's Magazine*, *The Atlantic Monthly*, and elsewhere. These pithy, entertaining pieces were published simultaneously with major scientific papers. In 1936, for instance, he and his colleague Julia Bell were able to estimate, statistically, the distance on the X chromosome map between the loci for the genes for colour blindness and haemophilia—the first cartographical step towards the 'Human Genome Project'.[36] That same year, German troops moved into the Rhineland (directly contravening the Treaty of Versailles), the Rome–Berlin Axis was formulated, Mussolini conquered Abyssinia, the Germans and Japanese signed the Anti-Comintern Pact, and the Spanish Civil War began. As if in rebuke, JBS added *The Daily Worker* to his roster of publications the following year. He was now able to proclaim his views through the official newspaper of the Communist Party of Great Britain—though he was yet to join the party himself. MI5, the organisation which his uncle had initiated, had already opened a file under his name, but was continually frustrated by the lack of material with which to pin him down as a traitor. As a 1939 entry read, 'Professor HALDANE has been urged to declare himself a Party member... but he has not yet consented.'[37]

He had always been on the side of the underdog, and enjoyed causing a scene when he could—like the time, as a student, he disrupted the Oxford trams that continued to operate in the midst of a tram-driver strike with a loud recitation of the Athanasian Creed in the middle of Cornmarket Street; or the time he interrupted a heckler during a protest against the original version of the Treaty of Versailles by placing a finger in each of his nostrils and dragging him backwards out of the room, 'hooked and struggling like a salmon'.[38] When it came to the Spanish Civil War, there was a new opportunity for theatricality. It was not uncommon for his sister to dress herself in traditional peasant's attire, thinking herself earthy, but also to stand out and to show off (play writing and performing were, after all, her first artistic loves). Now it was JBS's turn consciously to create a costume for himself, before setting off to advise and fight with the Communist International Brigade against General Franco and his allies. His motor cyclist's cap, black leather jacket three sizes too small, and alarmingly tight breeches made him look a bit like a member of the Village People. His bristling moustache completed the outfit. Also in his bag was a tin hat with a broken chin-strap, a leftover from the trenches of the Western Front. It turned out to be 'the only tin hat in the whole [of] Republican Spain'.[39] He stood out all right.

JBS made three trips to Spain across 1936 and 1937. He was equal parts assistance and menace to the Republicans. On the one hand, he could advise and effectively improvise when it came to protection against gas attacks and air raids; he could ensure that the blood that was being donated by the residents of Madrid for the benefit of casualties and the sick was screened for infectious diseases; and he could act as an interpreter, once co-ordinating a conversation between an Italian who spoke French and a Hungarian who spoke German. On the other hand, according to Fred Copeman, the commander of the British Battalion of the International Brigade, JBS was 'more bloody nuisance than he was worth'. Copeman had been given instructions that JBS was not to get killed; he was too valuable as an advisor and a public exponent of the Republican cause. In an interview for the Imperial War Museum, Copeman recalled: 'I would go up, and every time I would say: "What bloody good do you think you are? First of all you're taking two blokes' room, two blokes can sit where your fat arse is, so get down out of it and get back to Brigade headquarters."'[40] Another fellow fighter described him as 'a big shaggy bear enjoying a picnic'.[41]

JBS's fellow Old Etonian George Orwell (Eric Arthur Blair) was also in Spain across the first half of 1937 to fight against Franco, but would go on to write critically in *Homage to Catalonia* of the pro-Stalinist communists fighting there. For Orwell, Stalin and his followers represented yet another form of the totalitarianism he was determined to resist. Naomi wrote to Orwell in appreciation, and Orwell responded outlining the socialist predicament. But there was another major writer of the twentieth century who was brought into contact with a Haldane because of the civil war, and this time with dramatic results. Indeed, JBS may rightly be remembered as the man who almost got Ernest Hemingway killed.

The American journalist Virginia Cowles, who was in Spain as a war correspondent, remembered being with fellow journalist

Martha Gellhorn, and Gellhorn's then lover (later husband) Hemingway, sheltering in a bomb-damaged house with no frontage, only to find JBS stomping up the stairs and dragging out from the debris a dilapidated red plush chair from which he could watch, through his field glasses, the tanks manoeuvring on a distant battlefield. With studied nonchalance, JBS placed the chair bang in the middle of the room to give himself full view of the action, and thus gave the tanks full view of him. Hemingway was not happy: 'Your glasses shine in the sun', he told the English visitor, 'they will think we are military observers.' JBS countered: 'My dear fellow, I can assure you there isn't any danger here in the house.' Ten minutes later, the tanks turned upon them. The Americans hit the deck for protection as the bombardment began. JBS swiftly made his way back down the stairs and ran out of range of the guns. Hemingway and the others, after nearly twenty minutes of shelling, eventually made it back to their hotel. Who should they find in the lobby but JBS, knocking back a beer. 'Hallo', he called to them amiably, 'let me buy you a drink.'[42]

* * *

Where did JBS get his (sometimes foolish) courage from? The answer, he believed, was his father, though one would be hard pressed to find John making the kind of blunders of which JBS was capable. Reflecting on his 'liking for war', JBS wrote:

> I get a definitely enhanced sense of life when my life is in moderate danger... I also find happiness in practising the virtue of courage. I am not a particularly brave man. I have not got the requisite courage to dive head first into water, and I am frightened by flying in bumpy weather... However, I was taught courage by my father, and am sufficiently self-conscious not to pretend that I am doing something else on the rare occasions when I am being brave.

He went on to add: 'I enjoy the comradeship of war. Men like war because it is the only socialised activity in which they have ever taken part. The soldier is working with comrades for a great cause (or so he believes). In peace-time he is working for his own profit or someone else's.'[43] This echoes Naomi's desire for what she, and the early Christian church, called *agape*—a Greek word which, in Naomi's hands, means something like 'a sharing, generous, unerotic love, and specifically... a communal meal taken in a spirit of love, mutuality and commemoration' (as explored in her 1939 novel, *The Blood of the Martyrs*).[44] The language of comradeship, initially so suggestive of communism, and the desire for something approaching *agape*, can also be traced to their father. For John, comradeship was a spiritual principle; it had nothing whatsoever to do with the atheistic dialectical materialism so beloved of the communists. John may have rejected organised religion, but the fundamental outlook of his parents and their forebears could not be extinguished in him. In his opening presidential address to the Institute of Mining Engineers in 1924, John stated:

> Neither high wages, high dividends, nor welfare schemes will satisfy them [miners who are treated as tools], but only discerning and sympathetic treatment, the treatment of comradeship in a common enterprise—such comradeship as existed in and between ranks during the war, or such comradeship as is taught in the Gospels... In fighting the difficulties and dangers of mining work; in fighting for the economic stability of mining undertakings, including the interests of shareholders; and in fighting for the highest welfare of those employed and their families, a mining engineer finds that spiritual reality in his comradeship in those around him.[45]

So JBS's and Naomi's socialism was an adaptation, if not necessarily a development, of a longstanding family commitment. When Naomi's friend, the outrageous and problematic Wyndham Lewis, teasingly inserted a crucifix into the background of his 1938 portrait of her (she was writing *The Blood of the Martyrs* at the time), she begrudged the addition. Much later, Naomi could say: 'I think he was perhaps right [to add the crucifix], he knew a bit more about me than I knew myself.'[46]

John did not live to see his son become a fully signed-up member of the CPGB. That would not happen until 1942. John died in 1936, and like his brother Richard he worked right up until the last. In his final year, with Elizabeth for company, he even toured Iran, Iraq, Greece, and Turkey to investigate heatstroke in oil refinery workers. But after a lifetime of inhaling poison gases, his lungs were in a bad way, and to add to his ailments he caught whooping cough from one of his grandsons. Then, one morning, he fell out of his high single bed and couldn't get up. Pneumonia followed, and there were still no antibiotics to put it right, nor to treat the cystitis with which his wife was suffering at the time. 'I managed to get my mother up and across to his room just once to see him', wrote Naomi. 'I remember how delighted he was, greeting her with words of love.'[47]

John showed immense interest in his own final illness, commenting on the curious dreams that fever brought him and talking through the medical details of his treatment with the doctors. He was thrilled to discover that his temperature, at one stage, had plummeted to a record low. Before long, he was in an oxygen tent—a most fitting setting for the final days of this pioneer of oxygen therapy. JBS joined his sister at Cherwell to watch over their father. It was hard to maintain a peaceful atmosphere. Naomi had told a reporter that John was seriously ill, which made her brother furious, expressing his disgust in the most stringent Marxist terms. The conflagration broke out in the dining room directly beneath John's bedroom, so they were forced to quarrel in whispers. Both already had a well-established violent streak (with Naomi even once tying up and beating a gay male friend at his request, which she quite enjoyed).[48] Conditions were now ripe for their old childhood scraps to re-emerge: 'I bit his arm; he twisted my wrist. Crazy unhappiness made us not care. Finally we broke apart and went soberly up to the sick room.'[49] Their unhappiness could not ward off the final hour. As Naomi recalled:

> My father died in the oxygen tent at exactly midnight. He had a look of intense interest on his face as though he were taking part in some crucial experiment in physiology which had to be carefully monitored. Jack and I watched him, one on each side. We could only go on the look, however much we longed to ask him. But it made me at least feel that here was an experience deeply worth having...[50]

It had been a remarkable life. As has been said of him, 'Men walked ocean beds, worked the deepest mines, dared scale Everest and envisage space flight, while doctors now had a bank of expertise and equipment to deploy in tending respiratory problems in their patients, all on the back of knowledge that he brought to the world.'⁵¹ John was determined that his body, even in death, would prove useful for the scientific endeavour, leaving his corpse to Oxford's Radcliffe Infirmary for dissection. His friends and students there could not bear to have it. Instead, there was a simple cremation service, where an extract from Plato's *Phaedo* was read out, along with a passage from one of John's books. Elizabeth was crushed, and made to feel even worse when she gathered with Naomi and JBS at Euston station before travelling north to Cloan with the ashes. On the platform, Jack, clutching the parcel with the ashes, tore into his aunt and sister for organising first-class sleeper tickets for themselves. What capitalists they were! No, he would have none of it, and would be travelling third, popping the parcel on the rack above him with no qualms whatsoever.

Some semblance of calm descended once they got to the little graveyard at Gleneagles, where a large crowd had gathered to see the great professor laid to rest beside his older brother. The beauty of the day was mirrored by the simple rendition of 'I to the Hills' in the old Scots fashion. 'Fair enough', wrote Naomi, 'we had not succumbed to religious orthodoxy, but allowed ourselves a little traditional comfort from our fellows.'⁵²

The following year, on Christmas Eve, Elizabeth died aged seventy-five. Naomi felt her aunt could have gone on longer had she been less active, but 'no Haldane likes sitting down and taking things easy'.⁵³ *The Scotsman* ran a long obituary, which began:

> The death of Miss Elizabeth Sanderson Haldane, C.H., LL.D.,... removes from the Scottish scene one of the most representative figures of her time. She was representative not because women of her stature were common in her day and generation, but because she admirably expressed in her life an outlook and ideals which were new and which she herself, in no small measure helped to formulate.⁵⁴

Her younger brother, Willie, was now the sole remaining child of Robert and Mary Haldane, and it was his turn to attach the words 'of Cloan' to his name, moving back to the turreted house of his boyhood and closing up Foswell for the time being (it would open up to Barnardo's when the war came, as would parts of Cloan). For his nephew and niece, the Cloan connection came largely to an end. JBS's last visit was made in 1937. Naomi observed: 'The links were snapping between me and Cloan... [Aunt Bay's] death was the end of something that mattered to me; I was sad for myself as well as her.' It was also the occasion for yet further tension between Naomi and her brother. Her aunt had left her some money, and in an act of attempted reconciliation she gave half of it to JBS. He donated the entire sum to the Communist Party. Naomi was disgusted: 'I never quite got over that slap in the face.'[55]

* * *

For all JBS's communist sympathies and the severing of the links with Cloan, when European tensions came finally to a head and war broke out in 1939, his scientific commitments only heightened the sense of continuity with the past. He may have despised the British government in many respects (they had recently turned a deaf ear to his campaign for underground air-raid shelters, preferring instead the above-ground Anderson shelters), but he was not going to pass up an opportunity to serve in the fight against fascism, especially when that fight could come in the form of physiological experiments. Like his father before him, JBS now put himself at the disposal of the defence services, bringing much sickness and pain upon himself. It brought excitement, too.

The sinking of HMS *Thetis* in the summer of 1939, before hostilities commenced, sparked JBS's involvement in the war effort. This disaster in Liverpool Bay was the result of an officer opening the inner hatch of one of the submarine's torpedo tubes, believing it to be dry when in fact its outer hatch was open to the sea. Two rooms were flooded, and the craft lost balance and ultimately sank. It cost the lives of ninety-nine men, forty-three of whom were civilians. It was JBS's grim job to determine, and to report to the government on, the conditions under which these men suffered as they re-breathed their own expired air, which was gradually poisoning them with carbon dioxide.

It must have been reassuringly familiar when JBS first entered the tiny compression chamber in which he could barely stand up; so reassuring that he stayed inside for fourteen-and-a-half hours.

This and following experiments were, in his opinion, 'merely extensions' of his father's old work.[56] Shortness of breath, headaches, photophobia, and vomiting were par for the course, and his subsequent recommendations on the improvement of submarine design and emergency procedures bore the stamp of long acquaintance with deadly environments. One of the recommendations was the addition of soda lime to a submarine's cargo, which would act as an absorbent for carbon dioxide. JBS told the government tribunal of inquiry, 'I think I was the first person to use soda lime in a submarine, and that was, I think, in the year 1905, when I was 12 years old.'[57]

This depth of knowledge and experience was invaluable to the government—though they could have done without the fact that JBS enlisted the help of some of his old comrades from the International Brigade during his experiments. Still, it was not enough to deter the Admiralty from asking him to carry out a series of further experiments of his own choosing that would help clarify, mitigate, and avoid physiological problems associated with the contingencies of submarine activity. The findings were to be classified. If JBS wanted to continue using for his investigations men and women who held suspicious political commitments, then there wasn't much the Admiralty could do. It was an eclectic band he gathered around him. It included his secretary, his lover (Helen Spurway), a German refugee, the exiled former Republican prime minister of Spain (Juan Negrín), and a handful of card-carrying communists. By 1942, JBS himself belonged well and truly to this last group. No one took a greater part in the experiments than he did.

In taking up these investigations, which resulted in more than a hundred pressure chamber tests, JBS would raise his father's old work to new levels of danger. 'I was on one occasion immersed in melting ice for thirty-five minutes', he wrote, 'breathing air containing 6 1/2 per cent of carbon dioxide, and during the latter part of the period also under ten atmospheres' pressure. I became unconscious. One of our subjects has burst a lung, but is recovering; six have been unconscious on one or more occasions; one has had convulsions.'[58] Sometimes the results were mainly comic: 'You feel pretty queer at ten atmospheres... your voice sounds very odd, as if you were trying to imitate a Yankee twang, and overdoing it very badly.'[59] The work was to have long-lasting consequences with regard to submarine escape routines. It also made possible further investigations by JBS and Helen Spurway that contributed both to the successful attack on the famous German battleship *Tirpitz* by British X-class midget submarines in September 1943, and to the operation to clear the time-bombs and underwater mines that blocked the Normandy ports.

JBS knew all about midget submarines. In the autumn of 1940, at Portsmouth Harbour, he and fellow volunteer Martin Case (an old friend from Cambridge days) were locked inside a crude mock-up of a miniature submarine cabin on three occasions and submerged beneath the water. It was less than 5 by 5 by 5 feet, and on their third submersion they had crammed in alongside them oxygen cylinders, boxes of soda lime, and equipment for gas analysis. Only one man could lie down at a time. They remained inside for three days, during which they experienced a host of inconveniences, including a water leak, disruption from a passing ship which set the craft at a jaunty angle, increasing wall condensation that left them soaked and shivering, and, as they were being hauled from the water, an air raid that halted the crane and left the cabin suspended and swinging in mid-air until the sirens ceased. By the end of their incarceration, JBS and Case had shown, invaluably, that 'with one oxygen cylinder and three containers, two men could live comfortably for three days. They could also live less comfortably, but without serious loss of efficiency, for twelve hours without any reconditioning of the air.'[60] As JBS's first biographer wrote, 'Perhaps only Haldane, with his family motto of "Suffer", could have used the word "comfortably".'[61]

There was, of course, less dramatic war work, embracing the mathematics of air raids, the theory of random patrolling for German U-boats, and the tactics for shooting down V-1 flying bombs. The RAF, the Ministry of Aircraft Production, and the army all sought him out. One well-known general even asked his advice on whether or not, in the event of invasion, the sea could be coated with oil and set on fire. No wonder JBS became, according to one reader of *Nature*, 'the most romantic figure in the biological world of today' in the eyes of the younger generation.[62] This appeal to his juniors was very noticeable. Isaiah Berlin said of himself and other rising intellectuals of his age that JBS was 'one of our major intellectual emancipators'.[63] They admired his commitment to uncovering the truth by empirical investigation and his refusal to let convenient illusions soften the blow of reality. But where did ideology fit in? JBS appeared not even to wince when Russia signed their nonaggression pact with Germany in 1939, and his reaction was just as unintelligible when he later discovered that Nikolai Vavilov, the man who had once hosted him in Russia, had been taken prisoner on Stalin's orders and subsequently died of malnutrition in a forced labour camp in 1943. Vavilov's crime? Defending the discipline of genetics against its greatest detractor, Trofim Lysenko, Stalin's favoured 'biologist'. JBS's response? Silence, sprinkled with prevarication. Ideology had taken the upper hand.

It would be natural to ask if JBS may have been a spy for Russia. How could a committed pro-Stalin communist working on secret investigations for the British government resist spilling the scientific beans to his Russian friends? There have been books written that claim he did.[64] In fact, the evidence that JBS was a traitor to his country is very slim indeed, if non-existent. His voluminous MI5 file contains nothing which could genuinely incriminate him. The unredacted intercepts of an American counterintelligence programme known as 'Venona' do have references to JBS, but even these don't give us much to go on. Venona is known for uncovering the Cambridge Five and other high-profile cases of espionage. It also exposed the far less exciting or effective Gruppa Iks (X-Group). It was once believed that JBS, using the code name INTELLIGENTSIA, was the leader of this rather underwhelming group of British agents, but the Venona intercepts reveal that the name belonged to JBS's friend, Ivor Montagu—known for his filmmaking and a love of table tennis. The intercepts also show that JBS handed Montagu a copy of his eight-page report to the Admiralty 'on his experience relating to the length of time a man can stay underwater'.[65] That is the extent of JBS's known involvement. There is not even evidence to show that he handed the report over in the knowledge that it would find its way into Soviet hands. Samanth Subramanian states the position well: 'If espionage involves the deliberate transfer of secrets to another state, nothing stains Haldane's innocence at all.'[66] Still, enough MPs and MI5 officials held him in suspicion that by the 1950s his name was removed from the governmental subcommittees on which he served. They could no longer trust him to keep classified information to himself. Even if they were wrong, it is certainly true that JBS was capable of holding highly problematic, sometimes reprehensible, political views. But that is for our next chapter.

* * *

While JBS was busy re-enacting his father's career, Graeme Haldane spent the war years following up on his Uncle Richard's concerns over energy and defence. He was involved, for instance, in meetings with the difficult genius (Sir) Frank Whittle concerning the development of the gas turbine, which would go on to revolutionise aviation. Graeme's preference, however, was for his work at the National Physical Laboratory at Teddington, home of Richard's brainchild the Advisory Committee for Aeronautics, and other specialist groups. Here, Graeme and his team had been set the task of trialling what, on first hearing, sounds like a rather far-fetched idea: the possibility of disrupting overhead power-line networks by floating small hydrogen balloons across them, attached to which would be long lengths of wire which would do the disrupting. Ultimately, the plan was to fly such balloons across Germany, though this never transpired. To ascertain the practicalities, the team at Teddington rigged up a dummy section of high-voltage line, over which they floated the balloons. Importantly, they stationed a man with a shotgun at the boundaries of the laboratory's land, where he shot down the balloons once they'd completed their job. Things did not always go to plan. As Graeme later wrote:

> These balloons carried not only wire but other quite heavy equipment. One day two balloons were accidentally released simultaneously; the gun man duly shot down the first to reach him, but the second was well outside the grounds before he could explode it. There was a great crash as the wire and equipment fell through a glass conservatory of a private house nearby. As ill-luck would have it an old lady had been evacuated there from a bombed east London district and, though unhurt, was very much alarmed. The NPL Director had a great difficulty in pacifying her and at the same time keeping the nature of the work secret.[67]

Graeme was made a partner in Merz & McLellan in 1941, after the tragic death of Charles Merz and his family in the blitz. The loss of his admired mentor was offset by Graeme's marriage to Leslie Janet Wilkie, known as Billee, in 1942, and the two set up home together in Esher, Surrey—in Merz's former house, in fact. The family story goes that Graeme and Billee had met at a 'Meet' before a fox hunt, with the former on horseback and the latter on foot. They were reintroduced some weeks later, and Graeme was forced to admit he did not remember the young New Zealander (she had emigrated, penniless, to Britain in 1928, arriving on the day of her twentieth birthday). The only thing he remembered from the hunt was that a horse had bitten his bottom. Quick as a flash, Billee responded: 'Well, I bet if I had bitten your bottom you would have remembered me!'

That was Billee—intelligent, quick, open, and blunt. Later, her son Dick's friends would find her frankness highly entertaining and somewhat alarming. One young woman, in a relationship with Dick's best friend, upon being introduced to Billee was asked, 'Well, what sort of contraception do you use?' Whenever Dick mentioned he had a new girlfriend, his mother would reply, 'And have you slept with her yet?' These questions, along with her passion for modern technology, suggest a lady with advanced views, and yet in other matters Billee was ferociously traditional. The experience of her own parents' separation gave her no tolerance for divorcees (her mother was the twice-married Claire Georgetti, a flamboyant concert pianist). Billee refused to have a divorced person in her house. Interracial relationships were also unacceptable in her eyes, but on this she was less vocal. Her forcefulness may have been the reason for Graeme's attraction, for he did not find it easy to speak with women. Billee made that job easier.

Another attractive quality was the career success Billee had achieved in her own right. Amongst her many accolades, she had set up the advertising section of *Harper's Bazaar* and served as personal private secretary to Geoffrey Shakespeare, Minister of Health, Pensions and Unemployment, and as Radium Officer in charge of the Radium Department at the Royal Cancer Hospital. It was also at the RCH that she acted as administrative secretary to Constance Wood, Director of Radium Beam Therapy Research, whose reference for Billee when she applied for her next job stated, 'In writing this testimonial I am seeking to rob myself of the ablest assistant we have ever had.' In the three years directly before her marriage, she was chief administrator of the A&E department at the Elizabeth Garrett Anderson Hospital. Sadly, with the exception of a seven-year stint as a magistrate at the family court in Kingston upon Thames, her entry into the Haldane family signalled an end to this impressive list of titles, a fact that she seemed to resent. A month before she died, in her eighty-first year, she revealed these career successes for the first time to her daughter Robin, and remarked, 'So you see, I did achieve a little before I got married!'[68]

Billee's flatmate in the years before her marriage was Janet Macrae Simpson-Smith, known as Jan, a lawyer from Huddersfield of middle-class origins. She had met Archie in London through a friend of Billee's, and the two were married in December 1941 (around the same time as Pearl Harbor, as they liked to point out). Jan was a shy, self-effacing woman but she could be tough. She had been an apprentice to one of the UK's first female solicitors, Mary Sykes, in Huddersfield, and then went through numerous rejections by London law firms before she was eventually taken on by W. F. Tweedie, who accepted her simply because they were intrigued by the prospect of a female lawyer. After their marriage, Jan moved to Scotland to join Archie in Edinburgh and Cloan. The latter, where Willie and Edith still lived, had become quite a different place since the outbreak of war. Much of it had served as army divisional headquarters for a brief period, before Barnardo's moved into some of the ground floor and the whole of the second floor. A partition wall was added to the hallway to keep the dining room and library private for the family, who also had the run of the first floor. Elsie's son, Pat Campbell Fraser, remembers visiting Cloan as a small boy during these war years. What stood out more than anything was Willie's chain-smoking—he would smoke his cigarettes right down until they almost burnt his fingers—and the very particular smell of his tobacco. Neither can Pat forget the breakfast routine, with the children made to eat their porridge standing: a tradition from Willie's own childhood which he rigidly enforced. The children would walk around the table as they ate, and only once they were finished could they sit down for their cooked breakfast.

Archie initially continued to work at the legal office in Edinburgh, but after some underwhelming attempts to find war work, he was offered a job as a Principal in the Ministry of Production in London, with Jan gaining a similar post at the Ministry of Supply (they always felt their titles would have been more appropriate the other way round!). They found comfortable lodgings in Knightsbridge, but it was not a happy time for Archie: 'I did not take kindly to life in the Civil Service which seemed very like a return to school with the absurd rules as to whether one might or might not have a carpet in one's room, depending strictly on rank.'[69] By 1943, his trials in London were over, and new ones were encountered up north. His mother had died that year and Jan and he returned to Scotland to support Willie in the office and at Cloan, where staff were short.

When in Edinburgh, Jan worked at the Royal Botanical Gardens, and continued in good Haldane fashion by insisting on equal pay with the male employees. At weekends, she oversaw the running of Cloan. It was a struggle. 'Advancing years had not made my father any easier', wrote Archie, 'while the presence for a time of a competent, well-meaning but somewhat overbearing Miss Mackenzie who had come to us as a companion in my Mother's time did little to lessen difficulties.'[70] One of the challenges of living with Willie was that he was very tight with his money, or, as Archie would say, he 'looked at two sides of a shilling'. When a new fridge became an absolute necessity at Cloan, he refused to have one, point-blank. Much to her credit, Jan simply went out and made the requisite purchase. When Willie returned to find the buzzing white box installed in the kitchen, he was outraged. But there was nothing he could do. The fridge stayed put.

Archie found consolation throughout the war in his writing. *By Many Waters* (1941) beautifully records his pre-war fishing holidays, often in Graeme's company, while *The Path by the Water* (1944) tells the story of his early fishing adventures with his brother Pat. These publications, which were commercially successful, revealed Archie to be in possession of a striking literary talent. He had an exceptional ability to describe the sights, sounds, smell, and touch of nature, and to evoke transcendent but fleeting happiness, the remembrance of which both sustained and haunted him.

* * *

Graeme and JBS were not the only ones tracing the footsteps of their elders during the war. Naomi was heir to Mary Haldane just as much as she was to her Aunt Bay. The Mitchisons' purchase of the Carradale estate on the Kintyre peninsula in late 1937 was a decisive step towards a new matriarchy. Interestingly, Naomi drove west from Cloan with Graeme and Archie (the family legal firm were acting for the sellers) to view the property directly after Elizabeth's funeral, just at the time her close links with Cloan were coming to an end. It must have been a welcome sight when she first spotted Carradale House, with its Cloan-like turrets sprouting up here and there. Less welcome was the discovery that, as at Cloan, it was hard to make a profit from the land, though decent shooting and fishing were to be had (as much to Dick Mitchison's pleasure as it was to Archie and Graeme's). At just under 300 acres and in fairly poor condition, the estate was only a shadow of its former self, most of it already having been sold off. It still brought multiple responsibilities. There were staff and redundancies to deal with, as well as tenancies, land improvements, house renovations, farming, and a garden in desperate need of taming.

Naomi relished this last task, though most of it was done by a three-man team of gardeners, headed by the aptly named Mr MacGregor. Naomi was proud of their early efforts:

> with the walled garden hoed into weedlessness and all ivy and escallonia clipped or fastened back, the greenhouses painted and never a broken pane, the paths in the wild garden cleared..., the long stretches of grass mowed, even the croquet lawn almost level. There was also a splendid wire fruit cage for the soft fruit, with enormous currant bushes and row on row of raspberries.

Tellingly, she adds: 'So it was all rather like Cloan, only more so.'[71]

With responsibilities came possibilities, too. Ironically, despite Naomi's role as a significant landowner (Dick's too, but he was rarely in residence), Carradale offered the chance to put certain socialist principles into action. Some objectives were easy to accomplish, such as opening the estate to the public, providing an annual campsite for the Glasgow Young Communist League, turning a blind eye to poaching, and starting a local Labour Party branch. These things may have been easy, but they were radical in the context. According to one close family friend from that time, it was as if 'the cultural bedrock had been ripped up from underneath the village'.[72] A less easy task was to find a way of living alongside the locals who had been there for generations, and to do so in such a manner that Naomi wasn't viewed as an upper-class imposter from the South. She felt that the move to Carradale had strengthened her 'growing feeling of being a Scot and a Haldane at that'.[73] But would the reticent fishermen and their wives embrace her as one of them? One only has to listen to a recording of her wonderfully plummy voice (on her 1991 'Desert Island Discs', for instance) to realise how challenging it was going to be.

Could there be trust or common ground? Could she be 'respected as a worker'?[74] Ironically, in a letter back to her mother in 1939, her attempt to show that she was beginning to surmount some of the barriers falls almost immediately into classic aristocratic mode:

> I find that in talking with me now, they [the fishermen] are much less careful to use 'English' and they produce the most lively and poetic phrases and words which I knew in books; they remind me very much of some of the miners whom Uffer used to bring back. I seem to have been told so much about Carradale now that I might have been there for a generation. Oddly enough, there is probably a very remote family connection, for the castle on the golf course was built by a Lennox who is, I think, the Lennox who comes into the Haldane family tree, and, knowing the habits of fifteenth century earls, it seems highly likely that he has descendants in Carradale.[75]

Despite these possible family connections, the Carradale enterprise offered an opportunity to start afresh. Initially it was simply viewed as a spring–summer residence where family and friends could assemble over the holidays. Rivercourt in London would remain the Mitchisons' real home. But war soon came, forcing people out of London, and Naomi was fast falling in love with a romanticised version of West Highland life, especially in remote fishing communities. Their simple communal ways of living seemed to combat her growing disillusion with the grand socialist experiments going on elsewhere and with the compromises of day-to-day Labour Party politics. Moreover, Naomi was now out of favour on the English literary scene. *We Have Been Warned* was repeatedly turned down by publishers before its appearance in 1935. Its depiction of rape, abortion, and the use of 'rubber goods' was what made it controversial, but it was an unwieldy novel anyway. When *The Blood of the Martyrs* appeared in 1939, it mustered praise in certain quarters, but left some readers feeling that her depiction of the early Christians smacked of 'a Fabian summer school captured by white slavers'.[76]

Disenchanted with the South, Naomi began to reconnect with her Scottish roots at a time when there was an artistic and literary renaissance taking shape in Scotland. Into this she readily elided. Her long poem 'The *Alban* Goes Out: 1939', already shows Naomi (with a touch of wishful thinking probably) embedded in her new community, one of the fishermen, belonging to a people in a way she never had before: 'When all our hands are as net-cut, and our eyes as / sore from the spray, / How can we think of our neighbours except in a / neighbourly way?' Her early efforts towards a consciously Scottish literary craftsmanship marked the start of an affectionate correspondence with Neil Gunn—the leader, one could argue, of the new movement in Scotland, after Hugh MacDiarmid's removal to Sodom (of all places) in Shetland—and she would soon form a close friendship with another leading light of the renaissance, Eric Linklater. That said, in Naomi's own opinion, 'I was definitely not one of the bright and coming-up young people.'[77] Instead, scholars of the Scottish Renaissance would come to see her as a 'dual inspiration for male and female writers of that Renaissance'. Professor Douglas Gifford was convinced she had made a 'colossal contribution to this movement in Scottish culture'.[78]

Arguably, her greatest contribution came in the form of her novel *The Bull Calves*, begun in 1941 and published in 1947. It did not sell well, but it is something of a masterpiece. Set in Gleneagles, the family home of the central branch of the Haldanes, in the aftermath of the second failed Jacobite uprising of 1745, the book tells us as much about Naomi's feelings for her family both historic and present (since certain characters are modelled on her immediate relations) as it does about Scottish history, Naomi's politics, and her literary talent. Of her family, she is at turns unflattering ('Black William sat himself down at his wife's feet, his head against her knee, with that kind of grace that a Highlander could have so lightly, but none of the Haldanes had');[79] critical ('We were aye thinking of the anger of the Lord, since we had no right understanding of His Love';[80] the Haldanes have a 'sometimes intolerable serious-mindedness');[81] perceptive ('We Haldanes had aye stood for liberty of conscience and against the Bishops and the great nobles and any kind of divine or unreasonable rights, either of kings or others');[82] and extremely fond. Her love for her family is nowhere more evident than in the following passage, shining a light not only on eighteenth-century life at Gleneagles, but on her memories of Cloan and Cherwell and Naomi's present world of the Carradale dining room:

> By and bye James caught her [Helen Haldane] up on a theological matter of which she knew little, and contradicted her. At that, the young Haldane and half Haldanes all joined in, leaning across the table and talking in loud voices, baying to their own satisfaction and never listening for more than a moment to one another. Kirstie [the novel's version of Naomi] laughed, enjoying it all, for it went away back to her own childhood, the same kind of jokes, it seemed to her, the heavy punning on words and misquotations from the scriptures or Horace, the younger ones picking it up, year after year, trying now to make their own points and snubbed by their slightly elders, Elizabeth rather indelicately scratching her midge-bites.[83]

Naomi's feelings for her brother—the model for the notorious Patrick Haldane in the book—also flicker between the lines, and sometimes burst through forcefully. Patrick, 'the curse of Scotland' (see Chapter 2), was 'aye seeing the worst side of folk and how easy they could be turned and twisted by money and privilege'.[84] He often spoke 'with a kind of simple scorn and complacency that must be let go, aye, must be taken as part of his nature, part of the Haldane nature maybe'.[85] Naomi captures Patrick's complexity (and by extension, JBS's) and in so doing gives him as positive a depiction as one is likely to find in any history book. In her notes on the novel, she writes of having 'a certain fellow-feeling for the black sheep' of the family.[86] So, approvingly, she has Patrick saying: 'I like folks better than I like either the laws of God or the laws of Scotland. Or any of your kings and loyalties and oaths.'[87] But 'with his sudden childish pride', he can also say: 'I have the most peculiar and exceptional hatred… and never for the reasons which are commonly considered adequate or honourable.'[88] This was as true of JBS as it was of Patrick.

The Bull Calves was Naomi's statement to her fellow Scottish writers that a new literary presence was on the block. It was a major part of her efforts to press the restart button, a working out and clarification of her Scottish roots and connections, a statement of her own Scottishness. When she visited the National Library of Scotland in Edinburgh at the outset of her research in 1941, she saw the effort—characteristically—in rather grandiose terms, egged on (or so she felt) by the principal librarian, Dr Meikle:

> Meikle saw me as part of Scottish history, descendant and representative of the Haldanes and indeed of all the great families whose blood is mixed in mine—for indeed there is scarcely one of them that isn't represented, Highland and Lowland. And I felt in turn the pride and responsibility, immediately, that I had to write the hell of a good book, that I had to explain something very important, that it was laid on me.[89]

So much for her companionship with the proletariat! For all that, *The Bull Calves* is a novel born in a crucible of suffering, and this may account for its power. War had now engulfed the world, there were evacuees to take in at Carradale, food production intensified, her older children were of an age to be called up, and the terrors of 1914–18 had to be faced anew. She was even put on the Gestapo's *Sonderfahndungsliste GB*, a special blacklist of individuals singled out for arrest and imprisonment in the event of the planned Nazi invasion of Britain in 1940 (JBS and his then wife Charlotte also featured on the list). 'At first I thought I would try to convince them I really loved Germany', Naomi wrote, imagining the scene, 'but that would never have worked, so then I thought I might be able to shoot one or two of them before I was shot myself.'[90]

Naomi would meticulously document these challenges, as well as her tingling flirtations and stolen kisses with some of the local Carradale men, in her diary for the Mass-Observation project—an endeavour started in 1937 by some of Naomi's friends and acquaintances, who were looking to capture the details of ordinary life across Britain. Of course, Naomi's life in the 'Big House' (or *Tigh Mòr*, as she liked to call it in the Gaelic) was far from ordinary, but her privileges weren't enough to keep her free from pain. She fell pregnant in 1939, the same year she moved permanently to Carradale, at the age of forty-two. A girl, Clemency Ealasaid, was born on 4 July 1940. The baby seemed weak; something was not quite right. The next day she died of a heart defect. She was taken out in a local fishing boat, the *Cluaran*, and buried at sea.

Naomi was distraught and broken, and Dick was away (we have no record of his feelings at the time). 'The ghost of the cot is still there when I turn to my right', she wrote that month in a poem of devastating honesty and intensity, named after her dead daughter, 'And when I turn to my left, there is the sea, there is Carradale Bay, and the sea-deep, / Dark and alone where the Cluaran dropped her, my dear, my daughter, / Not in my arms, not in my womb: in the box Angus made, a small weight.' Inevitably, she could not keep this loss free from the other losses she felt approaching:

> Now I am trying to bargain, to say take her death, my grief,
> But save me the others, from bombs, shells, from pandemic
> Disease, save me children and husband...
> Clutching out for lives on the spread bargain counter, clutching
>   them to my heart,
> But looking up I see
> No bargainer on the far side of the counter, nothing: only another
> projection.

Like her Aunt Bay before her, contemplating the consequences of the blockades and reparations that were forced upon Germany after the First World War, Naomi had the presence of mind to see past the simplified rhetoric of a battle between good and evil. Her baby's death had stung her into a heightened objectivity:

> This winter we hope to starve
> France, Belgium, Holland, Denmark, Norway, Poland:
> Harvest of dead babies, disease, hatred: no sense.
> My breasts tingle and stab with milk that no one wants,
> Surplus as American wheat, surplus and senseless.
> Not her soft kind mouth groping for me. Useless, senseless.
> If my baby had been starved by England, would I ever forgive?

Not even Carradale was exempt from her damning, if now less objective, insight: 'How shall I stay here, how go on with the little things, / How not hate Carradale, the flowery betrayer, / Dagger in fist?' And yet, in a delicate balance between consolation and despair, Naomi could write, 'The roughest day is not yet.'[91]

There was something in her newfound love of Scotland that saw her through these years, even when the realities of life on the edge of a small village exhausted her and when the locals, in whom she invested so much significance, seemed to let her down. Again, her Aunt Bay was a model. She became heavily involved in local committees and projects, especially the campaign for a proper harbour and the building of a village hall—where, harking back to her adolescence, she and her friends performed in plays that she wrote throughout this period. The influence of her Uncle Richard, with his passion for devolving power wherever possible, can also be detected in her Carradale commitments. He would have uttered a hearty Amen to her comments of 1944:

> democracy must start in the home—with responsibility, choice and freedom of thought for the children—must go on to the school, the factory and the village. Then build up if you like. But it's not good enough to have a central plan and delegating small things to small bodies; that's the wrong way round.

He may not have agreed with her next sentence: 'Yet the other way of it will only come after a break up, a revolution.'[92] Her longing for revolution was at least tempered with a welcome dose of reality and humour: 'The bore is that any "New Order" will mean that I have to do much more washing up and mending and shall then have no time to write!'[93] She could also flare into anger, even thirst for blood: 'all I wanted was revolution and the chance of killing people myself'.[94] Perhaps she had been influenced by JBS, who had written to her: 'you (and the Labour Party) will have to realise that construction... can't start till the necessary destruction is done'.[95]

Ultimately, however, her urge was to be kind, to welcome, to mother even. There was no truer monument to this than Carradale House itself, a veritable melting pot of waifs and strays, as well as writers, scientists, politicians, and, above all, family. If Naomi had once been accused of not caring sufficiently for her children, her wartime diary reveals her deep concern for them (though her youngest, Val, resented her mother for sending her to the local Carradale primary school, while her siblings were receiving expensive educations in England). They were all growing into remarkable people, with the eldest two boys more than filling the Haldane shoes by this stage—though it was their father Dick, more than Naomi, who pushed for the children's intellectual achievement. Denny joined the Young Communist League in his late teens, painted red hammers and sickles wherever he could, and bolted from his German exchange school on Lake Constance. In Paris he met up with his mother, who found him 'looking really remarkably dirty even for one of my children, and we went to visit some old revolutionary—which? He had assassinated someone, no doubt deservedly, and Denny was thrilled.'[96] His fervour didn't stop him taking a first-class degree in natural sciences at Trinity College, Cambridge, where he was awarded a senior scholarship to study medicine before being 'rusticated' (sent away for a term) for having a woman in his rooms. That woman was Ruth Gill, 'the best medical student of her year'.[97] The Dean of Trinity took Ruth aside, wrote a short note about her being 'discovered' and told her to deliver it to the Dean of her own college, Girton, adding that he thought the incident would end her student career. Ruth simply went away and shredded the note, with no further consequences.[98] She and Denny were soon married, and children swiftly followed. Denny went on to complete his medical degree (and thus avoid military service) at University College, London, in 1943.

Murdoch meanwhile excelled in the academic hothouse of Winchester (his parents had told him he could only go to a conventional public school if he won a scholarship, which he did with ease), and then followed his brother up to Trinity, Cambridge, again as a scholar, to study medicine. Having secured his first within two years (though failing to qualify medically on account of his poor marks in anatomy), he too escaped front-line service, serving in Operational Research as a civilian from 1941 until 1943, at which point he received his commission into the army—though, to Naomi's relief, he continued in the same field. His work revolved around gunnery, armoured vehicle design, and—strangely—the impact of mud viscosity on tank movements. Murdoch claimed to be known as 'the designated officer in charge of mud'.[99]

* * *

Naomi's wish for revolution didn't stop her from engaging with real-world politics. Though she never fully embraced Scottish nationalism, her concern for devolution and her respect for nationalist figures such as John MacCormick led her to support certain SNP ventures. During the war, this took the shape of MacCormick's initiation of the all-party Scottish Convention, with Naomi not only in attendance in Glasgow but also joining the Convention's education committee. It was the start of long service, in numerous forms, to Scotland's people. It also gave Naomi some sense of value while Dick was busy pursuing worthy causes in London, not least his research for William Beveridge's ground-breaking report of 1942, setting the stage for the welfare state. Naomi sometimes felt belittled by Dick and his London friends, notably Douglas and Margaret Cole. She found it hard to deny 'the sense of inferiority that one tends to feel when confronted with hard-working left wingers'.[100] Yet Dick remained her mainstay, and she wished she could see more of him (he only came to Carradale during holiday periods). While he was away, they wrote to each other practically every day. She was satisfied when he finally became the MP for Kettering in 1945, beating the not yet scandalous John Profumo. Dick now had a purpose and a sense of success that, until that point, had been lacking in his life.

That year, 1945, brought the end of the war, but it also brought the end of the togetherness of community life that the war had engendered. Naomi closed her wartime diary in a way perhaps only a Haldane could:

> I know we are going to have hell trying to work the peace, trying to give people a worth-while-ness in their peace time lives comparable with the worth-while-ness of working together during the war. We shall probably fail. I think we are in for a civilization based on communism with its new system of classes. It may be unpleasant and its immediate values are not those I care for. However I think if we accept it and work from within in the sphere of values (and bloody well see that we and our children are in the ruling class—technocrats and commissars) the new civilization will have a pretty good chance. It means taking the long view. That, at near fifty, is hard. The short view is the County Council and all that implies.[101]

Once again, the Haldanes were determined to make the future their own.

11

THE LONG VIEW

1945 ONWARDS

Naomi was elected to the Argyll County Council in 1945, but it hardly offered obvious steps to revolution. '[P]erhaps I influenced a few useful decisions', she later wrote. The example she then offers is not exactly inspiring: she stopped the spraying of verges with weed-killer. Having said that, her Aunt Bay, a pioneer of public lending libraries, would have enthused over her other success: the instigation of the Argyll Collection of pictures, 'the first travelling school collection in Scotland'.[1] Still, it all felt a bit small fry; she longed for a bigger stage. In articles and essays she pushed for more devolution, a Scottish Parliament, a burst of money and initiative in fishing and agriculture, public ownership of the land, and a reassessment of the education system. Her pleas seemed to disappear into the ether. She was delighted, therefore, to receive an invitation in 1947 to join the post-war Labour government's newly formed Highland Panel, set to advise the Scottish Office on matters concerning fishing, agriculture, forestry, transport, and social issues in the Highlands. Here she could be of national, practical use. 'We would be able to do so much', she thought initially, 'for the people of the Highlands.'[2] Or would they?

It didn't take long for her to discover that the Panel would have 'no power and no money' and therefore 'it would be totally unable to achieve anything and so would not in the end bother anybody'. Failing power and money, Naomi turned to tears as a tried and tested way of getting people to do what she wanted:

> I managed to cry over [Arthur] Woodburn who was then in charge [at the Scottish Office] and this always made him so uncomfortable

that some little thing might have to be looked at. But I never went into tears twice on the same floor of the Scottish Office. That would have been counter-productive.[3]

But really, Naomi's recollections of her time on the Panel, especially when her focus was on rejuvenating Scottish fishing, are one long litany of failures and unfulfilled plans. The Panel's 'suggestions about measures for fish conservation came to nothing or very little';[4] their 'detailed proposals' over grants and loans for modern boats and fishing methods 'never got enough official backing to go through';[5] their campaign against trawling fell on deaf ears. When it came to social issues, Naomi was aware that the Panel's interventions would face resistance from the deeply religious communities in the west of Scotland, and she herself was aware that the changes they were proposing were morally ambiguous. Still, it didn't stop her from having a bit of fun with those who were dead set against the Panel's ambitions:

> Well, a deputation arrived, I think both of them F[ree] P[resbyterian] Ministers, to remonstrate with the Panel... They were against village halls, the singing of songs other than religious or Gaelic, and promiscuous—that is to say boys and girls—dancing. I asked in a rather shocked voice if they preferred men dancing together; this was picked up with a few friendly twinkles by other Panel members but not by the deputation, buggery being uncommon in the Islands where, I think, sheep are preferred, or small cows.[6]

The fun continued, as did her frustration, in her novel *Lobsters on the Agenda* (1952), which explores the complex issues at stake in Highland intervention. Naomi even inserted a fictional version of herself, 'short and solid', into the story.[7] It is she who says bluntly, 'I'm allergic to Ministers.'[8]

Ultimately, what really struck Naomi again and again was the difficulty of making positive changes in the Highlands when so many decisions still emanated from Whitehall (her Uncle Richard, that great advocate of ever-greater devolution, would have felt similarly perturbed). Looking back in 1986, she gives a perfect example:

> There was a time when They (but a more remote They, geographically several hundred miles, a night's journey even from Edinburgh,

let alone the Ness), decided that all rail traffic north and west of Inverness must cease. We pointed out little obvious difficulties like one-track roads easily snow-blocked in winter, not suitable for the buses which had been imagined in a Home Counties setting. There was no response. At that time the Jock [Lord Cameron, Senator of the College of Justice] was our Chairman and he persuaded some of us... to agree that we must face them with the threat of a strike and good media publicity. We would simply walk out on the rail closures... The thing was a success and there were no more rail closures. Not for the moment. But today? Will the South ever listen to us?[9]

These reflections on her time on the Highland Panel have Naomi written all over them and show quite clearly where she continued on, and diverged from, traditional Haldane lines. There is the same passionate regard for changing society (in her own image?) and for the dispersal of power; the same provocative disregard for convention. Where she differs is in her capacity for realism at the outset of a new venture. While her father and his siblings were optimists, they were always aware of the enormous obstacles that stood in their way and that, whatever was achieved, it would only be a step in the right direction, never the end goal itself. In most of what Naomi undertook she seemed to think a new world was on the horizon. 'The pattern becomes all too clear', observed Douglas Gifford, 'idealism and vision untampered by prosaic realism destined... to result in as much disillusion as success.'[10] This was as true of her time on the County Council as it was of her time on the Highland Panel. When, as a result of a slanderous local campaign, she lost her Council seat to a Conservative after almost twenty years of service, she was never quite able to forgive the Carradale community. She felt she had worked tirelessly on their behalf, even securing them a new fishing harbour, and this was their thanks. In the end, it left her with 'mixed feelings about Scotland'.[11]

* * *

A similar pattern of ambition and disappointment emerges when we look to her brother's political commitments, though JBS was reluctant to admit it himself. As the 1940s and 1950s rolled on, Stalin's crimes became ever clearer to the world, as did JBS's talent for obfuscation when challenged on the matter. In fact, the show trials, the purges, the starvation, the total disregard for freedom and justice that reigned in the Soviet Union barely seemed to rock his communist creed at all. When his first wife, Charlotte—the first British woman to be a war correspondent—returned in 1941 from her time reporting in Russia, she recounted to her husband her first-hand experience of the truth behind Soviet propaganda:

> My reports caused him, undoubtedly, considerable surprise and mental uneasiness. But he was intellectually and emotionally incapable of assessing their objective value; tied, as he still was but I no longer, to the propaganda of King Street, to Party discipline, and to the sacred texts of Communism, the works of Marx, Engels, Lenin and Stalin.[12]

Even towards the end of his life, when it was all too clear that people he had known and respected had lost their careers and even died at Stalin's orders, JBS could tell a former colleague at University College: 'As you know, I disagreed, during Stalin's lifetime, with some of his actions. But I thought, and think, that he was a very great man who did a very good job. And as I did not denounce him then, I am not going to do so now.'[13]

It was not the inhumanity of Stalin's actions that rocked the boat for JBS (we remember what he told Naomi about the necessity of destruction before construction); no, it was Stalin's attitude to science that ultimately unnerved him. Having once waxed lyrical about Russia's glorification of science, JBS slowly witnessed a revolution of an altogether darker kind unfold. For all his communism, JBS basically held to his Uncle Richard's view on the relationship between politicians and scientists, as expressed in the Haldane Principle.[14] When politicians overruled scientists with regard to research, questions ought to be asked. The problem was that the art of questioning was not easy for members of the Communist Party, especially not the chairman of the editorial board of *The Daily Worker* (as JBS was from 1940 until 1950).

Matters came to a head in the summer of 1948 at Moscow's Central House of Scientists, where the Lenin All-Union Academy of Agricultural Sciences was meeting for its annual conference. The

Academy's president, Trofim Lysenko, a Ukrainian peasant who was also director of the Institute of Genetics, addressed the 700-strong assembly and, with his words and consequent actions, changed the face of Soviet science. Lysenko proceeded to denounce, piece by piece, the orthodoxies that governed the Western world's practice of genetics. Genes did not actually exist, chromosomes did not carry the information of heredity, statistics were of no value, mutations were irrelevant. To think otherwise, so Lysenko and the Soviet authorities' argument went, you would have to deny the basic Marxist assertion that nature, even human nature, is at the command of human hands, that the future can be manipulated, *perfected* in fact, according to the human will.

Lysenko's rise through the ranks under Stalin was a result of the fact that he claimed he could do just that, having conducted experiments on wheat that showed—or so he said—that acquired characteristics could pass down from one generation to the next. Organisms could be changed, he said, by changing the environment itself, and the changes would last. Mendel was out, Lamarck was in. The Soviet people, well acquainted with famine, were told that the wheat that had once withered in the Siberian winters now flourished due to Lysenko's interventions, and it would continue to do so. The reality was quite other. When forced to follow suit and apply Lysenko's methods, catastrophe struck for Soviet agriculture. Crops failed over and over again. The loss of human life was immense. And for the Russian scientists who disagreed with Lysenko, there was no chance for debate. If you were lucky, you simply lost your job, as thousands did. For others, there was prison or the psychiatric hospital. Some even went the way of Lysenko's predecessor at the Academy of Agricultural Sciences and the Institute of Genetics, Nikolai Vavilov. Deviation could mean death.

Back in Britain, JBS was deeply concerned by these developments but didn't want to let on publicly. It was the middle of the Cold War, and anything that could be taken as a mini-victory for the Americans was to be avoided. He was afraid that by speaking out he would undermine the Communist Party and himself, even though more and more left-leaning scientists were parting company with the communists over the affair. Appearing that November on the BBC alongside three other well-respected geneticists to discuss

Lysenko's address, JBS gave probably the most shameful broadcast of his life. Instead of denouncing Lysenko for the crank that he was, as the other panellists basically did, JBS offered a host of evasions and circular arguments masquerading as open-mindedness and even-handedness. 'I think that a number of Lysenko's views, both positive and negative, are seriously exaggerated', he told viewers. 'But so, I think, is the view that you cannot change heredity in the direction you want... I do not think it will be such an easy job as Lysenko believes. But that does not mean that we can neglect his work.'[15] The repeated 'Buts' confounded his audience. Here was JBS speaking of a man whose beliefs, if true, made a mockery of JBS's own career. Even more confusing, perhaps, was his attitude to his old acquaintance Vavilov, whose death by starvation was widely reported by this stage. JBS simply brushed off the reports and changed the topic.

Oddly, there is an element of JBS's BBC contribution that, if he were here today, he might point towards in his defence. It is undoubtedly true that Lysenko's methods were unscientific and his results were unverified. What is remarkable, however, is that certain of his intuitions have proved, fairly recently, to be true in some measure. The growing study of epigenetics provides evidence that genes can be turned on or off inside cells and that environmental cues are the fingers on the switches. In some rare situations, changes brought on by the environment can pass from parent to offspring, or even grandparent to grandchild, skipping a generation. Does this vindicate Lysenko?

No, it does not. Epigenetics relies on a belief in the existence of genes, which Lysenko did not share. And whatever changes do pass across the generations, they are never permanent, as Lysenko insisted they must be. As for JBS, epigenetics may vindicate his call for open-mindedness, but beyond that it provides no defence for his BBC performance. JBS's opinion carried international weight. By providing a level of cover for Lysenko's lies, he helped to prolong them. As Naomi wrote to him the day after the broadcast, there were many, including herself, 'who were worried, willing to suspend judgement, but also anxious not to condone the kind of thing which they condemned in the Nazi scientists'.[16] JBS allowed that suspension of judgement to continue, in a situation where Lysenko's falsehoods could indeed be compared to Nazi falsehoods. Lysenko's beliefs, when applied wholescale to a state's agricultural practices, led to hundreds of thousands, if not millions of deaths. And yet, even in 1964, JBS was writing, 'In my opinion, Lysenko is a very fine biologist.'[17] In 2017, one writer in *The Atlantic* put it rather differently: 'Trofim Lysenko probably killed more human beings than any individual scientist in history.'[18]

Although, in many ways, JBS's broadcast words were uncharacteristic—tight logic and the exposure of lies and half-truths were his forte—there was also something strangely predictable going on, given the contradictory nature of his character. His cousin Graeme's assessment of his paradoxes says it all:

> Though fascinated by his intense originality I couldn't bring myself to approve of his general behaviour—his rudeness to intellectual inferiors, lack of consideration for other's [sic] feelings and above all his want of objectivity outside his own scientific field. The latter involved such a contrast; within the field of science Jack was meticulously careful, cautious and objective, whereas in politics he tended to accept unverified suppositions and to ignore unpalatable facts.[19]

Behind the scenes, JBS was actually facing up to some—though only some—of the unpalatable facts. There are articles, private letters, and personal encounters that show his growing disillusion, both with Soviet science and with Communist Party practice in Britain.[20] His disagreement with certain beliefs and actions grew to such an extent that he apparently left the CPGB around 1950, though there is no concrete evidence for him doing so other than his own later claims. Whatever the case might be, he remained broadly supportive of Stalin all his life, and one gropes around in vain to find an excuse for it.

All of this has to stand alongside his numerous acts of kindness, especially when it came to money. JBS would fund or augment out of his own pocket colleagues' salaries, departmental expenses, others' research trips. And he could cultivate intense devotion in those around him. The famous evolutionary biologist John Maynard Smith, who worked under JBS at UCL in the late 1940s and early 1950s, could say quite simply, 'I loved him.'[21] And this was despite the fact that being with JBS 'was like living with an unexploded bomb'.[22] Later, in India, a young Krishna Dronamraju—who would go on to lead the Foundation for Genetic Research in Houston, Texas—was so enthralled by JBS's personality that he would devote much of his life to promoting the thought and eccentricities of his beloved mentor.

As Graeme Haldane saw, JBS's political beliefs somehow also have to be viewed alongside his intense originality and scientific talent. The post-war years saw the release of seven further books from JBS's pen (not counting his posthumous publications) and a raft of further contributions to the fields of genetics and evolutionary theory. Major articles appeared on the mutation rate of the gene for haemophilia (1947), the evolutionary basis of disease (1949), the measurement of natural selection (1954), the statistics of evolution (again, 1954), and the cost of natural selection (1957; adding significantly to the concept of 'genetic load'). In 1947, JBS also suggested the term 'darwin' as a unit of evolutionary change, which is now established in the vocabulary of the discipline. When Nobel Prize-winner and president of the Royal Society Edgar Adrian presented the Society's Darwin Medal to JBS in 1952, Adrian was not wrong to say that 'the conclusions derived from his [JBS's] research have permeated practically every field of evolutionary discussion [while] his ideas have fundamentally altered our knowledge of evolutionary change'.[23]

None of this was enough to satisfy JBS's polymathic interests. To take a fairly random sampling from the hundreds of articles he produced in these years, we might mention his controversial, though plausible, 'A Quantum Theory of the Origin of the Solar System' of 1945; 'The Mechanical Chess Player', which accompanied 'The Origin of Language' in 1952; 'Educational Problems of the Colonial Territories', 'Some Alternatives to Sex', and 'Aristotle's Account of Bees' "Dances"'—three of his twenty-three articles of 1955; and, in 1959, 'Suggestions for Research on Coconuts' alongside 'The Non-Violent Scientific Study of Birds'. In 1963, the year before his death, big questions were brought to the fore, with 'Life and Mind as Physical Realities' holding its place next to 'Biological Possibilities for the Human Species in the Next Ten Thousand Years'. The themes of *Daedalus* were as present to JBS as ever.

* * *

THE LONG VIEW

The massive intellect of JBS—or what Naomi called his 'heroically proportioned' personality—has tended to obscure some other members of the family, whose own intellects have remained unsung.[24] Graeme Haldane, had he not been so continually self-effacing, could just as easily have spoken of his own intense originality and scientific talent. It could even be argued that his work in the realm of energy production is now as topical as anything JBS brought to the table, if not more so.

The years after 1945 saw Graeme and his firm immersed in the creation of the Supergrid, bringing voltages in excess of 200,000 volts to the British electricity transmission system; he was in top-secret correspondence with the man who split the atom, Sir John Cockcroft, and his colleagues at the Atomic Energy Research Establishment, making early suggestions about the use of uranium in pelletised form as a nuclear fuel (sharing the family passion for research, Graeme also instigated an atomic energy research unit within his firm Merz & McLellan);[25] and he oversaw the engineering consulting process for the development of the North of Scotland Hydro-Electric Board. Such was the importance of this hydro-electric initiative that Scotland has subsequently become the largest producer of renewable energy in the United Kingdom. In connection with this work, Graeme was a major voice in the promotion of pumped storage—that is, storing excess energy generated by renewables, by pumping water between two reservoirs at different elevations, creating something like a vast water battery. Though slow to catch on, Graeme's pleas were eventually taken up at the Cruachan and Foyer power stations in Scotland. Pumped storage is now an established practice throughout the world, and accounts for 95 per cent of all utility-scale energy storage in the USA.[26] Critically, as we face the current climate crisis, pumped storage hydro facilities allow grid operators to plug the gaps created by the intermittent nature of renewable energy, instead of turning to the standard practice of relying on fossil fuels to tide the grid over.

Graeme also chaired the Electrical Research Association Wind-Power Committee and orchestrated the establishment of a 100-kilowatt experimental plant at Costa Head in the Orkneys, though work there eventually had to be abandoned due to difficulties with expanding wind-power on a scale that would meet the country's needs. Thankfully, those difficulties are now being overcome. His work in New Zealand in the late 1950s and early 1960s, bringing geothermal power to the Wairakei plant near Lake Taupo, meant that a large proportion of the North Island's energy requirements could be met eventually through this renewable supply of energy. Geothermal power comes from steam and/or boiling water emitted by boreholes sunk thousands of feet into volcanic strata. Though limited to areas in tectonically active regions, it now meets a significant share of the electricity demand in not only New Zealand, but also El Salvador, the Philippines, and Kenya. In Iceland, it covers over 90 per cent of heating demand.[27] Unlike other renewables, it is not dependent on weather conditions and has extremely high capacity factors.

As with his early work on the heat pump in the late 1920s, Graeme's advocacy of hydropower, pumped storage, wind-power, and geothermal energy shows a man well ahead of his time. He has rightly been called 'a visionary pioneer of rational electricity supply and sustainable energy use'.[28] But in some areas his ideas never quite caught on. As drilling for oil was still essential in the 1970s, Graeme gave his attention to the problems associated with oil rig construction—though he was in his eighties by this stage. His son, Dick, explains Graeme's bold, left-field idea:

> Huge quantities of steel were needed for construction of the rigs and equally huge amounts of concrete were/are required to anchor them to the sea-bed. Dad suggested that the rigs should be constructed from ice—and frozen to the sea-bed! The energy required to create the ice and keep it frozen would come from the large amounts of waste gas which is burnt off at source. Twice I drove him to Newcastle University where so much of the early research, design & development took place, to progress his ideas, but eventually the weight of vested interest combined (as he put it) with a reluctance to think outside the box (both financially and environmentally) won the day. He was an old man, no longer with the energy to force his thinking through. But I still feel that this was a classic example of how he'd been all his life—always seeking new technologies or coming up with ideas for how to improve old.[29]

Dick was also amused to find his father pressing the deep freeze at Cloan into the service of his research. Graeme's wife, Billee, was

THE LONG VIEW

less amused, opening the freezer lid one day only to find the thing crammed to the brim with reinforced ice.

Graeme and Billee had moved permanently from their home in Esher to Cloan with their two young children, Dick and Robin, in 1958, following the death of Graeme's father Willie in 1951, aged eighty-seven (with Archie inheriting Foswell). Willie was the longest-living of all Mary and Robert's children, and as the years drew on, he became increasingly difficult. His continuing hatred of being early for anything, especially the departure of a train (a waste of precious time in his eyes), exercised his children and carers no end. When Willie sensed their agitation, say when he was taking far too long tying up his boots before leaving the house, he simply went even more slowly.

But Willie's professional life had been tremendously valuable. And, though he could be described as the odd one out amongst Mary's children, he had promoted his own advanced ideas. One such, that never saw the light of day, was the idea of a 'forest university' that would act as a springboard for upward mobility in the forestry industry—an industry which had always held to a sharp class divide between the foresters, who had not received a university education, and the managers, who often had. But, as Naomi wrote of Willie's idea, 'the class structure was too firmly in control to be moved in his day'.[30]

Willie was still alive to see Graeme propose one of his most forward-thinking and ultimately successful ideas: a high-voltage cross-Channel cable connecting Britain with continental Europe, allowing energy to flow between their respective grids—a key step towards the Common Market. Graeme first publicly discussed the concept in his Presidential Address to the Institution of Electrical Engineers—an organisation some 33,000 strong—in 1948. By 1961, the cross-Channel interconnector was an accomplished fact. His speech, however, was far more than a technical discussion on the future of engineering and energy supply. It was characteristic of a Haldane to be ahead of the trend, but it was equally characteristic to turn an address to a scientifically minded body into a philosophical excursion.

Despite the twenty years that had passed since his Uncle Richard's death, Graeme still largely held as sacred his uncle's metaphysical views. The two had been very close, and Graeme had even worked intimately with Richard in the writing of his 1921 magnum opus, *The Reign of Relativity*, while still an undergraduate at Cambridge. Even so, it is remarkable how closely Graeme's words in 1948 resemble the words his uncle used as far back as Victoria's reign. Graeme told his fellow engineers:

> I felt then [at Cambridge], and have never ceased to feel, the urge to seek the correlation of the various branches and categories of knowledge and experience. It seemed so unsatisfying to partition human knowledge into a series of watertight compartments completely divorced from one another, and to have no scale of values to apply to such widely differing subjects as physics, biology, religion and art… There is, I feel, clear evidence that the march of physics has brought this branch of knowledge [metaphysics] into a realm where the distinction between scientific and metaphysical conceptions has become somewhat blurred. Moreover, I feel it is right and proper to encourage the study of these broad problems during the student period, whatever may be the ultimate field of specialization. Our survival as a nation depends not so much on learning as on character, and the less our outlook is confined the more we are likely to assist character-formation.[31]

If there is a creed that summarises the intellectual outlook of the Haldanes of Cloan, then this is it. Richard and John's joint essay of 1883 said much the same. JBS took a similar line, too. As a young Oxford don in the early 1920s, he had worked with colleagues to create a degree course—never to come to pass—that would unify science and philosophy. In the words of Ronald Clark, JBS was ever 'perceiving the inter-relationships of science and politics, of politics and philosophy, and of philosophy and science, a unity which he had often suspected'.[32] In his late essay 'Life and Mind as Physical Realities' (1963), JBS brought together his own and his father's views and postulated the existence of 'only one science, of which physics, biology, and psychology are different aspects'.[33] The British Idealists of the late nineteenth century, with their belief in 'degrees' or 'categories' within knowledge, could not have agreed more.

Where JBS parted company with his father, uncle, and cousin was his rejection of the spiritual significance of reality—his Marxist materialism would not allow for that, though his stance would soften at the end of his life, when, as the editor of the *New Statesman*, Kingsley Martin, put it, 'the balm of Sanskrit philosophy... assuaged the burns of Marxism'.[34] Graeme, on the other hand, was absolutely in tune with the preceding generation of the family, and indeed the generations well before that, when he spoke in his 1948 speech of 'spiritual development' as that which should be each person's 'ultimate objective'.[35]

Graeme's siblings, Elsie and Archie, ironically parted from the above tradition by being traditionalists. Rather than looking ahead to some future synthesis of knowledge, they took the old ways, tried and tested, as their guide. In Archie this found expression in a desire to return to a careful study of Scottish history. He had already been awarded an honorary DLitt from the University of Edinburgh in 1950 for his exquisite descriptions of an angler's life, but an examination of Scotland's old drove roads called for a different set of skills, such as the minute study of historical records and manuscripts, which he had first learnt as an undergraduate in Oxford. The book that subsequently appeared in 1952 has been called 'one of the great classics of Scottish history'.[36]

Archie adored the research—all seven years of it—but it did have the odd hair-raising moment. His legal work meant that access to the National Library of Scotland was not possible during normal opening hours, but through Dr Meikle (the principal librarian who had so encouraged Naomi in her research for *The Bull Calves*), Archie was able to arrange for the night watchman to let him into the library at 8 pm and let him out again at 10.30 pm. It sounded like the perfect solution. On one occasion, however, it was not such a success:

> All went well and I was soon deeply engrossed in the books I wished to consult. Time passed unheeded and suddenly I realised to my alarm that the time was 11 p.m. I hurried to the door but there was no sign of the watchman who had no doubt continued on his round, to return I knew not when. A great Library is neither the most cheerful nor the warmest place in which to pass the night, and the season was late Autumn. The consolations of tobacco were of course in such a place not available and the prospect of the company through the night hours of the ghosts of the literary and legal giants of the past was singularly unpleasing.[37]

Thankfully, the National Library is connected to Edinburgh's Signet Library, and there Archie found a telephone, called for help, and was eventually released from his book-bound prison. The experience was evidently not too traumatic; he became a Queen's Trustee of the National Library in 1962.

Two other historical works followed, one for each decade, covering the development of transport routes in the Highlands as well as the early days of the Scottish postal service.[38] This output earned Archie a revered place amongst Scottish historians, but it was not this that brought him a CBE in 1968; that was a result of his role as vice-chairman of the Trustees Savings Bank and chairman of its inspection committee. Archie topped off his literary career with a return to his beloved fishing—*By River, Stream and Loch* appeared in 1973.

All this gives the impression of unremitting success. Behind the scenes, however, things looked different. Archie particularly struggled with depression—what he called, following Churchill, his 'black dog'. He hated unpredictability, and any sort of change could bring it on; even the prospect of a holiday would consign him to his bed. Ironically, it was a holiday that his doctor prescribed him as a cure. Twice in the 1960s Archie and Jan travelled to South Africa to combat the bleakness, and would be gone for as long as three months (their children, Jennifer and John, were at boarding school by this stage). His colleagues at the office would simply have to pick up the workload.

* * *

While Archie travelled to South Africa to combat his depression, Naomi found in Africa an answer to some of her own longing. She had continued to travel the world after the Second World War, notably another journey through the USSR in 1952, this time with a group of writers from the Authors' World Peace Appeal, including Doris Lessing, with whom she shared a room—bed even—in Leningrad. The two would become firm friends. There were also trips to India and Pakistan. The first came in 1951, when Naomi went to see her daughter Lois who was teaching in Karachi. She went again in 1958 to see JBS, who had moved to Calcutta with his wife Helen the year before (of which more anon), and she made a final journey in 1964 to visit Helen—and prevent her from committing suicide—after JBS's death. But nothing caught her imagination as Africa did.

A visit to Ghana in 1957 to cover the independence celebrations for the *Manchester Guardian* proved momentous. The 'constant bath of happiness' she experienced amongst the dancing, rejoicing Ghanaians gave her a sense of a culture far removed from the buttoned-up respectability of the Brits. When, three years later, a twenty-five-year-old man on a visit to Carradale House with the British Council introduced himself as the paramount chief designate of the Bakgatla people, a tribe stretching across the frontiers of South Africa and Bechuanaland (Botswana since 1966), Naomi found herself in the presence of someone she instinctively wanted to mother. This was Linchwe, future Kgosi Linchwe II, and he too found someone he could respond to in Naomi:

> I remember very well that at that time I was not used to mixing freely with white people, and she struck me straight away, she did not strike me as a white woman, she struck me as a mother, just a human being... the way she was approaching me, she was relaxed, I felt very comfortable with her, I felt at home.[39]

It was the start of a remarkable relationship, and one of the most important phases in Naomi's life. From the early 1960s until the 1990s, Naomi travelled most years to visit Linchwe and the tribe in Mochudi. On only her second visit in 1963 she found the title 'mother of the tribe' conferred upon her: a white stranger propelled into the front ranks of a tight-knit community and relishing the fact. (It was a title that meant much more to her than 'Lady Mitchison', as she became upon her husband Dick's life peerage the following year.) Again, as with Carradale, she felt a sense of responsibility. What could she do as the tribe made their 'difficult jump into the modern world', against a backdrop of challenging economic and environmental circumstances—everything there depended on rainfall—and a political situation that was far from straightforward?[40] The British Protectorate of Bechuanaland was moving towards independence, and over the border in South Africa, where some of the tribe dwelt, apartheid was still very much a reality. These were just the kind of circumstances to appeal to Naomi's saviour complex.

Soon she was busy setting up a library, writing to the *New Statesman* appealing for books; and then there was a secondary school that needed building and classes that needed to be taught, both of which she took a hand in; and, of course, she spent plenty of time discussing the role of women and their right to birth control. When not thus occupied, Naomi found the odd moment for a love affair too.

The fact that the tribalism she encountered had similarities to her conception of true socialism also helped—and not just in bringing, for a time, a sense of long-awaited belonging. It also fuelled her pen for a new surge of literary work. Between 1965 and 1970, she produced, in quick succession, *When We Become Men* (1965), *Return to the Fairy Hill* (1966), *African Heroes* (1968), and *The Africans* (1970). She was, frankly, obsessed. Her grandchildren would offer her money for every hour she did not mention her new passion. One other reason it mattered so much to her was that it gave her something into which she could rub the noses of the shallow capitalists back home. When Linchwe was installed as chief of the Bakgatla in 1963, Naomi wrote a piece in *The Scotsman* declaring him 'the nearest thing that exists today to Plato's dream of a philosopher king'. That word 'dream' ought to have given her a clue that her hopes for Linchwe, and for the tribe more widely, were perhaps a little beyond the reasonable. Once again, the old pattern emerged. She had entered into a society bound by traditions, and this presented her with a conundrum that she never quite overcame—she wanted to modernise, but she didn't want to lose the magic of the old ways. Tribal members often felt the same way, but on some issues Naomi found no readiness for change. As Jenni Calder put it, 'Her efforts to stir women out of submissiveness often brought little reward... She saw herself as their champion, but it was a championing that must have seemed irrelevant to many women's lives.'[41]

Despite the setbacks, Naomi made a genuine difference to the conditions in Mochudi. The library, the school—these prospered, and who knows what seeds she planted in women's minds about their status and dignity (though, as Naomi pointed out in a letter to Calder, 'The interesting thing about Botswana is that all the art is among women').[42] Well into her nineties, Naomi could write: 'I still go there in my dreams, but that doesn't help... I did so much that [it] was the best part of my life.'[43] That is not to say that she forgot Scotland: 'It was a new life, running with the old one.'[44] Indeed, between 1966 and 1976, in the thick of her African involvement, Naomi was a vocal member of the Highlands and Islands Development Consultative Council.

What is especially interesting is the fact that Naomi made such a close connection with a foreign culture in this period, just a few years after her brother's adoption of a foreign culture in India. JBS's claim in *The Times* that he and Helen were moving to India on account of Britain's behaviour in the Suez Crisis of 1956—Britain was now a 'criminal state' in his mind—was a piece of attention-grabbing of the type that the public had come to expect from him, though JBS certainly believed what he was saying.[45] As Peter Medawar wrote of him, 'the trouble was that his extravagances became self-defeating. He became a "character", and people began laughing in anticipation of what he would say or be up to next.'[46] In reality, JBS's India plans were long in the making. He had harboured a soft spot for the country ever since his convalescence there during his wartime service. Now, post-independence, JBS saw in India a basically socialist state that was working for peace, and he found in Pandit Jawaharlal Nehru, its first prime minister, the kind of secular political saint that he'd been waiting for all his life, calling Nehru a 'rationalist with a halo'.[47] The two had actually met in 1934, at one of Naomi's typically unconventional London dinner parties, and JBS wrote to him after his first visit to India in the winter of 1951–2, offering to help with the 'development of human physiology and of the more academic side of genetics'. Might a position be made available?—he gently implied. The son of Kathleen Haldane then added: 'I fully realise that the time has ceased when an Englishman can claim any right to advise Indians. If such a view is taken, I can make no complaint. If it is not, perhaps I may be of some service to India.'[48]

Nothing came of the inquiry, but that didn't stop JBS. Another visit in 1954 had confirmed his love for the place, with its luscious plant life and abundance of animals—'wouldn't any biologist like to live in a country where one can find chameleons in the garden?'[49]— and he was soon writing to Professor Mahalanobis, director of the Indian Statistical Institute in Calcutta, requesting posts for himself and Helen. The response was positive, and the Haldanes accepted the Professorship (for JBS) and Readership (for Helen), well before

Britain's 'criminal' activity in Egypt. But Britain was letting them down in other ways. UCL had been miserly with its funds and resources, thought JBS; the settlement of his divorce from Charlotte was not conducive to a buoyant bank balance; Helen had been charged for drunk and disorderly behaviour and for assaulting a police officer; and his health was flagging. In Samanth Subramanian's words, 'All in all, the decade after the war was humid with stress and dejection.'[50]

JBS and Helen moved to India in 1957, bringing plenty of opportunities for further theatricality. Soon, JBS, still moustachioed and bespectacled, was stalking about Calcutta unshod ('sixty years in socks is enough'), wearing his dhoti and kurta—a mix between Groucho Marx and Gandhi. Vegetarianism followed, and 'Bomber Haldane' from the trenches was now advocating a strict philosophy of non-violence. That philosophy was central to his and his students' biological work at the Indian Statistical Institute, work which mainly consisted of the patient watching and recording of animal and plant life. Indeed, this was Helen's particular skill. 'She was a meticulous observer', recalled John Maynard Smith:

> She was a damned good geneticist, because to be a good geneticist you've got to have the animals, they've got to be alive, they've got to breed, and you've got to write down precisely what happened. And that kind of honesty about the facts is what I learnt from Helen.[51]

In the Haldanes' Indian residence, the cats upon every surface and the four tortoises ('to remind me that if I cannot be good, I should be careful', as JBS wrote to Aldous Huxley)[52] were not simply the beloved pets of two animal enthusiasts; they were the embodied complement to the books and journals on the shelves, all 60,000 of them. Even a wasp hive in the bathroom was ripe for study.

The Edenic circumstances were not quite what they seemed. It didn't take long for JBS to fall out with Indian bureaucracy and the people he held responsible for it, especially the ISI's director Mahalanobis. By 1962, a year after they received their Indian citizenship, JBS and Helen had worked out alternative arrangements for themselves. They would move 270 miles south-west to Bhubaneswar, capital of the state of Orissa, to found a new genetics and biometry laboratory. Here they could do almost as they pleased, but it came at a cost—they'd have little money and resources to do it with. Observation of animals and plants was cheap, so that could continue. But they couldn't hope to compete with the big labs of the West. True to form, JBS dug deep into his own pockets to help combat the limitations. Winning Italy's Feltrinelli Prize in 1961, worth over £250,000 in today's money, he decided to plough two-thirds of the prize money into his new venture. He did much the same upon the death of his mother Kathleen, at ninety-eight years of age, that same year, using his inheritance—all £30,000 of it, which is roughly equivalent to £720,000 today—to establish a fund for the Royal Society on the one hand and to finance more equipment for the Bhubaneswar laboratory on the other. It must have given JBS particular delight to use his inheritance in this way. Kathleen, whose relationship with her son had broken down disastrously ever since JBS's involvement in the Spanish Civil War, had seen India as the jewel in the crown of Britain's vast Empire. With her money, JBS was now helping to establish an institute that could, after his own death, be run by Indians for Indians, free of colonial bonds. That said, he himself was a Brit, and not immune from a sense of entitlement. As one biographer notes, 'He expected the rules, the silly as well as the sensible ones, not to apply to him.'[53]

And here we get into the strange psychology of brother and sister as they set out to connect to foreign cultures in the second halves of their lives.[54] To some extent, they were each surely making an attempt, even if an unselfconscious one, to atone for what they saw as their mother's sins, and the sins of her culture. They wanted to encourage grassroots movements, to build their communities from the bottom up. Naomi lamented the incoming whites who visited Mochudi to paint the walls of schools and so on; why couldn't the locals do this for themselves? Equally, JBS lamented the lack of understanding amongst young Indian students about how to conduct research; his job, as he saw it, was to build up that basic understanding so that Indian science would flourish and compete with, perhaps even outstrip, the West. But surely there was something going on with a pot and a black kettle here. That is to say, their involvement can also be seen as another version of Kathleen's colonialism. They could never quite tear themselves away completely from the role of *white* knight.

Like Kathleen, they had a shared faith in utopias. Kathleen's was the British Empire; theirs were at the other end of the spectrum. But unlike Kathleen, they were resolved to play a role in their founding. Yes, playing a role, that was key. Their foreign allegiances provided a stage where they could stand in the limelight. Their clothing, their behaviour, everything was a statement. 'Pay attention, I am important', they seemed to cry. As Av Mitchison once said of his mother, 'She was a terrible show-off.'[55] Maynard Smith could say of his old mentor, 'He was very vain, you have to understand.'[56]

But in a sense, for JBS, the utopian dream did come true. Bhubaneswar—with the evenings full of the egrets' wings, the elephants visible in the woods, and a time-altering cannabis-milk mixture called *bhang*—was the closest thing to paradise he'd ever found. He still travelled away from time to time. A trip to Israel was particularly important to him. It was there that he visited the Valley of Elah, where David is said to have taken the stone with which to fell Goliath. JBS made sure he returned to India with his own stone from the valley, and it went with him everywhere thereafter. It was for him a vital symbol of the underdog against the ruling powers. When, in the autumn of 1964, his body finally began to succumb to the cancer that had been detected only the year before, JBS was determined to hold on to that stone until the very end. He would roll it about his hand as he sat upon the veranda of his house in Bhubaneswar, 'looking at flowering trees and birds in the sunshine'.[57] As Helen remembered, 'When he dropped it, I knew he'd died.'[58]

It is a touching image, but it is not necessarily the one that he desired to leave behind. His cancer had required him to undergo a colostomy some months earlier ('My rectum is a serious loss to me', he would write in his uproarious poem, 'Cancer's a Funny Thing': 'But I've a very neat colostomy, / And hope, as soon as I am able, / To make it keep a fixed time-table').[59] The procedure took place in London. Maynard Smith visited for the final half hour before the surgery. A nurse took JBS briefly away to shave the area that would come under the knife and to clean him. When he was wheeled back in, he wore a strange look on his face. He had evidently been thinking about what his last words ought to be, in the event that he didn't make it through the operation. Knowing that whatever he said now might be repeated countless times over, hopefully down through the ages, he looked Maynard Smith straight in the eye: 'Well Smith, just had me last shit.' He refused to utter another word.[60]

In JBS's final years, despite the distance, he had not isolated himself from the West. Visitors were common, and included Julian Huxley, Ernst Mayr, and Jacques Monod. Nor had he cut the ties with his family. Naomi visited in 1958—and swam with her brother at night in a tank they shared with the kitchen waste. In fact, Denny and his family lived in Madras for a few years in the late 1950s, while Denny helped establish a laboratory there for the treatment of tuberculosis (the Madras trial was revolutionary, producing the first solid evidence that TB could be effectively treated on an outpatient basis). His son Terence, aged about six at the time, remembers a visit they received from his great-uncle. The servants had spent hours and hours preparing an enormous goat curry. JBS sniffed the air upon arrival and said, 'I hope you remember that I'm a vegetarian.' The cooking had to start all over again.

It was at this time that JBS began to form a close bond with Terence's older brother, Graeme Mitchison, then in his mid-teens. Amongst Naomi's twenty grandchildren, Graeme was, in many ways, the most obvious inheritor of the classic Haldane characteristics, showing a remarkable facility with numbers and a wide range of interests beyond mathematics, especially in the sciences, literature, and music. Whenever JBS returned from India to visit Britain in the early 1960s, he made a point of seeing Graeme, who went up to Oxford in 1962. When JBS died two years later, he left a substantial sum in his will for this favourite great-nephew. Graeme was, in Terence's words, 'the nearest thing to a son that JBS had ever had'.[61] After Graeme's untimely death from a brain tumour in 2018, his friend the novelist Ian McEwan (Graeme played Rachmaninoff on the soundtrack for the film adaptation of *On Chesil Beach*) put into words what he conceived to be Graeme's 'private manifesto', namely 'his delight in harmonious friendships, in the synthesis of all music, art and science, and in the dance of a free mind and great and generous spirit'.[62] That word 'synthesis' tells us obliquely from which family he hailed.

Not that the talent had skipped a generation between JBS and Graeme. Naomi and Dick had made it perfectly clear to their children that their expectations were high. It was taken for granted that all five would win places at Oxford or Cambridge, which they did. But their careers, especially the boys', must surely have surpassed the hopes of their parents. While Lois became a writer and teacher, and Val a journalist (were the girls copying their mother by turning to writing for their profession?), all three sons became not just scientists, but professors of science—Denny as Professor of Bacteriology at the Royal Postgraduate Medical School in London, while also directing a Medical Research Council unit on drug sensitivity in TB; Murdoch as Professor of Zoology at the University of Edinburgh, where he served additionally as Dean of the Faculty of Science for a time (his wife Rosalind, or 'Rowy', was also an Edinburgh Professor in Economic History, and a one-time tutor to Gordon Brown); and Av as Jodrell Professor of Zoology and Comparative Anatomy at UCL, where he had once worked as a teenage lab technician under his uncle. Both Murdoch and Av became Fellows of the Royal Society, to the slight annoyance of Denny, whose more practical work in the field of TB treatment seemed to preclude his election to that august body.

Still, Denny's achievements in his field were legion. He orchestrated clinical trials across the world, the results of which—undergirded by rigorous statistical analysis—allowed him to develop the standard short-course drug treatment for TB, which has been used worldwide. Indeed, experts have concluded that his work saved millions of lives.[63] Though no FRS followed his name, he was proud to receive the British Thoracic Society medal, the International Union Against TB medal, the Stop TB Kochon Prize and the CMG. Denny continued active research until he was ninety-five.

Murdoch, meanwhile, focused on the control of cell division, isolating a type of yeast that made this sort of study eminently practicable, and released a book on the matter, *The Biology of the Cell Cycle*, in 1971. According to the Nobel Prize-winner Sir Paul Nurse, who studied under Murdoch, this book had a 'major impact on researchers of the time', not only because it showed 'how important the cell cycle was as the basis for the growth and reproduction of all living organisms', but also for its 'grand vision about cell growth and reproduction that was central to the life sciences'.[64] Murdoch was a founder member of the European Molecular Biology

40. Graeme Haldane speaking at the Fifth World Power Conference, Vienna, 1956. Graeme was a pioneer in the field of renewable energy. As a young man, he and his Uncle Richard had bonded over their shared interest in energy production, and even more so in philosophy.

41. Carradale House from the air, 1962. In some ways, the house represented Naomi's attempt to recreate the atmosphere at Cloan, with her at the centre as matriarch, just as her grandmother Mary had been.

42. Three generations of the Mitchison family on the steps at Carradale, 1963. Naomi stands close to the top left in a cardigan. Denny (two along on Naomi's left), Murdoch (on Naomi's right, with his father Dick behind him), and Av (sitting two below Murdoch) all became professors in the sciences, following their uncle and grandfather. Two of Av's children, Tim (standing above Av) and Hannah (b. 1964), have followed suit. Neil Mitchison, Murdoch's son (on Naomi's immediate left), bought Cloan from his relation Dick Haldane in 2015.

43. JBS, looking at home in India, early 1960s.

44. Naomi in Botswana, looking cosy with Kgosi Linchwe II, chief of the Bakgatla people, 1970s. Linchwe's wife Kathy is likely to be the woman on the right.

45. Archie (ARB) Haldane with wife Jan at their home, Foswell, 1970s. Though a lawyer by profession, Archie's books earned him enormous respect as an historian. He is also considered one of the finest writers on the joys of fishing.

46. A one-year-old Dick Haldane with his mother, Billee, and grandfather, Sir William (Willie) Haldane, at Cloan, 1948.

47. Dick Haldane, aged eleven, with his father, Graeme, 1958.

48. Dick Haldane and his new bride, Jenny Livingstone-Learmonth, on their wedding day, 1970.

49. Dick Haldane, centre, running into Moscow's Red Square during the Great Russian Race, 2005. The concept, organisation and successful completion of the race put to bed Dick's years of self-doubt over his place in the Haldane family.

50. Aage Bertelsen, Danish explorer and painter and Dick Haldane's biological grandfather, 1908. Dick's adopted status, which he was determined to keep secret, plagued him for many years. The discovery of such an accomplished and versatile relation as Aage, and of his Danish half-siblings in 2009, changed all this.

51. Cloan as it is today.

Organisation, Jenkinson Memorial Lecturer at Oxford, president of the British Society for Cell Biology, and a member of the Royal Commission on Environmental Pollution and of the Government's Advisory Committee on the Safety of Nuclear Installations. Not a bad CV, and yet it hardly captures the breadth of Murdoch's polymathic knowledge. His nephew, Graeme, gives us a glimpse of it:

> I remember, when I was in my teens, that we were walking along the beach towards the Point [at Carradale Bay] when someone asked what kinds of rocks we were looking at. 'Metamorphic mica schist' said Murdoch, without so much as a pause. This answer stuck in my mind partly because of the harmonious words… but also because of the sense that everything in the world could be subject to reason and knowledge. Boswell could not have been better pleased by Dr Johnson than I by my uncle.[65]

Unsurprisingly, the youngest of Naomi's sons, Av, would say, 'I had no choice but to become a biologist… it was sort of a family business.'[66] He could certainly show very similar behaviour to his uncle. Professor Martin Raff, who studied under Av at the National Institute for Medical Research in London in the late 1960s, recounts: 'I read a biography of JBS after I'd been with Av for a year or two, and it was like a description of Av. I mean they were *so* similar… both remarkably eccentric.' As an example of Av's eccentricities, Raff recalls:

> We were up in the animal room once, taking thymus glands out of mice, and he had just had a technician starting, and you could see that she was very squeamish about all this—you know, cutting open a mouse, taking out the thymus—and just to make her see how trivial this all was, he took a test-tube full of these thymuses, and went 'glug': one gulp, all the thymuses down, and this poor technician just about passed out.[67]

Though he was based in London, Av's work—covering the fields of immunological tolerance, tissue transplantation, immunoregulation, immunogenetics, and rheumatology—took him all over the world, as is reflected in his many international honours. In Germany, he won the prestigious Paul Ehrlich and Ludwig Darmstaedter Prize, as well as the Robert Koch Gold Medal, and even served as the founding scientific director of the Deutsches Rheuma-Forschungszentrum in Berlin, where there is now an Avrion Mitchison Prize for rheumatology. In America, Av is a Foreign Honorary Member of the American Academy of Arts and Sciences and a Foreign Associate of the National Academy of Sciences. In Switzerland, Novartis, one of the world's largest pharmaceutical companies, awarded him their Sandoz Prize for Immunology; while in Poland, he was made a Foreign Member of the Polish Academy of Arts and Sciences. In Israel, the Weizmann Institute of Science honoured Av with an honorary doctorate.

Naomi wouldn't have been happy if she felt she'd been outdone by her children. But she had nothing to fear. From the 1970s onwards, four of Scotland's more modern universities awarded her honorary degrees, and she was made an Honorary Fellow of two Oxford colleges (St Anne's and Wolfson). In 1981, having already turned down an OBE, she accepted a CBE, thinking it would give her greater influence. The enemy of Empire was now a commander of it.

She was certainly the commander at Carradale, though it was something of a sinking ship, growing more and more dilapidated as the years drew on. Formalities were kept up—no children in the drawing room, everyone dressed for dinner—but they hardly masked the challenges of the place. Writing during a visit in 1991, her daughter-in-law Rowy paints a vivid picture:

> For lunch Naomi produces nine slices of salami for 14 people. Fortunately a grandchild has arrived with a cargo of quiches... The trouble is that we come here not knowing what type of deficiency is going to dominate life. Will it be electric lightbulbs, wine, fruit or even bread?... The dishwasher, installed in April after mice destroyed the last one, has a faulty part and leaks. It has to be stood in everyone's way so that it can be drained... The missing part of the liquidiser, ordered two months ago, has still not arrived.[68]

By this stage, Naomi had been alone for twenty years. Dick had died in February 1970, after two strokes and a heart attack in swift succession, leaving behind not just his wife and children but also his mistress of thirty years, Tish Rokeling. He had not quite lived the life for which he had hoped. Some had once viewed him as 'the coming man of the Labour Party', and his 1934 book, *The First*

Workers' Government, had shown just how optimistic he was about the practical possibilities of building a new socialist state within his lifetime.[69] Dick's nineteen years as an MP and his brief stint in minor office as parliamentary secretary to the Ministry of Land and Natural Resources in the mid-1960s did not meet those expectations. He was a witty and cutting debater in the Commons and a talented drafter of parliamentary bills, but this still felt underwhelming. His peerage may have appeared to others as an honour, but Dick had always been a keen advocate for the abolition of the House of Lords, and by placing him there, Harold Wilson had in fact pushed Dick to the sidelines, rendering him less politically effective.

Yet Dick had been essential to Naomi. 'Without Dick as the fixed centre of her life', wrote Calder, 'it is hard to imagine how Naomi's excursive existence could have brought the challenges and rewards that it did. Their affection for each other was deep and constant.'[70] His grandchildren remember him as a far more conventional grandfather than Naomi was ever a conventional grandmother. At times, he could display old-fashioned attitudes that stood in contrast to those of his wife. Terence recalls the Carradale dinners in Dick's time, with Dick sitting at one end of the long dining table and Naomi at the other, the usual gaggle of family and friends in-between. Dick would make a point of sitting a good-looking young woman on one side of him—but very definitely on the side of his deaf ear—and a political friend on his other, and for this friend he would reserve more serious discussion. Other grandchildren have different, more flattering memories of such dinners. All are convinced that he remained an enlightened and generous man in many respects, not least in his willingness to use his wealth to sponsor Jewish refugees from Nazi Germany and to fund the defence of the leaders of the African National Congress who were facing trial in apartheid South Africa.

It's not surprising that the memories of Dick and Naomi's grandchildren go back to the Carradale dining table, for it symbolised something important. The house was fundamentally convivial. It was essential to Naomi that she was the centre of that conviviality, and in this she was aware of a family precedent: 'I think to some extent I am consciously treading the footsteps of my Haldane grandmother who always gathered her family around her.'[71] Like Cloan,

Carradale was a place where the exchange of ideas was paramount, where breadth of interest and regard for culture counted. Just as Naomi and Dick made sure interesting people came to visit, so it was with their children. At the table, you might see the influential economist Robert Neild, or perhaps James Watson of DNA fame. In fact, Watson wrote his controversial, world-famous book *The Double Helix* while staying at Carradale in the 1960s, and dedicated it to Naomi.

While intellect mattered, so did erudite humour. There were games of all sorts and an atmosphere of intense competition, especially amongst Naomi's grandchildren. Someone would write the first two lines of a poem, and then hand it on, and each guest around the table would have to contribute something before it was finally read out. 'The aim was to amuse and to show off at the same time', Terence remembers.[72] There were complicated literary and verbal games, and Naomi always enjoyed getting out the Scrabble board, of which she was the undisputed queen, usually winning by producing some obscure Scots word.

The atmosphere was invigorating for some, intimidating for others. Those who were shy or less academically able could easily feel out of place. If you didn't stand out for some special characteristic, you could be forgotten or think you were a let-down. (She would say to Terence in his student years, 'You've never been on a demonstration. You've never even been arrested!')[73] A number of Naomi's grandchildren felt they missed out on her attention because they weren't interesting enough to her. Her gaze was like a searchlight going around the room, alighting on those she liked, and simply ignoring everyone else.[74] And even those she liked felt a good deal of projection. Murdoch's daughter, Sally, was a favourite, partly because Naomi thought she resembled her younger self, but when she'd say to her granddaughter, 'I know you'd like a nice bit of fish tonight for your dinner', it would actually mean, 'I'd like a nice bit of fish tonight for my dinner', or if she said, 'I know this is your favourite bedroom', it would really mean, 'This is my favourite bedroom.'[75] As for the non-family members that Naomi didn't take to, she could drone on about their failings. For those she strongly disliked or disagreed with, she could be vicious. It was not unheard of for her to bite people. But she was not spiteful and her aggression didn't last.

On the whole Naomi was a lover of people, and it is this that family and friends always come back to. For all the difficulties Rowy records, she could still speak of 'Naomi's extraordinary warmth and generosity, the sudden darts of perception and sympathy'.[76] Doris Lessing, who visited Carradale a number of times in the 1950s, sums this up, as she does the atmosphere of the place:

> Naomi has the gift of friendship, and with many different kinds of people—who were very happy to be invited… where they might find thirty or forty people in a house that seemed to have no limit to its capacity, that had never heard of 'the two cultures'. Scientists, poets, artists, novelists, politicians, journalists, not to mention town councillors and the local fishermen, would all be there together. People came from Africa, from the Soviet Union—during the Cold War—from Canada and the United States; and there were, too, what seemed to be dozens of children. There must be hundreds of people from all over the world who remember Carradale House with affection. Naomi was surely the most original and warm-hearted hostess of her time.[77]

When not busy entertaining, Naomi kept up her writing, sitting at her desk on the edge of the bustling drawing room, clicking away at her little Olivetti. The post-war years were not commercially successful for Naomi, and critics in England had all but forgotten about her, but there was one genre with which she was now drawing in a fairly sizeable readership. Her regard for the young and her connection to her own inner child (her dreams were often contorted scenes from her early years) were expressed through an extensive output of children's fiction, the best of which is perhaps *The Big House* (1950)—a story that draws directly on Carradale life and explores class consciousness through a child's topsy-turvy experience of magic, time-travel, and friendship in a remote community. Scotland still dominated her imagination until Africa took up her field of vision. But she wasn't afraid to take on issues outside the worlds in which she moved. From the early 1960s, she became something of a science fiction writer.

Memoirs of a Space Woman (1962) examines what it is to show goodwill to non-human life forms, while *Solution Three* (1975) sees Naomi return to the family fascination with genes, as she envisions a world in which population problems are overcome by conditioning people to homosexuality. The novel even takes on the vexed question of eugenics and the preservation of gene banks. It is a pity JBS wasn't alive to read it. He would have had something to say, too, about her 1983 novel, *Not By Bread Alone*, where genetic engineering appears to provide the answer to the world's food production problems, but is ultimately undermined by uncontrollable biological and social consequences. All these stories have women at their centre. In *Not By Bread Alone* the main protagonist is a professional scientist and a lesbian. And yet Naomi was refusing by this stage to be called a feminist. Such a label would put her in a box— that, she could never allow.

After the frontiers of genetics, Naomi again confounded expectations and returned to pre-history with her novella *Early in Orcadia* (1987), recreating the world of Orkney's earliest settlers. She was almost ninety, but it wasn't the last thing to appear from her pen. That honour belonged to the short historical novels *The Oath-Takers* and *Sea-Green Ribbons*, both published in 1991, the year in which Naomi turned ninety-four. In the face of her own coming end, the gentle optimism of these last works implies, perhaps, that even this woman, who spent her life bound up with her own ego, believed that a future without her could still be a good one.

That end did come, but not until Naomi had celebrated her hundredth birthday in 1997 with a party at Carradale House, where she 'sat on one of the drawing-room sofas receiving with pleasure tribute and presents but at the same time looking strangely isolated from the conviviality'.[78] It is an apt image. For all her vivaciousness, Naomi never quite *belonged*. Like her brother, she was unique amongst her generation, and this is partly because she was always somewhere further down the road, signalling the way forward as she saw it. She herself put it rather well: 'It is always a bore being ahead of one's time.'[79]

After her death at Carradale on 11 January 1999, the house was put up for sale. On 2 August, the very final day of Mitchison ownership, Dick Haldane joined Naomi's daughters, Lois and Val, to say goodbye to the house. While they were thus engaged in the drawing room, Dick's mobile phone rang. He excused himself, went into the hallway, and looked out through a glass door onto the lawn and on down to the sea through a rhododendron-lined path. Enter fox from right. The orange visitor looked up at Dick and then disappeared into the bushes. Once Dick had completed his call, he returned to the drawing room and told Lois and Val of his sighting. Just then the fox reappeared for all to see through the window. Strange, Lois said. In all the years they had been coming to Carradale—over sixty of them—they had never once seen a fox. Perhaps, she conjectured, it was their mother returning to see if her beloved garden was being properly cared for.

Of course, in a chapter like this, there are many other deaths that one could record. Some will be mentioned in the closing chapter, others will pass unsaid. That is not because they do not matter, obviously. There is the question of space, but there is also another factor at play. Too much emphasis on death would overshadow the key message of the preceding pages. The tradition established all those years ago by the first Haldanes of Cloan is alive and well. Adapting, changing, yes; but unmistakably present. Look at Tim Mitchison, Av's son and J. S. Haldane's great-grandson, who is Hasib Sabbagh Professor of Systems Biology at Harvard and whose work in cell biology is having a major impact on the treatment of cancer today. Or look at Tim's sister, Hannah Mitchison, Professor of Molecular Medicine at UCL, whose lab focuses on how different genetic mutations can give rise to different clinical outcomes for ciliopathy patients, and seeks to translate this research to the bedside by means of new genetic-based therapies. The old Haldane combination of detailed research coupled with practical, life-changing outcomes is evident yet again. And for polymaths, take Neil Mitchison, who now lives at Cloan: mathematician, risk analyst, formerly Deputy Commissioner for Scotland for the EU, and parliamentary candidate. His five multilingual children were raised with Gaelic as their first language, adding a new string to the Haldane/Mitchison bow.

We'll never know how much of this is in the blood. The nature versus nurture debate will not be settled here. But what if you were adopted into such a family? Could you ever feel yourself to be a true Haldane of Cloan? It is with this sensitive and difficult question that our final chapter deals.

12

WHAT MAKES A HALDANE?

If the preceding pages have been rather full of glowing Haldane achievements, their faults and failings should have become clear too. Mary, for all her piety, imposed restrictions on her daughter Elizabeth that were not just painful, but in some ways hypocritical. One Mitchison descendant even wonders whether Mary's intense interest in her children and grandchildren was indicative of a controlling and interfering nature (I am not sure Mary's letters bear this out). Richard could irritate people with his omniscience and the confidence he placed in his own abilities. John was excessively absent-minded and at almost all times stubbornly convinced he was right, even in cases where the evidence went against him. As Graeme Haldane wrote to Naomi, after reading some recollections she put together of her father:

> You refer to his Haldane characteristic of being convinced he was right. This, I remember, came out very definitely when late in his life, I tried so unsuccessfully to get him to accept Thermo-dynamic principles... He seemed to regard the 2nd law... as a sort of conspiracy against common sense![1]

Elizabeth could be bossy, and always wanting to lead on things. Sir Edmund Gosse's wife, Nellie, thought her 'terribly domineering'.[2] Her local title, 'The Queen of Perthshire', was not entirely benign. Willie was tight with his money, grew wilfully more difficult with age, and showed a maddening obsession with his farms and forests.

We need hardly comment on Naomi and JBS's shortcomings, but Graeme, Archie, and Elsie had theirs too. Graeme struggled with personal relations and was buttoned-up even with his closest family.

It did not come naturally to Elsie to show warmth, and Archie was a worrier. As he himself admitted, he 'allowed the more sombre periods to affect unduly not only my own outlook but, too often, the lives of others'.[3]

None of this undermines what the family achieved. In some ways, the humanity of their failings is reassuring. They were real people, who shared the complexity and mess of life with the rest of us. It would have been to the good, however, if their frailties had been more widely commented on amongst their relations. Growing up a Haldane or a Mitchison, so I'm told by the present generation, you were never left in any doubt about the distinctions of other family members. Even if it went unsaid, pressure and expectations were high.

* * *

This was felt keenly by the boy who was set to inherit Cloan, Graeme and Billee's son, Dick Haldane. Across the early years of her marriage Billee had suffered a number of miscarriages, quite possibly as a result of her time working in the Radium Department at the Royal Cancer Hospital. She consulted the eminent gynaecologist (Sir) John Peel, who would deliver, or help to deliver, all four of the Queen's children. At the time that Billee saw him, in the years immediately after the war, Peel had a young theatre sister serving under him, named Anne Lysbeth Amsden, who had recently become pregnant to a visiting Danish doctor, Arne Bertelsen, during a short-lived affair. Arne was a talented doctor, who had already turned down the Chair of Anatomy at the University of Aarhus to pursue his dream of becoming a surgeon. He was in England to study under (Sir) Archibald McIndoe, famed for his pioneering plastic surgery on burns victims during the Second World War. Arne subsequently became the first surgeon authorised to use plastic surgery in Denmark.

Arne was short of build, darkly handsome, with a protruding, Habsburg lower lip, and extremely charming. Anne Amsden was petite, beautiful, and a highly competent nurse, who had trained at Addenbrooke's Hospital in Cambridge during the war. When the two met at the Queen Victoria Hospital sometime in 1946, there was an instant attraction. One early date involved an amusing lecture on 'male types'—the tall, stooping type; the sportsman type; the short and stocky type. Arne leaned over to Anne and whispered in her ear that the third type made the best lovers.

Another date took the pair to the Seven Sisters, the dramatic sea cliffs on the East Sussex coast, where Arne began to sing his favourite arias into the wind. According to Anne, whose own mother was an accomplished musician who had performed for the troops during the First World War, Arne 'sang beautifully... for me & the English Channel!'[4] They knew their time together would be short-lived—Arne already had a passage to America booked—so when a further date took them to Burlington Arcade in London, Arne bought a fine amber drop jewel and pressed it into Anne's hand, telling her to take it as a sign that their relationship 'was sealed and safe for all time'. For Anne, it was 'a great comfort', easing their inevitable separation. By the time that separation did come, they knew a baby was on the way and Anne decided that she would give it up for adoption. Arne wrote to her every day of his Atlantic crossing, deeply unhappy and with no distractions to take his mind off the situation. The two did not meet again until 1961. Upon his return to Denmark, Arne almost immediately fathered twins by his wife, with whom he already had two children.

John Peel evidently came to understand the plight of his young assistant and offered to deliver the baby himself. Simultaneously, knowing that his patient Billee Haldane would likely never bring a child to full term, Peel arranged for Billee and Graeme to be the adoptive parents (without revealing this to Anne). Anne insisted the birth would take place under anaesthetic, as she felt she would never be able to give her baby up otherwise. A boy was born on 6 May 1947. Anne had requested that he be called Richard. His new parents were more than happy to keep the name, which, for other reasons, meant so much to them. Dick, as he was known from the off, was adopted at one day old.

Arne had written a letter to Peel supplying the details of his life, and this, with the name redacted, accompanied the adoption papers and birth certificate that were handed over to the Haldanes. They made no attempt, as Dick grew up, to hide the fact of his adoption nor the fact that he had a Danish father, who was a doctor. (The coincidence, however, of Dick literally being a half-Dane—long believed to be the origin of the Haldane name itself—did not seem to register with them.) Billee and Graeme quickly came to know the name of their son's biological father, and later something of his professional success as a professor. Dick knew nothing about his birth mother, and if Billee did speak about her, she would always refer to her, somewhat patronisingly and without basis, as 'a poor little thing'. Though details about Arne were known, Dick never thought of trying to establish contact with him. He was much too devoted to his adoptive parents, especially his father whom he adored beyond all others, and to the Haldane name. But as a boy Dick felt proud of having a Danish professor as his birth father. He also felt proud of being adopted, ever since his mother had told him that he was different from other children because he had been chosen especially.

* * *

The pride did not last. To the old families of Perthshire, bloodlines mattered. Though he does not remember it, Dick was later told by his nurse that, during one of their holidays at Cloan in 1951, a visitor burst through the front door early one morning. It was Alex(ander) Chinnery-Haldane of Gleneagles, head of the principal branch of the family. He found Dick, aged just four at the time, playing in the hall and asked him pointedly where his *stepmother* was. Dick's nurse ushered the visitor through into the kitchen, where Billee was busy with some chore. Without any preamble, the Haldane chief, who had no direct male heir, announced, 'I've come to tell you there is no possibility of that little boy out there inheriting Gleneagles.'

It was not uncommon at that time to view or treat adoptees differently from natural children. Child adoption had only gained legal status in Britain in 1926. Dick's Uncle Archie, who'd inherited the Foswell estate after Willie's death in 1951, and Aunt Elsie both held traditional, if qualified, views on the subject. In 1952, when Dick was five, Archie wrote to Graeme requesting, with the support of his sister, that what they called the 'heirlooms'—a number of things of particular family interest at Cloan, mainly connected with their

WHAT MAKES A HALDANE?

Uncle Richard and Aunt Elizabeth—should 'remain in the family', as Archie regrettably put it, instead of passing to Dick and his sister Robin (also adopted) along with the rest of the contents of Cloan on Graeme's death. Archie added, 'When I say this I am well aware of the change which has, quite rightly, taken place in the general attitude to adoption even since Uncle Richard's time, but I do not think this change extends to the sort of things we have in mind.'[5] Graeme's response was clear. It was not for others to decide whether his children were in the family or not. Just as importantly, he told Archie that he believed their 'Uncle Richard and Dada [Willie]... would have taken the advanced viewpoint for which they rightly had a high reputation.' His siblings' request was therefore refused, though Graeme did promise to return to Archie two special family portraits, which had once hung at Foswell, should he, Graeme, predecease him. They were not of great monetary value, but their sentimental value was significant. Much later, for reasons he perceived to be valid, Graeme changed his mind on the pictures, and stipulated in writing that they were to remain at Cloan. He also made the ill-fated decision not to tell Archie, leaving his lawyers to break the news after his death. As Archie considered Graeme's original promise to be morally binding, and as Dick was not prepared to do anything but respect his late father's wishes, the consequences were not happy for the two families, and sadly rumble on to this day.

But with the exception of some perceived coldness from his Aunt Elsie, it was not until the early 1960s, when he was sixteen or so, that Dick became conscious of any issues with his adoption. It was then that he began attending dances which brought together the youth of Perthshire's landed families. Dick was aware that the Haldanes were the most ancient of that select circle and were thus held in high regard. Suddenly, at one of these balls, the fear hit him: what if people knew he was adopted? Would they think he wasn't really a Haldane? Would he count? Would he be accepted?

The insecurities seeped through into his school life. A multi-instrumentalist and fine singer, Dick sat a musical scholarship to Rugby School in Warwickshire when he was thirteen. His educational prospects looked bright. But his final two terms were blighted by a series of offences, one of which involved him leading a platoon attack upon the schoolmaster who was overseeing a night operation of the Combined Cadet Force. It was, in Dick's words, 'a shockingly stupid thing to do'.[6] The headmaster, Walter Hamilton, considered expelling him but chose instead to have Dick 'speckled'; in other words, he was stripped of his status as a prefect. Dick had only possessed the title for two weeks.

Dick's housemaster felt let down, though relations were already sour. He had called Dick 'the dirtiest boy in the House', because he had attempted to grow his hair and sideburns (it was the mid-1960s). Dick outdid him with cruelty, calling him 'the Cripple' because of his bad limp, a nickname that spread across the school and stuck, and he left school with a despairing final report from Hamilton. Four years later, Dick announced his engagement to Jenny Livingstone-Learmonth, a distant Haldane cousin, whom he had first met at a family wedding.[7] It turned out that Jenny's brother knew Hamilton through university connections. When he told the old man one day, 'My sister has just got engaged to a chap named Haldane', there followed a slight pause before Hamilton responded, in his deep and lugubrious voice, 'Oh, is that a good idea?'

Hearing of this later, Dick felt ashamed and promptly wrote to his old housemaster apologising for his behaviour at school. The housemaster replied with gratitude, ending his letter with the words, 'The important thing is you've seen that you had a chip on your shoulder, and have got rid of it.' Dick had never thought of his behaviour in these terms before, and couldn't help wondering if the chip came from his insecurities over his short stature, for which he had been bullied when younger, or whether it was in fact a result of carrying the burden of his adoption, that feeling of not quite belonging.

By the time Dick's twenty-first birthday came around, his feelings had crystallised. On the one hand, he was determined to keep his adoption a secret to those outside the family; on the other, he was determined to prove to his relations that he could live up to the Haldane name. In a speech at his birthday dinner, he vowed as much to the family.

* * *

Determined he may have been, but Dick had been causing some anxiety to his elders by his behaviour. Academically, his attempt to emulate his beloved father by studying electrical engineering at Imperial College London (Graeme was Crown Nominee on the governing body) had not gone well; he failed his first year before taking successful resits. Graeme and his Uncle Archie had persuaded him to continue his studies and Dick did finally take his degree. Socially, things had been even more precarious. Through family trusts vested in him on his eighteenth and twenty-first birthdays, Dick was extremely well provided for financially, but had still managed to live beyond his means in a vain attempt to keep up with an old school friend, one of the super-rich. Girlfriends had also seemed to follow one after the other with a remarkable frequency. His parents were delighted when he returned home for the Christmas holidays of 1969, announcing his intention to marry Jenny—which he did in July 1970, less than two months after his graduation.

By the following year, the two were splitting their time between Edinburgh and the Garden Cottage at Cloan. One evening, they invited Graeme and Billee over to the cottage for supper. At the end of the meal, Graeme produced an obituary and a photograph. It was the obituary of Arne Bertelsen, who had died in Copenhagen at the age of just sixty-one. The photograph was the first image Dick had ever seen of his birth father. He was scared by the resemblance. The lower lip in particular was nearly identical. Reading the obituary, Dick was struck by Arne's eminence as a professor, surgeon, and politician.[8] The obituary made no mention of his family life, nor the cause of death.

While Dick found it reassuring to know that his biological father had intellectual weight, particularly after all the educational mishaps of his own life (perhaps there was still hope for him, he wondered), he was nevertheless 'too much engaged in wanting to become a young gentleman named Haldane in Perthshire' to want to delve any deeper into Arne's life. In fact, he wanted the obituary and photograph destroyed and asked his father to take them away and do this for him. In a macabre thought, Dick knew that if he found the material amongst his father's possessions after his death it would be too confusing and emotionally draining for him. No, there was to be no more evidence of this man Arne Bertelsen. Dick was a Haldane and that was that.

Except of course it wasn't. Over the first ten years of his marriage Dick was often weighed down with a sense of failure. He brought his work in the engineering world to an end in 1973 and decided to study management at Heriot-Watt University. Simultaneously he was getting a fish-farming business off the ground ('I think you should forget about it as quickly as you thought of it', said his father upon hearing the idea) and began to act as a director of the family-run hotel in Ballachulish. He and some colleagues even bought a failing knitwear company and turned it round, before it ultimately fell into administration. The fish farming, contrary to Graeme's expectations, proved to be a genuinely good and profitable idea, and later it is what made maintaining and living at Cloan financially viable (by 2005, the company was the UK's largest hatchery business, producing over 40 per cent of the country's total requirement, roughly 12 million six-month-old trout per year). But Dick was unsatisfied and restless. His personal life was chequered by deep and sometimes suicidal depression, an increasing addiction to alcohol, and an extra-marital affair, demanding exceptional forbearance and resilience from Jenny. He felt, with shame, that he must have inherited something of his Danish father's genes. Thankfully, after many years he learnt to turn his back upon alcohol entirely. Another addiction of sorts was his love of fast cars. At one time or another an Aston Martin DB7, four Porsches, many BMWs, and a 400-horse power Range Rover all graced his garage. This only heightened the sense of a man seeking a thrill to fill a hole.

The cars were funded by his booming fish-farming business, but this didn't stop money from being an issue. He had always struggled to show restraint in this department, and matters became much worse when, in 1976, he became a member of Lloyds of London— as many of his other friends had done, to their apparent profit. It was the world's oldest insurance market, but, hit with an avalanche of asbestosis cases in the 1980s, its underwriters were increasingly exposed to loss. At that time, 'a Name'—a member who began underwriting, as Dick did—had unlimited liability. By the mid-1990s it became clear that Dick had lost nearly £500,000, at a time when 34,000 other Names lost between £120,000 and £5 million each, a total of £8 billion.

His only asset at the time was the 3,250-acre Cloan estate, which he had inherited on the death of his father in 1981. The only way he could cover his losses was to sell the 2,500 tenanted acres to the farmer who had been there since 1945. The figure he received, £250,000, was about 50 per cent of the land's open-market value had it been tenant-free. In 2019, he watched on with pain as the same land was sold for forestry development for £7.5 million.

* * *

The year of Graeme's death had been a seismic one for Dick. His love and respect for his father were unparalleled. In the final weeks of Graeme's illness, Dick wrote this letter to him:

> Dear Dad,
>
> This is just a brief note to attempt to put down on paper what I find myself incapable of expressing with the spoken word. Indeed, lying in bed last night, thinking of you and me and all of us, I couldn't help wondering if the root of any problems we may ever have had is our failure to communicate. I think we're all poor at it... I know that no son has ever had a better father... I love you very very dearly, and I thank you from the bottom of my heart for all you do for me, and have done for me, and for having been the father that you are. God bless,
>
> Dick

Graeme died on 24 June 1981. On 8 October, a memorial service took place at the Queen's Chapel of the Savoy in London, followed by a lunch at the nearby Institution of Electrical Engineers of which Graeme had been president in 1947. Another past president, C. T. Melling, CBE, gave an address at the service, summing up his colleague's achievements:

> Graeme Haldane was a visionary, a fore-runner of later practice... [he] had a long-term view, a gift of prophecy... But, more important, he had charity; not merely the occasional act of charity, but a fundamental philosophy, inspiring devotion to his family, friendship with those who knew him, a kindly regard for his fellow-men and a strong desire to achieve the good of his country and a better and fairer society.[9]

A year later, it was Archie's turn to be remembered; a very different character from Graeme, certainly, and one whose views on adoption have failed to pass the test of time. But he was also a man of wide-ranging talents, of extraordinary lyrical facility, of good humour. His historical works will long remain unsurpassed, and no fisherman or nature lover will fail to find refreshment in the books that document and express Archie's profound love of his native rivers, lochs, and streams.

* * *

With the relatively unexpected death of Billee, aged eighty, in 1988, Dick was now parentless—or so he thought. In 1990, he decided to change his lawyers, who, as part of the process, handed over a number of family documents which Dick had never seen before, including his adoption papers and those of his sister Robin. Dick's papers contained his adoption certificate, birth certificate, and the letter from Arne to John Peel, confirming details about him, minus his name. Dick now discovered he had at least two older half-siblings. The letter also noted, as had the obituary in 1971, that Arne's father was Aage Bertelsen, a well-known explorer and artist who had exhibited at the Royal Geographical Society in London in 1910. Dick found that one of the paintings from the exhibition was still held in the Society's archives. He travelled to London specially to see it and subsequently took to watercolour painting himself, with some success.

Arne's letter also noted that Aage had been made a Ridder (a Danish Knight, as Arne himself would go on to become). Dick took pride in the fact that his natural grandfather had been honoured just as Willie, his Haldane grandfather, had been. Indeed, Dick was also proud to find that—in counterpoint to his famous Haldane forebear, Admiral Adam Duncan, Viscount Duncan—one of his great-great-great-grandfathers had been a Commander in the Danish Navy which had fought Nelson at the First Battle of Copenhagen in 1801. More significantly, Dick's adoption papers now revealed his birth mother's full name—Anne Lysbeth Amsden. With Billee gone, he felt ready to find his other mother. He turned to a friend noted for her sleuthing abilities, Shellard Campbell, and asked if she might be able to uncover any further details that might allow him to track her down. Shellard set to the task with a will. First, she spent hours hunting down Anne's birth certificate in St Catherine's House in London, eventually discovering that her parents had owned a sweet shop in south London. A visit to this location brought encounters with old neighbours who had known the family, and even remembered Anne being pregnant and coming to live with her parents. But then the trail went cold. Where was she now?

Through a deeper dive into the marriage registers, Shellard discovered that an Anne L. Amsden had married a Robert Cameron relatively late in life, in December 1971. The telephone directory contained two R. Camerons, one living in Wimbledon, the other in Romsey, Hampshire. Pretending to be a picture framer touting for business, Shellard telephoned both. On the second call, a woman picked up and Shellard managed to ascertain her initials. They were A. L. Boldly, Shellard asked what the first letter stood for. Anne was the answer. Having got so far, Shellard could not quite see a way of asking about the L without breaking her cover.

What she did find out was that the farmhouse in which Anne and her husband lived was a rented National Trust property. Looking it up on the map, Dick was amazed to discover that he had driven past the house countless times. Still, the question of what the L stood for had to be answered before he made any approach. Shellard thus phoned the National Trust and was put through to a secretary in their Isle of Wight office. Here, the lease for the Hampshire farmhouse was found. The secretary read the name out over the phone: Anne Lysbeth Amsden. On 26 June 1991, just over five weeks after her search began, Shellard called Dick: 'I've found her.' Her diary notes his reaction: 'pleased, distracted, apprehensive'.[10]

The following day, Dick wrote to Anne:

Dear Mrs. Cameron,

This I suspect will prove to be the most difficult letter I have ever sat down to write—I have agonized over how to address you. The contents are extremely sensitive and it may be you will wish to read this in private.

My name is Richard Haldane, though I'm known to my friends as Dick. I was born on 6th May 1947 and was shortly afterwards adopted. My father was Danish, by name Bertelsen, and my mother was Anne Lysbeth Amsden, born 9th October 1922.

> Unless I am very much mistaken—in which case apologies are useless and my confusion will be total—you are Anne Amsden—and I am your son.

The letter goes on to detail how he found her and to summarise the key events of his life, stressing that he bore no resentments. He adds:

> It is very hard for me to express my feelings now that I have found my 'natural' mother... All I do know is that I am both excited and frightened—nervous of possibly introducing complications into both your and my life... I also know that I must meet you—and after that we can decide whether or not we wish to get to know each other better.

The letter concludes, 'And now I'm left with the same dilemma as faced me when I started this letter—how to end it? Forgive me for the familiarity, but I shall end it as a son should... with love.' Anne attempted a response on paper, but couldn't manage it and chose to call Dick instead. 'I just had to talk to you', she later wrote to him; '[I] couldn't bear the thought of you waiting and wondering. It was quite some moment waiting to hear your voice. I feel tingles even now when I think about it.'

The two arranged to meet at Anne's home the following month. He had brought photographs of his family and of himself—as a little boy, as a grown man, and, though he left this for Anne to look at once he'd left, his christening photograph at just a few weeks old. The image 'completely undid' her.

Anne had bought a half bottle of champagne for the occasion. Drinking it side by side, Dick noticed that their hands were identical. It became clear as they chatted that Anne had known details of Dick's life almost from day one. On her way to her first day back at work with John Peel after the birth, she happened to glance through the announcements of births and deaths in *The Times*. There she noticed that a boy, Richard, had been adopted by Mr and Mrs T. G. N. Haldane. When Anne arrived in Peel's office, there on the table was a file, bearing the title 'Haldane'. She was therefore able, throughout the intervening years, to collect various bits of information about him, including the announcement of his marriage to Jenny, and she had these kept carefully in a folder. As she told Dick of her successful rise through the nursing profession, she also told him of the time when, as Sister in Charge at London's Royal Eye Hospital, the papers for Dick's eye-squint correction operation had passed across her desk. She knew that it was her son going to theatre.

Now Dick was able to discover the facts behind the affair that led to his birth. It was quite clear that Anne was still, after forty-four years, in love with Arne. She had met him only one other time after he sailed for the United States, in 1961. She was convinced his return had been to find out more about his British son, whom he called 'Richard the Lion Heart', and that he was unsatisfied with the little information that Anne was able to give him. She could reassure Arne that their boy was settled with a good family, but 'he wanted detail'. Anne also told Dick of the twins Arne had fathered upon his return to Denmark, but this did not seem to dim Anne's admiration for her former lover. The impression she gave Dick was of a man who, though mischievous, was fundamentally lovable and good. That impression would be nuanced, in Dick's mind, by later revelations.

Dick and Anne continued to correspond by letter, with Dick now calling her 'ALM' for Anne Lysbeth Mother. They both felt a slight sense of shame in that the experience was almost like the early days of a new romance—'When will I hear from him?' 'Will she write?' There was relief in finding the feeling to be mutual. Anne visited Cloan on two happy occasions, but Anne's home life in the farmhouse in Hampshire was far from happy. Her husband, Robert, was a retired police officer, a divorcee, and a serial adulterer. The reason they were renting a property with the National Trust was that Anne had sold her old house to pay off his debts. It was not enough to earn his faithfulness. She was miserable, tired of being messed around. But what was she to do if she divorced him? She would be alone, with little money, and—she feared—would become a burden to her newly found son. In the days between Christmas and New Year's Eve of 1992, Anne contemplated a different route out.

On 1 January 1993, two police officers arrived at Dick's door at Cloan. They asked if they could speak inside. Dick took them through to the drawing room, and there they told him that his mother had taken her own life the night before. Anne had fed the car exhaust through a pipe and into the car, where she and her old dog, Saxon, spent their final minutes together. She was found dead by her husband. A short while before her suicide, she wrote her final letter to Dick:

> My dearest Richard,
>
> How do I write this to you? We have just found each other and now I have to 'disappear'. After all your searching and you/our/my delight in discovery, it is cruel beyond understanding. You know the reason for my going—without truth & respect, life has no meaning and suspicion, anger, resentment soil one's soul. I know I shall be with Arne and truly I know no fear. I am certain that the bridge between the two worlds is built on love. I have had a good life… And I have a son for whom I am full of admiration. God bless you darling Richard & be happy. I shall be watching you.
>
> My love always,
>
> ALM

There was guilt as well as grief for Dick. He had known she was unhappy in her marriage. Could he have made it clear that he would have let her come and live with him and his family at Cloan? Would he have even done that? Jenny had already spent most of her adult life in the close vicinity of Billee; could Dick thrust another mother-in-law into her midst? And, of course, the secret of his adoption would have been impossible to maintain to the outside world. Had a snobbish pride kept him from offering a refuge to Anne? Dick worried that the answer was yes. But he had no regrets about having looked for his mother.

* * *

Meeting Anne had not solved Dick's restlessness. He still felt a need to prove himself and was hungry for a challenge that would make his name. He and others had, in 1996, taken one hundred runners to Greece to run on the hundredth anniversary of the first Olympic marathon, and this had sparked a tantalising thought:

> My initial, somewhat naive and uninformed idea was, 'Britain is about 800 miles tall and 500 miles wide, and therefore has a perimeter of 2,600 miles. Why not repeat the exercise, with the same

team of 100 runners, this time each to run a marathon, as a relay, around the coast of Great Britain?'[11]

'Uninformed' was the right word. He soon found out that a runnable British coastline amounts to around 4,200 miles. It was back to the drawing board. Dick formed a trust with the intention of organising a celebratory run around Britain for the Queen Mother's hundredth birthday in the year 2000. The trust's patron was HRH The Princess Royal, who told Dick upon their first meeting at Buckingham Palace that 'her office did not believe we could do this'. Now Dick really did have his challenge.

What emerged was 'The Island Race', a hundred-day relay run that raised £1.2 million for over sixty charities. In the words of the chairman of the British Association of Road Runners, the event 'represented a quantum leap in road running-races'. It gave Dick a taste of personal fulfilment that he had barely known before. Only a year after the Race, he had a new idea—running the length of Russia. It sounded like madness. Dick was determined to prove it wasn't.

Again, he put together a powerful board of trustees, which in time came to include the British Ambassador to the Russian Federation, Sir Roderic Lyne, who told Dick, 'you know everyone here thinks you're barking mad!' Sebastian Coe, who had served on the trust for the Island Race, made a reappearance too. Getting the right backing was crucial. Soon, even the Russian Ambassador in London was inspired, and introduced Dick to the Russian Minister of Sport. The British Olympic Committee also gave its support. The intention of the trustees was twofold. Sport in Russia had traditionally been the preserve of elite athletes, and so their first aim was to promote, across the breadth of the country, the theme of sport and well-being for all. There would always be two teams of runners running, one Russian, one British. The British contingent would be composed of runners of varying ability, many of whom would be very far from competitive standard. In other words, the Brits were out to show the joy of amateur running. The Russians, true to culture, formed a far more 'professional' outfit.

Another characteristic noted in Russian society was a suspicion of charitable giving. It was often viewed as a way for dubious characters to line their own pockets, so Dick and his colleagues set about trying to change that mind set. Their goal was to raise, through their endeavour, a large sum to support the care of Russian orphans and homeless children, and to prove wrong the widespread suspicions.

The organisational aspect was immense, lasting from 2002 until the race year of 2005. It was called 'The Great Russian Race' and took place across fifteen weeks. Fifteen teams of British and Russian runners, each running in turn 750 kilometres in a week, relayed from Vladivostok to St Petersburg, a distance of 11,000 kilometres. The race crossed eight different time zones and covered a third of the world's circumference. Conditions were often extremely difficult, with the weather rarely falling below 30 degrees and mosquitos the size of small birds. The teams averaged just under three consecutive marathons a day, six days a week, with one rest day. Dick himself accumulated a total of roughly 540 kilometres, including 120 kilometres in the last week, and crowned it all by running the Moscow Marathon a day after the race's official end.

For the British runners, it was a revelatory experience. One of their number, Elizabeth Malloy, ran her 120-kilometre share of the first 740 kilometres from Vladivostok, along the Chinese border, to near the city of Khabarovsk. She loved the way the event brought her into contact with Russian runners, 'a crew of hardy, serious athletes' with whom she 'joked, chatted, commented and lived, sweated and experienced this whole journey together'.[12] What struck her most were the thousands of children that waited for the runners along the roadside and greeted them at the beginning and the end of the day, sometimes joining in for a mile or two. Elizabeth's memories of Dick are particularly enlightening:

> When I heard about the man who initiated this, and learned that he is the Trout Czar of the UK, living in a castle in Scotland, I was sceptical. And when I met him, his superb elocution put me off further—I could not imagine how this man's composure and pressed shirts would hold up. But this guy was one of the nicest gifts of the trip: full of humor even in the face of the Russian organizers crashing the Land Rovers and generally ignoring most of the agreed conditions... and despite the Russians' attempts to keep him in his senior rank by limiting him to the air conditioned Land Rovers, he soon escaped and crawled over to the dark side to hang out with us in our sweaty chamber in the Ural truck. But he was our spokesman, attending museum visits and, most notably, a trip

to the local water bottling plant at 1 am in order to get free water for us. But he still managed to pull out pressed shirts and blazers for the occasional official meeting. What I consider to be the true definition of elegance!

On their arrival in St Petersburg, having successfully completed their epic task, the mayor of the city read out to the assembled runners and citizens the following telegram (which makes for especially interesting reading now, as I write in the first months of the Russian invasion of Ukraine in 2022):

> President of Russian Federation—September 8, 2005
>
> To the Participants and the Organizers of the Russian-British Race—'The Great Russian Race'
>
> I welcome the Russian and the British athletes who have successfully completed the Race from Vladivostok to St Petersburg. It is symbolic that this grandiose project was carried out in 2005, the year which was declared by the General Assembly as the International Year of Sport and Physical Education. I am confident that this truly interesting and significant Race, uniting so large a number of professional and amateur runners, will serve as an example of a healthy mode of life, as a strengthening of human contacts and as a further development of international cooperation in the field of sport.
>
> I wish you new achievements and all the best!
>
> V. Putin

When an MBE followed in the 2006 New Year list of honours, for services to charity and the Great Russian Race, Dick finally felt that the vow he had made to his Haldane relatives all those years ago on his twenty-first birthday had come true. In the words of the British Ambassador to Russia, he had pulled off a 'landmark sporting, charitable and Anglo/Russian event'. Having spent his life hearing his Haldane forebears hailed as extraordinary, it was now, for a brief moment, his turn. 'No one else—I firmly believe this—could have brought off the great run across Russia... a quite extraordinary job accomplished by an equally extraordinary friend', wrote a former head of MI6 and fellow trustee of the race. Dick may not have been a statesman or a scientist or a writer, in the classic Haldane mode, but he had contributed to the betterment of the world in a meaningful way. And he had done so using the techniques that had been practised over and over again by the hero of the family, Uncle Richard (as he was always known to Dick, though technically Richard was his great-uncle). What were these? Single-mindedness of purpose, certainly; thinking in advance and careful planning; mobilising powerful contacts; and cross-sector and, of course, international cooperation. These techniques provided the necessary realism to balance out that common Haldane attribute, an unstinting optimism—or, as a previous age would have called it, idealism.

And yet, the question of his identity continued to gnaw at him. Dick had grown not to expect security or peace on that front.

* * *

Then, in 2009, the unexpected happened. Once again, the link was Shellard Campbell. Visiting a friend of a friend in Devon, she happened to discover a connection between her host and Arne Bertelsen's plastic surgery work with Archibald McIndoe, and mentioned Dick. Ten days later, she received a phone call from her Devon contact, who told her: 'This is extraordinary—I've just come across this internet post on Facebook.' It read as follows:

DENMARK calling ENGLAND.

Hello Half-brother! Are you out there?

I think you have a right to your ancestors! I think you have a right to know about your own genes. Your Fathers name: ARNE BERTELSEN (1910–1971). After world war 2 your father went to England to learn plastic surgery and orthopaedic surgery—between 1945–47… I think you were born about 1947… I have been thinking about you. I would like to let you know about your roots…

It was Dick's younger half-sister who wrote this message into the ether. Stunned to find it reach him, Dick was immediate in response. The initial correspondence was a flurry of information swapping, clearing up long-unanswered questions, and trying to establish common ground. They found that ground very quickly.

Amongst the large volume of information shared was the fact that some of Dick's biological relations had suffered from problems with alcohol, just as he had, and some in the family believed it to be a genetical inheritance from Arne's maternal grandfather. He also learnt that a driving ambition, the desire to prove oneself, was a common family trait. Dick reflected that perhaps, like his relationship to alcohol, this streak in himself was not entirely bound up with his insecurities around his adoption. There was something liberating in the thought.

His siblings welcomed him with open arms as one of the family. For his younger half-brother, the impact was especially profound. After a joyous visit to Cloan with his wife in late 2009, his daughter wrote to Dick:

> It is clear to me that he... really feels strongly that he has found the brother that mirrors himself, and I have been surprised to see how important that feeling obviously is to him—to see sides of himself in you and feeling understood in a more profound way, I think. So to say that you, his new brother, are one of the best things that ever happened to my father would be an understatement.

Dick's half-brother was a practising GP. It turned out he also worked in diving medicine and knew of the pioneering work of John Scott Haldane. It was not the only surprising coincidence. Arne's mother had been called Karen, and Dick and Jenny had given their eldest child that very name.

Connecting to the Bertelsens occasioned further reading into the life of Dick's natural grandfather, Aage Bertelsen. More than just a talented painter, Aage had participated in the ill-fated Denmark Expedition to north-east Greenland between 1906 and 1908. As Dick learnt more about the expedition, from which three of Aage's fellow explorers never returned, he discovered a history of which he could be proud—just as proud as he could be of his Haldane heritage. Aage was honoured for his role in the Danes' mission by having a Greenland glacier named after him, as well as a headland in Queen Louise Land, which is known as Cape Aage Bertelsen. As Dick absorbed these past stories and achievements, and as he experienced the loving welcome from his 'new' siblings, the sense of shame that had built up in connection with his adoption fell from his shoulders. Indeed, having been brought up in a family where a traceable antiquity had counted for so much, he now discovered that he could trace himself back to a twelfth-century Danish ancestor, Ketil Urne—his great-grandfather twenty-four times over—whose rune stone, dated 1200, stands in the church at Bjolderup. With this and other discoveries, there was nothing left to hide. Learning that his Danish family were, like all families, not fault-free was part of the healing process. Their own stories, some very sad and moving, shed light on the darkness that Dick himself had battled, helping him to understand himself, to be kind to himself.

He needed all that kindness when, in 2015, he chose to sell Cloan to Murdoch's son, Neil Mitchison. It was a fundamental break with the past (it came, coincidentally, at roughly the same time that his cousin, John Haldane, sold Foswell). Dick had been as loyal to, and protective of, the place as any son could be, but it was a white elephant that was impossible to leave to his children. Building a new, more manageable house, Cloanden, further up the glen, and deciding to rear Highland cattle on the farmlands his Haldane great-grandfather had bought over 150 years previously, brought a steadying element of continuity—as did the unwavering support of Jenny, a rock not only to Dick, but, in her many charitable and educational endeavours, to the wider Auchterarder community. There has been continuity, too, in their four children, who carry on the Haldane tradition in their own unique ways. Now, Dick and Jenny have thirteen grandchildren, who love to return to Cloanden in the holidays. Amongst their number a strong artistic bent is discernable—a link, perhaps, to their Danish heritage. One way or another, the two pasts have woven into one.

* * *

The narration of Dick's story is not an attempt to test the nature versus nurture question. The rigours demanded for such a test simply cannot be provided. What his story *can* do is reinforce the fundamental complexity of family life, of inheritance, of what it takes to belong. In this sense, Dick's life follows a pattern latent within the lives of his Haldane predecessors. Adoption brings its own unique challenges, certainly, but each generation of the family had to work out its relation to the generation before in uncomfortable and disruptive ways. Mary Haldane was evidently tormented by the regime under which her cruel governesses had forced her to live as a child, and even towards the end of her long life she was still trying to process the complicity of her parents in this. Mary's children, especially Richard, John, and Elizabeth, faced the hard struggle of breaking free from the religious strictures which had so dominated their upbringing. Their challenge was to find ways of conceiving and practising the twin pillars of the family—service and sacrifice—in a manner that was both in keeping with their new philosophical commitments and acceptable to their beloved mother. As John wrote in that time of disquiet, 'In lives that are real there must always be pain as well as happiness.'[13] His children, JBS and Naomi, knew that pain, too. In leaving behind the High Tory politics of their mother, Kathleen, they opened a wound that never healed.

And yet each generation after Mary was conscious of the fact that they were carrying something on from the past into the future, something that was recognisably Haldane (and Burdon Sanderson), something intimately connected to that hallowed home, Cloan. This book has sought to capture those enduring elements: the desire to synthesise knowledge, especially philosophical and scientific, while displaying independence of mind; the sense of a calling to serve the public in some form, often through personal sacrifice; the conviction of being in the right; the drive to be ahead of the trend. These get us a good way towards understanding the connecting themes between individual Haldane lives, but we should not take them, collectively, as a catch-all for what makes a Haldane. Few within the family have embodied all four. It is difficult to ascribe any of them to some members. Archie doesn't fit the bill, for instance, and yet no one would ever consider him any less of a Haldane for that. The question of identity—what makes us who we are, what makes us one thing and not another—must always retain an element of mystery.

If Dick, then, doesn't match neatly with all four traits, we need to be cautious about taking that as a sign that his biological origins lie elsewhere. Similarly, just because his success in Russia arose from a wealth of skills that his Uncle Richard had perfected, that doesn't *automatically* indicate that he grew up a Haldane of Cloan. There are others, quite unconnected to Richard, who have shown the same organisational virtues. If we cannot draw straight lines like this, we can still affirm that Dick's Haldane heritage has had an enormous influence on his life and has made him who he is today. Yes, he is distinct, but so too are other members of the family in their own ways. These many forms of individuality mean that Dick's adoption does not carry the weight, within the overall arc of the narrative, that we might at first think it does. He has felt an outsider at times, that is true. But, as my interviews have shown, it is true of other members of the family as well. And it's important to remember that he had the privilege of growing up at Cloan itself, which neither Naomi nor JBS had, nor the Mitchisons after them. Undoubtedly, each generation has experienced the ambiguities of feeling that the search for belonging brings. In Dick's case, he has made his peace, by and large, with these ambiguities. The discovery of his Danish family was essential to this. It did not do away with the mystery inherent in identity, but it did answer many a long-asked question.

So, if you travelled to Perthshire now and wound your way up the hill from Auchterarder into the Ochil Hills, past the gates of Cloan with its peeping spires behind the trees, and walked on into the high fields, there, quite possibly, you would find an older gentleman in pressed shirt and mud-bespattered wellingtons moving amongst his cows, wearing a look of concentration as he counts his bovine friends. Do not be distracted by the three joyously unruly golden retrievers. Look more closely at the man in his old school tie. Behind the furrowed brow, a hard-won contentment lies. He is living the life his grandfather, Willie Haldane, knew and loved. He is in possession of a story and a family that finally make sense of who he is. He is content because he knows himself to be every bit a Haldane: the true half-Dane.

APPENDIX

THE FOREBEARS OF ROBERT AND MARY HALDANE OF CLOAN

The forebears of Robert and Mary Haldane of

as named in

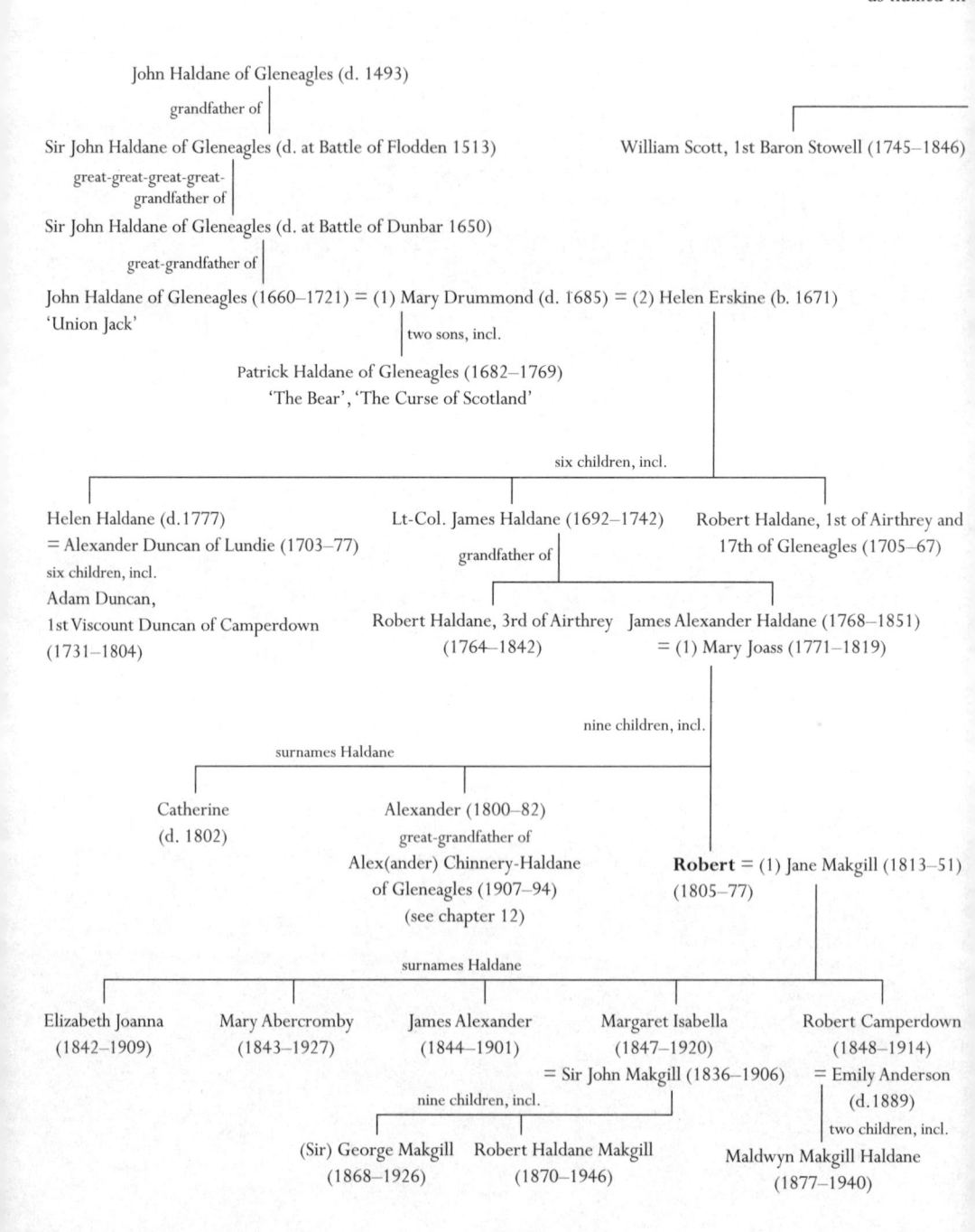

John Haldane of Gleneagles (d. 1493)
| grandfather of

Sir John Haldane of Gleneagles (d. at Battle of Flodden 1513) — William Scott, 1st Baron Stowell (1745–1846)
| great-great-great-great-
| grandfather of

Sir John Haldane of Gleneagles (d. at Battle of Dunbar 1650)
| great-grandfather of

John Haldane of Gleneagles (1660–1721) = (1) Mary Drummond (d. 1685) = (2) Helen Erskine (b. 1671)
'Union Jack'
| two sons, incl.

Patrick Haldane of Gleneagles (1682–1769)
'The Bear', 'The Curse of Scotland'

six children, incl.

Helen Haldane (d.1777)	Lt.-Col. James Haldane (1692–1742)	Robert Haldane, 1st of Airthrey and
= Alexander Duncan of Lundie (1703–77)	grandfather of	17th of Gleneagles (1705–67)
six children, incl.		
Adam Duncan,	Robert Haldane, 3rd of Airthrey	James Alexander Haldane (1768–1851)
1st Viscount Duncan of Camperdown	(1764–1842)	= (1) Mary Joass (1771–1819)
(1731–1804)		

nine children, incl.

surnames Haldane

Catherine	Alexander (1800–82)
(d. 1802)	great-grandfather of
	Alex(ander) Chinnery-Haldane	**Robert** = (1) Jane Makgill (1813–51)
	of Gleneagles (1907–94)	(1805–77)
	(see chapter 12)	

surnames Haldane

Elizabeth Joanna	Mary Abercromby	James Alexander	Margaret Isabella	Robert Camperdown
(1842–1909)	(1843–1927)	(1844–1901)	(1847–1920)	(1848–1914)
		= Sir John Makgill (1836–1906)	= Emily Anderson
	nine children, incl.		(d.1889)
			two children, incl.
	(Sir) George Makgill	Robert Haldane Makgill	Maldwyn Makgill Haldane
	(1868–1926)	(1870–1946)	(1877–1940)

Cloan, with children and grandchildren of Robert's first marriage
chapters 1 and 2

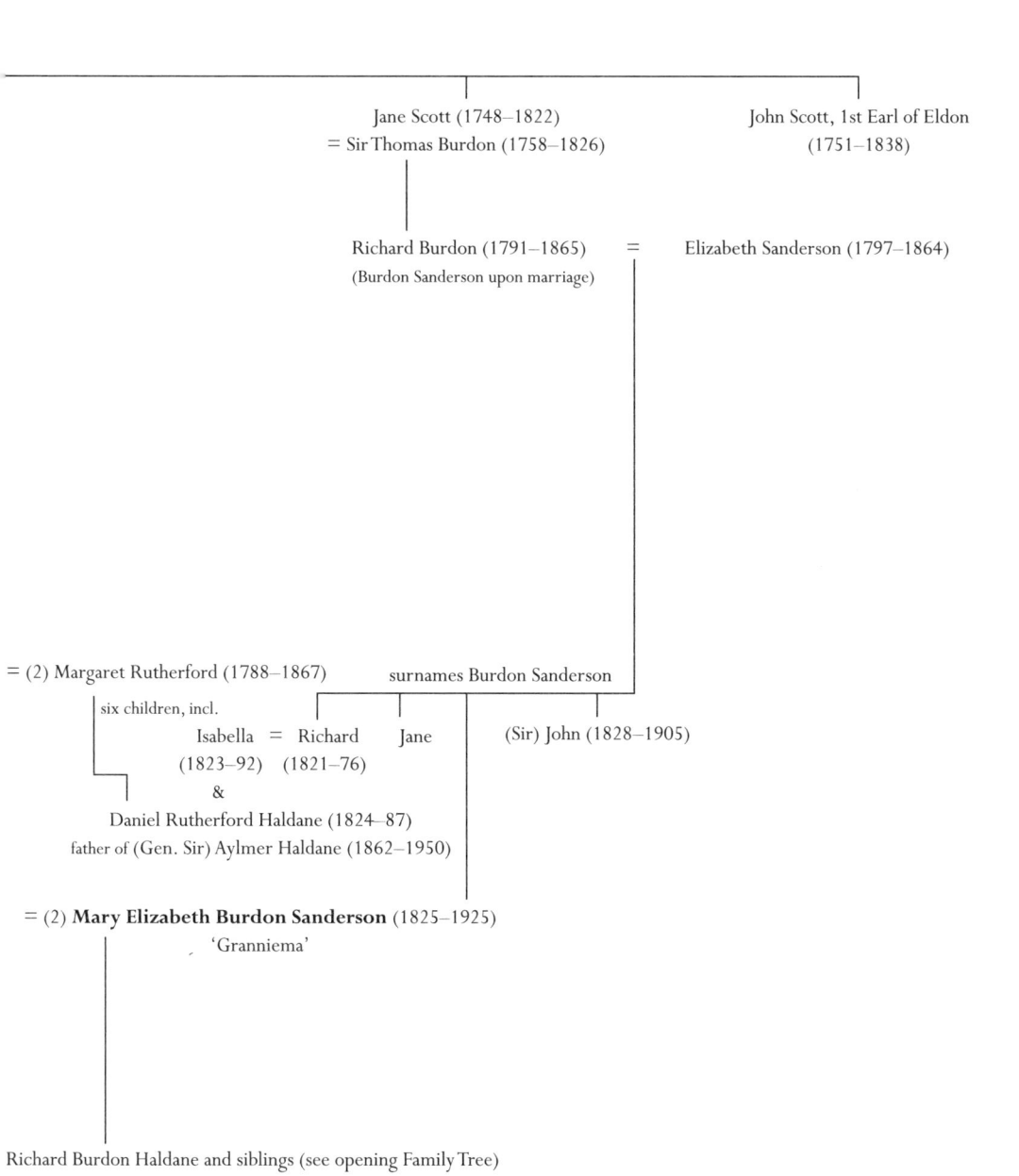

Jane Scott (1748–1822)   John Scott, 1st Earl of Eldon
= Sir Thomas Burdon (1758–1826)   (1751–1838)

Richard Burdon (1791–1865)   =   Elizabeth Sanderson (1797–1864)
(Burdon Sanderson upon marriage)

= (2) Margaret Rutherford (1788–1867)   surnames Burdon Sanderson

six children, incl.

Isabella   =   Richard   Jane   (Sir) John (1828–1905)
(1823–92)   (1821–76)
&
Daniel Rutherford Haldane (1824–87)
father of (Gen. Sir) Aylmer Haldane (1862–1950)

= (2) **Mary Elizabeth Burdon Sanderson** (1825–1925)
'Granniema'

Richard Burdon Haldane and siblings (see opening Family Tree)

LIST OF ILLUSTRATIONS

1. John Scott, 1st Earl of Eldon (1751–1838) by Sir Thomas Lawrence. He was Mary Haldane's great-uncle and a high Tory. Source: Wikipedia, public domain.

2. The itinerant preacher James Alexander Haldane (1768–1851) by George Zobel, after Colvin Smith stipple and line engraving, c. 1845. James Alexander was Robert Haldane of Cloan's father. Source: Wikipedia, Creative Commons Attribution-ShareAlike 3.0.

3. (Sir) John Burdon Sanderson FRS (1828–1905), c. 1870s. John was Mary's younger brother and first Waynflete Professor of Physiology at Oxford. Source: Wellcome Collection, public domain, photograph by Maull & Fox.

4. Robert Haldane of Cloan, early 1850s, surrounded by the children of his first marriage. Source: Richard Wilkie Haldane's private collection, photograph by Simon Jauncey.

5. A sketch of Cloan as it was in 1855, by Mary Haldane. Source: Richard Wilkie Haldane's private collection.

6. Cloan, shortly after the western extension in 1866, with Richard and Geordie on horseback, watched over by their mother Mary. Source: Neil Mitchison's private collection.

7. A young Richard Haldane in the arms of the family's beloved nurse, Betsy Ferguson (Baba), 1856. Source: Richard Wilkie Haldane's private collection, photograph by Justin Piperger.

8. Mary Haldane, with her second son, Geordie, 1858. Source: Richard Wilkie Haldane's private collection.

9. John, Richard and Geordie Haldane, c. 1870. Source: Richard Wilkie Haldane's private collection, photograph by Justin Piperger.

LIST OF ILLUSTRATIONS

10. John Haldane, seated far right, with fellow members of the Eureka Club, 1876. Source: The Edinburgh Academy Archives.

11. Mary and Robert's children, late 1870s. From left to right: John, Elizabeth, Willie and Richard. Source: Richard Wilkie Haldane's private collection, photograph by Justin Piperger.

12. Mary, surrounded by her three eldest children, Richard, John and Elizabeth, on the steps at Cloan, early 1880s. Source: Richard Wilkie Haldane's private collection, photograph by Justin Piperger.

13. Elizabeth and Richard Haldane, possibly during the 1907 army manoeuvres at Cloan. Source: Richard Wilkie Haldane's private collection, photograph by Justin Piperger.

14. The fields in front of Cloan, home to 1,000 soldiers and 500 horses during the army manoeuvres of 1907. Source: Richard Wilkie Haldane's private collection, photograph by Simon Jauncey.

15. Cloan, 1908, extended to make space for the increasingly well-to-do Richard Haldane's suite of rooms. Source: Scan of *The Woman at Home*, Jan. 1908, Richard Wilkie Haldane's private collection.

16. The drawing room at Cloan, 1908. Source: Scan of *The Woman at Home*, Jan. 1908, Richard Wilkie Haldane's private collection.

17. Richard's new study at Cloan, 1908. Source: Scan of *The Woman at Home*, Jan. 1908, Richard Wilkie Haldane's private collection.

18. Frances Horner, c. 1910s. Source: Richard Wilkie Haldane's private collection, photograph by Justin Piperger.

19. Jack (JBS) and Naomi Haldane, 1911, when Jack was Captain of the School at Eton. Source: Sally Mitchison's private collection.

20. John Haldane (left) and his team, including the pioneering Mabel Purefoy FitzGerald, during the Pikes Peak expedition, 1911. Source: http://blogs.bodleian.ox.ac.uk/archivesandmanuscripts/2016/03/03/mabelfitzgerald_1/

21. Richard Haldane, by now Viscount Haldane of Cloan, as Lord Chancellor, 1912. Source: Richard Wilkie Haldane's private collection, photograph by Justin Piperger.

LIST OF ILLUSTRATIONS

22. The cast of Naomi Haldane's play *Saunes Bairos* in the cloister of New College, Oxford, summer 1914. Featuring Naomi, her brother JBS Haldane, their mother Kathleen, Lewis Gielgud, Aldous Huxley, his brother Trevor, and Naomi's future husband, Dick Mitchison. Source: Sally Mitchison's private collection.

23. Voluntary Aid Detachment nurses in the improvised hospital at Cloan, formerly Robert Haldane's chapel, 1911. Source: Richard Wilkie Haldane's private collection.

24. Belgian soldiers at Cloan, where they were sent to recuperate in 1914. Source: Richard Wilkie Haldane's private collection.

25. JBS, otherwise known in the trenches as 'Bomber Haldane', 1914. Source: Sally Mitchison's private collection.

26. The 'Black Veil' respirator, created by John Haldane and Professor H. Brereton Baker, in 1915. This was the first gas mask to be used on the Front by British troops. Source: Wikipedia, public domain.

27. Oxygen apparatus developed by John Haldane, father of oxygen therapy, during WWI. Source: Science Museum, London. Attribution 4.0 International (CC BY 4.0).

28. Pat Haldane, Willie's eldest child, 1915. Source: Richard Wilkie Haldane's private collection.

29. A kneeling Sir William (Willie) Haldane and family, 1915. His youngest son, Archie, rests on his father's shoulder, with his older siblings Elsie and Graeme on the far side; Brodrick Chinnery-Haldane of Gleneagles and Willie's wife Lady (Edith) Haldane in the middle. Source: Richard Wilkie Haldane's private collection.

30. Lord Chancellor Richard Haldane and Albert Einstein on the steps at Richard's London home, 28 Queen Anne's Gate, during Einstein's first visit to the country, 1921. Source: Richard Wilkie Haldane's private collection, photograph by Justin Piperger.

31. JBS Haldane in oxygen breathing equipment, possibly taken in the 1920s. Source: Clare Mitchison's private collection.

32. John Haldane (right) with son JBS (centre) and Australian physiologist Harold Whitridge Davies, in John's private laboratory at his

LIST OF ILLUSTRATIONS

Oxford home, Cherwell, 1920s, where John and his team tested the first gas masks of the First World War. Source: National Library of Medicine / Science Photo Library.

33. Cherwell, the house built in 1907 by John and Kathleen Haldane, date unknown. Source: Wolfson College, Univ. of Oxford (Archives).

34. Mary Haldane, 1924, the year before she died, aged 100. Source: Richard Wilkie Haldane's private collection, photograph by Justin Piperger.

35. The Haldane family, gathered on the occasion of Mary Haldane's 100th birthday, 1925. Front row, left to right: John, Richard, Bruce (the dog), Elizabeth and Willie. Middle row: JBS, Edith (Lady Haldane), Archie, Elsie, Graeme, Agnes Chinnery-Haldane, Brodrick Chinnery-Haldane and (James) Brodrick Chinnery-Haldane of Gleneagles. Back row: Guy Bullough, Marjorie Bullough (née Chinnery-Haldane), Gen. Sir Aylmer Haldane, Alex(ander) Chinnery-Haldane, Katherine Chinnery-Haldane. Source: Richard Wilkie Haldane's private collection, photograph by Justin Piperger.

36. Naomi and Dick Mitchison's three eldest boys, 1925. Left to right: Denny, Murdoch and Geoff. Source: Sally Mitchison's private collection.

37. John, Elizabeth and Willie Haldane at the funeral of their brother Richard, 1928. Source: Richard Wilkie Haldane's private collection.

38. The Mitchison family, mid-1930s, at their London home, Rivercourt. Denny stands with his parents in the back row. Lois, Val, Av and Murdoch are seated left to right. Source: Sally Mitchison's private collection.

39. JBS Haldane in leather jacket, Spain, 1936. Source: Wikimedia Commons, Creative Commons CC0 1.0 Universal Public Domain Dedication (CC0).

40. Graeme Haldane speaking at the Fifth World Power Conference, Vienna, 1956. Source: Richard Wilkie Haldane's private collection.

41. Carradale House from the air, 1962. Source: Sally Mitchison's private collection.

LIST OF ILLUSTRATIONS

42. Three generations of the Mitchison family on the steps at Carradale, 1963. Source: Photograph by Lois Godfrey (nee Mitchison), Sally Mitchison's private collection.

43. JBS, looking at home in India, early 1960s. Source: estherlederberg.com, photograph by Esther M. Zimmer Lederberg.

44. Naomi in Botswana, with Kgosi Linchwe II, chief of the Bakgatla people, 1970s. Source: Neil Mitchison's private collection.

45. Archie (ARB) Haldane with wife Jan at their home, Foswell, 1970s. Source: Jennifer Halsey's private collection.

46. A one-year-old Dick Haldane with his mother, Billee, and grandfather, Sir William (Willie) Haldane, at Cloan, 1948. Source: Richard Wilkie Haldane's private collection.

47. Dick Haldane, aged eleven, with his father, Graeme, 1958. Source: Richard Wilkie Haldane's private collection, photograph by Simon Jauncey.

48. Dick Haldane and his new bride, Jenny Livingstone-Learmonth, on their wedding day, 1970. Source: Richard Wilkie Haldane's private collection, photograph by Simon Jauncey.

49. Dick Haldane, centre, running into Moscow's Red Square during the Great Russian Race, 2005. Source: Richard Wilkie Haldane's private collection.

50. Aage Bertelsen, Danish explorer and painter and Dick Haldane's biological grandfather, 1908. Source: Richard Wilkie Haldane's private collection.

51. Cloan as it is today. Source: Rettie sales brochure 2014, photograph by David Cemery.

ACKNOWLEDGEMENTS

My first thanks must go to John Campbell for supporting me so fully over the last two-and-a-half years as this book has taken shape. Our earlier collaboration on *Haldane: The Forgotten Statesman Who Shaped Modern Britain* was one of the great privileges and joys of my life, and he has made the present project an equal delight. While always ready with sage advice, he has not once sought to step on my toes—a remarkable achievement given his unparalleled passion for, and encyclopaedic knowledge of, all things Haldane. I have felt entirely free to go my own way with this book, but there is no doubt that his energy, kindness, and readiness to listen and enthuse have been some of the most fundamental sustaining factors in its production. Shellard Campbell and her sister Jo have also been firm supporters, and I am particularly grateful to Shellard for providing such a clear account of her involvement in the story which forms the focus of Chapter 12.

It would have been much harder to write this book without the assistance of the Haldane family itself, and thankfully they have been unfailing in their generosity and encouragement. Dick Haldane, the last of those bearing that surname to live at Cloan, eminently embodies these two attributes, having opened his personal and family papers, photographs, and memories to me without reserve, and sometimes at a significant emotional cost. I am deeply grateful to him and his wife Jenny not only for the hospitality they have extended at Cloanden, but also for the honesty they have shown in telling their side of the family story, with all the positives and negatives that reveals. This openness proved to be a feature of the family. It was there in abundance in Dick's sister Robin, and in his cousins Patrick Campbell Fraser, John Haldane, and Jennifer Halsey (and Jennifer's husband, Michael). To each of them, for their full and frank comments through conversation and correspondence, and

ACKNOWLEDGEMENTS

for access to further family papers and photographs, I give my thanks. The input of Dick's biological family in Denmark, the Bertelsens, and the practical support of Dick's daughter and son-in-law, Sally and Paul Rutkowski, have also been greatly appreciated.

The Mitchison side of the family has of course been essential. It was an honour to speak over the telephone with two of Naomi's children, Val Arnold-Forster and Professor Avrion Mitchison, both now in their nineties, providing a living link with a past that for so long had only existed for me in my head and on the printed page. My sincere thanks to them, and to their respective daughters, Kate Glennerster and Ellen Mortimer, for making these conversations possible. To Tabitha Lucas, Terence Mitchison, and Clare Mitchison, I owe my capacity to quote freely from the extensive papers of Naomi and her brother J. B. S. Haldane (some of which are held privately, some in public collections), and for this I am extremely grateful. I also enjoyed interviews with Tabitha and Terence, as well as with Sally Mitchison and her husband John Charlton; not forgetting my interviews, during a visit to Cloan, with Neil Mitchison, Neil's wife Aideen O'Malley, and his sister Harriet Mitchison. An old Mitchison family friend from Carradale days, Geoffrey Baxter, was equally giving of his time and memories over the phone. Tabitha, Clare, Ellen, and Sally came to my rescue when the moment arrived for gathering images for the book, and I must thank Sally especially for going to considerable lengths to locate particular photographs and providing high-quality scans. She and Terence gave even more of their time in reading an early draft of the manuscript to check the accuracy of my statements about the Mitchison side of the family. For whatever inaccuracies may remain, in any aspect of the story, I take full responsibility.

I have relied on a number of other kind-hearted individuals and generous institutions for reproducing quotes from various figures. Alison Metcalfe, on behalf of the National Library of Scotland, extended permission to quote from the Haldane Papers, and I am much in the debt of Alison and her colleagues Heidi Egginton and Colin McIlroy for assisting me in so many aspects of my research. Jeremy McIlwaine, on behalf of the Bodleian Library, Oxford, granted permission to quote from the diaries of Margot Asquith, and helped in other important respects. One of these was to establish

ACKNOWLEDGEMENTS

contact with Geoffrey Purefoy, who graciously allowed me to use an extract from the papers of Mabel Purefoy FitzGerald and shared with me his memories of his great-aunt. My thanks, too, to the Earl of Oxford and Asquith for permission to reproduce sections from the letters of R. B. Haldane to Frances Horner, and a letter from Frances to E. S. Haldane. Andrew McMillan, honorary archivist at the Edinburgh Academy, kindly looked for images of Mary's children at school, and to the school I am grateful for permission to use one of them here. I also thank Liz Baird, archivist at Wolfson College, Oxford, for granting permission to use the image of Cherwell, where the college now stands. Max Mills and Andrew Smith at Rettie helped me track down David Cemery, who took the brilliant photos of Cloan for the Rettie sales brochure in 2014. David warmly put the images at my disposal, and I am delighted that the final image of the book is one from his collection.

Copyright ownership is not always easy to uncover. I must thank Gay Sturt at the Dragon School in Oxford, Rafael Siodor at UCL Library Special Collections, Will Greenacre at the Wellcome Collection, and Alexandra Fisher at the Parliamentary Archives for helping me in my various quests. Sophie Bridges and Jessica Collins at the Churchill Archives Centre in Cambridge were wonderfully helpful in granting access to the previously classified papers of Graeme Haldane concerning his work on atomic energy. My friend Ambrogio Camozzi Pistoja at Harvard did me a great favour in tracking down hard-to-come-by texts. Thanks to Sandy Nairne, too, for his attempts to connect me with individuals potentially interested in my endeavour, and to Professor Lindsay Paterson for his reading suggestions and many a fascinating conversation.

I am deeply indebted to the groundbreaking work of previous biographers of Haldane family members. Jenni Calder and Samanth Subramanian have not only fielded innumerable questions from me, but also made available their personal research material with exceptional generosity of spirit. I have drawn extensively on Naomi's letters to Jenni, on Jenni's old copy of Naomi's USSR diary, and on the tape recordings of interviews that Jenni conducted with Naomi and other family members and friends. It was a privilege to read and listen to these items and to be able to quote from them. In addition,

ACKNOWLEDGEMENTS

the work of Martin Goodman has been vital to me; I only regret that I was not able to establish contact with him.

The team at Hurst have been fantastic. Thanks to Michael Dwyer for seeing the potential of this book; to Lara Weisweiller-Wu for her exemplary attention to detail and communication, and of course for offering the salutary plain-speaking of a true editor; and to Mei Jayne Yew, Daisy Leitch, Kathleen May, and Raminta Uselytė for their many forms of assistance. And it was a pleasure to work with the freelance copy-editor Rose Bell and indexer Alex Bell.

There have been many supporters amongst my friends, but I would like to single out Michael Osborne, Donald Mackintosh, Mikey Wood, and Will Ferguson for the refreshment I have found in their conversation and constant encouragement. (Will's father, James, must also be thanked for first introducing me to John Campbell.) As for family, my parents, Grahame and Rosaly, and my siblings and their families have been the most fantastic cheerleaders. My final thanks, however, must be reserved for my wife Sabrina, and our boys Magnus and Arvo. This book was written throughout the worst years of the coronavirus pandemic, forcing us to live on top of each other; I can't always have been the easiest person to be around, with my head so often lost in the clouds of this book. From my side, although writing conditions were not exactly ideal, every day spent in their company showed new dimensions to the meaning of the word 'family'. This has been the most valuable research tool I could have hoped for, given the focus of this book. And whenever I faced a brick wall or the writing became difficult, their love and laughter were the perfect restoratives. I dedicate this book to them.

LIST OF REFERENCING ABBREVIATIONS

FAMILY NAMES AND THEIR FREQUENTLY CITED WRITINGS

AH   **Alexander Haldane**

ML   *Memoirs of the Lives of Robert Haldane of Airthrey, and of his Brother, James Alexander Haldane* (New York: R. Carter, 1858).

ARBH   **Archibald Richard Burdon Haldane**

UM   *An Unfinished Memoir* (unpublished), Jennifer Halsey private collection.

ESH   **Elizabeth Sanderson Haldane**

D   Diary, typescript, Patrick Campbell Fraser private collection.

FOCTA   *From One Century to Another* (London: Alexander Maclehose & Co., 1937).

MEH   *Mary Elizabeth Haldane: A Record of a Hundred Years* (London: Hodder & Stoughton, 1925).

JBSH   John Burdon Sanderson Haldane

SWJSH   'The Scientific Work of J. S. Haldane', in S. A. Barnett and Anne McLaren (eds.), *Penguin Science Survey 1961*, Vol. 2 (London: Penguin, 1961).

JSH   **John Scott Haldane**

LEP   *A Letter to Edinburgh Professors* (London: David Stott, 1890), published anonymously under the title, 'A Medical Student'.

LKH   **Louisa Kathleen Haldane**

FK   *Friends and Kindred: Memoirs of Louisa Kathleen Haldane* (London: Faber & Faber, 1961).

LIST OF REFERENCING ABBREVIATIONS

MEH   **Mary Elizabeth Haldane**

MM   **Murdoch Mitchison**

TBHOD   *To the Beat of His Own Drum*, ed. Sally Mitchison (privately printed 2017).

NM   **Naomi Mitchison**

ACH   *All Change Here* (London: Bodley Head, 1975).

AYTN   *Among You Taking Notes: The Wartime Diary of Naomi Mitchison, 1939–1945* (London: Victor Gollancz, 1985).

BC   *The Bull Calves* (Glasgow: Richard Drew Publishing Ltd, 1985).

HPNHL   'The Haldanes: Personal Notes and Historical Lessons', *Proceedings of the Royal Institute of Great Britain*, 47 (1974), 1–22.

SSP   *Saltire Self-Portraits 2: Naomi Mitchison* (Edinburgh: Saltire Society, 1986).

ST   *Small Talk: Memories of an Edwardian Childhood* (London: Bodley Head, 1973).

USSR   USSR diary, 1932, typescript, Jenni Calder private collection.

YMWA   *You May Well Ask* (London: Flamingo, 1986).

RBH   **Richard Burdon Haldane**

PTR   *The Pathway to Reality: Stage the First* (London: John Murray, 1905).

RBH   *Richard Burdon Haldane: An Autobiography* (London: Hodder & Stoughton, 1929).

RWH   **Richard (Dick) Wilkie Haldane**

TGNH   **Thomas Graeme Nelson Haldane**

TGNHoC   *Thomas Graeme Nelson Haldane of Cloan, 1897–1981*, ed. Richard Wilkie Haldane (Edinburgh: Clark Constable, 1982).

WSH   **William Stowell Haldane**

SER   'Some Early Recollections', Richard (Dick) Wilkie Haldane private collection.

LIST OF REFERENCING ABBREVIATIONS

FREQUENTLY CITED SCHOLARS AND THEIR SECONDARY LITERATURE

JC **Jenni Calder**

BG *The Burning Glass: The Life of Naomi Mitchison* (Dingwall: Sandstone Press, 2019).

MG **Martin Goodman**

SAS *Suffer and Survive: Gas Attacks, Miners' Canaries, Spacesuits and the Bends: The Extreme Life of Dr. J. S. Haldane* (London: Pocket Books, 2008).

RC **Ronald Clark**

JBS *J. B. S.: The Life and Work of J. B. S. Haldane* (Oxford and New York: Oxford University Press, 1984).

SS **Samanth Subramanian**

DC *A Dominant Character: The Radical Science and Restless Politics of J. B. S. Haldane* (London: Atlantic Books, 2019).

PRIVATE COLLECTIONS (PC)

CM pc.	Clare Mitchison
EOA pc.	Earl of Oxford and Asquith
JC pc.	Jenni Calder
PCF pc.	Patrick Campbell Fraser
RWH pc.	Richard (Dick) Wilkie Haldane
TL pc.	Tabitha Lucas

INTERVIEWS CONDUCTED BY AUTHOR

AM int.	Avrion Mitchison, 5 Nov. 2020.
HM int.	Harriet Mitchison, 27 Aug. 2020.
JH int.	Jennifer Halsey, 13 Nov. 2020.
Neil M int.	Neil Mitchison, 27 Aug. 2020.
PCF int.	Patrick Campbell Fraser, 13 Nov. 2020.
RWH int.	Richard (Dick) Wilkie Haldane, 27 and 29 Jan. 2021.

LIST OF REFERENCING ABBREVIATIONS

SM int.	Sally Mitchison, 15 Sep. 2020.
TL int.	Tabitha Lucas, 20 Oct. 2020.
TM int.	Terence Mitchison, 13 Oct. 2020.

LIBRARIES, ARCHIVES, AND DICTIONARIES

BLO	Bodleian Library, Oxford
BLL	Brotherton Library, Leeds
EA Arch.	Edinburgh Academy Archives
NLS	National Library of Scotland
ODNB	*Oxford Dictionary of National Biography*
PA	Parliamentary Archives
WC	Wellcome Collection

NOTES

INTRODUCTION

1. See ESH, *FOCTA*, 26. The scene is dated to the late 1870s, but this seems unlikely given the age and station of the so-called 'big boys' by then. It must have been earlier in the decade. The paragraphs which follow in the main text above are extrapolations from photographs and descriptions gathered from various sources.
2. NM, *HPNHL*, 20.
3. Terence Mitchison, as quoted in Neil M int. The origins of this quip seem to lie with Naomi, who apparently once said: 'She was the only mother to have given birth to a third of a ton of Biology Professors.' See MM, *TBHOD*, 164.
4. 'Obituary—Professor Denny Mitchison', Stop TB Partnership.
5. See David Banks, 'Dr T. G. N. "Graeme" Haldane—Scottish Heat Pump Pioneer', *International Journal for the History of Engineering & Technology*, 85:2 (Jul. 2015), 168–76.
6. Ian J. Deary, *Intelligence: A Very Short Introduction* (Oxford: Oxford University Press, 2020), 57.
7. 'Edinburgh Engineer Crowned Young Woman Engineer', School of Engineering, University of Edinburgh.
8. The same cannot be said of the principal branch of the family, the Haldanes of Gleneagles. See Neil Stacy, *The Haldanes of Gleneagles: A Scottish History from the Twelfth Century to the Present Day* (Edinburgh: Birlinn, 2017). There is also Aylmer Haldane's *The Haldanes of Gleneagles* (Edinburgh and London: William Blackwood & Sons, 1929), which is more of a highly detailed family tree.
9. Noel Annan, *The Dons: Mentors, Eccentrics and Geniuses* (London: HarperCollins, 1999), 320.
10. See Laura Trevelyan, *A Very British Family: The Trevelyans and Their World* (London and New York: I. B. Tauris, 2012); Tim M. Berra, *Darwin and His Children: His Other Legacy* (Oxford: Oxford University Press, 2013); Ronald W. Clark, *The Huxleys* (London: Heinemann, 1968).
11. *The Times*, 28 Dec. 1937.

12. The original is to be found in Goethe's *Natur und Kunst* as '*Wer Großes will, muss sich zusammenraffen*'. A more literal translation than Lord Haldane's could be, 'He who wants to do great things must pull himself together.'
13. 'JBSH', quoted at the end of NM, *HPNHL*, 21.
14. JBSH, *SWJSH*, 11.
15. NM, *HPNHL*, 2.
16. Clark, *op. cit.*, 179.
17. This was openly recognised by Mary's great-grandchildren Pat Campbell Fraser, Dick Haldane, and Jennifer Halsey, in conversation with the author, 13 Nov. 2020.

1. HARD TIMES

1. ESH, *MEH*, 39. In a letter to her son, Richard, on 18 March 1911, Mary paints a rather gloomier picture of her birth: 'My advent into this world was a disappointment and my grandfather did not reply to the announcement, as I was to have [been] named after him and been his heir had I been a son.' NLS, MS 6009.
2. 7 Apr. [n.d., but likely 1926], NLS, Acc. 10306.21.
3. Cotton Mills Regulation Act 1825.
4. Ian Anstruther, *The Scandal of Andover Workhouse* (Stroud, Glos.: Sutton Publishing Ltd., 1984), 35.
5. There is some debate as to whether the surnames should be hyphenated or not. I am following the form in which they are found in most publications by family members—that is to say, unhyphenated. See, for example, RBH, *RBH*, and Lady Burdon Sanderson's *Sir John Burdon Sanderson: A Memoir* (Oxford: Clarendon Press, 1911).
6. ESH, *MEH*, 32.
7. It is now a central block in a newly created luxury apartment complex, known as La Sagesse after the Roman Catholic private girls' school that occupied the building in the second half of the twentieth century. The 'township of Jesmond' was formally added to the city of Newcastle upon Tyne in 1835.
8. See Mary's description of Otterburn Dene in Burdon Sanderson, *op. cit.*, 16.
9. ESH, *MEH*, 59–60.
10. Burdon Sanderson, *op. cit.*, 15.
11. ESH, *MEH*, 4.
12. This is the version told in Mary's memoirs (*ibid.*, 30). According to Lady Burdon Sanderson, wife of Mary's distinguished brother Sir John Burdon Sanderson, the prose recitations were simply omitted that year. See Burdon Sanderson, *op. cit.*, 10.

13. See Burdon Sanderson, *op. cit.*, 13.
14. ESH, *MEH*, 36.
15. *Ibid.*, 29.
16. *Ibid.*
17. Burdon Sanderson, *op. cit.*, 19.
18. ESH, *MEH*, 98.
19. *Ibid.*, 42.
20. *Ibid.*, 44.
21. Psalm 139, verses 23–4, King James Version.
22. ESH, *MEH*, 45.
23. *Ibid.*, 46.
24. *Ibid.*, 47.
25. Burdon Sanderson, *op. cit.*, 17.
26. *Quarterly Review*, Nov. 1831, quoted in A. N. Wilson, *The Victorians* (London: Arrow Books, 2003), 34–5.
27. ESH, *MEH*, 53.
28. *Ibid.*, 55.
29. *Ibid.*, 62.
30. *Ibid.*, 63.
31. *Ibid.*, 64.
32. Quoted in T. C. Smout, *A Century of the Scottish People, 1830–1950* (London: Fontana Press, 1987), 30.
33. Quoted in Smout, *op. cit.*, 31.
34. ESH, *FOCTA*, 64. Mary's son, Richard, would write in 1918: 'Unless a man has a decent home for his wife and his children and himself you will never get a good family, and without good families you will not get a good State.' RBH, 'The Future of Democracy' (London: Headley Bros., 1918), 10.
35. Richard's acquisition of two chapels is a detail found in a letter of James Alexander Haldane, the father of Robert Haldane of Cloan. See AH, *ML*, 580.
36. ESH, *MEH*, 80.
37. Quoted in Burdon Sanderson, *op. cit.*, 18.
38. ESH, *MEH*, 82.
39. From the 1861 census on Scotland's housing. See Smout, *op. cit.*, 34.
40. Quoted in *ibid.*, 34.
41. Smout, *op. cit.*, 95.
42. Wilson, *op. cit.*, 78.
43. *Ibid.*, 81.
44. *Ibid.*, 79.
45. *Ibid.*, 29.
46. ESH, *FOCTA*, 19.

47. ESH, *MEH*, 86.
48. Burdon Sanderson, *op. cit.*, 18.
49. ESH, *MEH*, 91.
50. *Ibid.*, 82.
51. *Ibid.*, 62–3.
52. *Ibid.*, 86.
53. NM, *ST*, 38.
54. ESH, *MEH*, 171–2.
55. 6 Jun. 1915, NLS, MS 6009.

2. FAMILY MATTERS

1. AH, *ML*, 153.
2. RBH, *RBH*, 9.
3. Frances Horner quoted in Andrew Gailey, *Portrait of a Muse: Frances Graham, Edward Burne-Jones and the Pre-Raphaelite Dream* (London: Wilmington Square Books, 2020), 223.
4. A. L. Drummond, *Robert Haldane at Geneva, 1816–1817* (Edinburgh: Scottish Church History Society, 1947), 73.
5. A. J. Campbell, *Two Centuries of the Church of Scotland, 1707–1929* (Paisley: Alexander Gardner, 1930), 160.
6. Deryck W. Lovegrove, 'Unity and Separation: Contrasting Elements in the Thought and Practice of Robert and James Alexander Haldane', *Studies in Church History Subsidia*, 7 (1990), 154.
7. AH, *ML*, 272.
8. Lovegrove, *op. cit.*, 154.
9. AH, *ML*, 387.
10. *Ibid.*, 372.
11. *Ibid.*, 60–2.
12. See Neil Stacy's list of the Lairds and Ladies of Gleneagles, in Appendix III of *The Haldanes of Gleneagles: A Scottish History from the Twelfth Century to the Present Day* (Edinburgh: Birlinn, 2017).
13. See George F. Black, *The Surnames of Scotland: Their Origin, Meaning, and History* (New York: New York Public Library, 1946), 337, and Aylmer Haldane, *The Haldanes of Gleneagles* (Edinburgh and London: William Blackwood & Sons, 1929), 1.
14. The details of the most credible version of the Haldane origins are taken from Stacy, *op. cit.*, 1–19.
15. AH, *ML*, 26–7.
16. *Ibid.*, 268.
17. Lovegrove, *op. cit.*, 160.
18. Quoted in AH, *ML*, 283.

19. *Ibid.*, 282.
20. *Ibid.*, 284–5.
21. *Ibid.*, 580.
22. Aylmer was the son of Robert's half-brother, Daniel Rutherford Haldane. It is interesting to note that Winston Churchill's famous escape from imprisonment during the Second Boer War was made possible by a plan provided to him by two other imprisoned officers, one of whom was Aylmer, which prevented the two officers from using the plan themselves, 'much to their chagrin'. Aylmer did eventually make his own escape, but he 'later insisted that he never spoke to Churchill without the latter referring to the incident'. See 'Haldane, Sir (James) Aylmer Lowthorpe', *ODNB*.
23. Aylmer Haldane, *op. cit.*, 221.
24. NM, *BC*, 92.
25. It is conjecture within the family that Mary's money had paid, at least in part, for the 1866 extensions, which could explain Richard inheriting the estate. And yet Willie Haldane, in *SER*, 9, states, 'my father's income had been very ample and expense no concern to my mother all her married life'. This suggests the expansion of Cloan would have been within his means. Robert Haldane's will shows that each of the children by his first marriage was to receive £5,000, roughly equivalent to £600,000 today, but this was to be administered through a Trust. As letters in the National Library of Scotland suggest, the decisions of the trustees, who included Mary and Richard, were sometimes strongly disapproved of by the children.
26. RBH, *RBH*, 8–9.
27. Quoted in AH, *ML*, 597.
28. *Ibid.*, 600.
29. *Ibid.*, 369.
30. In 1822, James Alexander went on to marry Margaret Rutherford, daughter of Professor Daniel Rutherford (1749–1819), famed for the isolation of nitrogen. Margaret was also a cousin of Sir Walter Scott, her father being the writer's maternal uncle. The couple had six children, including Daniel Rutherford Haldane (1824–87), later president of Edinburgh's Royal College of Physicians.
31. All quotes in the preceding paragraph are taken from ESH, *MEH*, 89–90.
32. *Ibid.*, 97.
33. *Ibid.*, 98.
34. *Ibid.*, 100.
35. The quotes concerning this story are all taken from either *ibid.*, 100, or ESH, *FOCTA*, 65.
36. ESH, *FOCTA*, 65–6.

37. MEH to RBH, 30 Jul. 1895 and 29 Jul. 1906, NLS, MS 6008.
38. See especially RBH to MEH, NLS, MS 5930, and JSH to MEH, NLS, MS 20655.
39. 13 May 1880, NLS, MS 5930.
40. James A. Haldane to Robert Haldane, n.d., c.1864, NLS, MS 6101.
41. 'Story: Makgill, Robert Haldane', Te Ara—The Encyclopedia of New Zealand.

3. THE WORLD IN BLACK AND WHITE: 1860s AND 1870s

1. ESH, *FOCTA*, 43.
2. WSH, *SER*, 5.
3. On Sunday mornings, the Haldanes attended the Free Church of Scotland.
4. ESH, *FOCTA*, 60–1.
5. Elizabeth, however, writes: 'our ground-work was religious, not mercantile or utilitarian as was much of the hardworking Puritanism of the early nineteenth century'. *Ibid.*, 74.
6. *Ibid.*, 63–4.
7. *Ibid.*, 66.
8. *Ibid.*, 53.
9. *Ibid.*, 63.
10. NM, 'My Father', in James Campbell (ed.), *New Edinburgh Review Anthology* (Edinburgh: Polygon Books, 1982), 11.
11. ESH, *FOCTA*, 43.
12. *Ibid.*, p. 29.
13. T. C. Smout, *A Century of the Scottish People, 1830–1950* (London: Fontana Press, 1987), 33.
14. ESH, *FOCTA*, 5.
15. *Ibid.*, 84.
16. *Ibid.*, 12.
17. *Ibid.*, 14.
18. ESH, *MEH*, 110.
19. ESH, *FOCTA*, 2.
20. RBH, *RBH*, 9.
21. MEH, handwritten reminiscence, NLS, MS 20150.
22. ESH, *FOCTA*, 2.
23. *Ibid.*, 7.
24. *Ibid.*, 93–4.
25. *Ibid.*, 53.
26. *Ibid.*, 9.

27. *Ibid.*, 10.
28. *Ibid.*, 3.
29. The 'mildly Whig' quote is from *ibid.*, 4.
30. *Ibid.*, 5–6.
31. *Ibid.*, 54. It took until 1916 for women at Edinburgh's medical faculty to become full members of the University. This was still ahead of Oxford, where women were allowed to matriculate in 1920, and well ahead of Cambridge, where they could not receive degrees until 1948. See Graeme Morton, *Ourselves and Others: Scotland, 1832–1914* (Edinburgh: Edinburgh University Press, 2012), 187.
32. RWH pc.
33. ESH, *FOCTA*, 54.
34. *Ibid.*, 14–15.
35. *Ibid.*, 28.
36. Smout, *op. cit.*, 216.
37. *Ibid.*, 217.
38. George Davie, *The Democratic Intellect* (Edinburgh: Edinburgh University Press, 1961).
39. Henry Brougham, 1st Baron Brougham and Vaux, quoted in Randall Thomas Davidson, *Life of Archibald Campbell Tait, Archbishop of Canterbury* (London: Macmillan, 1891), 19.
40. Smout, *op. cit.*, 216.
41. ESH, *FOCTA*, 50–1. The definitive account of the Scottish educational tradition between 1750 and 1918 can be found in R. D. Anderson, *Education and the Scottish People, 1750–1918* (Oxford: Clarendon Press, 1995).
42. Quoted in Davidson, *op. cit.*, 21.
43. ESH, *MEH*, 102.
44. It is noteworthy that Robert Camperdown Haldane, youngest son of Robert Haldane's first marriage, was an Academy contemporary of Robert Louis Stevenson.
45. D'Arcy Wentworth Thompson, MacTutor History of Mathematics Archive, St Andrews University.
46. NM, 'My Father', 12.
47. 'The Edinburgh Academy Chronicle', 1909, 54–5, EA Arch.
48. 'The Edinburgh Academy Chronicle', 1936, 131, EA Arch.
49. Alongside Sir D'Arcy Wentworth Thompson, Professor of Natural History at St Andrews for thirty-one years, and J. S. Haldane, the other two future Fellows of the Royal Society were Diarmid Noël Paton, Regius Professor of Physiology at Glasgow, and William Abbott Herdman, first holder of the Derby Chair of Natural History at Liverpool University College.

50. 22 Jul. 1881, NLS, MS 5932.
51. ESH, *FOCTA*, 18.
52. *Ibid*.
53. *Ibid.*, 15.
54. *Ibid.*, 16–17.
55. ESH, *MEH*, 108.
56. ESH, *FOCTA*, 2.
57. *Ibid.*, 93–4.
58. RBH, *RBH*, 8.
59. ESH, *FOCTA*, 98.
60. *Ibid.*, 27.
61. Violet Markham, *Friendship's Harvest* (London: Reinhardt, 1956), 51.
62. ESH, *FOCTA*, 69.
63. *Ibid.*, 4.
64. *Ibid.*, 121.
65. Markham, *op. cit.*, 43.
66. RBH, *RBH*, 14.
67. 8 May 1874, NLS, MS 5927.
68. Quoted in Frederick Maurice, *Haldane, 1856–1915: The Life of Viscount Haldane of Cloan K.T., O.M.* (London: Faber & Faber, 1937), 10.
69. 'Hermann Lotze', *The Stanford Encyclopedia of Philosophy*.
70. RBH, *Universities and National Life* (London: John Murray, 1910), 29.
71. *Ibid.*, 19.
72. Quoted in Maurice, *Haldane, 1856–1915*, 18.
73. Quoted in *ibid.*, 23.
74. RBH, *RBH*, 18.
75. For 'the Great Goethe' quote see RBH to Edmund Gosse, 6 Dec. 1916, Gosse Archive, BLL, BC MS 19c Gosse.
76. RBH, *RBH*, 17.
77. Ibid, 17, 20, 302.
78. MEH, handwritten reminiscence, NLS, MS 20150.
79. RBH, *RBH*, 24.
80. WSH, *SER*, 10.
81. NM, 'My Father', 12.
82. MEH to RBH, 11 Mar. 1893, NLS, MS 6008.
83. MEH, handwritten reminiscence, NLS, MS 20150.
84. RBH, *RBH*, 25. See also MG, *SAS*, 59.
85. See MG, *SAS*, 60–1.
86. RBH to MEH, 10 Mar. 1896, NLS, MS 5955.
87. RBH, *RBH*, 27.
88. RBH to MEH, 12 Jun. 1880, NLS, MS 5928.
89. 6 Dec. 1881, NLS, MS 5931.

90. ESH, *FOCTA*, 59.
91. WSH, *SER*, 9.
92. 12 Apr. 1911, NLS, MS 6009.
93. 13 Dec. 1877, NLS, MS 5927.
94. WSH, *SER*, 10.
95. NM, 'My Father', 12.
96. 6 Apr. 1896, NLS, MS 5955.
97. MG, *SAS*, 59–60.
98. RBH to MEH, 13 Jul. 1877, NLS, MS 5927.
99. RBH to MEH, 15 Feb. 1878, NLS, MS 5928.
100. 6 Mar. 1913, NLS, MS 6009.
101. *The Times*, 28 Dec. 1937.
102. ESH, *FOCTA*, 73.
103. *Ibid.*, 61.
104. *Ibid.*, 71.
105. RBH to MEH, 15 Nov. 1881, NLS, MS 5932.
106. The quote is from ESH, *FOCTA*, 145.
107. *Ibid.*, 73.
108. Markham, *op. cit.*, 48.
109. JSH, *The Sciences and Philosophy: Gifford Lectures, University of Glasgow, 1927 and 1928* (London: Hodder & Stoughton, 1928), v.
110. *Ibid.*, 165–6.
111. MG, *SAS*, 370. It is interesting to note, however, that in his preface to *The Sciences and Philosophy* (p. vi) John writes: 'Deeply as I am indebted to post-Kantian idealism, my own standpoint must be described as realistic rather than idealistic, though to me there is nothing truer than Hegel's saying, which my brother often quoted, "Das Geistige allein ist das Wirkliche" [The spiritual alone is the real].' He explains in a later publication that his insistence on realism comes from the fact that he 'treats the universe as depicted by the sciences, not as "mere appearance", but as the real universe imperfectly depicted'. JSH, *The Philosophy of a Biologist* (Oxford: Clarendon Press, 1935), preface.
112. JSH, *LEP*, 20.

4. THE DECLARATION OF INDEPENDENCE: 1880s AND 1890s

1. On 27 January 1881, he writes to his mother: 'I am going to put myself in the hands of an Italian to have my voice made deeper' (NLS, MS 5931). The topic re-emerges in a letter, again to Mary, of 9 March 1896: 'You asked about my voice. It is, I think, both fuller in tone & easier. Madame Bebube is greatly pleased with her work on it & with the result of the operation… She says I have got three new tones as a result of the excision' (NLS, MS 5955).

2. 23 Mar. 1881, NLS, MS 5931.
3. 13 Oct. 1881, NLS, MS 5932.
4. JSH to MEH, 12 Jul. 1883, NLS, MS 20231.
5. JSH to MEH, 11 Jul. 1883, NLS, MS 20231.
6. 13 Jul. 1883, NLS, MS 5902.
7. 12 Jul. 1883, NLS, MS 20231. The reference to money is surprising given the family's financial troubles after Robert's death.
8. ESH, *FOCTA*, 144.
9. 17 May 1883, NLS, MS 5934.
10. ESH, *FOCTA*, 64.
11. Vernon Bogdanor, 'Oxford and the Mandarin Culture: The Past that is Gone', *Oxford Review of Education*, 32:1 (Feb. 2006), 147–65.
12. T. H. Green, 'Essay on Christian Dogma', in R. L. Nettleship (ed.), *Works of Thomas Hill Green*, Vol. 3: *Miscellanies and Memoirs* (Cambridge: Cambridge University Press, 2011), 161–85, see especially 162–3.
13. 1 May 1891, NLS, MS 5945.
14. JSH, *The Philosophy of a Biologist* (Oxford: Clarendon Press, 1935), preface.
15. Quoted in S. C. Carpenter, *Church and People, 1789–1889*, Vol. 3 (London: SPCK, 1959), 483.
16. RBH and JSH, 'The Relation of Philosophy to Science', in Andrew Seth and R. B. Haldane (eds.), *Essays in Philosophical Criticism* (London: Longmans, Green & Co., 1883), 44; hereafter abbreviated 'RPS'.
17. A. G. Gardiner, *Prophets, Priests, and Kings* (London: J. M. Dent & Sons, 1914), 283.
18. RBH and JSH, 'RPS', 46.
19. Ibid.
20. Ibid., 42.
21. Ibid., 56.
22. RBH, *PTR*, xiii.
23. Ibid., 132.
24. RBH and JSH, 'RPS', 58. See also Steve Sturdy, 'Biology as Social Theory: John Scott Haldane and Physiological Regulation', *British Journal for the History of Science*, 21:3 (1988), 315–40.
25. RBH and JSH, 'RPS', 61.
26. JSH, *LEP*, 1.
27. JSH, *Organism and Environment as Illustrated by the Physiology of Breathing* (New Haven, CT: Yale University Press, 1917), 119.
28. RBH and JSH, 'RPS', 65–6.
29. JBSH, A. D. Sprunt, and NM, 'Reduplication in Mice', *Journal of Genetics*, 5 (1915), 133–5.
30. 'Remembering Graeme Mitchison', openDemocracy.

31. *The Scotsman*, 14 Oct. 1933, 10.
32. ESH, *FOCTA*, 107.
33. RBH, *RBH*, 22–3.
34. Quoted in MG, *SAS*, 74–5.
35. ESH, *FOCTA*, 107–8.
36. *Ibid.*, 111.
37. *Ibid.*
38. 22 Mar. 1882, NLS, MS 5930.
39. 28 Nov. 1892, NLS, MS 5948.
40. 10 Nov. 1891, NLS, MS 5946.
41. The critical nature of Richard's friendship with Grey has recently been articulated in great detail by T. G. Otte in his *Statesman of Europe: A Life of Sir Edward Grey* (London: Allen Lane, 2020).
42. For Frances as 'High Priestess', see Jane Abdy and Charlotte Gere, *The Souls: An Elite in English Society, 1885–1930* (London: Sidgwick & Jackson, 1984), 127.
43. See especially chapter 2 of John Campbell's *Haldane: The Forgotten Statesman Who Shaped Modern Britain* (London: Hurst, 2020), 27–56, and Andrew Gailey's *Portrait of a Muse: Frances Graham, Edward Burne-Jones and the Pre-Raphaelite Dream* (London: Wilmington Square Books, 2020). Two points are worth noting about Gailey's work. *Portrait of a Muse* reveals that Frances's affections (and Gailey thinks even physical affections) had already been given to Richard's closest friend of these years, the future prime minister H. H. Asquith—a fact of which Campbell was unaware at the time of writing *Haldane*. But Campbell's research would suggest that Richard's relationship with Frances eclipsed that of Asquith, both by its longevity and its depth. Secondly, on the basis of a single letter from Marie Belloc Lowndes to her daughter, written almost twenty years after Richard's death, Gailey claims (223 and 402, n. 39) that both Richard's sister and mother were antagonistic to her, disapproving of their beloved Richard's affection. Such a claim seems highly unlikely when the other evidence is considered. The tone of the references to Frances in Elizabeth's diaries is entirely positive, with the two lunching and dining together. Frances's letters to Elizabeth on Richard's death are deeply familiar and caring. She signs off, 'your loving friend FH' (23 Aug. 1928, NLS, MS 6033). As for Mary, Richard could write to Frances in October 1905, 'My mother was talking of Margot [Asquith, second wife of H. H. Asquith] today—critically. "How different" she said "are the characters of Mrs Horner & the late Lady Tweedmouth. These represent the serious view of life"' (EOA pc.). Could this really have been said by someone who, in the words of Belloc Lowndes, 'hated' Frances?

44. 20 Sep. 1897, EOA pc. All subsequent letters from RBH to Frances are in this collection.
45. See Jill Pellew, 'A Metropolitan University Fit for Empire: The Role of Private Benefaction in the Early History of the London School of Economics and Political Science and Imperial College of Science and Technology, 1895–1930', in Mordechai Feingold (ed.), *History of Universities*, Vol. 26/1 (Oxford: Oxford University Press, 2012), 201–45; and Campbell, *op. cit.*, 207–12.
46. 'Sanderson, Sir John Scott Burdon, baronet', *ODNB*.
47. JSH, *LEP*, 2.
48. Quoted in MG, *SAS*, 79.
49. C. G. Douglas, 'John Scott Haldane, 1860–1936', *Obituary Notices, Fellows of The Royal Society*, 5:2 (1936), 136.
50. MG, *SAS*, 341.
51. JBSH, *SWJSH*, 3.
52. Thomas Carnelley, JSH, and A. M. Anderson, 'The Carbonic Acid, Organic Matter, and Micro-Organisms in Air, more especially of Dwellings and Schools', *Philosophical Transactions of the Royal Society of London*, 178 (Jan. 1887), 61–111; Thomas Carnelley and JSH, 'The Air of Sewers', *Proceedings of the Royal Society of London*, 42:251–7 (Jan. 1887), 394–6.
53. These are the words of Dr Louis Parkes in the 'Discussion' section of JSH's paper, 'The Air of Buildings and Sewers', *Transactions of the Sanitary Institute of Great Britain*, 9:1 (1887), 413.
54. MG, *SAS*, 98.
55. Quoted in *ibid.*, 103–4.
56. JSH, *LEP*, 2.
57. JSH to MEH, 31 Dec. 1893, NLS, MS 20231.
58. NM, *The Listener*, 8 Feb. 1973.
59. LKH, *FK*, 105.
60. *Ibid.*, 150.
61. 14 Nov. 1891, NLS, MS 5946.
62. MG, *SAS*, 120.
63. LKH, *FK*, 154–5.
64. 3 May 1893, NLS, MS 20659.
65. D'Arcy Wentworth Thompson, quoted in RC, *JBS*, 17.
66. RC, *JBS*, 17.
67. NM, *ST*, 123.
68. JSH, talk to Wigan mining students, 18 Oct. 1919, quoted in MG, *SAS*, 157.
69. JSH, *Report to the Secretary of State for the Home Department on the Causes of Death in Colliery Explosions and Underground Fires, with Special Reference to*

the Explosions at Tylorstown, Brancepeth and Micklefield (London: HMSO, 1896), 32.
70. Douglas, *op. cit.*, p. 119.
71. ESH, *FOCTA*, 142–3.
72. *Ibid.*, 143.
73. 'Octavia Hill: Her Life and Legacy', The National Trust.
74. ESH, *FOCTA*, 113.
75. *Ibid.*
76. ESH, 'Registered Friendly Societies for Women', *The National Review*, 28:166 (Dec. 1896), 566.
77. ESH, *FOCTA*, 117.
78. 9 Nov. 1891, NLS, MS 5946.
79. JH int.
80. PCF int.
81. 8 Sep. 1898, NLS, MS 5960.
82. 2 Nov. 1889, NLS, MS 5943.
83. 2 Jun. 1896, NLS, MS 5955.
84. 24 Apr. 1897, NLS, MS 6008.

5. A NEW CENTURY: 1900–1905

1. Many of the details for the opening two paragraphs are taken from NM, *ST*, 31.
2. Mia Carter, *Archives of Empire*, Vol. 2: *The Scramble for Africa* (Durham, NC: Duke University Press, 2003), 668.
3. LKH, *FK*, 195.
4. JSH to MEH, 10 Jun. 1902, NLS, MS 20231.
5. MG, *SAS*, 162.
6. The quote is from RBH to MEH, 19 Nov. 1900, NLS, MS 5964. On Richard's ambivalent attitude to the Second Boer War see John Campbell, *Haldane: The Forgotten Statesman Who Shaped Modern Britain* (London: Hurst, 2020), 157–61.
7. RBH, *RBH*, 71.
8. H. Rashdall, '*The Pathway to Reality*. Being the Gifford Lectures Delivered in the University of St Andrews in the Session 1902–3. By Richard Burdon Haldane', *Mind*, NS, 12:48 (Oct. 1903), 527.
9. 27 Jan. 1905, BLO, MS. Eng., d. 3204, ff. 11–12.
10. JBSH, *SWJSH*, 20.
11. *Ibid.*, 20–1.
12. *Ibid.*, 21.
13. *Ibid.*, 22.

14. Steve Sturdy, 'Biology as Social Theory: John Scott Haldane and Physiological Regulation', *British Journal for the History of Science*, 21:3 (1988), 328.
15. C. G. Douglas, 'John Scott Haldane, 1860–1936', *Obituary Notices, Fellows of The Royal Society*, 5:2 (1936), 124.
16. *Ibid.*
17. 24 Nov. 1905, NLS, MS 5974.
18. ESH, *D*, Jan. 1906.
19. G. Monger, *The End of Isolation: British Foreign Policy, 1900–1907* (London: Thomas Nelson & Sons, 1963), 82.
20. RBH, *RBH*, 182.
21. 27 Jan. 1901, NLS, MS 6008.
22. WSH, *SER*, 18–19.
23. Prof. Jiji Suzuki, 18th Hereditary Head of the Soami School of Imperial Design, Japan, 1925, quoted in 'Background', The Japanese Garden at Cowden.
24. 'Background', The Japanese Garden at Cowden.
25. 20 Dec. 1905, NLS, MS 5974.
26. *New York Times*, 30 Aug. 1913.
27. 'How it All Began', LEYF.
28. JBSH, *SWJSH*, 21.
29. NM, *ST*, 27.
30. *Ibid.*, 19.
31. Quoted in *SS*, DC, 65.
32. RC, *JBS*, 19.
33. According to the website Autism Speaks, 'Asperger Syndrome… is a previously used diagnosis on the autism spectrum. In 2013, it became part of one umbrella diagnosis of autism spectrum disorder (ASD) in the Diagnostic and Statistical Manual of Mental Disorders 5'. 'What is Asperger Syndrome?' Autism Speaks.
34. Email to author, 13 Jan. 2022.
35. JBSH, *SWJSH*, 21.
36. LKH, *FK*, 221.
37. NM, *ST*, 19.
38. *Ibid.*
39. *Ibid.*, 20.
40. *Ibid.*, 11.
41. TGNH, 'J. B. S. H', RWH pc.
42. NM, *ST*, 34.
43. *Ibid.*

6. THE HALDANE MISSIONS, PART ONE: 1906–1914

1. Roy Hattersley, *The Edwardians* (London: Abacus, 2006), 2. Nicely balanced historical assessments of this claim can be found in Samuel Hynes, *The Edwardian Turn of Mind* (London: Pimlico, 1992), and David Powell, *The Edwardian Crisis: Britain, 1901–1914* (Basingstoke: Palgrave, 1996).
2. See G. R. Searle, *A New England? Peace and War, 1886–1918* (Oxford: Clarendon Press, 2005), 516–17.
3. 'Education (Scotland) Bill', *House of Commons Debates*, 5 May 1908, vol. 188, cols. 101–2.
4. RBH to MEH, 4 May 1910, NLS, MS 5983.
5. The fullest account of Richard's achievements at the War Office remains Edward M. Spiers's *Haldane: An Army Reformer* (Edinburgh: Edinburgh University Press, 1980).
6. ESH, *MEH*, 12.
7. RBH to Edmund Gosse, 17 Dec. 1905, Gosse Archive, BLL, BC MS 19c Gosse.
8. 24 Jan. 1910, NLS, MS 5909.
9. LKH, *FK*, 175–6.
10. JBSH, *SWJSH*, 24–5.
11. *Ibid.*, 25.
12. See JBSH, *Keeping Cool and Other Essays* (London: Chatto & Windus, 1944), 60.
13. NM, *ST*, 120.
14. JSH, *Report of a Committee appointed by the Lords Commissioners of the Admiralty to Consider and Report upon the Conditions of Deep-Water Diving* (London: HMSO, 1907).
15. NM, *ST*, 123.
16. *Ibid.*, 55.
17. L. S. R. Byrne, Eton College report for J. B. S. Haldane, German and History, Lent 1910, TL pc.
18. L. S. R. Byrne, Eton College report for J. B. S. Haldane, History-German Specialist, 21 Jul. 1910, TL pc.
19. Eton College report for J. B. S. Haldane, Science, 26 Jul. 1908, TL pc.
20. NM interview with JC, 13 Jun. 1992, JC pc.
21. Quoted in SS, *DC*, 74.
22. NM to Victor Gollancz, 31 Aug. 1932, quoted in JC, *BG*, 179.

7. THE HALDANE MISSIONS, PART TWO: 1906–1914

1. 14 Apr. 1908, NLS, MS 6001.
2. 12 May 1910, NLS, MS 5983.

3. Quoted in MG, *SAS*, 272–3.
4. 28 Oct. 1913, NLS, MS 5990.
5. ESH, *D*, Oct. 1913.
6. WSH to Lloyd George, 20 Oct. 1913, PA, Lloyd George Papers, c/4/18/1. My thanks to John Campbell for visiting these archives on my behalf.
7. '100th Anniversary of the Anglo-American Expedition to Pikes Peak', Physiological Society.
8. *New York Times*, 3 Sep. 1911.
9. Quoted in J. B. West, 'Centenary of the Anglo-American High-Altitude Expedition to Pikes Peak', *Experimental Physiology*, 97:1 (Jan. 2012), 3.
10. C. G. Douglas, JSH, Yandell Henderson, Edward C. Schneider, 'Physiological Observations Made on Pike's Peak, Colorado, with Special Reference to Adaptation to Low Barometric Pressures', *Philosophical Transactions of the Royal Society of London*, 203 (1913), 191.
11. Martin Goodman, 'The High-Altitude Research of Mabel Purefoy FitzGerald, 1911–13', *Notes and Records of the Royal Society of London*, 69:1, Special issue: Women and Science (20 Mar. 2015), 90.
12. Mabel Purefoy FitzGerald to Laurie FitzGerald, 18 Jul. 1911, Mabel Purefoy FitzGerald Papers, BLO, Box 3.
13. *Colorado Springs Gazette*, 19 Jul. 1911.
14. MG, *SAS*, 245.
15. West, *op. cit.*, 9.
16. Vanessa Heggie, 'Experimental Physiology, Everest and Oxygen: From the Ghastly Kitchens to the Gasping Lung', *British Journal for the History of Science*, 46:1 (Mar. 2013), 133.
17. MG, *SAS*, 338.
18. Goodman, *op. cit.*, 88.
19. West, *op. cit.*, 7.
20. JSH to Mabel Purefoy FitzGerald, 22 Aug. 1911, Mabel Purefoy FitzGerald Papers, BLO, Box 28.
21. Quoted in Goodman, *op. cit.*, 94. Earlier quotes on the same page account for Sir Peter Ratcliffe's suggestion that the papers were published separately because of FitzGerald's slowness in writing up her findings. See 'Watch J. S. Haldane Lecture: A hundred years on: 21st Century Insights into Human Oxygen Homeostasis', Department of Physiology, Anatomy & Genetics, University of Oxford, at 05.50 mins.
22. Mabel Purefoy FitzGerald, 'The Changes in Breathing and the Blood at Various High Altitudes', *Philosophical Transactions of the Royal Society of London*, 203 (1913), 351–71.
23. R. W. Torrance, 'Major Breathing in Miners', in John T. Reeves and Robert F. Grover (eds.), *Attitudes on Altitude* (Boulder, CO: University Press of Colorado, 2001), 71.

24. 'Watch J. S. Haldane Lecture'. The quote from FitzGerald can be found on p. 364 of her Royal Society paper, 'The Changes in Breathing and the Blood at Various High Altitudes'.
25. RBH, *RBH*, 220–1.
26. ESH, *D*, 25 May 1911.
27. RBH, *RBH*, 224.
28. 'A Palace in Westminster', *The Times*, 25 Aug. 2017.
29. NLS, MS 20069, f. 27.
30. NLS, MS 20069, f. 25.
31. *Daily Chronicle*, 12 Feb. 1912, NLS, MS 20069, f. 27.
32. 6 Feb. 1912, NLS, MS 5987.
33. 11 Feb. 1912, NLS, MS 5987.
34. 15 Feb. 1912, NLS, MS 5987.
35. 7 Mar. 1912, NLS, MS 5987.
36. 14 May 1912, NLS, MS 5987.
37. See RBH, *Selected Addresses and Essays* (London: John Murray, 1928), 49–93.
38. John Campbell, *Haldane: The Forgotten Statesman Who Shaped Modern Britain* (London: Hurst, 2020), 301–14. A more polemical reading can be found in Frederick Vaughan, *Viscount Haldane: 'The Wicked Step-Father of the Canadian Constitution'* (Toronto: University of Toronto Press, 2010).
39. G. E. Sherington, 'The 1918 Education Act: Origins, Aims and Development', *British Journal of Educational Studies*, 24:1 (Feb. 1976), 66–85.
40. H. A. L. Fisher to Edmund Gosse, 8 Dec. 1916, in F. Russell Bryant (ed.), *Coalition Diaries and Letters of H. A. L. Fisher, 1916–1922*, Vol. 1 (Lewiston, NY: Mellen Press, 2006), 84.
41. ESH, *FOCTA*, 260–1.
42. Ibid., 228–9.
43. NM interview with JC, 13 Jun. 1992, JC pc.
44. JBS to R. E. J. Pembrey, 21 Dec. 1961, CM pc.
45. Lesley A. Hall, *Naomi Mitchison: A Profile of Her Life and Work* (Seattle, WA: Aqueduct Press, 2007), 3.
46. NM, *ACH*, 76–7.
47. Ibid., 37.
48. Ibid., 78–80.
49. Ibid., 78.
50. Ibid., 80.
51. ARBH, *The Path by the Water* (Edinburgh: Thomas Nelson & Sons Ltd, 1944), 52.
52. Ibid., 53.

53. ESH, *MEH*, 114; Campbell, *op. cit.*, 38.
54. ARBH, *Path by the Water*, 53–4.
55. ESH, *FOCTA*, 289.
56. TGNH, *TGNHoC*, 4.
57. See LKH, *FK*, 221.
58. C. G. Douglas, JSH, and JBSH, 'The Laws of Combination of Haemoglobin with Carbon Monoxide and Oxygen', *Journal of Physiology*, 44:4 (Jun. 1912), 275–304.
59. 'Was Ma Hump to Blame', *LRB*, 11 Jul. 2002.
60. NM, *ACH*, 72.
61. *Ibid.*, 71.
62. Gervas Huxley, *Both Hands: An Autobiography* (London: Chatto & Windus, 1970), 69.
63. JC, *BG*, 47.

8. THE MOTTO COMES TRUE: 1914–1918

1. ESH, *FOCTA*, 301–2.
2. *Ibid.*, 303.
3. *Ibid.*, 304.
4. JBSH, 'Why I Am a Cooperator', Appendix 1 to Gavan Tredoux, *Comrade Haldane is Too Busy to Go on Holiday: The Genius who Spied for Stalin* (New York and London: Encounter Books, 2018), 251.
5. NM interview with JC, 13 Jun. 1992, JC pc. Naomi's narrative contrasts somewhat with what she writes in *ACH*, 101.
6. RBH, *RBH*, 274–5.
7. ESH, *D*, 8 Aug. 1914.
8. There is another well-known, if disputed, story about Asquith playing bridge at an inappropriate time—a Monday morning three weeks before the Somme offensive—which can be accessed at 'Asquith and the Liberal Legacy', Liberal History.
9. John Buchan, *Memory Hold-the-Door* (London: Hodder & Stoughton, 1940), 151.
10. For the story of the Ballin letter, see RBH, *RBH*, 270–3.
11. Stephen E. Koss, *Lord Haldane: Scapegoat for Liberalism* (New York: Columbia University Press, 1969), 144–5.
12. ESH, *D*, 27 Mar. 1915.
13. *Ibid.*, 4 Jun. 1915.
14. John H. Johnson, 'The Reform of Real Property Law in England', *Columbia Law Review*, 25:5 (May 1925), 614.
15. Robert Joseph Gowen, 'Lord Haldane of Cloan (1856–1928): Neglected Apostle of the League of Nations', *Il Politico*, 36:1 (Mar. 1971), 162.

16. ESH, *D*, 9 Apr. 1915.
17. Quoted in MG, *SAS*, 280.
18. MG, *SAS*, 285.
19. Jon Agar, *Science in the Twentieth Century and Beyond* (Cambridge: Polity Press, 2012), 103.
20. See JBSH, *Callinicus: A Defence of Chemical Warfare* (London: Kegan Paul, 1925), 67.
21. NM, *ACH*, 112.
22. Sources differ as to the exact profile of the solution. I have opted for the list provided at 'Black Veil Respirator: The British Army', Australian War Memorial.
23. See MG, *SAS*, 289–90.
24. 'April [1915] was one of the happiest months of my life.' JBSH, 'Why I Am a Cooperator', 252. Later in the same piece (p. 272), JBS wrote, 'I think war is a monstrous evil, and yet admit that I enjoy it.' He felt his father would have too: 'One of my first thoughts', he wrote recalling his first experience under enemy shell fire, 'was "How my father would enjoy this!"' JBSH, *On Being the Right Size and Other Essays* (Oxford: Oxford University Press, 1985), 169.
25. RC, *JBS*, 37.
26. JBSH, *Callinicus*, 68.
27. RC, *JBS*, 40.
28. ESH, *D*, 16 May 1915.
29. *Ibid.*
30. Philip B. James, *Oxygen and the Brain: The Journey of Our Lifetime* (Florida: Best Publishing Company, 2014), 77–8.
31. *Ibid.*, 82.
32. JBSH, 'Why I Am a Cooperator', 254.
33. *Ibid.*, 255.
34. *Ibid.*, 256.
35. SS, *DC*, 97.
36. The quoted words are from a 1914 letter simply dated 'Tuesday', RWH pc.
37. Edith Haldane, 23 Jan. 1917, handwritten diary, PCF pc.
38. *Ibid.*
39. *Ibid.*
40. *Ibid.*
41. 17 June 1915, NLS, MS 5994.
42. ARBH, *UM*, 16.
43. *Ibid.*, 17.
44. TGNH, *TGNHoC*, 5.
45. 2 Nov. [Richard mistakenly wrote Oct.] 1914, NLS, MS 5992.

46. TGNH to WSH, 25 Dec. 1914, RWH pc.
47. 6 Jan. 1915, RWH pc.
48. TGNH, *TGNHoC*, 16.
49. *Ibid.*, 17.
50. *Ibid.*
51. *Ibid.*, 6.
52. 11 Jul. 1915, RWH pc.
53. TGNH, *TGNHoC*, 23–4.
54. *Ibid.*, 24.
55. *Ibid.*, 19.
56. *Ibid.*, 25.
57. *Ibid.*, 33.
58. NM, *ACH*, 102.
59. *Ibid.*, 111.
60. *Ibid.*
61. RC, *JBS*, 33.
62. John Charlton, *Making Middle England: The History of an English Family* (London: History & Social Action Publications, 2017), 11.
63. NM, *ACH*, 103.
64. *Ibid.*, 106.
65. *Ibid.*, 110.
66. *Ibid.*, 127.
67. *Ibid.*, 122.
68. *Ibid.*, 145.
69. Sally Mitchison, email to the author, 13 Jan. 2022.
70. 18 Nov. 1918, NLS, MS 6013.
71. ESH, *D*.
72. *Ibid.*
73. 'Report on the Physical Welfare of Mothers and Children', Wellcome Collection.
74. ESH, *D*, 2 Sep. 1917.
75. *Ibid.*, 10 July 1915.
76. *Ibid.*, 22 Mar. 1917.
77. *Ibid.*, 24 Oct. 1915.
78. *Ibid.*, 29 May 1915.
79. *Ibid.*, 20 Sep. 1917.
80. *Ibid.*
81. *Ibid.*, 10 Oct. 1915.
82. *Ibid.*, 1 Aug. 1915.
83. RBH to MEH, 9 Oct. 1915, NLS, MS 5994.
84. ESH, *D*, 23 Jul. 1916.
85. *Ibid.*, 14 Jun. 1917.

86. *Ibid.*, 20 Jan. 1918.
87. J. E. B. Seely to ESH, 22 Aug. 1928, NLS, MS 6033.
88. ESH, *MEH*, 123.
89. *Ibid.*, 132.
90. *Ibid.*, ix–x.

9. CHANGING OF THE GUARD: 1918–1930

1. 'The Centenary of the Armistice', Assets Publishing Service.
2. 12 [Richard writes 13] Nov. 1918, NLS, MS 6000.
3. 5 Dec. 1918, NLS, MS 6013.
4. Camillo von Klenze, 'Life of Goethe by P. Hume Brown', *Journal of English and Germanic Philology*, 20:4 (Oct. 1921), 560.
5. RBH to MEH, 19 Dec. 1918, NLS, MS 6000.
6. RBH to MEH, 15 Jun. 1918, NLS, MS 6000.
7. 21 Nov. 1915, NLS, MS 6000.
8. See RBH to MEH, 3 Apr. 1919, NLS, MS 6001; 12 Dec. 1918, NLS, MS 6000; 8 May 1919, NLS, MS 6001; 28 Jul. 1919, NLS, MS 6002.
9. Major-General Sir John Davidson, quoted in Dudley Sommer, *Haldane of Cloan* (London: G. Allen & Unwin, 1960), 370. On the timing of Haig's gestures, which Richard combines into one occasion in his autobiography, see John Campbell, *Haldane: The Forgotten Statesman Who Shaped Modern Britain* (London: Hurst, 2020), 394, n. 90.
10. RBH, *RBH*, 288.
11. 29 Apr. 1919.
12. ESH, *D*, 10 Mar. 1919.
13. *Ibid.*, 12 Feb. 1919.
14. See Johan Findlay, *All Manner of People: The History of the Justices of the Peace in Scotland* (Edinburgh: Saltire Society, 2000), 114, 117.
15. ESH, *D*, Jan. 1920.
16. The quote is from a letter from RBH to Sir Edmund Gosse, 17 Aug. 1926, Gosse Archive BLL, BC MS 19c Gosse.
17. 30 Dec. 1926, quoted in Joan C. Tonn, *Mary P. Follett: Creating Democracy, Transforming Management* (New Haven, CT and London: Yale University Press, 2003), 436.
18. See NM, *YMWA*, 70, and JC, *BG*, 86.
19. NM, 'J. S. Haldane and his Son', NLS, Acc. 10889, 7.
20. JC, *BG*, 28, 390.
21. NM, *YMWA*, 62.
22. JC, *BG*, 86.
23. NM, *The Conquered* (London: Jonathan Cape, 1929), 13.
24. NM interview with JC, 13 Jun. 1992.

25. Isobel Murray (ed.), *Scottish Writers Talking 2* (East Linton: Tuckwell Press, 2002), 71.
26. H. C. Harwood, 'New Books', *Outlook*, 3 May 1923.
27. Quoted in NM, *YMWA*, 101.
28. Murray, *op. cit.*, 72.
29. Mary Chamberlain (ed.), *Writing Lives: Conversations between Women Writers* (London: Virago, 1988), 172.
30. NM, *When the Bough Breaks* (London: Jonathan Cape, 1924), 133–4.
31. Samuel Hynes, *The Auden Generation: Literature and Politics in England in the 1930s* (London: Pimlico, 1992), 20.
32. Chamberlain, *op. cit.*, 174. See also Lucy Pollard, *Margery Spring Rice: Pioneer of Women's Health in the Early Twentieth Century* (Cambridge: Open Book Publishers, 2020).
33. NM, 'Comments on Birth Control', *Criterion Miscellany*, 12 (London: Faber & Faber, 1930), 25.
34. NM, *YMWA*, 166.
35. Quoted in JC, *BG*, 118.
36. JC, *BG*, 93.
37. RBH to MEH, 6 June 1921, NLS, MS 6004.
38. See especially, Andrew Robinson, *Einstein on the Run: How Britain Saved the World's Greatest Scientist* (New Haven, CT and London: Yale University Press, 2019), 74–83, and Campbell, *op. cit.*, 66–9.
39. 13 Jun. 1921, NLS, MS 6004.
40. RBH to MEH, 2 Jul. 1921, NLS, MS 6004.
41. TGNH, 'Viscount Haldane of Cloan: T. G. N. Haldane's Recollections', Nov. 1937, RWH pc.
42. 19 Dec. 1923, NLS, MS 6013.
43. 12 [possibly 11] Dec. 1923, NLS, MS 6006.
44. RBH to Edmund Gosse, 4 Jan. 1924, BLL, BC MS 19c Gosse.
45. *Ibid.*
46. See Henry Hemming, *M: Maxwell Knight, MI5's Greatest Spymaster* (London: Arrow Books, 2017), 36.
47. RBH to MEH, 4 Nov. 1924, NLS, MS 6007.
48. 10 Mar. 1925, NLS, MS 6007.
49. Ministry of Reconstruction, 'Coal Conservation Committee: Final Report' (London: HMSO, 1918), 9. For Graeme's own history of the establishment of the National Grid, which became operative over most of the country by 1934, see his book *The Socialization of the Electrical Supply Industry* (London: Victor Gollancz, 1934), published under the initials G. H. on behalf of the New Fabian Research Bureau.
50. The quote on Einstein can be found in JBSH, 'Daedalus, or Science and the Future', in Krishna R. Dronamraju (ed.), *Haldane's Daedalus Revisited* (Oxford: Oxford University Press, 1995), 26.

51. C. M. Bowra, *Memories, 1898–1939* (London: Weidenfeld & Nicolson, 1966), 106.
52. JBSH, 'Daedalus', 39.
53. *Ibid.*, 30.
54. For quotes in this paragraph see SS, *DC*, 137–40.
55. Quoted in Dronamraju, *op. cit.*, 55–6.
56. This is my translation of the following: 'Haldane offenbart mit Meisterhand den erschütternden Gegensatz zwischen technischem and geistigem Können und [zwischen] der in kleinlichen und schädlichen Leidenschaften wurzelnden Gebundenheit des menschlichen Wollens.' Quoted in a letter by the Director of the Drei Masken Verlag AG., München, to JBSH, 12 Sep. 1925, CM pc.
57. NM, *HPNHL*, 14.
58. 29 Apr. 1919.
59. 19 Dec. 1923, NLS, MS 6013.
60. Julian Huxley, *Memories* (London: Harper & Row, 1970), 137–8.
61. JBSH, 'Sex Ratio and Unisexual Sterility in Hybrid Animals', *Journal of Genetics*, 12 (Oct. 1922), 101–9.
62. 'Population Genetics', Nature Portfolio.
63. I'm grateful to JBS's biographer, Samanth Subramanian, for helping me clarify the essence of JBS's genius on this issue.
64. JBSH, *The Causes of Evolution* (London: Longmans, Green & Co., 1932), 6.
65. SS, *DC*, p. 125.
66. Rose Scott-Moncrieff, 'The Classical Period in Chemical Genetics: Recollections of Muriel Onslow, Robert and Gertrude Robinson and J. B. S. Haldane', *Notes and Records of the Royal Society of London*, 36:1 (Aug. 1982), 127.
67. JBSH, 'The Biochemistry of the Individual', in Hans Naurath (ed.), *Perspectives in Biochemistry* (Washington: American Chemical Society, 1989), 4.
68. Stéphane Tirard, 'J. B. S. Haldane and the Origin of Life', *Journal of Genetics*, 96:5 (Nov. 2017), 736.
69. See JBSH, 'The Origin of Life', *The Rationalist Annual* (1929), 3–10.
70. MG, *SAS*, 340–1.
71. RBH to MEH, 27 Jun. 1924, NLS, MS 6007.
72. 13 [Richard writes 12] Oct. 1924, NLS, MS 6007.
73. ESH to Edmund Gosse, 8 Apr. 1925, BLL, BC MS 19c Gosse.
74. 9 Apr. 1925, BLL, BC MS 19c Gosse.
75. RBH to Edmund Gosse, 11 May 1925, BLL, BC MS 19c Gosse.
76. 20 May 1925, BLL, BC MS 19c Gosse.
77. Aldous Huxley, *Point Counter Point* (New York: Modern Library, 1928), 487.

78. NM interview with JC, 19 Jun. 1994, JC pc.
79. SM int.
80. TM int.
81. My thanks to Sally Mitchison for pointing this out to me.
82. Obituary, Lord Haldane, *The Times*, 20 Aug. 1928.
83. See Campbell, *op. cit.*, 336–8.
84. 23 Aug. 1928, NLS, MS 6033.

10. LIVING TRADITION: 1930–1945

1. 1940s, WC, HALDANE/5/1/1/43.
2. MM, *TBHOD*, 26.
3. *Ibid.*, 27.
4. Denny Mitchison, 'Growing up with Murdo', in MM, *TBHOD*, 82.
5. TL int.
6. AM int.
7. JC, *BG*, 244.
8. NM quoted in Johanna Alberti, 'Elizabeth Haldane as a Women's Suffrage Survivor in the 1920s and 1930s', *Women's Studies International Forum*, 13:1/2 (1990), 117.
9. JBSH, 'What I Think About', *The Nation* (May 1931), 525.
10. NM, *USSR*, 4.
11. *Ibid.*, 5.
12. 'Mending the Curtains', *LRB*, 24 Jan. 1991.
13. NM, *USSR*, 4–5.
14. *Ibid.*, 246.
15. *Ibid.*, 251.
16. *Ibid.*, 253.
17. *Ibid.*, 252.
18. *Ibid.*, 251.
19. *Ibid.*, 105.
20. Quoted in JC, *BG*, 157.
21. *News Chronicle*, 4 Jun. 1931.
22. The novel also picks up again on the theme of erotic sibling connection. So, Erif can share this moment with her brother Berris: 'He laughed suddenly and threw his arms round her waist and squashed her softly against him; the heat and excitement passed from his skin to her; her throat and breast and belly began to throb. He reached up a hand behind and pulled her dress loose from one shoulder. He let her go, staggering and laughing...' NM, *The Corn King and the Spring Queen* (Edinburgh: Canongate Classics, 1990), 529.
23. Typescript of letter from NM to John Pilley, NLS, TD. 2980 2/5.

24. See TGNH, *TGNHoC*, 59–60. See also David Banks, 'Dr T. G. N. "Graeme" Haldane—Scottish Heat Pump Pioneer', *International Journal for the History of Engineering & Technology*, 85:2 (Jul. 2015), 168–76.
25. This note is mentioned but not quoted in Jill Benton, *Naomi Mitchison: A Century of Experiment in Life and Letters* (London: Pandora, 1990), 82. It is also mentioned in an unpublished draft version of Jenni Calder's *The Nine Lives of Naomi Mitchison*, which was kindly shared with me by Graeme's son, Dick Haldane. In the late 1990s, Dick still felt uneasy about publishing the details of this incident and asked Calder to remove his father's name from the account. He is now happy for the full details to be revealed.
26. Quoted in draft version of Jenni Calder's *The Nine Lives of Naomi Mitchison* (see footnote above).
27. NM, *YMWA*, 195. For details of Naomi's trip to Austria, see her *Vienna Diary* (London: Victor Gollancz, 1934).
28. NM, WWII diary, typescript, 538, quoted in JC, *BG*, 233.
29. TGNH, *TGNHoC*, 64.
30. TGNH, 'National Defence in the U. S. A.', 1 Feb. 1939, RWH pc.
31. *Ibid.*, 76.
32. ARBH, *UM*, 17.
33. It is Graeme who mentions the nickname in this form (*TGNHoC*, 97–8); others in the family claim it was the 'Rear Light' or the 'Tail Lamp'.
34. *New York Herald Tribune*, 30 Oct. 1938, WC, HALDANE/5/1/2/1/29.
35. See Krishna Dronamraju, *Popularizing Science: The Life and Work of J. B. S. Haldane* (New Delhi, India: Oxford University Press, 2017), 35.
36. Julia Bell and JBSH, 'Linkage in Man', *Nature*, 138 (Oct. 1936), 759–60, and 'The Linkage between the Genes for Colour Blindness and Haemophilia in Man', *Proceedings of the Royal Society of London*, 123B (1937), 119–50.
37. Quoted in SS, *DC*, 220.
38. Quoted in RC, *JBS*, 56.
39. Virginia Cowles, *Looking for Trouble* (London: Hamish Hamilton, 1941), 21.
40. Quoted in SS, *DC*, 217.
41. Quoted in RC, *JBS*, 120.
42. Cowles, *op. cit.*, 33–4.
43. JBSH, 'Why I Am a Cooperator', Appendix 1 to Gavan Tredoux, *Comrade Haldane is Too Busy to Go on Holiday: The Genius who Spied for Stalin* (New York and London: Encounter Books, 2018), 271–2.
44. The definition is Jenni Calder's. See JC, *BG*, 244.
45. JSH, 'Presidential Address: The Values for which the Institution Stands', *Transactions of the Institution of Mining Engineers*, 68 (1924–5), 359–61.

46. NM, *YMWA*, 144.
47. Ibid., 211.
48. Ibid., 78–9.
49. Ibid., 211.
50. Ibid., 211–12.
51. MG, *SAS*, 377.
52. NM, *YMWA*, 213.
53. Ibid.
54. *The Scotsman*, 27 Dec. 1937.
55. NM, *YMWA*, 213.
56. Quoted in RC, *JBS*, 135.
57. Quoted in SS, *DC*, 246.
58. Quoted in RC, *JBS*, 138.
59. Quoted in *ibid.*, 142.
60. JBS's official report, quoted in RC, *JBS*, 150.
61. RC, *JBS*, 150.
62. Quoted in SS, *DC*, 251.
63. Quoted in *ibid.*, 5.
64. Nigel West, *Venona: The Greatest Secret of the Cold War* (London: HarperCollins, 2000) and Tredoux, *Comrade Haldane is Too Busy to Go on Holiday*.
65. Quoted in SS, *DC*, 254.
66. SS, *DC*, 257.
67. TGNH, *TGNHoC*, 79–80.
68. The details and quotes in this paragraph were kindly provided to me by Billee's daughter, Robin Haldane.
69. ARBH, *UM*, 76.
70. Ibid., 77.
71. NM, *YMWA*, 218–19.
72. Geoffrey Baxter, son of Tom Baxter—Dick Mitchison's election agent for the King's Norton elections and the Labour Party's East Midlands Organiser—and his wife Bettie (one of Naomi's best friends), in interview with the author, 30 Oct. 2020. Geoffrey was very much one of the family at Carradale.
73. NM, *SSP*, 3.
74. NM to Tom Harrison, 6 Oct. 1942, Mass-Observation Diary, quoted in JC, *BG*, 205.
75. NM to LKH, 1939, NLS, Acc. 4549/4, quoted in Helen Lloyd, 'Witness to a Century: The Autobiographical Writings of Naomi Mitchison', PhD thesis, University of Glasgow (2005), 125.
76. John Mair, 'New Novels', *New Statesman and Nation*, 7 Oct. 1939.
77. NM, *SSP*, 9.

78. Douglas Gifford, 'A Woman of Many Ages who was Always Ahead of Her Time', review of Jenni Calder's *The Nine Lives of Naomi Mitchison*, newspaper source unknown, RWH pc.
79. NM, *BC*, 24.
80. *Ibid.*, 40.
81. *Ibid.*, 417.
82. *Ibid.*, 39.
83. *Ibid.*, 136.
84. *Ibid.*, 81–2.
85. *Ibid.*, 267.
86. *Ibid.*, 412.
87. *Ibid.*, 267.
88. *Ibid.*, 290.
89. NM, *AYTN*, 169–70.
90. Graham Ogilvy, 'Under the Nazi Jackboot', newspaper source unknown, RWH pc.
91. The poem is printed at the start of *The Bull Calves* (NM, *BC*).
92. NM to John B. Torrance, 'Sunday 23rd' [April 1944], Imperial War Museum, Department of Documents, Mitchison Papers, quoted in Lloyd, *op. cit.*, 129.
93. NM, *AYTN*, 114.
94. NM, WWII diary, typescript, 1044, quoted in JC, *BG*, 239.
95. Quoted in RC, *JBS*, 117.
96. NM, *YMWA*, 195–6.
97. *Ibid.*, 234.
98. My thanks to Terence Mitchison for telling me his mother's version of this incident, which differs from Naomi's in *YMWA*, 234.
99. MM, *TBHOD*, 164.
100. NM quoted in JC, *BG*, 212.
101. NM, *AYTN*, 338.

11. THE LONG VIEW: 1945 ONWARDS

1. NM, *SSP*, 8.
2. *Ibid.*, 10.
3. *Ibid.*
4. *Ibid.*, 23.
5. *Ibid.*, 12.
6. *Ibid.*, 18.
7. NM, *Lobsters on the Agenda* (London: Victor Gollancz, 1952), 167.
8. *Ibid.*, 178.
9. NM, *SSP*, 30–1.

10. Douglas Gifford, 'A Woman of Many Ages who was Always Ahead of Her Time', review of Jenni Calder's *The Nine Lives of Naomi Mitchison*, newspaper source unknown, RWH pc.
11. NM, *SSP*, 33.
12. Charlotte Haldane, *Truth Will Out* (New York: Vanguard Press, 1950), 259.
13. Quoted in RC, *JBS*, 248.
14. See 'John Maynard Smith', Web of Stories.
15. *The Listener*, 9 Dec. 1948.
16. NM to JBSH, 1 Dec. 1948, WC, HALDANE/5/1/2/8/40.
17. JBSH, 'Self-Obituary', 1964, Appendix 3 to Gavan Tredoux, *Comrade Haldane is Too Busy to Go on Holiday: The Genius who Spied for Stalin* (New York and London: Encounter Books, 2018), 309.
18. 'The Soviet Era's Deadliest Scientist is Regaining Popularity in Russia', *The Atlantic*, 19 Sep. 2017.
19. TGNH, 'J. B. S. H', RWH pc.
20. See SS, *DC*, 260–1 and 266. See also 'John Maynard Smith', Web of Stories; and Alison Macleod, *The Death of Uncle Joe* (London: Merlin Press, 1997), 26–7.
21. 'John Maynard Smith', Web of Stories.
22. *Ibid*.
23. Quoted in RC, *JBS*, 193.
24. NM, 'Portrait of a Biologist: J. B. S. Haldane', *Transition*, 26 (1966), 23.
25. Graeme's correspondence on this (at the time) sensitive issue has only recently been opened, having been closed since it came into the possession of the Churchill Archives Centre, Cambridge, in 1982. It can be found there now under 'The Papers of Thomas Graeme Nelson Haldane', TGNH 6/1 and TGNH 6/2.
26. 'Pumped Storage Hydropower', Office of Energy Efficiency and Renewable Energy.
27. 'Geothermal Energy', International Renewable Energy Agency.
28. David Banks, 'Dr T. G. N. "Graeme" Haldane—Scottish Heat Pump Pioneer', *International Journal for the History of Engineering & Technology*, 85:2 (Jul. 2015), 176.
29. RWH, email to author, 28 Nov. 2021.
30. NM, *SSP*, 26.
31. TGNH, 'Means and Ends', Presidential Address to the Institution of Electrical Engineers, pamphlet, 6, RWH pc.
32. RC, *JBS*, 99.
33. Quoted in *ibid.*, 249–50. For a fuller discussion on this topic, see Andy Hammond, 'J. B. S. Haldane, Holism, and Synthesis in Evolution', *Transactions of the American Philosophical Society*, 99:1 (2009), 49–70.

34. Kingsley Martin, 'Cuddly Cactus', *New Statesman and the Nation*, 7 Jan. 1956.
35. TGNH, 'Means and Ends', 8.
36. See 'The Drove Roads of Scotland', Birlinn.
37. ARBH, *UM*, 80.
38. ARBH, *New Ways through the Glens* (London: Thomas Nelson, 1962) and *Three Centuries of Scottish Posts* (Edinburgh: Edinburgh University Press, 1971).
39. Kgosi Linchwe interview with JC, 31 Oct. 1994, JC pc.
40. NM to JC, 11 Jun. [no year, but 1990s], JC pc.
41. JC, *BG*, 310.
42. 27 Jun. [no year, but 1990s], JC pc.
43. NM to JC [undated, but 1990s], JC pc.
44. NM to JC, 11 Jun. [no year, but 1990s], JC pc.
45. 'Prof. J. B. S. Haldane to Live in India', *The Times*, 21 Nov. 1956.
46. Introduction to RC, *JBS*, 9.
47. JBSH, 'A Rationalist with a Halo', *The Rationalist Annual* (1954), 14.
48. JBSH to Pandit Nehru, 15 Feb. 1952, WC, HALDANE/5/7/5, f. 80.
49. Quoted in SS, *DC*, 283.
50. SS, *DC*, 279.
51. 'John Maynard Smith', Web of Stories.
52. Quoted in SS, *DC*, 291.
53. SS, *DC*, 295.
54. It is noteworthy that their Uncle Richard's final philosophical article of 1928 sought to show the ways in which Western thinkers could learn from their Eastern counterparts. See RBH, 'East and West', *Hibbert Journal*, 26:4 (July 1928), 590–607.
55. 'Avrion Mitchison', Web of Stories.
56. 'John Maynard Smith', Web of Stories.
57. JBSH, quoted in RC, *JBS*, 263.
58. 'John Maynard Smith', Web of Stories.
59. JBSH, 'Cancer's a Funny Thing', *New Statesman*, 21 Feb. 1964.
60. See 'John Maynard Smith', Web of Stories.
61. TM int.
62. 'Remembering Graeme Mitchison', openDemocracy. Graeme wrote a fictional Nobel Prize presentation speech for a character in McEwan's novel *Solar*. McEwan also dedicated *Machines Like Me* to Graeme when he was dying.
63. 'Obituary—Professor Denny Mitchison', Stop TB Partnership.
64. MM, *TBHOD*, 165 and 167.
65. *Ibid.*, 154.
66. 'Avrion Mitchison', Web of Stories.

67. 'Martin Raff', Web of Stories.
68. 'Mending the Curtains', *LRB*, 24 Jan. 1991.
69. The quote is from a letter the Salford playwright Walter Greenwood wrote to Naomi after hearing Dick speak at a rally in Manchester in 1933 (NLS, Acc. 7721). See John Charlton, *Making Middle England: The History of an English Family* (London: History & Social Action Publications, 2017), 226.
70. JC, *BG*, 355.
71. NM quoted in JC, *BG*, 344.
72. TM int.
73. *Ibid*.
74. HM int.
75. SM int.
76. 'Mending the Curtains', *LRB*.
77. Doris Lessing, 'Letters', *LRB*, 13:4 (Feb. 1991).
78. JC, *BG*, 391.
79. *Ibid*., back cover quotation.

12. WHAT MAKES A HALDANE?

1. Draft letter, 16 Oct. 1979. This and all following letters and documents in this chapter are from Richard (Dick) Wilkie Haldane's private collection, unless otherwise stated.
2. Ann Thwaite, *Edmund Gosse: A Literary Landscape, 1849–1928* (London: Secker & Warburg, 1984), 460.
3. ARBH, *UM*, 95.
4. Anne Cameron to RWH, 28 Jul. 1991. All quotes in the next paragraph are taken from this letter.
5. Excerpts from this correspondence were kindly provided to me by John Haldane, Archie's son.
6. RWH int., as are all other quotes from Dick in this chapter unless otherwise stated.
7. Jenny is a descendant of the second marriage of Dick's great-great-grandfather, James Alexander Haldane.
8. Arne Bertelsen occupied the first Chair of Orthopaedic Surgery in Denmark from 1957 at the University of Copenhagen, where he became Dean of the medical faculty in the mid-1960s. He had been president of the Danish Orthopaedic Association between 1954 and 1956, and an Honorary Fellow of the British Orthopaedic Association from 1962. He was also a Member of the Danish Parliament between 1960 and 1962 and became a Ridder (Knight) in 1965.
9. 'Thomas Graeme Nelson Haldane', Address by Mr. C. T. Melling, CBE, at Memorial Service on 8 Oct. 1981.

10. Shellard Campbell, private diary.
11. RWH, 'Cloan—and The Island Race', RWN pc.
12. Elizabeth Malloy, 'The Great Russian Race—Sector 1', RWN pc.
13. Quoted in MG, *SAS*, 75.

BIBLIOGRAPHY

The bibliographic details of frequently cited works are given in the 'List of Referencing Abbreviations' section.

Books

Abdy, Jane, and Charlotte Gere, *The Souls: An Elite in English Society, 1885–1930* (London: Sidgwick & Jackson, 1984).

Agar, Jon, *Science in the Twentieth Century and Beyond* (Cambridge: Polity Press, 2012).

Anderson, R. D., *Education and the Scottish People, 1750–1918* (Oxford: Clarendon Press, 1995).

Annan, Noel, *The Dons: Mentors, Eccentrics and Geniuses* (London: HarperCollins, 1999).

Anstruther, Ian, *The Scandal of Andover Workhouse* (Stroud, Glos.: Sutton Publishing Ltd., 1984).

Benton, Jill, *Naomi Mitchison: A Century of Experiment in Life and Letters* (London: Pandora, 1990).

Berra, Tim M., *Darwin and His Children: His Other Legacy* (Oxford: Oxford University Press, 2013).

Black, George F., *The Surnames of Scotland: Their Origin, Meaning, and History* (New York: New York Public Library, 1946).

Bowra, C. M., *Memories, 1898–1939* (London: Weidenfeld & Nicolson, 1966).

Bryant, F. Russell (ed.), *Coalition Diaries and Letters of H. A. L. Fisher, 1916–1922*, Vol. 1 (Lewiston, NY: Mellen Press, 2006).

Buchan, John, *Memory Hold-the-Door* (London: Hodder & Stoughton, 1940).

Burdon Sanderson, Lady [Ghetal], *Sir John Burdon Sanderson: A Memoir* (Oxford: Clarendon Press, 1911).

Campbell, A. J., *Two Centuries of the Church of Scotland, 1707–1929* (Paisley: Alexander Gardner, 1930).

BIBLIOGRAPHY

Campbell, John, in collaboration with Richard McLauchlan, *Haldane: The Forgotten Statesman Who Shaped Modern Britain* (London: Hurst, 2020).

Carpenter, S. C., *Church and People, 1789–1889*, Vol. 3 (London: SPCK, 1959).

Carter, Mia, *Archives of Empire*, Vol. 2: *The Scramble for Africa* (Durham, NC: Duke University Press, 2003).

Chamberlain, Mary (ed.), *Writing Lives: Conversations between Women Writers* (London: Virago, 1988).

Charlton, John, *Making Middle England: The History of an English Family* (London: History & Social Action Publications, 2017).

Clark, Ronald W., *The Huxleys* (London: Heinemann, 1968).

Cowles, Virginia, *Looking for Trouble* (London: Hamish Hamilton, 1941).

Davidson, Randall Thomas, *Life of Archibald Campbell Tait, Archbishop of Canterbury* (London: Macmillan, 1891).

Davie, George, *The Democratic Intellect* (Edinburgh: Edinburgh University Press, 1961).

Deary, Ian J., *Intelligence: A Very Short Introduction* (Oxford: Oxford University Press, 2020).

Dronamraju, Krishna R., *Popularizing Science: The Life and Work of J. B. S. Haldane* (New Delhi: Oxford University Press, 2017).

Dronamraju, Krishna R. (ed.), *Haldane's Daedalus Revisited* (Oxford: Oxford University Press, 1995).

Drummond, A. L., *Robert Haldane at Geneva, 1816–1817* (Edinburgh: Scottish Church History Society, 1947).

Findlay, Johan, *All Manner of People: The History of the Justices of the Peace in Scotland* (Edinburgh: Saltire Society, 2000).

Gailey, Andrew, *Portrait of a Muse: Frances Graham, Edward Burne-Jones and the Pre-Raphaelite Dream* (London: Wilmington Square Books, 2020).

Gardiner, A. G., *Prophets, Priests, and Kings* (London: J. M. Dent & Sons, 1914).

Haldane, A. R. B., *The Path by the Water* (Edinburgh: Thomas Nelson & Sons Ltd, 1944).

——— *New Ways Through the Glens* (London: Thomas Nelson, 1962).

——— *Three Centuries of Scottish Posts* (Edinburgh: Edinburgh University Press, 1971).

Haldane, Aylmer, *The Haldanes of Gleneagles* (Edinburgh and London: William Blackwood & Sons, 1929).

Haldane, Charlotte, *Truth Will Out* (New York: Vanguard Press, 1950).

BIBLIOGRAPHY

Haldane, J. B. S., *Callinicus: A Defence of Chemical Warfare* (London: Kegan Paul, 1925).
—— *The Causes of Evolution* (London: Longmans, Green & Co., 1932).
—— *Keeping Cool and Other Essays* (London: Chatto & Windus, 1944).
—— *On Being the Right Size and Other Essays* (Oxford: Oxford University Press, 1985).
Haldane, J. S., *Organism and Environment as Illustrated by the Physiology of Breathing* (New Haven, CT: Yale University Press, 1917).
—— *The Sciences and Philosophy: Gifford Lectures, University of Glasgow, 1927 and 1928* (London: Hodder & Stoughton, 1928).
—— *The Philosophy of a Biologist* (Oxford: Clarendon Press, 1935).
Haldane, R. B., *Universities and National Life* (London: John Murray, 1910).
—— *Selected Addresses and Essays* (London: John Murray, 1928).
Haldane, T. G. N. (published anonymously under 'G. H.'), *The Socialization of the Electrical Supply Industry* (London: Victor Gollancz, 1934).
Hall, Lesley A., *Naomi Mitchison: A Profile of Her Life and Work* (Seattle, WA: Aqueduct Press, 2007).
Hattersley, Roy, *The Edwardians* (London: Abacus, 2006).
Hemming, Henry, *M: Maxwell Knight, MI5's Greatest Spymaster* (London: Arrow Books, 2017).
Huxley, Aldous, *Point Counter Point* (New York: Modern Library, 1928).
Huxley, Gervas, *Both Hands: An Autobiography* (London: Chatto & Windus, 1970).
Huxley, Julian, *Memories* (London: Harper & Row, 1970).
Hynes, Samuel, *The Auden Generation: Literature and Politics in England in the 1930s* (London: Pimlico, 1992).
—— *The Edwardian Turn of Mind* (London: Pimlico, 1992).
James, Philip B., *Oxygen and the Brain: The Journey of Our Lifetime* (Florida: Best Publishing Company, 2014).
Koss, Stephen E., *Lord Haldane: Scapegoat for Liberalism* (New York: Columbia University Press, 1969).
Macleod, Alison, *The Death of Uncle Joe* (London: Merlin Press, 1997).
Markham, Violet, *Friendship's Harvest* (London: Reinhardt, 1956).
Maurice, Frederick, *Haldane, 1856–1915: The Life of Viscount Haldane of Cloan K.T., O.M.* (London: Faber & Faber, 1937).
Mitchison, Naomi, *When the Bough Breaks* (London: Jonathan Cape, 1924).
—— *The Conquered* (London: Jonathan Cape, 1929).

―――― *Vienna Diary* (London: Victor Gollancz, 1934).

―――― *Lobsters on the Agenda* (London: Victor Gollancz, 1952).

―――― *The Corn King and the Spring Queen* (Edinburgh: Canongate Classics, 1990).

Monger, G., *The End of Isolation: British Foreign Policy, 1900–1907* (London: Thomas Nelson & Sons, 1963).

Morton, Graeme, *Ourselves and Others: Scotland, 1832–1914* (Edinburgh: Edinburgh University Press, 2012).

Murray, Isobel (ed.), *Scottish Writers Talking 2* (East Linton: Tuckwell Press, 2002).

Otte, T. G., *Statesman of Europe: A Life of Sir Edward Grey* (London: Allen Lane, 2020).

Pollard, Lucy, *Margery Spring Rice: Pioneer of Women's Health in the Early Twentieth Century* (Cambridge: Open Book Publishers, 2020).

Powell, David, *The Edwardian Crisis: Britain, 1901–1914* (Basingstoke: Palgrave, 1996).

Robinson, Andrew, *Einstein on the Run: How Britain Saved the World's Greatest Scientist* (New Haven, CT and London: Yale University Press, 2019).

Searle, G. R., *A New England? Peace and War, 1886–1918* (Oxford: Clarendon Press, 2005).

Smout, T. C., *A Century of the Scottish People, 1830–1950* (London: Fontana Press, 1987).

Sommer, Dudley, *Haldane of Cloan* (London: G. Allen & Unwin, 1960).

Spiers, Edward M., *Haldane: An Army Reformer* (Edinburgh: Edinburgh University Press, 1980).

Stacy, Neil, *The Haldanes of Gleneagles: A Scottish History from the Twelfth Century to the Present Day* (Edinburgh: Birlinn, 2017).

Thwaite, Ann, *Edmund Gosse: A Literary Landscape, 1849–1928* (London: Secker & Warburg, 1984).

Tonn, Joan C., *Mary P. Follett: Creating Democracy, Transforming Management* (New Haven, CT and London: Yale University Press, 2003).

Tredoux, Gavan, *Comrade Haldane is Too Busy to Go on Holiday: The Genius who Spied for Stalin* (New York and London: Encounter Books, 2018).

Trevelyan, Laura, *A Very British Family: The Trevelyans and Their World* (London and New York: I. B. Tauris, 2012).

Vaughan, Frederick, *Viscount Haldane: 'The Wicked Step-Father of the Canadian Constitution'* (Toronto: University of Toronto Press, 2010).

BIBLIOGRAPHY

West, Nigel, *Venona: The Greatest Secret of the Cold War* (London: HarperCollins, 2000).

Wilson, A. N., *The Victorians* (London: Arrow Books, 2003).

Articles, Book Chapters, Pamphlets, and Reports

Alberti, Johanna, 'Elizabeth Haldane as a Women's Suffrage Survivor in the 1920s and 1930s', *Women's Studies International Forum*, 13:1/2 (1990), 117–25.

Banks, David, 'Dr T. G. N. "Graeme" Haldane—Scottish Heat Pump Pioneer', *International Journal for the History of Engineering & Technology*, 85:2 (Jul. 2015), 168–76.

Bell, Julia, and J. B. S. Haldane, 'Linkage in Man', *Nature*, 138 (Oct. 1936), 759–60.

——— 'The Linkage between the Genes for Colour Blindness and Haemophilia in Man', *Proceedings of the Royal Society of London*, 123B (1937), 119–50.

Bogdanor, Vernon, 'Oxford and the Mandarin Culture: The Past that is Gone', *Oxford Review of Education*, 32:1 (Feb. 2006), 147–65.

Carnelley, Thomas, and J. S. Haldane, 'The Air of Sewers', *Proceedings of the Royal Society of London*, 42:251–7 (Jan. 1887), 394–6.

Carnelley, Thomas, J. S. Haldane, and A. M. Anderson, 'The Carbonic Acid, Organic Matter, and Micro-Organisms in Air, More Especially of Dwellings and Schools', *Philosophical Transactions of the Royal Society of London*, 178 (Jan. 1887), 61–111.

Douglas, C. G., 'John Scott Haldane, 1860–1936', *Obituary Notices, Fellows of The Royal Society*, 5:2 (1936), 114–39.

Douglas, C. G., J. S. Haldane, and J. B. S. Haldane, 'The Laws of Combination of Haemoglobin with Carbon Monoxide and Oxygen', *Journal of Physiology*, 44:4 (Jun. 1912), 275–304.

Douglas, C. G., J. S. Haldane, Yandell Henderson, and Edward C. Schneider, 'Physiological Observations Made on Pike's Peak, Colorado, with Special Reference to Adaptation to Low Barometric Pressures', *Philosophical Transactions of the Royal Society of London*, 203 (1913), 185–318.

FitzGerald, Mabel Purefoy, 'The Changes in Breathing and the Blood at Various High Altitudes', *Philosophical Transactions of the Royal Society of London*, 203 (1913), 351–71.

Goodman, Martin, 'The High-Altitude Research of Mabel Purefoy

BIBLIOGRAPHY

FitzGerald, 1911–13', *Notes and Records of the Royal Society of London*, 69:1, Special issue: Women and Science (20 Mar. 2015), 85–99.

Gowen, Robert Joseph, 'Lord Haldane of Cloan (1856–1928): Neglected Apostle of the League of Nations', *Il Politico*, 36:1 (Mar. 1971), 161–8.

Green, T. H., 'Essay on Christian Dogma', in R. L. Nettleship (ed.), *Works of Thomas Hill Green*, Vol. 3: *Miscellanies and Memoirs* (Cambridge: Cambridge University Press, 2011), 161–85.

Haldane, E. S., 'Registered Friendly Societies for Women', *The National Review*, 28:166 (Dec. 1896), 559–66.

Haldane, J. B. S., 'Sex Ratio and Unisexual Sterility in Hybrid Animals', *Journal of Genetics*, 12 (Oct. 1922), 101–9.

────── 'The Origin of Life', *The Rationalist Annual* (1929), 3–10.

────── 'What I Think About', *The Nation* (May 1931), 525.

────── 'A Rationalist with a Halo', *The Rationalist Annual* (1954), 14–22.

────── 'Cancer's a Funny Thing', *New Statesman*, 21 Feb. 1964.

────── 'The Biochemistry of the Individual', in Hans Naurath (ed.), *Perspectives in Biochemistry* (Washington: American Chemical Society, 1989), 1–10.

────── 'Daedalus, or Science and the Future', in Krishna R. Dronamraju (ed.), *Haldane's Daedalus Revisited* (Oxford: Oxford University Press, 1995), 23–50.

────── 'Self-Obituary', 1964, Appendix 3 to Gavan Tredoux, *Comrade Haldane is Too Busy to Go on Holiday: The Genius who Spied for Stalin* (New York and London: Encounter Books, 2018), 309.

────── 'Why I Am a Cooperator', Appendix 1 to Gavan Tredoux, *Comrade Haldane is Too Busy to Go on Holiday: The Genius who Spied for Stalin* (New York and London: Encounter Books, 2018), 251.

Haldane, J. B. S., A. D. Sprunt, and Naomi Haldane, 'Reduplication in Mice', *Journal of Genetics*, 5 (1915), 133–5.

Haldane, J. S., 'The Air of Buildings and Sewers', *Transactions of the Sanitary Institute of Great Britain*, 9:1 (1887), 395–413.

────── *Report to the Secretary of State for the Home Department on the Causes of Death in Colliery Explosions and Underground Fires, with Special Reference to the Explosions at Tylorstown, Brancepeth and Micklefield* (London: HMSO, 1896).

────── *Report of a Committee Appointed by the Lords Commissioners of the*

BIBLIOGRAPHY

Admiralty to Consider and Report upon the Conditions of Deep-Water Diving (London: HMSO, 1907).

———— 'Presidential Address: The Values for which the Institution Stands', *Transactions of the Institution of Mining Engineers*, 68 (1924–5), 356–61.

Haldane, R. B., 'The Future of Democracy' (London: Headley Bros., 1918).

———— East and West', *Hibbert Journal*, 26:4 (July 1928), 590–607.

Haldane, R. B., and J. S. Haldane, 'The Relation of Philosophy to Science', in Andrew Seth and R. B. Haldane (eds.), *Essays in Philosophical Criticism* (London: Longmans, Green & Co., 1883), 41–66.

Hammond, Andy, 'J. B. S. Haldane, Holism, and Synthesis in Evolution', *Transactions of the American Philosophical Society*, 99:1 (2009), 49–70.

Heggie, Vanessa, 'Experimental Physiology, Everest and Oxygen: From the Ghastly Kitchens to the Gasping Lung', *British Journal for the History of Science*, 46:1 (Mar. 2013), 123–47.

Johnson, John H., 'The Reform of Real Property Law in England', *Columbia Law Review*, 25:5 (May 1925), 609–27.

Klenze, Camillo von, 'Life of Goethe by P. Hume Brown', *Journal of English and Germanic Philology*, 20:4 (Oct. 1921), 558–60.

Lessing, Doris, 'Letters', *LRB*, 13:4 (Feb. 1991).

Lovegrove, Deryck W., 'Unity and Separation: Contrasting Elements in the Thought and Practice of Robert and James Alexander Haldane', *Studies in Church History Subsidia*, 7 (1990), 153–77.

Martin, Kingsley, 'Cuddly Cactus', *New Statesman and the Nation*, 7 Jan. 1956.

Ministry of Reconstruction, 'Coal Conservation Committee: Final Report' (London: HMSO, 1918).

Mitchison, Denny, 'Growing up with Murdo', in Murdoch Mitchison, *To the Beat of his Own Drum*, ed. Sally Mitchison (privately printed 2017).

Mitchison, Naomi, 'Comments on Birth Control', *Criterion Miscellany*, 12 (London: Faber & Faber, 1930).

———— 'Portrait of a Biologist: J. B. S. Haldane', *Transition*, 26 (1966), 23.

———— 'My Father', in James Campbell (ed.), *New Edinburgh Review Anthology* (Edinburgh: Polygon Books, 1982), 11–19.

Pellew, Jill, 'A Metropolitan University Fit for Empire: The Role of

BIBLIOGRAPHY

Private Benefaction in the Early History of the London School of Economics and Political Science and Imperial College of Science and Technology, 1895–1930', in Mordechai Feingold (ed.), *History of Universities*, Vol. 26/1 (Oxford: Oxford University Press, 2012), 201–45.

Rashdall, H., '*The Pathway to Reality*. Being the Gifford Lectures Delivered in the University of St Andrews in the Session 1902–3. By Richard Burdon Haldane', *Mind*, NS, 12:48 (Oct. 1903), 527–35.

Scott-Moncrieff, Rose, 'The Classical Period in Chemical Genetics: Recollections of Muriel Onslow, Robert and Gertrude Robinson and J. B. S. Haldane', *Notes and Records of the Royal Society of London*, 36:1 (Aug. 1982), 125–54.

Sherington, G. E., 'The 1918 Education Act: Origins, Aims and Development', *British Journal of Educational Studies*, 24:1 (Feb. 1976), 66–85.

Sturdy, Steve, 'Biology as Social Theory: John Scott Haldane and Physiological Regulation', *British Journal for the History of Science*, 21:3 (1988), 315–40.

Tirard, Stéphane, 'J. B. S. Haldane and the Origin of Life', *Journal of Genetics*, 96:5 (Nov. 2017), 735–9.

Torrance, R. W., 'Major Breathing in Miners', in John T. Reeves and Robert F. Grover (eds.), *Attitudes on Altitude* (Boulder, CO: University Press of Colorado, 2001), 59–85.

West, John B., 'Centenary of the Anglo-American High-Altitude Expedition to Pikes Peak', *Experimental Physiology*, 97:1 (Jan. 2012), 1–9.

Unpublished PhD Thesis

Lloyd, Helen, 'Witness to a Century: The Autobiographical Writings of Naomi Mitchison', PhD thesis, University of Glasgow (2005).

Websites

'100th Anniversary of the Anglo-American Expedition to Pikes Peak', Physiological Society, https://www.physoc.org/abstracts/100th-anniversary-of-the-anglo-american-expedition-to-pikes-peak/, last accessed 18 Jun. 2021.

'Asquith and the Liberal Legacy', Liberal History, https://liberalhistory.org.uk/wp-content/uploads/2014/10/61_Goldman_Asquith_liberal_legacy.pdf, last accessed 26 Jul. 2021.

BIBLIOGRAPHY

'Avrion Mitchison', Web of Stories, https://www.webofstories.com/playAll/avrion.mitchison?sId=13765, last accessed 15 Dec. 2021.

'Background', The Japanese Garden at Cowden, https://cowden-garden.myshopify.com/pages/background, last accessed 26 May 2021.

'Black Veil Respirator: The British Army', Australian War Memorial, https://www.awm.gov.au/collection/REL31825.002?image=1, last accessed 22 Jul. 2021.

'D'Arcy Wentworth Thompson', MacTutor History of Mathematics Archive, St Andrews University, https://mathshistory.st-andrews.ac.uk/Biographies/Thompson_DArcy/, last accessed 20 May 2022.

'Edinburgh Engineer Crowned Young Woman Engineer', School of Engineering, University of Edinburgh, https://www.eng.ed.ac.uk/about/news/20150108/edinburgh-engineer-crowned-young-woman-engineer-year#:~:text=Senior%20hardware%20engineer%20Naomi%20Mitchison,warning%20systems%20for%20military%20aircraft, last accessed 4 Nov. 2020.

'Education (Scotland) Bill', *House of Commons Debates*, 5 May 1908, vol. 188, cols. 101–2, https://api.parliament.uk/historic-hansard/commons/1908/may/05/education-scotland-bill, last accessed 24 May 2021.

'Geothermal Energy', International Renewable Energy Agency, https://www.irena.org/geothermal, last accessed 8 Dec. 2021.

'Haldane, Sir (James) Aylmer Lowthorpe', *ODNB*, https://www.oxforddnb.com/view/10.1093/ref:odnb/9780198614128.001.0001/odnb-9780198614128-e-95438, last accessed 5 May 2021.

'Hermann Lotze', *The Stanford Encyclopedia of Philosophy* (Winter 2018 Edition), Edward N. Zalta (ed.), https://plato.stanford.edu/archives/win2018/entries/hermann-lotze/, last accessed 5 Mar. 2021.

'How it all Began', LEYF, https://leyf.org.uk/about/history/, last accessed 25 May 2021.

'John Maynard Smith', Web of Stories, https://www.webofstories.com/playAll/john.maynard.smith?sId=7285, last accessed 10 Dec. 2021.

'Martin Raff', Web of Stories, https://www.webofstories.com/playAll/martin.raff?sId=51858, last accessed 15 Dec. 2021.

'Mending the Curtains', *LRB*, https://www.lrb.co.uk/the-paper/v13/n02/rosalind-mitchison/mending-the-curtains, last accessed 15 Dec. 2021.

BIBLIOGRAPHY

'Obituary—Professor Denny Mitchison', Stop TB Partnership, http://www.stoptb.org/news/announcements/2018/a18_001.asp, last accessed 5 Mar. 2021.

'Octavia Hill: Her Life and Legacy', The National Trust, https://www.nationaltrust.org.uk/features/octavia-hill-her-life-and-legacy, last accessed 26 Apr. 2021.

'Population Genetics', Nature Portfolio, https://www.nature.com/subjects/population-genetics, last accessed 31 Aug. 2021.

'Pumped Storage Hydropower', Office of Energy Efficiency and Renewable Energy, https://www.energy.gov/eere/water/pumped-storage-hydropower, last accessed 8 Dec. 2021.

'Remembering Graeme Mitchison', openDemocracy, https://www.opendemocracy.net/en/remembering-graeme-mitchison/, last accessed 30 Mar. 2021.

'Report on the Physical Welfare of Mothers and Children', Wellcome Collection, https://wellcomecollection.org/works/unj9kpkf, last accessed 30 Jul. 2021.

'Sanderson, Sir John Scott Burdon, baronet', *ODNB*, https://www.oxforddnb.com/view/10.1093/ref:odnb/9780198614128.001.0001/odnb-9780198614128-e-32177, last accessed 5 May 2021.

'Story: Makgill, Robert Haldane', Te Ara—The Encyclopedia of New Zealand, https://teara.govt.nz/en/biographies/3m39/makgill-robert-haldane, last accessed 3 Feb. 2021.

'The Centenary of the Armistice', Assets Publishing Service, https://assets.publishing.service.gov.uk/government/uploads/system/uploads/attachment_data/file/963267/Armistice_web__1__V2.pdf, last accessed 19 Aug. 2021.

'The Drove Roads of Scotland', Birlinn, https://birlinn.co.uk/product/the-drove-roads-of-scotland/, last accessed 9 Dec. 2021.

'The Soviet Era's Deadliest Scientist is Regaining Popularity in Russia', *The Atlantic*, 19 Sep. 2017, https://www.theatlantic.com/science/archive/2017/12/trofim-lysenko-soviet-union-russia/548786/, last accessed 7 Dec. 2021.

'Was Ma Hump to Blame', *LRB*, https://www.lrb.co.uk/the-paper/v24/n13/john-sutherland/was-ma-hump-to-blame, last accessed 25 Jun. 2021.

'Watch J. S. Haldane Lecture: A Hundred Years On: 21st Century Insights into Human Oxygen Homeostasis', Department of Physiology,

BIBLIOGRAPHY

Anatomy & Genetics, University of Oxford, https://www.dpag.ox.ac.uk/news/watch-j-s-haldane-lecture-a-hundred-years-on-21st-century-insights-into-human-oxygen-homeostasis, last accessed 22 Jun. 2021.

'What is Asperger Syndrome', Autism Speaks, https://www.autismspeaks.org/types-autism-what-asperger-syndrome, last accessed 4 Jul. 2022.

Newspaper Articles

'A Palace in Westminster', *The Times*, 25 Aug. 2017.
Colorado Springs Gazette, 19 Jul. 1911.
H. C. Harwood, 'New Books', *Outlook*, 3 May 1923.
JBS, 'Cancer's a Funny Thing', *New Statesman*, 21 Feb. 1964.
John Mair, 'New Novels', *New Statesman and Nation*, 7 Oct. 1939.
New York Times, 30 Aug. 1913.
New York Times, 3 Sep. 1911.
News Chronicle, 4 Jun. 1931.
Obituary, Lord Haldane, *The Times*, 20 Aug. 1928.
'Prof. J. B. S. Haldane to Live in India', *The Times*, 21 Nov. 1956.
The Listener, 9 Dec. 1948.
The Scotsman, 14 Oct. 1933.
The Scotsman, 27 Dec. 1937.
The Times, 28 Dec. 1937.

Documents in Private Collections

Douglas Gifford, 'A Woman of Many Ages who was Always Ahead of Her Time', review of Jenni Calder's *The Nine Lives of Naomi Mitchison*, newspaper source unknown, RWH pc.
Edith Haldane, 23 Jan. 1917, handwritten diary, PCF pc.
Elizabeth Malloy, 'The Great Russian Race—Sector 1', RWH pc.
Eton College report for J. B. S. Haldane, Science, 26 Jul. 1908, TL pc.
Graham Ogilvy, 'Under the Nazi Jackboot', newspaper source unknown, RWH pc.
——— Eton College report for J. B. S. Haldane, German and History, Lent 1910, TL pc.
L. S. R. Byrne, Eton College report for J. B. S. Haldane, History-German Specialist, 21 Jul. 1910, TL pc.
R. W. Haldane, 'July 18, 2005—Half Way There', RWH pc.

BIBLIOGRAPHY

——— 'Great Russian Race—Third Interim Report', RWH pc.
Shellard Campbell, private diary.
T. G. N. Haldane, 'J. B. S. H', RWH pc.
——— 'Viscount Haldane of Cloan: T. G. N. Haldane's Recollections', Nov. 1937. RWH pc.
——— 'Means and Ends', Presidential Address to the Institution of Electrical Engineers, pamphlet, 6, RWH pc.
——— 'National Defence in the U. S. A.', 1 Feb. 1939, RWH pc.
'Thomas Graeme Nelson Haldane', Address by Mr. C. T. Melling, CBE, at Memorial Service on 8 Oct. 1981, RWH pc.

INDEX

Abercromby, Robert, 35
Aboriginal Australians, 206
abortion, 223–4, 247
Abyssinia, 231
Adam, Robert, 31, 39
Addenbrooke's Hospital, Cambridge, 286
adoption, 288
Adrian, Edgar, 262
adults and children, divide between, 51–2
Advisory Committee for Aeronautics, 107, 129, 241
African Heroes (Mitchison), 270
Africans, The (Mitchison), 270
Agadir Crisis (1911), 124, 146
Agar, Jon, 168
agriculture, 101
air-raid shelters, 237
Airthrey Castle, Stirling, 30, 31
'*Alban* Goes Out, The' (Mitchison), 247
Albion Colliery disaster (1894), 96
Alexander I, Emperor of Russia, 15
Alexandra, Queen consort of the United Kingdom, 139–40, 214
Alps, 142
altitude sickness, 142–5

American Academy of Arts and Sciences, 278
American Bar Association, 149
Amsden, Anne Lysbeth, 286–8, 294–8
anaemia, 111
Ancient Order of Foresters, 99
ancylostomiasis, 111
Anderson, A. M., 91
Anderson, John, 228
Anderson shelters, 237
Anglicanism, 62
Annan, Noel, 5
Anne, Princess Royal, 299
Antic Hay (Huxley), 159
Argyll County Council, 255
Aristotelian Society, 130
Aristotle, 84
'Aristotle's Account of Bees' "Dances"' (Haldane), 262
Arnold, Matthew, 61
asbestos, 292
Asperger syndrome, 119, 338 n.33
Asquith, Anthony 'Puffin', 146
Asquith, Herbert Henry, 88, 109, 114, 123, 163, 165–6, 185, 186, 191, 335 n.43, 342 n.8
Asquith, Margot, 109, 335 n.43
Athanasian Creed, 231

INDEX

atheism, 14, 100
Atlantic, The, 261
Atlantic Monthly, The, 231
Atomic Energy Research Establishment, 263
Auchterarder, Perthshire, 4, 99–100, 117, 185, 304
Auden, Wystan Hugh, 8, 198, 201, 225
Austen, Jane, 72
Australia, 206
Austria, 227
Austria-Hungary, 162
Authors' World Peace Appeal, 268
Avrion Mitchison Prize, 278
Aytoun Hall, Auchterarder, 185

backboards, 19, 24
Baden-Powell, Robert, 129, 151
Baker, Herbert Brereton, 167, 169, 170
Bakgatla people, 269
Baldwin, Stanley, 203
Balfour, Arthur James, 88, 126
Balkan Wars (1912–13), 156, 161
Ballachulish, Highland, 292
Ballad of Reading Gaol, The (Wilde), 88
Ballater, Aberdeenshire, 60
Ballin, Albert, 164
Balliol College, Oxford, 61, 62, 157, 158, 229
bankruptcy, 16, 17
baptism, 85
Baptists, 31
Bar Association of Canada, 149
Bar, 75, 108

Barbarian Stories (Mitchison), 198
Barnardo's, 236, 243
Battle of Camperdown (1797), 35
Battle of Copenhagen (1801), 294
Battle of Dunbar (1650), 34
Battle of Flodden (1513), 34
Battle of Jutland (1916), 178–9
Battle of Loos (1915), 187
Battle of Ypres (1915), 167
Beatty, David, 179
Bechuanaland, 269–70, 273
Bedford Square, London, 16
Before the War (Haldane), 191
Beit, Alfred, 125, 130
Belgium, 163, 185, 250
Bell, Julia, 231
Ben Lawers, 59–60
Ben Vorlich, 153
bends, the, 91, 131–4
Berkeley, George, 63, 73
Berlin Mission (1912), 146–9, 164, 165
Berlin, Isaiah, 239–40
Bernal, John Desmond, 201
Bernard fitz Brian, 34
Bertelsen, Aage, 294, 303
Bertelsen, Arne, 286–8, 291, 294, 295, 297, 298, 302
von Bethmann Hollweg, Theobald, 147
Betts, Barbara, 201
bhang, 274
Bhubaneswar, Orissa, 272–5
bicycles, 72
Big House, The (Mitchison), 281
Bingham, Francis, 190

INDEX

'Biological Possibilities for the Human Species'(Haldane), 262
Biology of the Cell Cycle, The (Mitchison), 276
Birkbeck College, 213
Birkenhead, Frederick Edwin Smith, 1st Earl, 166
Birth Control Research Committee, 200
birth control, 3, 94, 199–200, 223–4, 242
Black Sparta (Mitchison), 198
Black Watch, 170, 171–6
Blackie, John Stuart, 62, 63
Blood of the Martyrs, The (Mitchison), 234, 247
Bloomsbury, London, 150
Board of Education, 150
Board of Film Censors, 199
Boat Race, 201
Boer War, Second (1899–1902), 105–7, 126, 213, 329 n.22
Bogdanor, Vernon, 78
Bohr, Christian, 93
Bohr, Niels, 8, 93
Bombay, India, 35
Bosanquet, Bernard, 202
Botswana, 269–70, 273
Bowra, Maurice, 205
Boy Scouts, 129
Boycott, Arthur Edwin, 131–2
Brave New World (Huxley), 206
breathing, regulation of, 111–12
bridge, 60, 163, 166, 342 n.8
Bridges, Robert, 181
Briggs, George Edward, 209
Briggs, Isobel, 194
Briggs-Haldane equation, 209

Bristol, England, 91
British Association for the Advancement of Science, 95, 213
British Association of Road Runners, 299
British Empire, 55, 105, 106, 124, 126, 273, 274
  Bechuanaland, 269
  Indian colonies, 8, 20, 32–3, 35, 110, 172–3
  South African colonies, 105–7, 126
British Expeditionary Force (BEF), 129, 163–4, 187–8, 190
British Idealism, 77–86
British Institute of Adult Education, 202
British Nurse in Peace and War, The (Haldane), 213
British Olympic Committee, 299
British Thoracic Society, 276
Brontë sisters, 72
Brown, James Gordon 276
Brown, Lancelot 'Capability', 31
Bruce of Grangehill Medal, 68
Brüning, Heinrich, 228
Bryce, James, 72
Buchan, John, 151, 164
Buckingham Palace Conference (1914), 162
Bull Calves, The (Mitchison), 39, 247–9, 267
Bumble Puppy (game), 230
Burdon Sanderson family, 9
Burdon Sanderson, Elizabeth, 14–15, 16, 17, 21, 23, 26, 27, 43

371

INDEX

Burdon Sanderson, Isabella (née Haldane), 37–8, 67
Burdon Sanderson, Jane, 17, 18, 19, 20, 21, 23, 24
Burdon Sanderson, John, 3, 18, 23, 25, 73, 89–90, 112–13
Burdon Sanderson, Richard (b. 1791), 14–18, 21, 22, 23, 27, 37–8, 40, 42–3
Burdon Sanderson, Richard (b. 1821), 17, 27, 37–8, 66–7
Burdon, Thomas, 18
Burghes, Charlotte, see Haldane, Charlotte
Burghes, Ronnie, 230
Burlington Arcade, London, 286
Burne-Jones, Edward, 88
Burning Glass, The (Calder), 5, 196, 221, 270,
By Many Waters (Haldane), 244
By River, Stream and Loch (Haldane), 268

Calcutta, India, 268, 271–2
Calder, Jenni, 5, 196, 221, 270, 349 n.25
Calvinism, 16, 32, 61, 83
Cambridge Five, 240
Cambridge University Press, 139
Cameron, John 'Jock', 257
Cameron, Robert, 295
Campbell, John, 5, 217, 335 n.43
Campbell, Shellard, 294–5, 302
Campbell Bannerman, Henry, 88, 106, 113–14, 123
Campbell Fraser, Alexander (b. 1819), 73

Campbell Fraser, Alexander (b. 1891), 229–30
Campbell Fraser, Mary Elizabeth 'Elsie' (née Haldane), 101, 154, 156, 217, 229–30, 267, 285–6, 288
Campbell Fraser, Patrick, 229, 243
Canada, 87, 149–50, 166
canaries, 91, 97
'Cancer's a Funny Thing' (Haldane), 274
cannabis, 274
Canterbury, Archbishop of
    Davidson, Randall, 151, 189, 214
    Tait, Archibald Campbell, 56
Capanna Margherita, Monte Rosa, 142
carbon dioxide, 111–12, 130, 143, 144, 238
carbon monoxide, 96, 143, 158
carbonic acid, 97
Carnegie, Andrew, 100
Carnegie Trust, 186, 213
Carnelley, Thomas, 91
Carradale estate, Kintyre, 245–6, 248, 249–53, 257, 269, 277, 279–83
Case, Martin, 239
Cassel, Ernest, 124, 191
Castle, Barbara, 201
Catto, Andrew Yule, 131–2
Causes of Evolution, The (Haldane), 209
Cave, George, 1st Viscount, 166, 203

372

INDEX

Cavendish Laboratory, Cambridge, 205
Cawnpore, siege of (1857), 20
Central Hotel, Glasgow, 110
Chamberlain, Arthur Neville, 204, 228
Chamberlain, Joseph, 107
Charlotte Square, Edinburgh, 39, 49, 51, 66, 71, 93
Charlottenburg, Germany, 108
Chatham House, 202
Cherwell, Oxford, 134, 135, 136, 158, 167–9, 171, 181, 220
Chevy Chase coach, 20
children and adults, divide between, 51–2
Chinnery-Haldane, Alexander, 288
chlorine gas, 167–71
chloroform, 134
cholera, 20
Chopin, Frédéric, *113*
Christian IX, King of Denmark, 93
Christianity
  Baptists, 31
  Burdon Sandersons and, 16, 20–21, 23, 25–7, 37
  Calvinism, 16, 32, 61, 83, 330 n.5
  Church of England, 62
  Church of Scotland, 31, 54, 202
  Congregationalism, 30–31
  Free Church of Scotland, 100
  Haldanes and, 29–32, 36, 37, 44, 47–8, 60, 62, 77, 80, 85–6, 330 n.5
  Methodism, 30
  Plymouth Brethren, 23
  Protestantism, 47–8, 330 n.5
  United Free Church of Scotland, 202
Christie family, 115–16
Church of England, 62
Church of Scotland, 31, 54, 202
Churchill, Winston, 128–9, 156–7, 167, 168–9, 186, 190, 199, 329 n.22
Civil Service, 140, 244
Clark, Ronald, 9, 170, 266
climate change, 226, 263
Cloan, Auchterarder, 1, 4–5, 21, 39–40, 49, 58–60, 71, 76, 102, 103–5, 151–6, 219
  acquisition (1851), 39
  Archie's writing on, 154–6
  army manoeuvres (1907), 128–9
  Barnardo's at, 236, 243
  carbonic acid experiments, 97
  chapel, 30, 47
  extension (1866), 39, 58, 104, 329 n.25
  extension (1904), 117–18
  Garden Cottage, 291
  Gorgonzola (ghost), 121
  heirlooms, 288–9
  indoor games, ban on, 60
  Initial Tree, 59
  meals at, 60, 153, 243
  Naomi's writing on, 152–4
  Neil Mitchison's purchase (2015), 304

INDEX

notable visitors to, 128–9, 151–2
tenanted acres, sale of, 292–3
Cloud Cuckoo Land (Mitchison), 198
Cluaran (fishing boat), 250
Coal Conservation Committee, 192, 205
coal mining, *see* mining
Cockcroft, John, 263
Coe, Sebastian, 299
Cole, (George) Douglas Howard, 182, 201, 253
Cole, Margaret, 201, 253
Colorado, United States, 142–5
colour blindness, 231
Columbia Law Review, 166
'Comments on Birth Control' (Mitchison), 200
Common Market, 265
communism, 198–9, 221–2, 232, 234–5, 237, 245, 252, 259, 266–7
Communist International, 198, 231
Communist Party of Great Britain (CPGB), 198–9, 231, 234, 237, 261
concentration camps, 105–7
Congregationalism, 30–31
Conquered, The (Mitchison), 183, 195–8
Conservative Party, 86, 94, 106, 107, 113, 127, 165, 203
Cooperazia, SS, 222
Copeman, Fred, 232
Copley Medal, 219

Corn King and the Spring Queen, The (Mitchison), 225, 348 n.22
Cornwall, England, 111, 113
correspondence courses, 71–2
Costa Head, Orkney Islands, 263
country houses, 105
Cowden estate, Clackmannanshire, 115–16
Cowles, Virginia, 232
Cowper, William, 36
Crewe, Robert Crewe-Milnes, 1st Marquess, 163
cricket, 19, 54
Crimean War (1853–6), 213
Croonian Lecturer, 113
Crown Agency, 116, 141, 175
Cruachan power station, Argyll and Bute, 263

Daedalus (Haldane), 205–8, 209, 210, 262
Daily Chronicle, 147
Daily Express, 187, 231
Daily Mail, 148, 165, 167, 231
Daily Worker, The, 231, 258
Dalai Lama, 115
Dalton, Hugh, 222
Damant, Guybon Chesney Castell, 132
Daphne plant, 214
Dartmouth, Devon, 156, 179
Darwin family, 5
Darwin, Charles, 90, 91, 209, 219
Davey, Horace, 87
Davidson, Randall, 151, 189, 214
Davie, George, 54

INDEX

death duties, 86, 125
decompression sickness, 91, 131–4
Defence, HMS, 179
Denmark, 93, 250, 286, 297, 303–4
Descartes (Haldane), 117
Descartes, René, 117, 139
Desert Island Discs, 246
Deutsches Rheuma-Forschungszentrum, Berlin, 278
Deveron river, 29
Dewey, John, 228
Dickens, Charles, 25, 49, 72
diphtheria, 66, 68–9, 90
disease, 89, 91–2, 110, 111, 206
diving, 91, 130–34
Dolcoath mine, Cornwall, 111, 113
Dominant Character, A (Subramanian), 5, 173, 206, 240
Doncaster Mining Research Laboratory, 145, 169
Doris, HMS, 176–8
Double Helix, The (Watson), 280
Douglas, Claude Gordon, 90, 142, 158, 169, 171
Downing Street, London, 161
Dragon School, Oxford, 118–19, 135, 195, 220
Drinker, Philip, 212
Dronamraju, Krishna, 262
Duncan, Adam, 1st Viscount, 35, 294
Dundee, Scotland, 91, 92
Dunkirk, France, 110

Durham Grammar School, 15
Dussek, Jan Ladislav, 19
Dyson, Freeman, 206–7

Early in Orcadia (Mitchison), 282
Early Oath-Takers, The (Mitchison), 282
East India Company, 32, 34
East Lothian, Scotland, 97
eating habits, 60, 110, 153, 243
ectogenesis, 206
Edinburgh, Scotland, 21–2, 24, 32, 38, 39, 44, 49
  Academy, 55–7, 100, 229
  Charlotte Square, 39, 49, 51, 59, 66, 71, 93
  High School, 38, 54
  Medical School, 92
  Moray Place, 57
  National Library of Scotland, 45, 249, 267–8, 329 n.25
  Royal Botanical Gardens, 244
  Royal College of Physicians, 329 n.30
  Royal Infirmary, 117
  Signet Library, 268
  University, 38, 68, 72–3, 100, 129, 266, 276
education, 19, 24, 51, 54–8, 60, 89
  Cassel Trust, 191
  correspondence courses, 71–2
  female medical students debate (1870s), 52–3
  schoolrooms, 24, 51, 59, 135, 155
  universities, 54, 108–9, 139, 150

INDEX

Education Act (1918), 150
Education (Scotland) Act (1872), 53
Education (Scotland) Act (1908), 125
'Educational Problems of the Colonial Territories' (Haldane), 262
Edward VII, King of the United Kingdom, 114, 124, 140, 186
Edward, Prince of Wales, 8
Edwardian era (1901–10), 104, 124, 139, 180
Egypt, 271, 272
Eighty Club, 86
Einstein, Albert, 3, 152, 202, 205, 206–7, 219
El Salvador, 264
Eldon, John Scott, 1st Earl, 14, 16, 17
Electrical Research Association, 263
electricity, 3, 205, 263–5, 346 n.49
Eliot, George, 72, 100, 213
Elizabeth Garrett Anderson Hospital, London, 243
Elizabeth, Queen Mother, 299
Encaenia ceremony (Oxford University), 15
Enchantress, 157
Entente Cordiale (1904), 126
Epidemiology and Infection, 110
epigenetics, 260
Equal Franchise Act (1928), 199
Esher Committee (1904), 126
Esher, Surrey, 242, 265

Essays in Philosophical Criticism, 77–86
Eton College, Berkshire, 55, 119, 135, 157
eugenics, 206, 282
Eugénie, Empress consort of the French, 43
Eureka Club, 57
European Economic Community (EEC), 265
European Molecular Biology Organisation, 276–7
evolution, 208–12, 262
experimental pathology, 90
Explosives Committee, 107

Fabian Society, 222, 247
Fair Play or a few words for the Lady Doctors (Haldane), 52–3
'fallen' women, 44
family tradition, 7, 60
famine, 14, 25
Faust (opera), 71
Feltrinelli Prize, 273
feminism, 19, 44, 94, 200
Ferguson Scholarship, 68
Ferguson, Betsey 'Baba', 49–50, 53–4, 66, 70
fevers, 91
Fichte, Johann Gottlieb, 63
First Worker's Government, The (Mitchison), 278–9
Fischer, Emil, 119
fish farming, 292
Fisher, Herbert Albert Laurens, 150
Fisher, John 'Jacky', 1st Baron, 107

INDEX

Fisher, Ronald, 208
fishing, 3, 118, 154, 166, 173, 176, 228–9, 244, 268
FitzGerald, Mabel Purefoy, 142–5, 210, 340 n.21
Follett, Mary Parker, 193–5
Forster, Edward Morgan, 197, 201
Forster, Miss (governess), 20–21, 23, 26
Foswell estate, Auchterarder, 101, 115, 121, 154, 175, 226, 229, 265, 288, 289, 304
Foundation for Genetic Research, 262
fox hunting, 19, 242
Foyer power station, Loch Ness, 263
France
    Agadir Crisis (1911), 124, 146
    Christianity in, 32
    Entente Cordiale (1904), 126
    plague, measures against, 110
    Revolutionary period (1789–1802), 35, 71
    World War I (1914–18), 163–76, 183–4
Franco, Francisco, 231–2
Franz Ferdinand, Archduke of Austria, 162
Frederick William III, King of Prussia, 16
Free Church of Scotland, 100
French Revolutionary Wars (1792–1802), 35
French, John, 129, 187
From One Century to Another (Haldane), 219

Fullerian Professorship in Physiology, 230
Fushiebridge Inn, Midlothian, 21–2
'Future of Democracy, The' (Haldane), 327 n. 34

Gailey, Andrew, 335 n.43
Gairdner, Alice, 210
Gaitskell, Hugh, 8, 227
Gallipoli campaign (1915–16), 177–8, 186
Gandhi, Indira, 201
Garden Cottage, Cloan, 291
gas masks, 2, 91, 167–71
Gas Referees, 97, 212
gas turbine, 241
Geddes, Eric, 199
Gellhorn, Martha, 233
General Electric Company, 125
genetics, 4, 84, 208–12, 231, 259–62, 282
Geneva, Switzerland, 32, 38
George IV, King of the United Kingdom, 16
George V, King of the United Kingdom, 124, 136, 141, 148–9, 166, 186, 214
Georgetti, Claire, *242*
geothermal power, 264
germ theory, 89, 91–2
Germany, 69, 73, 76, 108, 111
    Agadir Crisis (1911), 124, 146
    army, 127
    ancylostomiasis in, 111
    authoritarianism in, 111, 113
    economic growth, 124

INDEX

education in, 62–5, 73, 76, 108
Haldane Mission (1912), 146–9, 164, 165
Idealists, 79
Nazi period (1933–45), 228, 231, 238–40, 249, 260–61, 279
shipbuilding, 124, 148
Treaty of Versailles (1919), 192, 231, 250
World War I (1914–18), 163–88, 250
World War II (1939–45), 238–40, 249
Gestapo, 249
Ghana, 269
ghost stories, 155
Gibbon, Edward, 72
Gielgud, Lewis, 159
Gifford Lectures, 73, 82, 213
Gifford, Douglas, 247
Gill, Ruth, *see* Mitchison, Ruth
Girton College, Cambridge, 252
Glasgow, Scotland, 110
'Glen Path, The' (Mitchison), 219
Gleneagles, Perthshire, 33–4, 39, 60, 217, 236, 247, 248
God, 80–83
von Goethe, Johann Wolfgang, 6, 64, 73, 88, 129, 151, 190, 326 n.12
Gold Standard, 199
Goodman, Martin, 144, 212
Gorgonzola (ghost), 121
Gosse, Edmund, 214, 285
Gosse, Nellie, 285
governesses, 18, 20–21, 23, 26

Gowen, Robert Joseph, 167
Graham, J. Ivon, 169
Grampians, 60, 118
Grand Tour, 32
Gray Scholarship, 68
Great Reform Act (1832), 13, 20, 213
Greece, 234
Green, Thomas Hill, 61, 78–9, 82, 84
Greenland, 303
Grey, Edward, 88, 113–14, 126, 162, 163, 165, 186
Grotta del Cane, Italy, 98
Grove, Ned, 184
Gruppa Iks, 240
Gunn, Neil, 247
Guy Fawkes Day, 94

Habeler, Peter, 212
Hadden, Scottish Borders, 34
Haddingtonshire, Scotland, 86, 97
haemophilia, 231, 262
Haig, Douglas, 8, 129, 170, 187, 190, 191, 201
Haldane (Campbell), 5, 335 n.43
Haldane, Alexander, 32, 35, 36–7
Haldane, Archibald Richard Burdon ('Archie', 'ARB'), 3, 8, 9, 10
Characteristics:
　fishing, love of, 118, 154, 173, 244
　literary and historical talent, 154, 176, 244, 267, 294
　personality, 154, 176, 244, 266, 268, 285–6, 293–4

INDEX

Key life events:
  birth, 118
  upbringing and education, 118, 229
  becomes Writer to the Signet, 229
  wedding to Janet, 243
  Principal, Ministry of Production, 244
  publishes *By Many Waters* and *The Path by the Water*, 244
  publishes post-war historical works 266–8
  Trustees Savings Bank vice-chair, 268
  awarded CBE, 268
  death, 293–4
Relationships:
  children, 268
  Dick Haldane (nephew), 288–9, 291
  Elsie (sister), 229
  Graeme (brother), 228–9, 266, 288–9
  Jan (wife), 243–4
  Pat (brother), 118, 173–6, 229, 244
  Richard (uncle), 166, 217
  Willie (father), 229, 244, 265
Haldane, Aylmer, 38, 329 n.22
Haldane, Bernard, 34
Haldane, Catherine, 36
Haldane, Charlotte, 210–11, 215, 222, 230, 249, 258, 272
Haldane, Daniel Rutherford, 66, 329 n.22, n.30
Haldane, Edith, 101, 173–6, 217
Haldane, Elizabeth Joanna, 39, 45
Haldane, Elizabeth Sanderson ('Bay', 'Elsa'), 2, 6, 10, 13, 25, 42, 62, 67, 73–4, 103–4, 115, 128, 137, 207, 219, 245
Characteristics:
  appearance, 71, 104
  ghost stories, love of, 121
  intellect, 69–70, 76–7
  personality, 72, 140, 155, 192–3, 257, 285
  philosophical views, 62, 76–7, 78, 85
  women's rights, views on, 52–4, 140
  writing, 117, 219
Key life events:
  birth, 45
  upbringing and education, 47–61, 71–2
  Paris visit, 70–71
  denounces church membership, 85–6
  Treasurer, Scottish Women's Liberal Association, 97
  trains under Octavia Hill, 98
  co-founds Scottish Women's Benefit Society, 99
  establishes Auchterarder Public Library, 100
  John Burdon Sanderson's funeral, 113
  Board of Edinburgh Royal Infirmary, 117

379

INDEX

Auchterarder School Board work, 117
Honorary LLD, St Andrews, 117
runs Westminster Health Society, 117
Scottish Universities Committee, 139
establishes Territorial Force Nursing Service and VAD, 139, 182
Insurance Act work, 140
Royal Commission on the Civil Service, 140, 185
Kaiser Wilhelm's visit, 146
Trustee, Carnegie United Kingdom Trust, 100
World War I, 161–3, 170, 185–6
awarded Companion of Honour, 186
Perthshire Education Authority work, 193
Justice of the Peace, 193
Governor, Birkbeck College, 213
Member, General Council of Nursing, 213
death, 236

Relationships:
friends, 72, 190, 194–5, 186
John (brother), 97–8, 193, 234, 236
Mary (mother), 13, 22, 26, 50, 70–2, 193, 305
nephews and nieces, 103–4, 156, 166, 174–5, 193, 236–7, 245, 251, 255, 265–6
Richard (brother), 97–99, 165–6, 193, 217–18
Willie (brother), 98

Haldane, George Abercromby, 1–2, 44, 47, 52, 65–6, 68–9, 113, 204
Haldane, Helen, 230, 238–9, 248, 268–9, 271
Haldane, James Alexander (b. 1768), 29–38, 40, 329 n.30
Haldane, James Alexander (b. 1844), 39, 45
Haldane, Jane (née Makgill), 9, 38, 39, 40–41
Haldane, Janet Macrae (née Simpson-Smith), 243–4, 268
Haldane, Jennifer (née Livingstone-Learmonth), 290, 296, 298, 304
Haldane, Jennifer, *see* Halsey, Jennifer
Haldane, John 'Union Jack', 33–4
Haldane, John Burdon Sanderson ('Jack', 'JBS'), 3, 7, 8, 9, 10, 84, 91, 103–4, 110, 131, 152, 153, 162, 219, 245, 306

Characteristics:
appearance, 172
childhood precocity, 95, 119, 130, 132
eugenicist views, 206
India, views on, 271–4
personality, 119, 157, 209, 211, 231, 233, 240, 261–2, 271, 274–5, 285

INDEX

self-experimentation, 207, 212, 237–9
Soviet Union, views on, 257–61
women scientists, promotion of, 210
Key life events:
birth, 94
upbringing and education, 95, 119, 130, 132, 135–7, 157
World War I, 169–70, 171–3, 343 n.24
Fellow, New College, Oxford, 196
Reader in Biochemistry, Cambridge, 205
publication of *Daedalus*, 205–8
mathematical theory of evolution work, 208–9
Briggs–Haldane equation work, 209
joins John Innes Horticultural Institution, 209–10
wedding to Charlotte, 211
'origin of life' article, 211–12
Russian tour, 222
Fellow of the Royal Society, 230
Chair of Genetics, University College, London, 230
X chromosome mapping, 231
Spanish Civil War, 231–3
death of father, 234–6
World War II, 237–9
joins Communist Party, 234, 238
suspected as spy, 240–1
BBC debate on Lysenko, 259–61
awarded Darwin Medal, 262
moves to India, 268, 271–2
death of mother, 273
death, 269, 274
Relationships:
Charlotte (first wife), 210–11, 215–16, 230, 249, 258, 272
cousins, 120–1, 230, 266
friends, 157–9, 181
great–nephews, 275
Helen (second wife), 230, 238–9, 268, 271–4
John (father), 95, 118, 119, 130, 132–3, 158, 169–71, 207–8, 209, 233–6, 237–8, 266, 343n.24
Kathleen (mother), 120, 221, 271, 273–4, 305
Naomi (sister), 118–20, 134, 153–4, 159, 161, 181, 195–7, 222, 235–7, 271, 273–4
nephews, 276–7
Richard (uncle), 104, 221, 258, 266
students, 261–2, 274–5
Haldane, John Patrick, 268
Haldane, John Scott ('Johnnie', 'Uffer'), 2, 9, 10, 62, 70, 73–

381

INDEX

4, 86, 89, 100, 103–4, 115, 117, 152, 246, 283

Characteristics:
  appearance, 93, 120, 219
  Germany, views on, 73, 76, 111, 113
  inventiveness, 91, 169, 179
  oxygen therapy, pioneering of, 144, 171, 235
  personality, 90, 92, 93, 95–6, 120, 153, 155, 159, 235–6, 257, 285
  philosophical views 73, 77–84, 333n.111
  scientific views, 73, 79, 81–4, 333n.111
  self-experimentation, 90–1, 96, 111, 134, 168–70, 212, 234
  walking, love of, 59–60
  women scientists, promotion of, 142, 144–5, 210

Key life events
  birth, 44–5
  upbringing and education, 47–61, 72–3, 75–6
  death of Geordie, 68–9
  denounces church membership, 85
  work with Carnelley, 91–2
  moves to Oxford as Demonstrator in Physiology, 92
  wedding to Kathleen, 94
  Lecturer in Physiology Department, Oxford 95
  mining work, 96–7
  Metropolitan Gas Referee, 97
  Fellow of the Royal Society, 95
  Boer War camp conditions intervention, 106–7
  Fellow, New College, Oxford, 109
  co–founds *Journal of Hygiene*, 110
  regulation of breathing paper, 111–12
  diving work for Admiralty, 130–4, 303
  Reader in Physiology Department, Oxford 134
  building of Cherwell, 134
  Pikes Peak expedition 142–6
  gas mask development, 167–70
  spacesuit prototype design, 212
  Honorary professor in Mining, Birmingham 212
  UK Gas Referee, 212
  President, Institution of Mining Engineers, 212, 234
  delivers Gifford Lectures, 73, 213
  awarded Companion of Honour, 213
  awarded Copley Medal 219
  death, 234–6

Relationships:
  Elizabeth (sister), 70–2, 97–8, 234

INDEX

grandchildren, 220, 235
Graeme (nephew), 285
JBS (son), 95, 118–19, 130, 132–3, 158, 169–71, 207–8, 233–4
Kathleen (wife), 93–4, 134, 235
Mary (mother), 305
Naomi (daughter), 120, 219, 234
Richard (brother), 77, 79, 89, 142, 147, 266
students, 92
Haldane, Leslie 'Billee' (née Wilkie), 9, 226, 242, 264–5, 286–8, 291, 294, 298
Haldane, Louisa Kathleen (née Trotter), 93–5, 103, 106, 118, 120, 134, 141, 207, 211, 220, 271, 273–4, 305
Haldane, Maldwyn Makgill, 45
Haldane, Margeret (née Rutherford), 329 n.30
Haldane, Margaret Isabella, 39, 45
Haldane, Mary (née Joass), 35, 36, 41
Haldane, Mary Abercromby, 39, 45
Haldane, Mary Elizabeth 'Elsie', *see* Campbell Fraser, Mary Elizabeth
Haldane, Mary Elizabeth (née Burdon Sanderson), 1, 4, 6, 8, 9, 10, 11, 13–15, 17, 45, 47, 58–9, 74, 100, 101–2, 104, 117, 153

Characteristics:
appearance, 42, 155
education, views on, 26–7, 55–6, 72, 96
military company, love of, 129
as mother, 50, 102, 193, 214
personality, 19, 20, 25–8, 43–4, 70, 155–6, 188, 214, 285, 304–5
poverty, views on, 49
religious views, 20–1, 27, 42, 48, 55, 62, 65, 77, 78, 188
women's rights, views on, 19, 44, 52

Key life events:
birth, 13, 326 n.1
upbringing and education, 18–25
rejects suitor, 42
wedding to Robert, 29, 43
birth of children, 44–5
death of Geordie, 65–6, 68–9
death of elder brother, 67
death of husband, 67
Paris visit, 70–71
death of younger brother, 112–3
World War I, 187, 188
centenary year, 213–14
death, 214

Relationships:
Elizabeth (daughter) 50, 70–2
grandchildren, 155–6, 175–6, 245, 270, 279–80

383

INDEX

John (son), 305
Richard (son), 50, 102, 148–9, 188
Richard's friends, 4–5, 156, 188, 214
Robert (husband), 42–3
step-children, 68, 329 n.25
Willie (son), 48, 101–2

Haldane, (Nancy) Robin, 243, 265, 289

Haldane, Richard Burdon, 'Bo', 1st Viscount, 1, 2, 6, 7, 10, 39, 72, 73–4, 94, 100, 101, 106, 117–18, 139, 154, 156, 236

Characteristics:
appearance, 75, 104, 109, 152–3
busyness, 88, 107–8, 129, 234
education, views on, 64
Germany, views on, 62, 64, 113, 164, 191–2
health issues, 75, 129, 165, 216–17
personality, 87, 109, 153, 155, 164, 257, 285, 289, 302, 305
philosophical views, 63–4, 77–84, 126, 353n.54
scientific views, 79, 81–4
voice, 75, 165, 333 n.1
walking, love of, 59–60
women's rights, views on, 64, 86, 185

Key life events:
birth, 44
upbringing and education, 47–65, 68

death of Geordie, 66–9
denounces church membership, 85
'Devils' for Horace Davey, 87
elected MP for Haddingtonshire, 86
QC, 87
meets Frances Horner, 88
helps establish LSE, 88
refashions University of London, 89
instigates Explosives Committee, 107
success at the Bar, 108
Trustee, Carnegie Trust for the Universities of Scotland, 100
delivers Gifford Lectures, 73, 108
Privy Counsellor, 108
instigates Civic University boom, 108
instigates University Grants Committee, 108–9
Relugas Compact, 113–14
enters Government as War Secretary, 89, 108
influences Liberal social reforms, 125
remodels British defence system, 126–9, 157, 163–4, 187–8, 231
founds Imperial College, London, 108, 130
chairs University Education Commission, 130, 147, 150

INDEX

Eton visit, 135
raised to peerage, 125, 146
Berlin Mission, 146–9, 164
outbreak of war, 162
Lord Chancellor, 27, 150, 166–7
President of the Judicial Committee, 87, 150, 166
Montreal Address, 149–50, 171
ejection from Government and press vilification, 27, 164–6, 187
Order of Merit, 166
Wartime committee work, 184–5
Machinery of Government Report, 'Haldane Report' 185
post–war vindication and public work, 189–91, 201–2, 217
Lord Chancellor in first Labour Government, 203–4
death of mother, 214
death, 217
Relationships:
dogs, 118, 128, 324
Elizabeth (sister) 97, 98, 99
Frances Horner, 88–9, 114, 217–18, 335 n.43
friends, 88, 109, 126, 151, 162–3, 165, 189–90, 193–4, 202, 214
half-siblings, 45, 68, 329n.25

John (brother), 77, 79, 89, 142, 147, 207, 266
Mary (mother), 50, 102, 148–9, 188, 213–14, 305
nephews and nieces, 104, 153, 155, 157, 187, 204–5, 207, 217, 229, 241, 251, 256, 258, 266
Robert (father) 67
Royalty, 114, 128, 140, 148, 186
Willie (brother) 101, 116, 141
Haldane, Richard Wilkie ('Dick'), 5, 10, 226–7, 282, 286–306
Characteristics:
appearance, 290, 291, 300–1
personality, 289–92, 300–2
Key life events:
birth 287
adoption, 287
upbringing and education, 287–91
wedding to Jenny, 291
establishes fish farm, 292
death of father, 293
death of mother, 294
tracks down Anne (biological mother), 295
death of Anne, 297–8
Lloyds crash, 292
sells majority of Cloan estate, 292–3
organises 'The Island Race', 298–9
organises 'The Great Russian Race', 299–302

385

INDEX

  discovers Danish half–sib-
    lings, 302
  sells Cloan, builds
    Cloanden, 5, 304
  Relationships:
    Anne (biological mother),
      287, 294–8
    Archie (uncle), 288–9
    Billee (mother), 287–8, 294
    children, 304
    Elsie (aunt), 288–9
    Graeme (father) 264–5,
      287–9, 291–3
    grandchildren 304
    half–siblings, 302–4
    Jenny (wife), 290–2, 298,
      304
    Naomi (father's cousin),
      226–7
    Robin (sister), 289
Haldane, Robert, 1, 4, 8, 9, 11,
16, 21, 22, 28, 29, 32, 36, 47,
52, 53, 58–9, 61, 62, 68, 71,
104
  Characteristics:
    appearance, 39
    personality, 38–9, 40, 67,
      70
    religious views and practices,
      30, 42, 48
  Key life events:
    birth, 29
    upbringing and education,
      35–7, 38
    death of mother, 41
    wedding to Jane, 39
    birth of children, 39
    death of father, 40

    death of Jane in childbirth,
      40
    purchase of Cloan, 39
    wedding to Mary, 43
    death of Geordie, 66
    death, 45, 67
  Relationships:
    Mary (second wife), 42–3
    children of first marriage,
      45, 68, 329n.25
    children of second marriage,
      22–3, 44–5, 49, 53, 66
Haldane, Robert Camperdown,
  39, 45, 331 n.44
Haldane, Robert Patrick 'Pat',
  9–10, 101, 118, 157, 173–6,
  178, 229
Haldane, Robert, 3rd of Airthrey,
  30, 31, 32, 34
Haldane, (Thomas) Graeme
  Nelson, 3, 8, 10, 62, 203, 229,
  245
  Characteristics:
    appearance, 176
    inventiveness, 179
    personality, 176, 264–6,
      285, 293
  Key life events:
    birth, 101
    upbringing and education,
      156–7, 205
    World War I, 176–80
    enters Merz & McLellan,
      204–5
    develops heat pump, 3, 226
    Russian tour, 225–7
    Swedish tour, 227
    US tour, 227–8

INDEX

World War II, 241
Partner, Merz & McLellan, 242
wedding to Billee, 242
energy production work, 263–5
President, Institution of Electrical Engineers 265, 293
inception of cross-Channel cable idea, 265
death 292–3

Relationships:
Archie (brother), 228–9, 266, 288–9
Billee (wife) 226, 242, 264–5, 286–8
cousins, 120–1, 211, 225–7, 230, 261–2
Dick (son), 264–5, 286–8, 291, 293
Elsie (sister), 266
John (uncle), 285
Naomi (cousin), 8, 225–7
Pat, 178
Richard (uncle), 204–5, 217, 241, 265–6, 289
Robin (daughter), 265
Willie (father), 178–9, 265, 289

Haldane, William Stowell, 2, 3, 11, 65, 71, 85, 118, 120, 229, 306

Characteristics:
appearance, 100, 243
personality, 100–1, 115, 243–4, 265, 285, 289

Key life events
birth 45
upbringing and education, 47–61, 100
death of Geordie, 68
becomes Writer to the Signet, 100
establishes W. & F. Haldane, 101
wedding to Edith, 101
buys Foswell estate, 101
Christie case, 115–16
Crown Agent, 116
Prison Commissioner, 116–17
Rural Development Commission, 140–1
knighthood, 141
Land Reform work with Lloyd George, 141
moves back to Cloan, 236
death of Edith, 244
death 265

Relationships:
Archie (son), 229
Edith (wife), 101, 229
Elizabeth (sister), 101
Elsie (daughter), 229
Graeme (son), 156, 176–7, 229
Mary (mother), 48, 101–2
Pat (son), 115, 173–6
Richard (brother) 101, 116, 141, 217

Haldane boxes, 91, 97
Haldane Haemoglobinometer, 91
Haldane Mission (1912), *see* Berlin Mission

387

INDEX

Haldane Principle, 185, 258
Haldane's sieve, 208
Haldanus, 34
Hall, Lesley, 152
Halsey, Jennifer, 101
Hamilton, Walter, 290
Handa, Taki, 116
Hansson, Per Albin, 227
Harmsworth, Alfred, 1st Viscount Northcliffe, 165
Harper's Bazaar, 242
Harper's Magazine, 231
Harrison, Edward, 170
Harvard University, 283
Harwood, H. C., 197
Hattersley, Roy, 124
Haudene, 34
Haydn, Franz Joseph, 19
health insurance, 123
heating systems, 226, 264
Hegel, Georg Wilhelm Friedrich, 73, 79, 80, 108, 148, 333 n.111
heirlooms, 288–9
Hemingway, Ernest, 8, 232–3
Henderson, Yandell, 142
Herdman, William Abbott, 331 n.49
Heretics Club, 205
Heriot-Watt University, 292
High School of Edinburgh, 38, 54, 55
Highland cattle, 304
Highland Panel, 255–6
Highlands and Islands Development Consultative Council, 271
Hill, Octavia, 98–9

Hiroshima, atomic bombing of (1945), 212
Historiographer Royal, 70, 151
History of Ancient Art (Winckelmann), 104
History of the Decline and Fall of the Roman Empire, The (Gibbon), 72
Hobhouse, Emily, 106
Holland, Henry Scott, 79, 81
Holtby, Winifred, 225
Holy Roman Empire, The (Bryce), 72
Homage to Catalonia (Orwell), 232
Home Office, 110–11
Homer, 17, 157
homosexuality, 282
Honiton lace, 43
hookworm, 111
Hoover Dam, 228
Horner, Frances, 88–9, 114, 192, 207, 214, 217–18
Horner, John, 88
House of Lords, 123, 125, 141
    Lord Chancellorship, 14, 16, 69, 27, 114, 153, 157, 162, 166, 203–4
    Parliament Act (1911), 123, 125, 141
Housing (Financial Provisions) Act (1924), 204
Human Genome Project, 231
Hume Brown, Peter, 70, 151–2, 189–90
hunting, 19, 242
Huxley family, 5, 158–9

INDEX

Huxley, Aldous, 8, 158–9, 168, 182, 206, 215, 272
Huxley, Gervas, 158, 159
Huxley, Julian, 158, 159, 201, 207, 275
Huxley, Thomas Henry, 9, 158
Huxley, Trevenan, 158, 159
hydrogen fuel cell, 205
Hynes, Samuel, 198

Icarus (Russell), 208
idealism, 77–86
Imperial College London, 89, 108, 130, 167, 291
Imperial General Staff, 129
Imperial War Museum, 232
Imperialists, 94, 106–7, 114
Indefatigable, HMS, 179
India, 8, 20, 32–3, 35, 110, 172–3, 268, 271–5
indoor games, 60
inheritance tax, 86, 125
Institut Pasteur, 110
Institute of Mining Engineers, 234
Institution of Electrical Engineers, 265, 293
Institution of Mining Engineers, 212–13
intelligence, 4
International Brigade, 232, 238
International Union Against TB, 276
internationalism, 220–21
Invincible, HMS, 179
Iran, 234
Iraq, 234
Ireland

Buckingham Palace Conference (1914), 162
Great Famine (1845–52), 14, 25
Home Rule movement, 86, 124, 156, 161–2
Land Law Bill (1887), 86
iron lung, 212
Isle of Wight, 43, 295
Israel, 274, 278
Italy, 98, 231

Jacobite risings
1715–16, 34
1745–46, 247
James III, King of Scots, 34
James, Philip, 171
Japan, 231
Japanese Garden, Cowden, 115, 116
Jenkinson Memorial Lecturer, 277
Jewish people, 205, 211, 279
John Innes Horticultural Institution, 209–10
Johnson, Louis, 227
Journal of Genetics, 84
Journal of Hygiene, 110
Jowett, Benjamin, 61
Judicial Committee, Privy Council, 87, 130, 150, 166, 194
Julius Caesar (Shakespeare), 133
Justices of the Peace, 193

Kaiser (dog), 128, 151, 202, 214
Kant, Immanuel, 63, 79, 333 n.111
Kellas, Alexander, 212

389

INDEX

Kenya, 264
Keogh, Alfred, 168
Kettering, Northamptonshire, 253
Khabarovsk, Russia, 300
King's College, London, 56
King's Norton, Worcestershire, 223
Kintyre, Scotland, 245
Kipling, Rudyard, 220
Kitchener, Herbert, 1st Earl, 105–6, 167, 168, 170, 187
Knox, John, 54
Kyles of Bute, Scotland, 132

Labour Movement, The (Hobhouse), 106
Labour Party, 123, 199, 201, 203, 223, 245, 246, 278
Lake District, 66
Lake Taupo, New Zealand, 264
land reform, 141
Land Transfer Bill (1895), 86
landlordism, 98
Lang, Cosmo, 151, 188, 214
Lansdowne, Henry Petty-Fitzmaurice, 5th Marquess, 107
Larken, Frank, 178
Lausanne, Switzerland, 45
League of Nations, 167, 184
Learning and Work Institute, 202
Leine river, 62
Lessing, Doris, 8, 268, 281
Letter to Edinburgh Professors, A (Haldane), 92
Lewis, Percy Wyndham, 234
Liberal Party, 86, 97, 105, 113–14, 123, 125, 126–7, 141, 165, 203
libraries, 100

'Life and Mind as Physical Realities' (Haldane), 262, 266
Life of Goethe (Hume Brown), 190
Linchwe II, Kgosi of the Bakgatla, 269
Linklater, Eric, 247
Linton Road, Oxford, 134
Liverpool, Robert Banks Jenkinson, 2nd Earl, 13
Livingstone-Learmonth, Jenny, *see* Haldane, Jennifer
LLD (Legum Doctor), 117
Lloyd George, David, 99, 123, 128, 140, 141, 166, 186
Lloyds of London, 292
Lobsters on the Agenda (Mitchison), 256
Local Authorities (Land Purchase) Bill (1891–2), 86
Loch Ridden, 132
London Early Years Foundation, 117
London Library, 130
London School of Economics, 89, 129
London Underground, 95
Lord Advocate, 116
Lord Chancellorship, 14, 16, 69, 27, 114, 153, 157, 162, 166, 203–4
Lotze, Hermann, 63–4, 73, 89, 164
Low Wood, Windermere, 66
Lowndes, Marie Belloc, 335 n.43
Lucas, Auberon Thomas Herbert, 9th Baron, 162
Lucretius, 157
Luther, Martin, 48

INDEX

Lyne, Roderic, 299
Lysenko, Trofim, 240, 259–61

Macaulay, Thomas Babington, 1st Baron, 14
MacCormick, John, 253
MacDiarmid, Hugh, 247
MacDonald, Ramsay, 199, 203–4
Machinery of Government Committee, 185, 203–4
Madras, India, 275
Magdalen College, Oxford, 113
Mahalanobis, Prasanta Chandra, 271, 272
Makgill, George, 45, 204
Makgill, John, 39
Makgill, Robert Haldane, 45
Mallory, George, 212
Malloy, Elizabeth, 300
Manchester Guardian, 231, 269
marathons, 298–302
Markham, Violet, 62, 72
Married Love (Stopes), 183
   1923 film version, 199
Martin, Kingsley, 267
Marxism, 198, 235, 259, 266–7
Mary, Queen consort of the United Kingdom, 214
Mass Observation, 249
Maxwell, James Clerk, 56
Maynard Smith, John, 261, 272, 273
Mayr, Ernst, 275
McEwan, Ian, 84, 275
McIndoe, Archibald, 286, 302
meals, 60, 110, 243
'Mechanical Chess Player, The' (Haldane), 262

mechanism, 79, 81–2, 143
Medawar, Peter, 8, 271
Medical Research Council, 276
medical students, 52–3
Memoirs of a Space Woman (Mitchison), 281
Mendel, Gregor, 208–9
meningitis, 215
Menon, Krishna, 201
Meredith, George, 88
Merz & McLellan, 204, 227, 242, 263
Merz, Charles, 204, 242
Messner, Reinhold, 212
Methodism, 30
Methuen, Paul, 23
Metropolitan Railway, 95, 97
MI5, 45, 129, 231, 240
MI6, 129, 301
miasma theory, 91–2
midwifery, 76
Milner, Alfred, 107
Milton, John, 17
mind, 80
Mines Act (1842), 24
minimum wage, 123
mining, 24, 91, 96–7, 111, 113, 192, 212–13
Ministry of Aircraft Production, 239
Ministry of Land and Natural Resources, 279
Ministry of Production, 244
Ministry of Supply, 244
Mitchison, Avrion, 4
Mitchison, Clemency, 250
Mitchison, Denis, 3, 195, 216, 220, 252, 275

INDEX

Mitchison, Geoff, 195, 215–16, 220
Mitchison, Gilbert Richard 'Dick', 159, 180–84, 200, 223, 245, 252, 278–9
Mitchison, Graeme, 84
Mitchison, Hannah, 283
Mitchison, (John) Murdoch, 195, 216, 220, 226, 252, 276–7
Mitchison, John, 181
Mitchison, Naomi 'Nou' (née Haldane), 3, 6, 7, 8, 9, 13, 45, 48, 68, 84, 103–5, 132, 133, 136, 137, 156, 168, 207, 232, 306
Characteristics:
   appearance, 180–1, 231
   imagination, 121, 152, 154
   liberty with truth, 93, 152, 162, 197
   literary talent, 152–4, 197–8, 225, 247
   personality, 180–1, 197, 201, 222, 251, 255–7, 269–70, 278–82, 285
   women's rights, views on, 198–201, 222–4, 270, 282
Key life events:
   birth, 95
   upbringing and education, 120, 134–5, 180
   wedding to Dick, 183
   World War I, 180–4
   publication of first novel, 195, 197–8
   death of Geoff, 215–16
   publication of *The Corn King and the Spring Queen*, 225
   Russian tour, 222–7
   travels in Austria and US, 227
   death of father, 235–6
   purchase of Carradale estate, 245–6
   death of Clemency, 250
   World War II, 249–53
   publication of *The Bull Calves*, 247–9
   Argyll County Council, 255, 257
   Highland Panel, 255–7
   post–WWII travels, 268–9
   Botswana connection, 269–71
   Highlands and Islands Council, 271
   death of Dick, 278
   centenary year, 282
   death, 282
Relationships:
   Charlotte and Helen (sisters-in-law), 215, 269
   children, 184, 195, 215–16, 220, 222, 249–52, 268, 275–8, 282–3, 325n.3
   cousins, 120–1, 154, 225–7, 245
   Dick (husband), 180–4, 199–201, 226, 253, 275–6, 278–9
   Elizabeth (aunt), 221, 237, 245, 251, 255
   friends, 157–9, 199, 201, 247

INDEX

Graeme (cousin), 8, 225–7
JBS (brother), 118–20, 134, 153–4, 159, 161, 181, 195–7, 215–16, 222, 225, 235–7, 248–9, 251, 260, 268, 271, 273–4, 282
John (father), 120, 219, 234–6
Kathleen (mother), 120, 134, 180, 219–20, 221, 246, 273–4, 305
Linchwe (Bakgatla chief), 269–70
lovers, 200–1, 224–5, 227, 249, 270
Mary (grandmother), 13, 245
Richard (uncle), 153, 251, 256
Mitchison, Neil, 5, 283, 304
Mitchison, (Nicholas) Avrion 'Av', 216, 220, 274, 277–8
Mitchison, Rosalind 'Rowy', 223, 278, 281
Mitchison, Ruth, 252
Mitchison, Sally, 119, 216, 280
Mitchison, (Sonja) Lois, 215, 216, 268, 276, 282, 283
Mitchison, Terence, 275, 280
Mitchison, Tim, 283
Mitchison, Valentine, 216, 251, 276, 282, 283
Mochudi, Botswana, 269–70, 273
Monod, Jacques, 275
Montagu, Ivor, 240
Montague Street, London, 16

Monte Rosa, Alps, 142
Montreal, Quebec, 149–50, 171
Moral Basis of Politics, The (Mitchison), 221
Moray Place, Edinburgh, 57
Morgan, John Harcourt Alexander, 228
Morgan, John Pierpont, 150
Motherhood and its Enemies (Haldane), 215
Mount Everest, 144, 212, 235
mountain climbing, 142–5, 212
Mozart, Wolfgang Amadeus, 19
Mrs Gaskell and her Friends (Haldane), 219
Munro-Ferguson, Val, 87
music, 19
Mussolini, Benito, 231
My Friend Mr Leakey (Haldane), 230
mystery, 73, 209

Naples, Italy, 98
Napoleon III, Emperor of the French, 43
National Academy of Sciences, 278
National Efficiency, 127
National Grid, 3, 205, 263, 346 n.49
National Institute for Medical Research, London, 277
National Institute of Industrial Psychology, 202
National Insurance Act (1911), 99, 140
National Library of Scotland, 45, 249, 267–8, 329 n.25

INDEX

National Physical Laboratory, 241
National Review, The, 99
National Service League, 128
National Trust, 295
National Unemployed Workers' Movement (NUWM), 199
Nature, 208, 239
Nazi Germany (1933–45), 228, 231, 238–40, 249, 260–61, 279
Negrín, Juan, 238
Nehru, Jawaharlal, 8, 271
Neild, Robert, 280
Nelson, Thomas, 101
Netherlands, 250
neurodiversity, 119, 216
New College, Oxford, 109, 157, 196
New State, The (Follett), 194
New Statesman, 267, 270
New York Times, 142
New York, United States, 150
New Zealand, 264
Newdigate Prize, 14, 15
Newton, Isaac, 202
Nigg, Highland, 172
Nine Lives of Naomi Mitchison, The (Calder), 5, 349 n.25
Nobel Prize, 8, 107, 225
'Non-Violent Scientific Study of Birds, The' (Haldane), 262
Northcliffe, Alfred Harmsworth, 1st Viscount, 165
Norway, 250
Not By Bread Alone (Mitchison), 282
Novartis, 278

nuclear power, 263, 277
Nurse, Paul, 276
nursing, 51, 139, 172, 182–6, 213, 229, 297

Ochil Hills, 59, 115
oil, 205, 234, 264
Olympic Games, 298
On Chesil Beach (2017 film), 275
open marriages, 8, 200–201
Order of Merit, 166
Order of the Companions of Honour, 186
organisational theory, 193
Oriel College, Oxford, 15
'Origin of Language, The' (Haldane), 262
Orissa, India, 272
Orkney Islands, 263, 282
Orwell, George, 21, 232
Osborne House, Isle of Wight, 156
Otterburn Dene, Northumberland, 14–15, 21
Outline for Boys and Girls and their Parents, An, 224
Outlook, 197
Ovingham, Northumberland, 15
Oxford, Oxfordshire, 91, 94, 95, 103, 134–6, 158–9
   Cherwell, 134, 135, 136, 146, 158, 167–9, 171, 181, 220
   Dragon School, 118–19, 135, 195, 220
   University, *see* University of Oxford
Oxford House, London, 78
Oxford Times, 184

INDEX

oxygen secretion, theory of, 143
oxygen therapy, 144, 171, 235

Pakistan, 268
Palace of Westminster, London, 91
Paradise Lost (Milton), 17
Paris, France, 43, 70–71
Parliament Act (1911), 123, 125, 141
Pasteur, Louis, 91
Path by the Water, The (Haldane), 154, 244
Pathological Institute, Berlin, 92
Pathway to Reality, The (Haldane), 108
Paton, Diarmid Noël, 331 n.49
Patriotic Society, 175
Paul Ehrlich and Ludwig Darmstaedter Prize, 277
Pearl Harbor attack (1941), 243
Peel, John, 286–8, 294, 296
pensions, 123
People's Budget (1909), 123
Phaedo (Plato), 236
Philby, Harold 'Kim', 227
Philippines, 264
Philosophical Works of Descartes, The, 139
philosophy, 56, 61, 77–86
phosphates, 228
Pikes Peak, Colorado, 142–5
Pilley, John, 224–5
plague, 110
Plato, 84, 236
playing cards, 60
Plymouth Brethren, 23
Plymouth, Devon, 42–3

Point Counter Point (Huxley), 159, 215
Poland, 250, 278
poor law, 117
Pop club (Eton College), 136
Pope, Alexander, 17
Portrait of a Muse (Gailey), 335 n.43
Portsmouth, Hampshire, 239
poverty, 24–5, 48, 98–9, 105
Pre-Raphaelites, 88
Preyer, William Thierry, 73
Priestley, John Gillies, 111–12
Prison Commissioners, 116–17
Privy Council, 87, 108, 130, 139, 150, 166, 184, 194
Profumo, John, 253
Protestantism, 47–8
Prussia, 16
Psalms, 139
Puerto Rico, 111
Punch, 152
Putin, Vladimir, 301

'Quantum Theory of the Origin of the Solar System, A' (Haldane), 262
Quebec, 87, 149–50, 171
Queen Anne's Gate, London, 147, 162, 170, 191, 202
Queen Mary, HMS, 179
Queen Victoria Hospital, East Sussex, 286
Queen's Chapel, Savoy, 293

Radcliffe Infirmary, Oxford, 236
radium, 242
Raff, Martin, 277

INDEX

Ratcliffe, Peter, 145, 340 n.21
Rationalist Annual, The, 211
rats, 110
Rayleigh, John William Strutt, 3rd Baron, 107
reading, 19, 25, 48, 60, 72, 120, 220
Reconstruction Committee, 185
Red Cross, 182, 185, 186
Regius Chair of Medicine, 90, 112
Reign of Relativity, The (Haldane), 202, 266
'Relation of Philosophy to Science, The' (Haldane), 65, 77–86, 99, 266
Relugas Compact (1905), 114
renewable energy, 205, 264
Reports on the Sanitary Condition of the Labouring Population of Scotland, 22
Representation of the People Act (1918), 123
Respiration (Haldane), 212
respiratory system, 111–12, 207
Return to the Fairy Hill (Mitchison), 270
Reuters, 125
rheumatology, 278
Rivercourt, London, 202, 216, 220
Robert Koch Gold Medal, 277
Roberts, Frederick, 1st Earl, 128, 129
Roebuck House, Cambridgeshire, 215–16
Rokeling, Tish, 278

Romaine, William, 16
Roosevelt, Franklin, 3, 227
Rotherfield, East Sussex, 13
Rothschild, Emma, Baroness, 88
Rothschild, Nathan, 1st Baron, 88
Royal Academy, 56
Royal Air Force, 212, 239
Royal Botanical Gardens, Edinburgh, 244
Royal Cancer Hospital, London, 242, 286
Royal Commissions, 6, 10
  on civil service, 140
  on environmental pollution, 277
  on health and safety in mines, 134
  on metalliferous mines and quarries, 145
  on rural development, 140–41
  on university education, 130, 147, 150, 185
Royal Economic Society, 129–30
Royal Eye Hospital, London, 297
Royal Flying Corps, 129
Royal Geographical Society, 294
Royal Infirmary, 117
Royal Institute of International Affairs, 202
Royal Institution, 230
Royal Medal, 113
Royal Navy, 124, 127
Royal Postgraduate Medical School, London, 276
Royal Society of Literature, 130
Royal Society, 3, 56, 57, 95, 97,

INDEX

112–13, 129, 145, 171, 219, 262, 273, 331 n.49
Rugby School, Warwickshire, 55, 289
Rural Development Commission, 140–41
Russell, Bertrand, 208
Russell, James Burn, 24
Russell Square, London, 16
Russian Empire, 15
Russian Federation, 299–302
Russian Revolutions (1917), 198
Russian Soviet Socialist Republic, *see* Soviet Union
Rutherford, Daniel, 329 n.30
Rutherford, Ernest, 205
Rutherford, Mark, 85

Sadler's Wells Theatre, London, 213
Saint Ronan's Well (Scott), 22
Salisbury, Robert Gascoyne-Cecil, 3rd Marquess, 107
Sandoz Prize for Immunology, 278
Sass, Henry, 18
Savoy, London, 293
scarlet fever, 90
Schlote, Helene, 64
Schneider, E. C., 142
schoolrooms, 24, 51, 59, 135, 155
Schopenhauer, Arthur, 87, 100, 114
science, 77–86
Sciences and Philosophy The (Haldane), 333 n.111

Scotland of our Fathers, The (Haldane), 219
Scots Gardens in Old Times (Haldane), 219
Scotsman, The, 40, 84, 236, 270
Scott-Moncrieff, Rose, 210
Scott, John, 16
Scott, Walter, 22, 72, 329 n.30
Scottish National Party (SNP), 253
Scottish Office, 255–6
Scottish Parliament, 255
Scottish Renaissance, 247
Scottish Universities Committee, 139
Scottish War Savings Committee, 186
Scottish Women's Benefit Society, 99
Scrabble, 280
Sea-Green Ribbons (Mitchison), 282
Secret Service Bureau, 129
Seely, John Edward Bernard, 188
Selborne, William Palmer, 2nd Earl, 113
Sellar, William Young, 55, 61
Serbia, 162
Seth Pringle-Pattison, Andrew, 77
sewers, 91
Sex Disqualification (Removal) Act (1919), 193
sex viri, 210–11
sex, 8, 88, 183, 196, 200–201, 225–7
Shairp, John Campbell, 55
Shakespeare, Geoffrey, 242

INDEX

Shakespeare, William, 133, 152, 157
sharecroppers, 227
Shelley, Percy Bysshe, 14
sick pay, 123
Siege of Cawnpore (1857), 20
Signet Library, Edinburgh, 268
Silliman Lectures, 171
Simeon, Charles, 16
Simpson-Smith, Janet Macrae, *see* Haldane, Janet Macrae
Simpson, James Young, 76
Smith, Adam, 87
Smith, Colvin, 33
Smith, James Lorrain, 92–3
smoking, 48
Smout, Thomas Christopher, 54
Smuts, Jan, 213
Social Union, 98
socialism, 8, 83, 182, 201, 204, 221–4, 234, 246, 270
Society for Propagating the Gospel at Home, 31
Sodom, Shetland, 247
Solution Three (Mitchison), 281
'Some Alternatives to Sex' (Haldane), 262
'Song of the House', 1
South Africa, 105–7, 126, 213, 268
Soviet Union, 198, 221–7, 240, 257–61
spacesuits, 91, 212
Spanish Civil War (1936–9), 231–3, 238, 273
Spanker, HMS, 132
Spectator, 231
sports, 19, 54

Spring Rice, Margery, 199, 200
Spurway, Helen, *see* Haldane, Helen
St Anne's College, Oxford, 180, 278
St Catherine's House, London, 295
St Cuthbert's, Edinburgh, 44
St Helena, 33
St Thomas's hospital, London, 182
Stalin, Joseph, 223, 232, 240, 257–8, 261
Stanford Encyclopedia of Philosophy, 63
Stephen, Leslie, 88
Stevenson, Flora, 53
Stevenson, Robert Louis, 331 n.44
stocks, 19, 24
Stop TB Kochon Prize, 276
Stopes, Marie, 183, 199
Stowell, William Scott, 1st Baron, 14, 17
Strachey family, 153–4
Strachey, Amabel, 153
Strachey, Celia, 201
Strachey, John, 201
Strasburger, Eduard, 73
submarines, 130, 237–8
Subramanian, Samanth, 5, 173, 206, 240
Suez Crisis (1956), 271, 272
'Suffer' motto, 134, 188, 239
'Suggestions for Research on Coconuts' (Haldane), 262
sulpho-carbolate of soda, 90
Sunday Tramps, 88
supertax, 123

INDEX

Sweden, 227
Switzerland, 32, 278
Sykes, Mary, 243

Tabernacles, 32
Taff Vale case (1900–01), 108
Taft, William Howard, 171
Tait, Archibald Campbell, 56
Tait, Peter Guthrie, 55
Taylor, Miss (governess), 18
Technische Hochschule, Charlottenburg, 108
Teddington, Surrey, 241
Tennessee Valley Authority, 228
Territorial and Reserve Forces Act (1907), 127
Territorial Force Nursing Service, 139, 186
Territorial Force, 127–9, 187, 190, 217
Theory of Relativity, The (Einstein), 205
Thetis, HMS, 237
Thompson, D'Arcy Wentworth, 56, 213
Thomson, Joseph John, 3, 205
Tiger, HMS, 179
Times, The, 6, 56, 95, 117, 147, 164, 165, 168, 217, 271
Tirpitz sinking (1943), 239
von Tirpitz, Alfred, 147, 148
Torrance, Robert, 145
Toryism, 94, 106, 127, 305
Toynbee Hall, London, 78
Trade Disputes Act (1906), 108
Treaty of Versailles (1919), 192, 231, 250
tree climbing, 51, 54

tree, perception of, 80–81
Trevelyan family, 5
tribalism, 270
Trinity College, Cambridge, 205, 252
Trustees Savings Bank, 268
Truth, 8
tuberculosis, 3, 134, 275
Tunbridge Wells, Kent, 13, 17
Turkey, 177–8, 234
tutors, 51, 60
Tweedie, W. F., 243
Tylorstown disaster (1896), 96

U-2 spy plane, 212
Ukraine, 301
unemployment, 14, 123, 192
UNESCO, 39
United Free Church of Scotland, 202
United States, 124, 150, 227–8
   sharecroppers, 227
   Venona, 240
   World War I (1914–18), 189, 191
   World War II (1939–45), 240
universal male suffrage, 16
universities, 54, 108–9, 130, 139, 147, 150, 185
University College, Dundee, 91
University College, Liverpool, 108
University College, London, 230, 252, 261, 272
University Grants Committee, 109
University of Aarhus, 286
University of Berlin, 92

399

INDEX

University of Birmingham, 212
University of Bristol, 108, 224
University of California, Berkeley, 230
University of Cambridge, 56, 62, 139, 196, 197, 205, 207, 210–11, 252
University of Edinburgh, 38, 68, 72–3, 100, 129, 266, 276
University of Glasgow, 73, 213
University of Göttingen, 62–5
University of Jena, 73
University of Leeds, 108
University of Liverpool, 108
University of London, 86, 150
University of Manchester, 108
University of Oxford, 61, 62, 78
   Archie Haldane at, 229
   J. S. Haldane Lecture, 145
   John Burdon Sanderson at, 90, 112–13
   John Burdon Sanderson Haldane at, 109, 157–8, 196, 196, 231
   Murdoch Mitchison at, 277
   John Scott Haldane at, 92, 95, 134, 146
   Naomi Mitchison at, 180, 278
   Richard Burdon at, 14, 15, 27
   Patrick Haldane at, 157
University of Reading, 108
University of Sheffield, 108
University of St Andrews, 73, 108, 117, 213, 217
University of Stirling, 31
Urne, Ketil, 304
utilitarianism, 64

V-1 flying bombs, 239
Valiant, HMS, 179
Vavilov, Nikolai, 222, 240, 259–60
Venona, 240
ventilation, 109–10, 130
Venus flytrap, 90
Verbindung, 62
Victoria, Queen of the United Kingdom, 124
Victoria Cross, 56
Victoria University, Manchester, 108
Voltaire, 14
Voluntary Aid Detachment, 139, 182–3, 185, 229

W. & F. Haldane, 101
Waddell, John, 176
Wade-Gery, Theodore, 200–201
Wairakei plant, New Zealand, 264
walking, 59–60, 153
Wall Street Crash (1929), 199
War Office, 114, 167
Watson, James, 8, 280
Waynflete Chair of Physiology, 90, 146
We Have Been Warned (Mitchison), 224, 246–7
Webb, Beatrice, 189
Webb, Sidney, 86, 89, 108
'Wee Frees' case, 108
Weizmann Institute of Science, 278
welfare, 51, 99, 105, 123
Wernher, Julius, 124–5, 130
Wesley, Charles, 30
Wesley, John, 30

INDEX

West Jesmond, Northumberland, 14, 18, 19, 23, 24, 37, 129, 326 n.7
West Point, New York, 150
West, John, 144
Westminster Health Society, 117
Wheatley, John, 204
When the Bough Breaks (Mitchison), 196, 198
When We Become Men (Mitchison), 270
Whigs, 8
White, William Hale, 85
Whitefield, George, 32
Whittle, Frank, 241
Wilde, Oscar, 7, 88
Wilhelm II, German Emperor, 113, 124, 146–9, 164
William I 'the Lion', King of Scotland, 34
Wilson, Henry, 164
Wilson, James Harold, 279
Wilson, Woodrow, 191
Winchester College, Hampshire, 229
Winckelmann, Johann, 104
Windermere, Lake District, 66
de Winton, Dorothea, 210
Wolfson College, Oxford, 278
women; women's rights, 2, 19, 44, 51, 54, 69–70, 222–4
   birth control, 3, 94, 199–200, 223–4
   education, 19, 52–3, 57–8
   'fallen' women, 44
   feminism, 19, 44, 94, 200
   medical students debate (1870s), 52–3, 331 n.31
   sports and, 19, 54
   suffrage, 86, 99, 123, 199, 213
Women's Industrial League, 86
Women's Liberal Association, 97
Woodburn, Arthur, 255
Woolf, Virginia, 88
Woolsack, *see* Lord Chancellorship
Wordsworth, William, 66
workhouses, 25
Working Men's College, 87
World as Will and Idea (Schopenhauer), 100
World War I (1914–18), 2, 8, 27, 105, 123–5, 161–88, 190–92, 213, 250, 287
   Battle of Jutland (1916), 178–9
   Battle of Loos (1915), 187
   Battle of Ypres, Second (1915), 167
   Gallipoli campaign (1915–16), 177–8, 186
   gas masks, 2, 91, 167–71
   Mesopotamia campaign (1914–18), 172
   Pat, death of (1915), 10, 173–6, 178
   Voluntary Aid Detachment, 139, 182–3, 185, 229
World War II (1939–45), 238–53
Wright, Sewall, 208
Writer to the Signet, 38, 100, 229

X chromosome, 231

INDEX

Yale University, 171
York, Cosmo Lang, Archbishop of, 151, 188, 214
You May Well Ask (Mitchison), 196
Young Communist League, 245, 252
Young Woman Engineer of the Year, 5